高等院校电子信息科学与工程类
·专业基础课教材·

光电子技术专业英语

主编 徐朝鹏 王朝晖 焦斌亮
主审 毕卫红

北京邮电大学出版社
·北京·

内 容 简 介

本书是光电子技术方面的专业英语教材。本书主要介绍了科技英语的特点、翻译方法和技巧，半导体物理和器件，电磁场和电磁波，光学原理，激光原理，非线性光学原理，集成电路制备，光通信，全息数据存储，光镊，光子晶体光纤，科技文献检索以及英语科技论文写作等内容。每一章分别从基本概念、原理、分类、技术优势和挑战等方面对现有的光电子技术进行阐述。

本书可作为高等院校电子科学与技术、光学工程、光信息科学与技术、光学等专业的本科生以及研究生的教材和参考书，也可作为非光电子类读者了解光电子学基本知识的参考书，还可作为读者投稿国际光电子类学术期刊的"投稿指南"。

图书在版编目(CIP)数据

光电子技术专业英语/徐朝鹏,王朝晖,焦斌亮主编. --北京:北京邮电大学出版社,2010.9(2022.12 重印)

ISBN 978-7-5635-2242-2

Ⅰ. ①光… Ⅱ. ①徐…②王…③焦… Ⅲ. ①光电子技术—英语—高等学校—教材 Ⅳ. ①H31

中国版本图书馆 CIP 数据核字(2010)第 142116 号

书　　名：	光电子技术专业英语
主　　编：	徐朝鹏　王朝晖　焦斌亮
责任编辑：	陈岚岚
出版发行：	北京邮电大学出版社
社　　址：	北京市海淀区西土城路 10 号(邮编:100876)
发 行 部：	电话:010-62282185　传真:010-62283578
E-mail：	publish@bupt.edu.cn
经　　销：	各地新华书店
印　　刷：	保定市中画美凯印刷有限公司
开　　本：	787 mm×1 092 mm　1/16
印　　张：	19.25
字　　数：	481 千字
版　　次：	2010 年 9 月第 1 版　2022 年 12 月第 11 次印刷

ISBN 978-7-5635-2242-2　　　　　　　　　　　　　　　　　　定　价：35.00 元

· 如有印装质量问题,请与北京邮电大学出版社发行部联系 ·

前 言

  光电子技术专业英语是继大学基础英语之后为提高光电子各专业学生读写英语文献的能力而开设的专业必修课,是大学阶段学习英语以及专业课的重要环节。通过本课程的学习,可以进一步增进学生对专业英语词汇、语法和结构的了解,增强学生对科技论文的写作能力,为将来从事光电子领域英文资料的查阅、翻译和写作打下坚实的基础。

  在高等教育面向21世纪的改革中,学生基本素质和实际工作能力的培养受到了空前重视,国家教育部也提出要培养创新式人才。对于非英语专业的学生而言,学好英语,尤其是专业英语,是获取专业信息、掌握学科发展动态、参加国际间学术交流的基本前提。可见,英语水平和能力的培养不仅是文化素质的重要部分,在很大程度上也是能力的补充和延伸。在此背景下,教育部制定了有关规范,使外语教学更加受到重视。教材是教学的基本要素之一,特别是国家对学科进行调整之后,光电子等交叉学科专业的出现和发展,使专业英语的教材缺乏问题显得尤为突出。

  考虑到专业英语一般在大三上学期开设,学生刚开始接触专业课,所以本书的专业内容定位在专业教材和科普读物之间,即不是用原版英语教材进行专业课教学,而是用英语介绍广泛的专业内容和知识。从专业的角度看,本书可称做"光电子技术概论"。

  光电子学是发展十分活跃,又尚未完善的一门学科。作者在汇集国内外学者的研究成果和总结作者若干年的教学与科研工作的基础上,编写了这本教材,力求做到:基本概念清晰,基本内容深入浅出、易于理解。既有基本原理的阐述和必要的理论知识分析与讨论,也有典型应用事例、国内外近期发展状况与趋势。希望在有限的篇幅里让读者对电子与光电子领域的基本原理、主要知识体系及应用能够有所了解和掌握。同时每章还对重点词汇和疑难句进行了解析,并为词汇标注了音标,以方便读者阅读。

  本书内容丰富,选材合理,涵盖光电子学基本理论和实际应用两部分内容。这两方面无所偏重,基本平衡。在基础部分,介绍了半导体物理、电磁场与电磁波、光学原理、激光原理、非线性光学等学科的基础知识;在应用部分,既介绍了"集成电路"这样目前广泛应用的高新技术,又介绍了"体全息存储"、"光镊"、"光子晶体光纤"这样的前沿题目,还涉猎到了"星间链路"这样的光波技术应用的核心领域。通过阅读本书可使读者在不知不觉间进入到光电子学研究的前沿。

  本书共分13章,第1章主要讲述科技英语的特点、翻译方法和技巧;第2章是半导体物理和器件;第3章是电磁场和电磁波;第4章是光学原理;第5章是激光原理;第6章是非线性光学原理;第7章是集成电路制备;第8章是光通信;第9章是全息数据存储;第10章是光镊;第11章是光子晶体光纤;第12章是科技文献检索;第13章是英语科技论文写作。为了拓展知识面,本书配备了必要的补充材料,包括英语中常用的前缀和后缀、常用的数学符号和单位、SCI和EI收录的光电类有关期刊等。

本书由燕山大学信息科学与工程学院徐朝鹏、王朝晖、焦斌亮主编,刘兆伦、谈爱玲、刘雪强和燕山大学财务处张文杰参与编写。其中第1章由王朝晖、徐朝鹏执笔,第4章由焦斌亮执笔,第5、8章由王朝晖执笔,第7章由刘雪强、徐朝鹏执笔,第10章由谈爱玲执笔,第11章由刘兆伦执笔,第12章由张文杰、徐朝鹏执笔,其余章节和附录由徐朝鹏执笔,刘雪强也参与整理了第2章文稿。全书由徐朝鹏统稿,由毕卫红教授统审。

燕山大学李文慧副教授和黄震博士为本书提供了重要的资料,并提出了宝贵的修改意见。研究生韩富兴、赵岩、巩洁、孙燕、张文娟、李涛在书稿的文字输入、编排和校对方面做了大量的工作,在此,编者对他们表示衷心的感谢。

本书得以付梓,离不开方方面面的支持。所有参编教师精诚团结,兢兢业业,几经易稿,终成此书。感谢燕山大学光电子工程系、里仁学院电子科技04级、05级、06级、07级全体学生的支持,他们提出的许多宝贵意见使本书能不断补充和更新,日臻完善。还应感谢燕山大学信息学院的各级领导,他们在经费和政策上的支持为本书的顺利完成提供了有力的保障。更要感谢本书所有引用文献的作者们,本书编者在编写过程中由于参考了国内外出版的许多相关书刊,从中选用的材料以及完美的语句使本书增色不少。

本书可作为高等院校电子科学与技术、光学工程、光信息科学与技术、光学等专业的本科生以及研究生的教材和参考书,也可作为非光电子类专业的读者了解光电子学基本知识的参考书,还可作为读者投稿国际光电子类学术期刊的"投稿指南"。

由于时间紧迫,本书涉及范围又很广,加之编者水平有限,本书定有许多疏漏和不妥之处,恳请读者提出宝贵意见,以便完善。

作　者

目 录

第 1 章 科技英语翻译技巧 ... 1
1.1 科技英语概念 ... 1
1.2 科技英语文体总貌 ... 1
1.3 科技英语词汇特点 ... 2
1.4 科技英语翻译方法和技巧 ... 4
1.4.1 科技英语翻译标准 ... 4
1.4.2 科技英语翻译过程中语法特点 ... 4
1.4.3 科技英语的翻译方法与技巧 ... 6
1.5 提高科技英语翻译能力的途径 ... 15

第 2 章 Semiconductor Physics and Device ... 17
2.1 Semiconductor Materials ... 17
2.2 Type of Solids ... 19
2.3 Crystal Structure ... 20
2.4 The Atomic Structure of Semiconductors ... 21
2.4.1 Electron Shells and Orbits ... 21
2.4.2 Valence Electrons, Conduction Electrons, and Ions ... 22
2.4.3 Metallic Bands ... 22
2.4.4 Covalent Bonds ... 23
2.4.5 Electrons and Hole Current ... 24
2.5 The PN Junction ... 25
2.5.1 Doping ... 25
2.5.2 The PN Junction ... 26
2.5.3 The Depletion Region ... 26
2.6 Biasing the Semiconductor Diode ... 27
2.6.1 Forward Bias ... 27
2.6.2 Reverse Bias ... 28
2.6.3 Peak Inverse Voltage (PIV) ... 29
2.6.4 Reverse Breakdown ... 29
2.7 Semiconductor Device-BJT and FET ... 30
2.7.1 Bipolar junction transistor ... 30
2.7.2 Field-effect transistor ... 31

2.8　Semiconductor Applications ………………………………………………… 32
2.9　Semiconductor Competition …………………………………………………… 33

第3章　Electromagnetic Field and Electromagnetic Wave ………………………… 37

3.1　The Concept of Electromagnetic Fields and Waves ………………………… 37
3.2　History of Electromagnetic Wave …………………………………………… 38
3.3　Basic Laws of Electromagnetic Theory ……………………………………… 41
　　3.3.1　Faraday's Induction Law …………………………………………… 41
　　3.3.2　Gauss's Law-Electric ………………………………………………… 45
　　3.3.3　Gauss's Law-Magnetic ……………………………………………… 47
　　3.3.4　Ampere's Circuital Law ……………………………………………… 47
　　3.3.5　Maxwell's Equations ………………………………………………… 50
3.4　Properties of Electromagnetic Wave ………………………………………… 51
　　3.4.1　Wave Model ………………………………………………………… 51
　　3.4.2　Particle Model ……………………………………………………… 52
　　3.4.3　Speed of Propagation ……………………………………………… 52
3.5　Electromagnetic Spectrum and Applications ………………………………… 53

第4章　Fundamentals of Optics ……………………………………………………… 60

4.1　A Brief History about Optics ………………………………………………… 60
　　4.1.1　The Views of the Antique Philosophers …………………………… 61
　　4.1.2　Classical Optics ……………………………………………………… 61
　　4.1.3　Modern Optics ……………………………………………………… 65
　　4.1.4　Moving Bodies Optics ……………………………………………… 67
4.2　Contents of Optics …………………………………………………………… 68
　　4.2.1　Rectilinear Propagation of Light …………………………………… 68
　　4.2.2　Reflection and Refraction …………………………………………… 72
　　4.2.3　Interference and Diffraction ………………………………………… 77
4.3　Optics Systems ………………………………………………………………… 78
　　4.3.1　Telescopes …………………………………………………………… 78
　　4.3.2　Retinal Acuity ……………………………………………………… 79

第5章　Fundamentals of Lasers ……………………………………………………… 84

5.1　Definition of Laser …………………………………………………………… 84
5.2　A Brief History of Laser ……………………………………………………… 85
5.3　Principle of Laser Generation ………………………………………………… 86
　　5.3.1　Spontaneous and Stimulated Emission, Absorption ……………… 86
　　5.3.2　The Laser Idea ……………………………………………………… 89
　　5.3.3　Pumping Schemes …………………………………………………… 91

5.4 Structure and Properties of Laser ……………………………………………… 94
    5.4.1 Structure of Laser ………………………………………………………… 94
    5.4.2 Properties of Laser Beams ……………………………………………… 98
5.5 Lasers Types ……………………………………………………………………… 103
5.6 Application of Laser …………………………………………………………… 104
    5.6.1 Industrial Applications …………………………………………………… 104
    5.6.2 Medical Applications …………………………………………………… 105

第 6 章 Nonlinear Optics ……………………………………………………… 109

6.1 Definition of Nonlinear Optics ………………………………………………… 109
6.2 History of Nonlinear Optics …………………………………………………… 112
6.3 Features of Interaction of Intense Light with Matter ……………………… 116
6.4 Theory Framework of Nonlinear Optics ……………………………………… 119
6.5 Descriptions of Nonlinear Optical Processes ……………………………… 121
    6.5.1 Second-Harmonic Generation ………………………………………… 121
    6.5.2 Frequency Mixing Generation ………………………………………… 123
    6.5.3 Sum-Frequency Generation …………………………………………… 124
    6.5.4 Difference-Frequency Generation …………………………………… 124
    6.5.5 Optical Parametric Oscillation ………………………………………… 125
    6.5.6 Third-Order Nonlinear Optical Processes …………………………… 126
    6.5.7 Intensity-Dependent Refractive Index ……………………………… 126
    6.5.8 Third-Order Interactions ………………………………………………… 127
    6.5.9 Parametric versus Nonparametric Processes ……………………… 128
    6.5.10 Saturable Absorption …………………………………………………… 129
    6.5.11 Two-Photon Absorption ………………………………………………… 130
    6.5.12 Stimulated Raman Scattering ………………………………………… 130
6.6 Application and Outlook ………………………………………………………… 130

第 7 章 Integrated Circuit Fabrication ……………………………………… 136

7.1 The Concept of Integrated Circuit …………………………………………… 136
7.2 History of Integrated Circuit …………………………………………………… 137
7.3 Integrated Circuit Fabrication ………………………………………………… 139
    7.3.1 Integrated Circuit Design ……………………………………………… 140
    7.3.2 The Manufacturing Process …………………………………………… 140
7.4 Application ………………………………………………………………………… 156
7.5 The Future ………………………………………………………………………… 157

第 8 章 Optical Communications …………………………………………… 160

8.1 The System Model ……………………………………………………………… 161

8.2	Optical Transmitters	163
8.3	The Transmitted Optical Field	165
8.4	Stochastic Fields	169
8.5	The Optical Channel	171
	8.5.1　The Unguided (Space) Channel	171
	8.5.2　The Guided (Fiberoptic) Channel	172
8.6	The Detected Optical Field	174
8.7	Background Radiation	180
8.8	Photodetection	180
8.9	Optical Intersatellite Links	183

第 9 章　Holographic Data Storage ······ 187

9.1	The Concept of Holography	188
9.2	History of Holographic Data Storage	189
9.3	Principle of Holographic Data Storage	191
9.4	Theory about Formation and Reconstruction of a Hologram	193
	9.4.1　Volume Grating and Bragg Diffraction	193
	9.4.2　Born's approximation	194
	9.4.3　Coupled Wave Theory	196
9.5	Hardware for Holographic Data Storage	198
9.6	Coding and Signal Processing	199
	9.6.1　Binary Detection	200
	9.6.2　Interpixel Interference	200
	9.6.3　Error Correction	201
	9.6.4　Predistortion	202
	9.6.5　Gray Scale	202
	9.6.6　Capacity Estimation	203
9.7	Associative Retrieval	203
9.8	Recording Materials	206
9.9	Two-color or Photon-gated Holography	209

第 10 章　Optical Tweezers ······ 215

10.1	Concept of Optical Tweezers	216
10.2	History of Optical Tweezers	216
10.3	Basic Theory of Optical Tweezers	217
10.4	System of Optical Tweezers	220
10.5	Application of Optical Tweezers	221
10.6	Future of Optical Tweezers	222

第 11 章 Photonic Crystal Fiber … 226

11.1 The Origins of PCFs … 226
11.1.1 Conventional Optical Fibers … 226
11.1.2 Photonic Crystal … 227
11.1.3 From Conventional Optical Fibers to PCFs … 229
11.2 The History of PCFs … 229
11.3 Guiding Light in PCFs … 231
11.3.1 Modified Total Internal Reflection … 231
11.3.2 Photonic Bandgap Guidance … 232
11.4 Properties of PCFs … 233
11.4.1 Solid Core PCFs … 233
11.4.2 Hollow Core PCFs … 237
11.5 Fabrication of PCFs … 237
11.5.1 Stack-and-draw Technique … 238
11.5.2 Extrusion Fabrication Process … 240
11.6 Application of PCFs … 241
11.6.1 High Power and Energy Transmission … 241
11.6.2 Fiber Lasers and Amplifiers … 241
11.6.3 Gas-based Nonlinear Optics … 242
11.6.4 Supercontinuum Generation … 243
11.6.5 Telecommunications … 243
11.6.6 Optical Sensors … 245
11.6.7 Gratings in PCF … 245
11.7 Future Perspectives … 246

第 12 章 科技文献检索 … 249

12.1 信息检索的含义 … 249
12.2 信息检索的基本原理 … 250
12.3 检索语言 … 250
12.4 文献检索工具 … 251
12.4.1 检索工具应具备的条件 … 251
12.4.2 检索工具的类型 … 251
12.5 检索文献资料的途径 … 251
12.6 文献检索的基本方法 … 252
12.7 文献检索的一般步骤 … 253
12.8 文献数据库检索 … 253
12.8.1 检索工具的类型 … 253
12.8.2 国内主要资源 … 255

12.8.3　国外主要资源 ... 255
12.8.4　进入数据库的方法和思路 ... 256
12.9　其他检索文献途径 ... 256

第13章　英语科技论文写作 ... 259

13.1　科技论文的概念和特点 ... 259
13.2　如何撰写英语科技论文 ... 259
13.2.1　构建论文写作提纲 ... 260
13.2.2　撰写英语科技论文 ... 260
13.3　英语科技论文的写作技巧 ... 266
13.4　投稿过程 ... 270
13.5　论文发表后的工作 ... 272

附录A　常用前缀、后缀和构词成分 ... 273

附录B　常用数学符号及数学式表达 ... 279

附录C　常用的符号和单位 ... 282

C-1　SI Base Units ... 282
C-2　SI Prefixes ... 282
C-3　Directly Derived Unit ... 282
C-4　Special Names of Derived Unit ... 283
C-5　Units to be Discouraged or Abandoned ... 283
C-6　Some Physical Constants ... 283

附录D　SCI收录的光电类期刊 ... 284

D-1　530　物理学 ... 284
D-2　537　光学 ... 285
D-3　539　应用物理学 ... 289
D-4　730　电工与电子技术 ... 289
D-5　736　电子技术 ... 293

附录E　2009年EI收录的中国科技期刊(光电类可投期刊) ... 296

第1章 科技英语翻译技巧

学习专业英语不仅仅是学习英语专业词汇,在科技英语中,专业词汇仅占20%,其余80%都是我们常用的词汇。科技英语的初学者往往会碰到这样的难题:借助字典查出了一个句子中的所有的词汇,所有的词意也都明白,但对整个句子的意思仍然模糊不清,这主要是由于没有掌握科技英语的语法特点和翻译方式。

科技英语主要应用于科技报告和论文的写作中,在表达上具有简洁、准确的特点,这使得科技英语在语法上具有一定的特殊性。通过专业文献的阅读翻译来掌握科技英语语法的基本特点,可以使我们在以后的文献阅读和科技英语写作中收到事半功倍的效果,这也是专业英语教学的主要目的之一。

下面将对科技英语的概念、文体总貌、词汇特点、翻译方法和技巧等方面进行简单阐述,以使读者尽快适应专业英语的学习。

1.1 科技英语概念

科技英语(English for Science and Technology, EST)诞生于20世纪50年代,是第二次世界大战后科学技术迅猛发展的产物。70年代以来,科技英语在国际上引起了广泛的关注和研究,目前已经发展成为一种重要的英语文体。

科技英语泛指一切论及或谈及科学和技术的书面语和口语,其中包括:一、科技著述、科技论文和报告、实验报告和方案;二、各类科技情报和文字资料;三、科技实用手册的结构描述和操作规程;四、有关科技问题的会谈、会议、交谈用语;五、有关科技的影片、录像、光盘等有声资料的解说词。

1.2 科技英语文体总貌

科技英语要求客观性、准确性和严密性,注重叙事逻辑上的连贯(Coherence)及表达上的明晰(Clarity)与畅达(Fluency),避免行文晦涩。作者应避免表露个人感情,避免论证上的主观随意性。因此,科技英语总是力求少用或不用描述性形容词以及具有抒情作用的副词、感叹词及疑问词。科技英语力求平易(Plainness)和精确(Preciseness),避免使用旨在加强语言感染力和宣传效果的各种修辞格,忌用夸张、借喻、讥讽、反诘、双关及押韵等修辞手段,以免使读者产生行文浮华、内容虚饰之感。

1.3 科技英语词汇特点

科技英语大量使用专业词汇和半专业词汇。专业词汇是指仅用于某一学科或专业的词汇或术语。每门学科或专业都有自己的一套含义精确而狭窄的术语。从词源角度来分析,专业词汇主要有两个来源,一个是来自英语日常词汇,另一个是来自拉丁语和希腊语词根及词缀的词汇。

1. 日常词汇

用于某一专业科技领域便成为专业技术用语,具有严格的科学含义。例如,mask 在日常生活中表示"面具,掩饰",被光电领域借用后表示"掩模";gray 在日常生活中表示"灰色的",被纺织业借用后表示"未漂染的,本色的"。借用日常词语表达专业技术概念,在语义学上属于以联想建立词义理据,即以引申或扩展的基本词义来给新的概念命名,符合英语一词多义和词性转化的历史传统。

2. 加缀词

除部分来自英语日常词汇外,绝大多数,尤其是名词术语则是由拉丁语和希腊语的词根(root)和词缀(affix)构成的。现以前缀 hyper-(超出,过度,在……上)和后缀-asis(或-osis)(表示疾病)分别举例如下:

hyperacid 胃酸过多的;酸过多的

hyperfocal distance 超焦距

psychosis 精神病

词根是英语词汇的基本组成部分。绝大多数的自由词根来源于古英语,这类词根在各类词素中是唯一的自由形式;而绝大多数的粘着词根来源于希腊语或拉丁语。由于粘着词根的构词力不强,所以由这种词根构成的词的词义比较专一、稳定,不含感情色彩,没有引申寓意,这些特点使由粘着词根加前后缀构成的词汇成为构成科学技术、学术文化所需要的专门术语的好素材。

3. 半专业词汇

指那些既用于日常英语,同时又是科技英语中常用的词汇。半专业词汇与专业词汇的主要区别在于半专业词汇一般不专用于某一学科,而是为各学科所通用。这些词汇用在不同学科中虽然基本含义不变,但其确切含义则存在较大差别。

例如,power 一词在日常英语中有"力量,权力"等词义,用在各专业中,则有"爆发力(体育),动力(机械),电力(电力),功率(物理)"等词义;carrier 一词,在日常英语中表示"搬运人、邮递员"等词义,而在各专业中,则有"托架、承载器(机械),航空母舰(海军),运输机(航空),载体(化学),载流、载波(无线电),带菌体、媒介体(医学)"等词义。以 power 为例:

(1) Power can be transmitted over a long distance.

电力可以输送到很远的地方。

(2) Energy is the power to do work.

能量就是做功的能力。

(3) Friction causes a loss of power in every machine.

摩擦能引起每台机器的功率损耗。

(4) The fourth power of three is eighty-one.

三的四次方是81。

(5) The combining power of one element in the compound must equal the combining power of the other element.

化合物中,一种元素的化合价必须等于另一种元素的化合价。

(6) This is a 20 power binocular microscope.

这是一架20倍的双筒显微镜。

4. 新词汇

近几十年来,在现有专业词汇和半专业词汇的基础上又出现了几种新的词汇,其构词方法主要有合成法(Compounding)、混成法(Blending)、截短法(Clipping)、缩略法(Acronym)、转化法(Conversion)等,现分述如下。

(1) 合成法,即将两个或两个以上的旧词组合成一个新词。科技英语中的合成词有合写式(无连字符)和分写式(有连字符)两种。例如:

greenhouse 温室

hardware 硬件

warm-up 预热

(2) 混成法,即将两个词中在拼写或读音上比较适合的部分以"前一词去尾、后一词去首"的方式,加以叠合混成新词,而混成的新词兼具两个旧词的形和义。例如:

bit＝binary＋digit 二进制位,二进制数字

transistor＝transfer＋resistor 晶体管

(3) 截短法,即删除某一旧词中的一个或多个音节,形成新词,其词义不变。例如:

auto＝automobile 汽车

maths＝mathematics 数学

quake＝earthquake 地震

(4) 缩略法,即将某一词语组合中主要词的第一个字母组成新词的构词方法。科技英语中广泛使用缩略词是因为它们简略、方便。例如:

laser＝light amplification by stimulated emission of radiation 激光

radar＝radio detecting and ranging 雷达

UPS＝uninterrupted power supply 不间断电源

(5) 转化法,即不通过任何词形上的变化,直接转化为另一个词。在转化过程中,词性有所改变而词义则与转化前的原义仍保留有若干联系。例如:

xerox 用静电复印法复印(由名词词义"静电复印法"转化而来)

clone 使无性繁殖;复制(由名词词义"无性繁殖,克隆"转化而来)

e-mail 发电子邮件(由名词词义"电子邮件"转化而来)

另外,科技英语在词法方面的显著特点是名词化倾向。名词化倾向主要指广泛使用能表示动作或状态的抽象名词或起名词作用的非限定动词,以求明确和简练,避免表达带有主观色彩。其中,抽象名词绝大多数是由动词派生而来的。在科技英语中与名词化倾向密切

相关的一种现象是名词前较多使用名词作修饰词。例如：

origination 起源

radio propagation forecast 无线电传播预报

1.4 科技英语翻译方法和技巧

翻译是把一种语言所表达的思维内容用另一种语言表达出来的跨语言、跨文化的语言交际活动。翻译包括口译（Interpretation）和笔译（Translation）。在笔译中，又可分为科技翻译、文学翻译、政论文翻译和应用文翻译等。

随着国际学术交流的日益广泛，科技英语已经受到普遍的重视，掌握一些科技英语的翻译技巧是非常必要的。科技英语作为一种重要的英语文体，与非科技英语文体相比，具有词义多、长句多、被动句多、词性转换多、非谓语动词多、专业性强等特点，这些特点都是由科技文献的内容所决定的。因此，科技英语的翻译也有别于其他英语文体的翻译。

1.4.1 科技英语翻译标准

关于翻译标准曾有过"信、达、雅"，"信、顺"，"忠实、通顺、易懂"，"等值"等多种提法。许多翻译工作者和研究者也曾对这些提法展开过广泛而激烈的争论和讨论。但就科技英语翻译而言，我们可以把翻译标准概括为忠实原作和译文通顺。

1. 忠实

译文应忠实于原文，准确地、完整地、科学地表达原文的内容，包括思想、精神与风格。译者不得任意对原文内容加以歪曲、增删、遗漏和篡改。

2. 通顺

译文语言必须通顺，符合规范，用词造句应符合本民族语言的习惯，要用民族的、科学的、大众的语言，以求通顺易懂。不应有文理不通、逐词死译和生硬晦涩等现象。

1.4.2 科技英语翻译过程中语法特点

科技英语是科学技术的载体，用其来客观表达科技的实质。这也要求科技文献的逻辑严密，能着重客观叙述文献作者的观点。所以，在科技文献中，一般现在时、情态动词 can 和 may、动词被动语态、非限定动词以及长句的使用频率较高，现分述如下。

1. 大量使用名词化结构

《当代英语语法》（A Grammar of Contemporary English）在论述科技英语时提出，大量使用名词化结构（Nominalization）是科技英语的特点之一。因为科技文体要求行文简洁、表达客观、内容确切、信息量大、强调存在的事实，而非某一行为。例如：

Archimeds first discovered the principle of displacement of water by solid bodies. 阿基米德最先发展固体排水的原理。句中 of displacement of water by solid bodies 系名词化结构，一方面简化了同位语从句，另一方面强调 displacement 这一事实。

2. 多用动词的现在时

科技英语中多用一般现在时来表示"无时间性"的"一般叙述"，即叙述事实或真理，客观地表述定义、定理、方程式、公式、图表等。例如：

(1) Action is equal to reaction but it acts in a contrary direction. 作用力和反作用力大小相等，方向相反。

(2) AIDS is spread by direct infection of the bloodstream with body fluids that contain the AIDS virus. 艾滋病传播是由血液和带有艾滋病病毒的体液直接感染引起的。

3. can 和 may 使用频率高

这是因为这两个情态动词可用来表示客观可能性，而其他则多突出主观性。例如：

(1) The best way to improve urban air may be to curb the use of cars, even though modern car are far cleaner than earlier ones. 改善城市空气质量最好的办法可能还是控制汽车的使用，尽管现代汽车比以前的汽车污染要小得多。

(2) According to a growing body of evidence, the chemicals that make up many plastics may migrate out of the material and into foods and fluids, ending up in your body. 越来越多的证据表明，许多塑料制品的化学成分会移动到食物或流体上去，最终进入人体内。

4. 广泛使用被动语句

根据英国利兹大学 John Swales 的统计，科技英语中的谓语至少 1/3 是被动语态。科技英语倾向于使用被动语态，这是因为科技英语注重对事实和方法、性能和特征做出客观表述。与主动语态相比，被动语态表达更为客观，有助于将读者的注意力集中在叙述中的事物、现实或过程上。因此尽量使用第三人称叙述，采用被动语态。例如：

(1) Atoms can be thought of as miniature solar systems, with a nucleus at the center and electrons orbiting at specific distances from it. 原子可被看成是一个微型的太阳系，原子核在其中心，而电子以一定的距离绕核做圆周运动。

(2) Care should be taken not to damage the instruments. 注意不要损坏仪器。

(3) Attention must be paid to the working temperature of the machine. 应当注意机器的工作温度。

5. 非限定动词的应用和大量使用后置定语

如前所述，科技文章要求行文简练，结构紧凑，因此，科技英语往往使用分词短语代替定语从句或状语从句；使用分词独立结构代替状语从句或并列分句；使用不定式短语代替各种从句；使用介词＋动名词短语代替定语从句或状语从句。这样既可缩短句子，又比较醒目。例如：

(1) What the TV camera does is to break the picture up into a number of lines consisting of very small points of light. 电视摄像机的功能就是把图像分解成许许多多由小光点组成的线条。

(2) Using density one can calculate the mass of a certain volume of liquid. 可以用密度计算一定体积的液体的质量。

6. 大量使用常用句型

科技文章中经常使用若干特定的句型，从而形成科技文体区别于其他文体的标志。例如：It—that—结构句型；被动态结构句型；分词短语结构句型；省略句结构句型等。举例如下：It is evident that a well lubricated bearing turns more easily than a dry one. 显然，润滑好的轴承，比不润滑的轴承容易转动。

7. 使用长句

为了描叙事物精确,要使用长句。为了表述一个复杂概念,使之逻辑严密,结构紧凑,科技文章中往往出现许多长句。例如:

Each chemical element had its number and fixed position in the table, and from this it became possible to predict its behavior: how it would react with other elements, what kind of compounds it would form, and what sort of physical properties it would have. 每个化学元素在周期表中都有一定的原子数和位置,可以据此来推测它所具有的特点:如何同其他元素发生反应,形成什么样的化合物,以及其物理性质如何。

8. 大量使用复合词与缩略词

大量使用复合词与缩略词是科技文章的特点之一,复合词从过去的双词组合发展到多词组合;缩略词趋向于任意构词,某一篇论文的作者可以就仅在该文中使用的术语组成缩略词,这给翻译工作带来一定的困难。例如:full-enclosed 全封闭的(双词合成形容词)。

综上所述,科技英语所具有的词汇和语法特点使其在实际运用中有别于日常英语和英语在其他语域中的实际运用。广大英语学习者应该在英语学习和实践中不断深入体会和把握科技英语的各项特点,这样将有助于提高英语水平,尤其是科技英语翻译水平。

1.4.3 科技英语的翻译方法与技巧

在语际交流过程中,原文语言叫原语(Source Language,SL),译文语言叫译语(Target Language,TL)。要提高翻译质量,使译文达到"忠实"、"通顺"这两个标准,就必须运用翻译技巧。翻译技巧就是在翻译过程中用词造句的处理方法,即翻译 SL 时在某些场合需要对 TL 作哪些相应的调整和改变。

翻译技巧的依据就是 SL 和 TL 在语言、语法及表达方式上的异同。即由于这两种语言的不同,用 TL 来表达 SL 信息时,需要在词句上作哪些改变才能表达出与原文相同的意思。

翻译技巧一般包括词类转换(conversion)、词序调整(inversion)、省略(omission)、增词(amplification)、重复(repetition)、反译法(negation)、选词用字(diction)、分译法(division)、综合法(Recasting)和语篇重构(textual reorganization)。

1. 词类转换

英语翻译中,常常需要将英语句子中属于某种词类的词,译成另一种词类的汉语词,以适应汉语的表达习惯或达到某种修辞目的。这种翻译处理方法就是转换词性法,简称词类转换。举例如下。

(1) Lasers are used in the treatment of retinal detachment.

激光用于治疗视网膜脱落。"treat 治疗"因作介词宾语需用名词 treatment,汉译时仍可用动词"治疗"。

(2) Maiman's invention of the laser provided new sources of very intense, coherent and highly directional light beams.

梅曼发明了激光器,提供了一种新光源,可产生极强的、相干的和高度定向的光束。"发明"英译时因作主语故用名词 invention。

(3) Planned economy is over and market economy is in.

计划经济制度已经废止,现在实行的是市场经济。原文用的是介词 over 和 in,汉译时根据需要分别改用动词"废止"和"实行"。

(4) In any case, the performance test have priority.

不管怎样进行,性能测试都要优先。这里将名词"priority"转译为动词"优先"。

2. 词序调整

有时候英语长句的叙述层次与汉语相反,这时就须从英语原文的后面译起,自上而下,逆着英语原文的顺序翻译。翻译时应根据 TL 的表达方式作一些有必要的调整。例如:

(1) Ningbo, China, August 2, 2009—China outclassed Russia in a hard-fought five-set match on Sunday in the 2009 FIVB World Grand Prix. (地点在前)

2009 年 8 月 2 日,在中国宁波举行的一场 2009 世界女排大奖赛的一场比赛中,中国队经过五局苦战,以 3∶2 战胜俄罗斯队。(时间在前)

(2) Rain or shine, we'll have to go tomorrow.

无论晴天下雨,我们明天非去不可。汉语先说"晴天",后说"下雨";英语则先说 rain 后说 shine。

(3) An insufficient power supply makes the motor immovable.

电源不足就会使马达停转。这里将"insufficient power"(不足电源)改序翻译为"电源不足"较为合理。

(4) ①There is an equilibrium between the liquid and its vapor, ②as many molecules being lost from the surface of the liquid and ③then existing as vapor, ④as reenter the liquid in a given time.

这个句子是由一个主句①、定语从句④以及两个分次独立结构组成,这个句子分为四层意思:①液体和蒸汽之间处于平衡状态,是主句,是全句的中心所在;②许多分子从液体表面逸出,成为蒸汽;③又有同样多的分子重新进入液体;④在一定时间内。

根据汉语表达习惯,"因"在前面,"果"在后,可逆原文翻译。

译文:在一定时间内,许多分子从液体表面逸出,成为蒸汽。又有同样多的分子重新进入液体,因此,液体和蒸汽之间处于平衡。

(5) ①Rocket research has confirmed a strange fact ②which had already been suspected, ③there is a "high-temperature belt" in the atmosphere, with its center roughly 30 miles above the ground.

分析:①是主句,②是定语从句,③是同位语从句做 fact 的同位语。按照汉语表达习惯,用逆译法翻译,更显得自然、流畅。

译文:大气中有一个"高温带",其中心在距地面约 30 英里高的地方。对此人们早就怀疑,利用火箭加以研究,这一奇异的事实已得到证明。

3. 增减词译法

翻译时对原文内容不应该作任何删节或增补。但由于两种语言表达方式不同,在把原文信息译成译文信息时,常常需要删去或增添一些词。这样做并不损害原意,反而可以使译文更为通顺,意思更为清楚。这种省略和增添不仅是许可的,而且常常看成是一种翻译技巧。增词就是在译句中增加或补充英语句子中原来没有或省略了的词语,以便更完善、更清楚地表达英语句子所阐述的内容。在英语句子中,有的词从语法结构上讲是必不可少的,但并没有什么实际意义,只是在句子中起着单纯的语法作用;有的词虽有实际意义,但按照字面译出又显多余。这样的词在翻译时往往可以省略不译。

(1) 省略

汉语没有冠词,代词、连词、介词用得也远较英语为少。上述词类汉译时往往可以省略不译,省略后意思并不含混反而更为简练明白。

① You cannot build a ship, a bridge or a house if you don't know how to make a design or how to read it.

不会制图或看不懂图纸,就不可能造船、架桥或盖房子。汉译中省略代词 you 和 it、冠词 a、连接词 if 和副词 how。

② Please take off the old picture and throw it away.

请把那张旧画取下来扔掉。汉译时省略了作宾语的代词。

③ University applicants who had worked at a job would receive preference over those who had not.

报考大学的人,有工作经验的优先录取。英语句子中有些短语重复出现,或者具有相同意义的词重复出现,英译汉时可按情况作适当省略。

④ There was no snow, the leaves were gone from the trees, and the grass was dead.

没有下雪,但叶落草枯。根据汉语习惯,译文中可以省略一些可有可无的词。

(2) 增词

英语没有量词、助词,汉译时应根据上下文的需要增加量词和助词。汉语名词没有复数的概念,动词没有时态变化,翻译时如有必要应增加表复数和表时态的词。英语中用了一些不及物动词意义就很完整,这些词在汉语中为他动词,必须增加宾语,否则意义就不完整。根据上述情况汉译时必须考虑增词。

① 英语中的某些抽象名词、不及物动词或代词,若单独译出,有时意思不够明确,可分别在其后增加"状态"、"工作"、"过程"、"现象"、"方式"、"情况"、"作用"、"部分"、"化"等词。例:

Oxidation will make iron and steel rusty.

氧化作用会使钢铁生锈。

Due care must be taken to ensure that the pulse signal itself shall show no irregularities and no interruptions.

应注意保证脉冲信号本身不出现不规则现象和中断现象。

② 英语中的名词为复数形式时,根据情况可增加适当的表示复数概念的词。如"们"、"之类"、"一些"、"许多"、"一批"、"这些"、"那些"、"各种"、"大量"、"几个"、"几次"等。例:

The first electronic computers went into operation in 1945.

第一批电子计算机于 1945 年投入使用。

In spite of the difficulties, our task was got over well.

虽然有各种困难,但我们的任务已顺利完成。

③ 如果分词短语或独立分词结构含有时间、原因、条件、让步等状语意义,翻译时可增加"当……时"、"……之后"、"因为……"、"由于……"、"如果……"、"假若……"、"虽然……

但……"等词。例:

Using a transformer, power at low voltage can be transformed into power at high voltage.

如果使用变压器,低压电就能转换成高压电。

The velocity increasing, the acceleration of a body is positive.

速度增大时,物体的加速度为正。

Being stable in air at ordinary temperature, mercury combines with oxygen if heated.

虽然常温下水银在空气中是稳定的,但给它加热的话,就与氧化合。

④ 当动词不定式和不定式短语表示目的或结果状语时,通常就可在其前面加"为了"、"要"、"以便"、"就"、"从而"、"结果"等词。例:

We made transistors by different means only to get the same effect.

我们用不同的方法制造晶体管,结果得到相同的效应。

Many lathes are equipped with multistage speed gearboxes to get different speeds.

为了得到不同的速度,许多车床装有多级变速齿轮箱。

⑤ 当动词不定式的被动形式作定语时,通常表示按计划或要求表示的动作,含有"将来"的意思。翻译时要增加"要"、"将"、"待"、"应"、"须"等词。例:

The cutting tool must be harder than the material to be cut.

刀具必须比待切的材料硬。

The chief difficulty to be overcome in aviation is that of renewing supplies of petrol while in the air.

航空上要克服的主要难题是空中加油问题。

⑥ 当被动语态句中的谓语是由表示"知道"、"了解"、"看见"、"认为"、"发现"、"考虑"等意义的动词来担任时,译时通常可在其前面增加"人们"、"我们"、"大家"、"有人"等词,变为主动语态句。例:

All matter is known to possess weight.

大家都知道,所有物质都具有质量。

Many elements in nature are found to be mixtures of different isotopes.

人们发现,自然界里许多元素,都是各种不同的同位素的混合物。

⑦ 当句中有几个成分并列时,可根据并列成分的数量增加数词,并在其后加入量词,如"个"、"者"、"种"、"方面"、"领域"等,使译文确切明白。例:

The frequency, wave length and speed of sound are closely related.

频率、波长和声速三者是密切相关的。

This report summed up the new achievements made in electron tubes, semiconductors and components.

本报告总结了电子管、半导体和元件三方面的新成就。

⑧ 英语中的动词时态,在译成汉语时,可视不同情况增加"正"、"正在"、"过"、"了"、"曾"、"曾经"、"已经"、"一直"、"将要"、"会"、"能"等词。例:

Contemporary natural sciences are now working for new important breakthroughs.

当代自然科学正在酝酿新的重大突破。

Before 15th century it was generally believed that the earth was the center of the universe.

15世纪前,曾普遍认为地球是宇宙的中心。

⑨ 英语中,用倒装语序表示的虚拟条件状语从句,译成汉语时,往往可增加"如果……便……"、"假如……就……"、"万一……就……"、"只要……的话,就……"等连词。例:

Hard there been no electronic computers, there would have been no artificial satellite or rockets.

如果没有电子计算机,就不会有人造卫星或火箭。

Should a DC system be used, the losses in transmission would be very great.

如果使用直流系统的话,输电线路上的损耗就会很大。

⑩ 不用连词,而以不变化的"be"开头的让步状语从句,英译汉时,往往增加"不论"、"不管"、"无论"等连词。例:

Be the shape of a body complicated, it is possible to find out its volume.

不论物体的形状如何复杂,总可以求出它的体积。

All magnets behave the same, be they large or small.

所有磁体,无论大小,其性质都一样。

⑪ 英语中无连词的并列句,只用一定的标点符号分开,翻译时,如果语气有突然的转折,可增加"但"、"但是"、"而"等词。例:

Liquids contract in freezing; water is an important exception to the rule.

液体冻结时收缩,但水却是这一规则的重要例外。

Adding heat does not make the molecules any larger; it makes the average distance between them larger.

增加热量不能使分子变大,而是使分子间的平均距离增大。

⑫ 英语中的祈使语气句,汉译时根据句子的不同情况,分别增加"要"、"请"、"应"、"须"、"试"、"千万"、"一定"、"务必"等词。例:

Remember that science requires the effort of a lifetime.

要记住,科学需要人们付出毕生的精力。

Compare the melting point and freezing point of a substance.

试比较一种物质的熔点和凝固点。

⑬ 为使句子前后连贯、意思通顺、逻辑严密,英译汉时可增加某些适当的词,包括语气助词、概括词、承上启下的词等。例:

The first term of a Fourier series is called the fundamental, the other terms the harmonics.

傅里叶级数的第一项称为基波,其他各项称为谐波。

Speed and reliability are the chief advantage of the electronic computer.

速度快和可靠性高是电子计算机的主要优点。

The propagation of such microwaves will be explained in term of Maxwell's equations.

这种微波的传播原理要用麦克斯韦方程来解释。

综上,词量增加归纳起来是 4 个方面的要求:词汇要求,语法要求,逻辑要求和修辞要求。其原则是增加原文中虽无其词,然有其意的词,不是随心所欲地任意增加。

(3) 汉译英时的增词情况

汉译英也有增词法,称"词的增补"。概括起来,汉译英需要增补的有下列 9 种情况。

① 汉语无主语视情况补出主语。例:

接到你的来信,非常高兴。

I was very glad to have received your letter.

② 增补物主代词。汉语里物主代词用得少,而且常常不用出现,但英语里凡说到一个人的器官和归他所有的或与他有关的事物时,总要在前面加上物主代词。例:

我们响应政府号召。

We respond to the call of our government.

工人们带午饭到工厂吃。

The workers take their lunches to the factory.

我用手蒙住脸。

I cover my face with my hands.

③ 增补作宾语的代词。按习惯,汉语常常可省略宾语,但英语里,凡及物动词都得有宾语。例:

请原谅,打断你一下。

Excuse me for interrupting you.

④ 增补连词。汉语有意合特点,即词、词组、分句或句子之间的关系可以通过上下文及语序来表示,较少用连词,但英语注意形合,连词不能少。例:

虚心使人进步,骄傲使人落后。

Modesty helps one to go forward, whereas conceit makes one lag behind.

⑤ 增补介词。英语句子十有八九都少不了介词。汉语中不需要介词的地方,英语也要用。所以,汉译英时注意补介词。例:

这些书,你们五个人分。

Divide these books among the five of you.

⑥ 增补冠词。汉语里无冠词。有冠词是英语的特点之一,名词前一般都有冠词,汉译英时要增补冠词。例:

我们对问题要作全面的分析,才能解决得妥当。

We must make a comprehensive analysis of a problem before we solve it properly.

⑦ 增补暗含的词语。由于习惯问题,汉语中有些词不需明言,意思都很清楚,但译成英语时,如果不补则意思不明,甚至会引起误会,这时应视情况补上适当的词。例:

要提倡顾全大局。

We should advocate the spirit of taking the whole situation into consideration.

⑧ 增补概括性的词语。例:

黄金白银,坚甲利兵,并非构成大国的要素。

Gold and silver, a strong army and powerful weapons—these are not the elements that constitute a great nation.

⑨ 增补注释性词语。汉语中的典故、谚语、政治名词、术语和简化说法,译时往往要适当加注释性词语。例:

三个臭皮匠,合成一个诸葛亮。

Three cobblers with their wits combined equal Zhuge Liang the mastermind.

4. 重复

英语要避免重复,而汉语则不怕重复。英语为了避免重复常常用一个动词接几个宾语或表语;用了一个动词,后面相同的动词便可以省略;或大量使用代词以避免重复名词。汉语不怕重复,遇到上述情况汉译时可以采用重复某词的手法。实际上,重复代词所代表的名词也是减少使用代词的一种方法。

① I had experienced oxygen and/or engine trouble.

我曾碰到过,不是氧气设备出故障,就是引擎出故障,或两者都出故障。本例属名词的重复。

② Happy families also had their own troubles.

幸福的家庭也有幸福家庭的苦恼。本例属代词的重复。英语中用物主代词 its、his、their 等以代替句中作主语的名词(有时附有修饰语)时,翻译时往往可以不用代词而重复其作主语的名词(有时附有修饰语),以达到明确具体的目的。

③ The positive charges do not move about; but the electrons do.

正电荷不能到处移动,可是电子却能到处移动。

在英语里,为了使文字简明生动,常常对重复部分予以省略或用词(如 do so 和代词等)代替。英译汉时,为了明确或便于表达,对省略或代替了的部分加以重复。

④ Once he took up his pen, writings began pouring down.

他一动笔,就洋洋洒洒,一发难收。

在重复法中,有时采用两字重叠、四字重叠或四字对偶等修辞手段,使译文更生动。

5. 反译法

由于汉英两种语言表达习惯不同而且均可以从正面或反面来表达同一概念,翻译时如果用正面表达译文有困难,欠通顺,则不妨用反面表达,或将反面表达改用正面表达,这样可以使译文比较通顺而与原意并无出入。

① I lay awake almost the whole night.

我几乎一夜没睡着。本例属正说反译。

② I can't agree with you more.

我极其赞同你的意见。本例属反说正译。

③ You cannot fail to arrive there before 8 o'clock tomorrow morning.

明天早上你务必在8点之前到达那里。有一些双重否定的句子在翻译的过程中也要译为肯定句。

④ That's a thing that might happen to anyone.

这种事任何人都不能幸免。有时,采用反译法可以加强修辞效果。本例也可译成"这种事可能发生在任何一个人身上",显然,前一种译法的修辞效果更好,更加符合原文的语气。

6. 选词用字

由于构词时联想不同,表达方式不同,两种语言表达同一种思想常常用词不同。因而在翻译时必须在理解原意的基础上,考虑表达这个意思的 TL 要用什么词最为恰当。选词用字恰当是翻译中的一个十分重要的问题。

① It caused devastation by burrowing and by devouring the herbage which might have maintained millions of sheep and cattle.

它们在地下打洞,吞食掉本来可以维持数百万只牛羊的牧草,从而造成了破坏。原文中的 cattle 有"牲畜"和"牛"二义,这里因与"羊"(sheep)对置,根据种属概念不能并列的逻辑规则,cattle 只能作"牛"解。

② Velocity changes if either the speed or direction changes.

如果(物体运动的)速率和方向有一个发生变化,则物体的运动速度也随之发生变化。velocity 和 speed 都可表示"速度",前者具专业色彩,一般用于科技,后者语域较宽,可用于科技或日常生活领域。如果将 velocity 和 speed 都理解为"速度",原文表述将失去意义,因此这里 velocity 和 speed 中必有一个词表示其他意义。物理学告诉我们,速度是矢量,有大小又有方向,而速率是标量,有大小而没有方向。据此,velocity 是速度,因为原文语境信息暗示它有方向(direction),speed 是速率。

③ Put a teaspoonful of tea in the pot and then you just add the boiling water to it and let it stand.

在茶壶内放一茶匙茶叶,冲上开水后待一会儿再喝。let it stand 是指沏完茶以后,"稍等片刻"再喝。

④ Studies serve for delight, for ornament, and for ability.

译文:a. 读书能给人乐趣、文雅和能力。
   b. 读书可以怡情养性,可以撷拾文采,可以增长才干。
   c. 读书可以怡情,足以博采,足以长才。

译文 a 既忠于原文,读起来也顺口。可算是很不错了!

但当我们读译文 b 时,相比之下,译文 a 逊色了。因为译文 b 能给人一种全新的、富有表现力的感受。这样翻译不仅符合了"信"、"达"的标准,还具有"传神"的效果。

当我们读了译文 c 时,又会情不自禁地拍案叫绝。比起译文 b,译文 c 又"更上一层楼"。因为这才是真正地体现了严复的"信、达、雅"三字翻译标准。

以上原文中的 studies 为何不约而同地被译为"读书"而不是"学习或研究"呢?这是受上下文制约的。"语境是决定语义的唯一因素,脱离了语境,则不存在语义。"语境不同,词义即有所不同。

7. 分译法

英语中长句比较多,有时英语长句中的主句与从句或主句与修饰语间的关系不十分密切,翻译时可按照汉语多用短句的习惯,把长句中的从句或短语化为句子,分开来叙述,将原句化整为零。为使译文通顺连贯,也可以适当加几个连接词。另外,有的词若按 SL 的结构翻译不好处理,这时如将这个词译成句子就能较准确地表达出原意,译文也比较通顺。

① The number of the young people in the United States who can't read is incredible about one in four.

大约有 1/4 的美国青年人没有阅读能力,这简直令人难以置信。

该句在英语中是一个相对简单的句子,但是如果我们按照原文的句子结构死译,就可能被翻译成:没有阅读能力的美国青年人的数目令人难以相信约为 1/4。这样,就使得译文极为不通顺,不符合汉语的表达习惯。

② Television, it is often said, keeps one informed about current events, allows one to follow the latest developments in science and politics, and offers an endless series of programs which are both instructive and entertaining.

人们常说,通过电视可以了解时事、掌握科学和政治的最新动态。从电视里还可以看到层出不穷、既有教育意义又有娱乐性的新节目。

在此长句中,有一个插入语"it is often said",三个并列的谓语结构,还有一个定语从句,这三个并列的谓语结构尽管在结构上同属于同一个句子,但都有独立的意义,因此在翻译时,可以采用分译法,按照汉语的习惯把整个句子分解成几个独立的分句。

③ An infrared system could be usable in both anti-air and anti-ship engagements, but its inherent disadvantages related to some dependence on optical visibility and to sensibility to interference from natural or man made sources make it less attractive in the surface than in the air role.

红外系统既可用于对空作战,也可用于对舰作战,但是它有两个固定的缺点:一是对光学可见度有一定的依赖性,二是易受天然或人工干扰源的干扰。因此,该系统的对空作用较之对舰作用更为诱人。

8. 综合法

对那些用某种翻译技巧无法译出的句子,应着眼于篇章,以逻辑分析为基础,有顺有序,有主有次地对全句进行综合处理。

Many man-made substances are replacing certain natural materials because either the quantity of the natural product can not meet our ever-increasing requirement, or, more often, because the physical property of the synthetic substance, which is the common name for man-made materials, has been chosen, and ever emphasized, so that it would be of the greatest use in the fields in which it is to be applied.

这个句子是由一个主句加上一个由 because 引导的原因状语从句,一个由 so that 引导的状语从句和 which 引导的非限制性定语从句及 in which 引导的定语从句所组成。

译文:人造材料统称为合成材料,许多人造材料正在替代某些天然材料,这或者是由于天然产品的数量不能满足日益增长的需要,或者往往是人们选择了合成材料的一些物理性质并加以突出而造成的。因此合成材料在应用的领域中将具有极大的用途。

9. 语篇重构

语篇重构就是对原文的结构和语言进行较大幅度的改动,脱离原句的层次和结构安排,按汉语叙事伦理的习惯重新组合句子,摆脱了原文的语序和句子形式的约束,使译文自然、流畅,更加符合汉语的表达习惯,以期在更深的层次上达到与原文的对等。

① Computer languages may range from detailed low level close to that immediately understood by the particular computer, to the sophisticated high level which can be rendered automatically acceptable to a wide range of computers.

译文:计算机语言有低级的也有高级的。前者比较烦琐,很接近特定计算机直接能动的语言;后者比较复杂,适用范围广,能自动为多种计算机所接受。

② The law of conservation and transformation of energy is the chief basis of physical, astronomical and chemical reasoning as well as of engineering practice.

译文:能量守恒和能量转换定律不仅是工程实践的主要基础,而且也是物理、天文以及化学等方面的主要基础。

另外,在科技英语长句中,很多都是专业方面的问题,除了上述的几种翻译技巧外,很多词在特定领域有特殊含义和约定俗成的翻译方法。需要加强专业的知识和素养。

1.5 提高科技英语翻译能力的途径

对于广大英语学习者来说,要想具有上述素质当然不可能一蹴而就,但只要努力,将来就一定能够成功。下面列出了几种提高科技英语翻译的途径,以供参考。

① 广泛阅读英汉报刊杂志,提高英汉两种语言基本功。

② 广泛涉猎中英文科技文章和新闻,有效地扩展自己的知识面。例如,学习者可收听VOA 中的科技新闻,阅读 Time、Newsweek 等原文期刊中科技栏目的文章,甚至上网搜索有关材料。在翻译时,如遇到有关专业背景知识不理解,要积极向专家请教,或认真查阅专业技术资料。

③ 认真学习本专业的基础课程,大量阅读本专业的中英文文献,提高自身的专业水平。

④ 认真学习有关科技英语翻译著作和刊物,切实掌握科技英语翻译方法和技巧,深入认识科技翻译中经常会遇到的问题。学习者可阅读《中国翻译》、《中国科技翻译》、《上海科技翻译》等学术刊物,以及《科技英语学习》、《英语沙龙》、《英语学习》、《英语世界》等涉及英汉翻译,尤其是科技英语翻译的刊物。

⑤ 在翻译实践中提高。正如其他语言学习一样,学习翻译,尤其是在打基础的阶段,实践是极其重要的。一方面,应注意在数量上提高,译得应快一些;另一方面就是要在质量上提高,译得好一些。学习者经过一定量的翻译实践后,随着个人对翻译技能体会的加深,翻译速度自然会逐渐提高。另外,学习者应琢磨做翻译的工作程序和方法,找出自己的薄弱环节,通过在方法上的改进来提高翻译速度。

下面介绍一个"定时定量翻译工作程序",供大家参考。

第一步:快速浏览原文一遍,了解文章大意即可。遇到生词除十分必要的以外都不要去查词典,可以在下面画线标出。

第二步:边看边译,每次处理一个自然段(如段落长,一次五六行左右)。具体步骤为:阅读原文,查阅词典,斟酌措辞,写下译文。如果有的地方一时还理解不好或找不到适当的表达方式,可以暂时空下,做个记号,等译完初稿后再补上。每段译文写下来后随手做些修改。有的地方一时修改不好就放下,但要在旁边做个记号。

第三步,初稿完成后即进行修改。首先是把空下来未译的地方补上,把原来未修改好的地方再修改一下。然后,从头再阅读一遍译文,修改错别字以及语句不通顺的地方。

要想在质量上提高,学习者在平时的科技翻译学习和实践中就应自觉运用已经学过的翻译知识、方法和技巧,防止重犯在过去的实践中曾经出现过的失误。因此,广大学习者应认真理解原文,对汉语表达字斟句酌,不厌其烦地反复修改。译文的质量没有止境,只有反反复复地修改才会发现自己存在的问题,从而提高翻译能力。修改本身就是个提高的过程,学习者不应该怕费事。另外,学习者也可翻译配有译文的原文,把自己的译文同所配译文相比较,找出差距和不足,这样也将有助于提高翻译质量。

本章参考文献

1. 冯梅. 英汉科技翻译. 哈尔滨:哈尔滨工业大学出版社,2000.
2. 严俊仁. 汉英科技翻译. 北京:国防工业出版社,2004.
3. 李学平. 科技翻译与英语学习. 天津:南开大学出版社,2005.

Semiconductor Physics and Device

第2章

PREVIEW

We often hear that we are living in the information age. Large amounts of information can be obtained via the Internet, for example, and can also be obtained quickly over long distances via satellite communication system. The development of the *transistor*[1] and the *integrated circuit*[2] (IC) has lead to these remarkable capabilities. The IC permeates almost every facet of our daily lives, including such things as the compact disk player, the fax machine, laser scanners at the grocery store, and the cellular telephone. One of the most dramatic examples of IC technology is the digital computer—a relatively small laptop computer today has more computing capability than the equipment used to send a man to the moon a few years ago. The semiconductor electronics field continues to be a fast-changing one, with thousands of technical papers published each year.

2.1 Semiconductor Materials

Semiconductors are special crystalline materials that have electrical *conductivity*[3] σ (and the corresponding *resistivity*[4] $\rho=1/\sigma$) between that of a *conductor*[5] and an *insulator*[6]. Insulators such as fused quartz and glass have very low conductivities, in the order of $1E-18$ to $1E-8$ S/cm; and conductors such as aluminum and silver have high conductivities, typically from 10^4 to 10^6 S/cm. The conductivity of a semiconductor is generally sensitive to temperature, illumination, magnetic field, and minute amount of *impurity*[7] atoms. This sensitivity in conductivity makes the semiconductor one of the most important materials for electronic applications. Semiconductors form the backbone of the electronics industry because they are rugged, inexpensive, and can form diodes, transistors, and other important electronic components.

The study of semiconductor materials began in the early nineteenth century. Over the years many semiconductors have been investigated. Two general classifications of semiconductors are the *elemental semiconductor*[8] materials and the *compound semiconductor*[9] materials. The elemental semiconductor materials, those composed of single species of atoms, such as *silicon*[10] (Si) and *germanium*[11] (Ge), can be found in Group Ⅳ of the periodic table. The compound semiconductor materials, most of which are formed from special combinations of group Ⅲ and group Ⅴ elements (Semiconductors can also be formed from combinations of group Ⅱ and group Ⅵ elements). Table 2-1 shows a portion of the periodic table related to semiconductors and Table 2-2 lists a few of the semiconductor materials.

Table 2-1 A portion of the periodic table related to semiconductors.

Ⅲ	Ⅳ	Ⅴ
B	C	
Al	Si	P
Ga	Ge	As
In		Sb

The elemental materials, those that are composed of single species of atoms, are silicon and germanium. Silicon is by far the most common semiconductor used in integrated circuits and will be emphasized to a great extent.

The two-element, or binary, compounds such as gallium arsenide (GaAs) or gallium phosphide (GaP) are formed by combining one group Ⅲ and one group Ⅴ element. GaAs is one of the more common of the compound semiconductors. Its good optical properties make it useful in optical devices. GaAs is also used in specialized applications in which, for example, high speed is required.

Table 2-2 A list of some semiconductor materials

Elemental semiconductors	Si	Silicon
	Ge	Germanium
Compound semiconductors	AlP	Aluminum phosphide
	AlAs	Aluminum arsenide
	GaP	Gallium phosphide
	GaAs	Gallium arsenide
	InP	Indium phosphide

We can also form a three-element, or ternary, compound semiconductor. An example is $Al_x Ga_{1-x} As$, in which the subscript x indicates the fraction of the lower atomic number element component. More complex semiconductors can also be formed that provide flexibility when choosing material properties.

Prior to the invention of the *bipolar transistor*[12] in 1947, semiconductors were used only as two-terminal devices, such as *rectifiers*[13] and *photodiodes*[14]. In the early 1950s, Ge was the major semiconductor material. However, Ge proved unsuitable in many applications because Ge devices exhibited high *leakage currents*[15] at only moderately elevated temperatures. In addition, germanium oxide is water soluble and unsuited for device fabrication. Since the early 1960s silicon has become a practical substitute and has now virtually supplanted germanium as a material for semiconductor fabrication. The main reasons we now use silicon are that silicon devices exhibit much lower leakage currents, and high-quality silicon dioxide can be grown thermally. There is also an economic consideration. Device grade silicon costs much less than any other semiconductor material. Silicon in the form of silica and silicates comprises 25% of the Earth's crust, and silicon is second only to oxygen in abundance. At present, silicon is one of the most studied elements in the periodic table; and silicon technology is by far the most advanced among all semiconductor technologies.

Many of the compound semiconductors have electrical and optical properties that are absent in silicon These semiconductors, especially GaAs, are used mainly for microwave and photonic applications. Although we do not know as much about the technology of compound semiconductor technology as we do about that of silicon, compound semiconductor technology has advanced partly because of the advances in silicon technology.

2.2 Type of Solids

*Amorphous[16], polycrystalline[17], and single crystal are the three general types of solids. Each type is characterized by the size of an ordered region within the material. An ordered region is a spatial volume in which atoms or molecules have a regular geometric arrangement or periodicity*①. Amorphous materials have order only within a few atomic or molecular dimensions, while polycrystalline materials have a high degree of order over many atomic or molecular dimensions. These ordered regions, or single-crystal regions, vary in size and orientation with respect to one another. The single-crystal regions are called *grains*[18] and are separated from one another by *grain boundaries*[19]. Single-crystal materials, ideally, have a high degree of order, or regular geometric periodicity, throughout the entire volume of the material. The advantage of a single-crystal material is that, in general, its electrical properties are superior to those of a nonsingle-crystal material, since grain boundaries tend to degrade the electrical characteristics. Two-dimensional representations of amorphous, polycrystalline, and single-crystal materials are shown in Fig. 2-1.

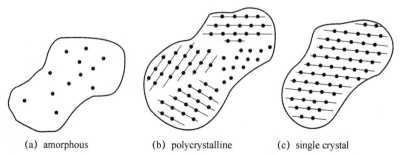

(a) amorphous　　　(b) polycrystalline　　　(c) single crystal

Fig. 2-1　Schematics of three general types of crystals.

2.3 Crystal Structure

The semiconductor materials we will study are single crystals, that is, the atoms are arranged in a three-dimensional periodic fashion. The periodic arrangement of atoms in a crystal is called a *lattice*[20]. In a crystal, an atom never strays far from a single, fixed position. The thermal vibrations associated with the atom are centered about this position. For a given semiconductor, there is a *unit cell*[21] that is representative of the entire lattice; by repeating the unit cell throughout the crystal, one can generate the entire lattice.

Fig. 2-2 shows some basic cubic-crystal unit cells. Fig. 2-2 (a) shows a simple cubic crystal; each corner of the cubic lattice is occupied by an atom that has six *equidistant*[22] nearest neighboring atoms. The dimension a is called the lattice constant. Only polonium is crystallized in the simple cubic lattice. Fig. 2-2 (b) is a *body-centered cubic*[23] (bcc) crystal, where in addition to the eight corner atoms, an atom is located at the center of the cube. In a bcc lattice, each atom has eight nearest-neighboring atoms. Crystals exhibiting bcc lattices include those of sodium and tungsten. Fig. 2-2 (c) shows a *face-centered cubic*[24] (fcc) crystal that has one atom at each of the six cubic faces in addition to the eight corner atoms. In an fcc lattice, each atom has 12 nearest neighboring atoms. A large number of elements exhibit the fcc lattice form, including aluminum, copper, gold, and platinum.

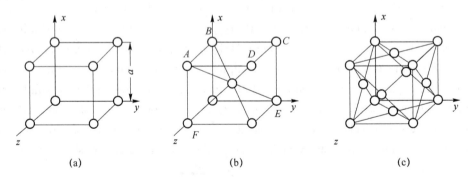

Fig. 2-2 Three cubic-crystal unit cells.

The element semiconductors, such as silicon and germanium, have a *diamond lattice*[25] structure. This structure also belongs to the cubic-crystal family and can be seen as two interpenetrating fcc sublattices with one sublattice displaced from the other by one quarter of the distance along a *diagonal*[26] of the cube (i.e., a displacement of $a\sqrt{3}/4$). All atoms are identical in a diamond lattice, and each atom in the diamond lattice is surrounded by four equidistant nearest neighbors that lie at the corners of a tetrahedron. Most of the III-V compound semiconductors (e.g., GaAs) have a *zincblende lattice*[27], which is identical to a diamond lattice except that one fcc sublattice has Column III atoms (Ga) and the other has Column V atoms (As).

Therefore, the crystal properties along different planes are different, and the electrical and other device characteristics are dependent on the crystal orientation. A convenient method of defining the various planes in a crystal is to use *Miller indices*[28]. These indices are obtained using the following steps:

(1) Find the intercepts of the plane on the three *Cartesian coordinates*[29] in terms of the lattice constant.

(2) Take the reciprocals of these numbers and reduce them to the smallest three integers having the same ratio.

(3) Enclose the result in parentheses (hkl) as the Miller indices for a single plane.

2.4 The Atomic Structure of Semiconductors

Electronic devices such as diode and transistors are constructed from special materials called semiconductors.

In this section, you will learn about the atomic structure of semiconductors.

2.4.1 Electron Shells and Orbits

The electrical properties of materials are explained by their atomic structure. In the early part of the 20th century, Neils Bohr, a Danish physicist, developed a model of the atom that showed electrons orbiting the nucleus. In Bohr's model of the atom, the electrons orbit only in certain discrete (separate and distinct) distances from the nucleus. The nucleus contains positively charged protons and uncharged neutrons. The orbiting electrons are negatively charged. Modern quantum mechanical models of the atom retain much of the ideas of the original Bohr model but have replaced the concept of electron "particles" with mathematical "matter waves", however, the Bohr model provides a useful mental picture of the structure of an atom.

Energy is the ability to do work and is subdivided into potential (position), kinetic (motion), and rest (mass). Electrons have potential energy because of their position within the atom. Electrons near the nucleus have less energy than those in more distant orbits. These discrete orbits mean that only certain energy levels are permitted within the atom. These energy levels are known as *shells*[30]. Each shell has a certain maximum permissible number of electrons. The differences in energy levels within a shell are much smaller than the difference in energy between shells. The shells are designated 1, 2, 3, 4, and so on, with 1 being closest to the nucleus, as illustrated in Fig. 2-3.

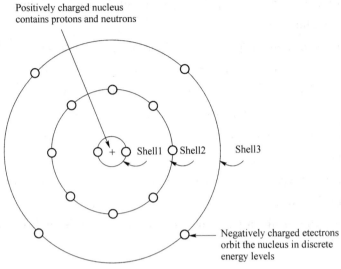

In this neutral silicon atom, 14 protons are in the nucleus and 14 electrons orbit the nucleus.

Fig. 2-3　Energy levels increase as distance from the nucleus increases.

2.4.2　Valence Electrons, Conduction Electrons, and Ions

Electrons in orbits farther from the nucleus are less tightly bound to the atom than those closer to the nucleus. This is because the force of attraction between the positively charged nucleus and the negatively charged electron decreases with increasing distance. Outer-shell electrons are also shielded from the nuclear charge by the inner-shell electrons.

An electron that is in the outermost shell is called a valence electron; valence electrons have the highest energy and are relatively loosely bound to their parent atom. A valence electron is identical to any other electron; it is so named because of its location only. For the silicon atom in Fig. 2-3, the third-shell electrons are the valence electrons.

Sometimes, a valence electron can acquire enough energy to break free of its parent atom. This free electron is then called a conduction electron because it is not bound to any certain atom. When a negatively charged electron is freed from an atom, the rest of the atom is positively charged and is said to be a positive ion. In some chemical reactions, the freed electron attaches itself to a neutral atom (or group of atoms), forming a negative ion. An ion is always an atom or group of atoms that has acquired a charge due to an imbalance in the number of protons and electrons.

2.4.3　Metallic Bands

Metals tend to be solids at room temperature. The nucleus and inner-shell electrons of metals occupy fixed lattice positions. The outer valence electrons are held loosely by all of the atoms of the crystal and are free to move about. This "sea" of negatively charged electrons holds the positive ions of the metal together, forming *metallic bonding*[31].

With the large number of atoms in the metallic crystal, the discrete energy level for the valence electrons is blurred into a band called the *valence band*[32]. These valence electrons are mobile and account for the thermal and electrical conductivity of metals. In addition to the valence energy band, the next (normally occupied) level from the nucleus in the atom is also blurred into a band of energies called the *conduction band*[33].

Fig. 2-4 compares the energy-level diagrams for three types of solids. Notice that for conductors, shown in Fig. 2-4 (a), the bands are overlapping. Electrons can easily move between the valence and conduction bands by absorbing light (and radiating light as they move back). This movement of electrons back and forth between the valence band and conduction band accounts for the *luster*[34] of metals.

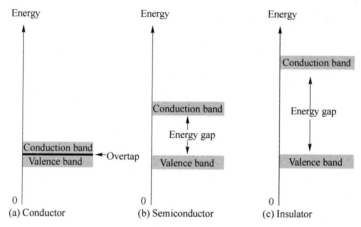

The upper level is the conduction band; the lower level is the valence band.

Fig. 2-4 Energy level diagrams for three types of materials.

2.4.4 Covalent Bonds

Atoms of some solid materials form crystals, which are three-dimensional structures held together by strong bonds between the atoms. In diamond, for example, four bonds are formed by the sharing of four valence electrons in each carbon atom with adjacent atoms. This effectively creates eight valence electrons for each atom and produces a state of chemical stability. This sharing of valence electrons produces strong *covalent bonds*[35] that hold the atoms together.

The shared electrons are not mobile; each electron is associated by a covalent bond between the atoms of the crystal. Therefore, there is a large energy gap between the valence band and the conduction band. As a consequence, crystalline materials such as diamond are insulators, or nonconductors, of electricity. Fig. 2-4 (c) shows the energy bands for a solid insulator.

Electronic devices are constructed from materials called semiconductors. The most common semiconductive material is silicon; however, germanium is sometimes used. At room temperature, silicon forms a covalent crystal. The actual atomic structure is similar to diamond, but the covalent bonds in silicon are not as strong as those in diamond. In silicon, each atom shares a valence electron with each of its four neighbors. As in the case of other crystalline materials, the discrete levels are blurred into a valence band and a conduction band, as shown in Fig. 2-4 (b).

The important difference between a conductor and a semiconductor is the gap that separates the bands. With semiconductors, the gap is narrow; electrons can easily be promoted to the conduction band with the addition of thermal energy. At absolute zero, the electrons in a silicon crystal are all in the valence band, but at room temperature many electrons have sufficient energy to move to the conduction band. The conduction band electrons are no longer bound to a parent atom within the crystal.

2.4.5 Electrons and Hole Current

When an electron jumps to the conduction band, a *vacancy*[36] is left in the valence band. This vacancy is called a *hole*[37]. For every electron raised to the conduction band by thermal or light energy, there is one hole left in the valence band, creating what is called an *electron-hole pair*[38]. Recombination occurs when a conduction-band electron loses energy and falls back into a hole in the valence band.

A piece of *intrinsic*[39] (pure) silicon at room temperature has, at any instant, a number of conduction-band (free) electrons that are unattached to any atom and are essentially drifting randomly throughout the material. Also, an equal number of holes are created in the valence band when these electrons jump into the conduction band. Pure silicon has electrons in the conduction band and holes in the valence band.

When a voltage is applied across a piece of intrinsic silicon, as shown in Fig. 2-5, the thermally generated free electrons in the conduction band are easily attracted toward the positive end. This movement of free electrons is one type of current in a semiconductor and is called electron current.

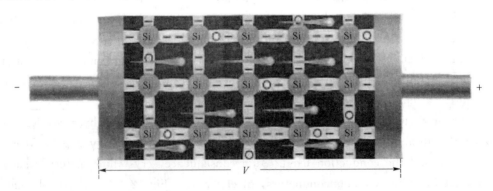

Free electrons are shown with "tail" to indicate mobility.

Fig. 2-5 Electron current in pure silicon.

Another type of current occurs at the valence level, where the holes created by the free electrons exist. Electrons remaining in the valence band are still attached to their atoms and are not free to move randomly in the crystal structure. However, a valence electron can move into a nearby hole, with little change in its energy level, thus leaving another hole where it came from. Effectively, the hole has moved from one place to another in the crystal structure, as illustrated in Fig. 2-6. This current is called hole current.

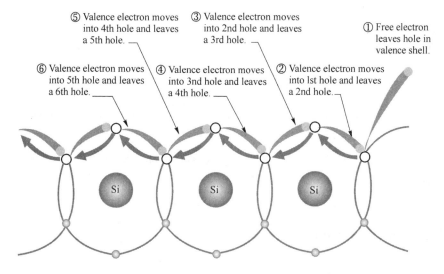

Fig. 2-6　Hole current in pure silicon.

2.5　The PN Junction

Intrinsic silicon is not a good conductor. By adding a small amount of impurity to the silicon crystal, its electrical properties can be changed dramatically. During manufacture, the silicon layers with different impurities are joined and form a boundary called the pn *junction*[40]. Amazingly, it is the characteristics of the pn junction that allow diodes and transistors to work.

2.5.1　Doping

The conductivity of silicon (or germanium) can be drastically increased by the controlled addition of impurities to the pure (intrinsic) semiconductive material. This process, called *doping*[41], increases the number of current carriers (electrons or holes), thus increasing the conductivity and decreasing the resistivity. The two categories of impurities are n-type and p-type.

To increase the number of conduction-band electrons in pure silicon, a controlled number of pentavalent impurity atoms called *donors*[42] are added to the silicon crystal. These are atoms with five valence electrons, such as arsenic, phosphorus, and antimony. Each pentavalent atom forms covalent bonds with four adjacent silicon atoms, leaving one extra electron. This extra electron becomes a conduction (free) electron because it is not bonded to any atom in the crystal. The electrons in these n materials are called the *majority carriers*[43]; the holes are called *minority carriers*[44].

To increase the number of holes in pure silicon, trivalent impurity atoms called *acceptors*[45] are added during manufacture. These are atoms with only three valence electrons, such as aluminum, boron, and gallium. Each trivalent atom forms covalent bonds with four adjacent silicon atoms. All three of the impurity atom's valence electrons are used in the covalent bonds. However, since four electrons are required in the crystal structure, a hole is formed with each trivalent atom added. With p materials, the acceptor causes extra holes in the valence band; the majority carrier in p materials is holes, and the minority carrier is electrons.

The process of creating n-type or p-type materials retains the overall electrical neutrality. With n-type materials, the extra electron in the crystal is balanced by the additional positive charge of the donor's nucleus.

2.5.2 The PN Junction

When a piece of intrinsic silicon is doped so that half is n type and the other half is p type, a pn junction is formed between the two regions. The n region has many free electrons (majority carriers) and only a few thermally generated holes (minority carriers). The p region has many holes (majority carriers) and only a few thermally generated free electrons (minority carriers). The pn junction forms a basic diode and is fundamental to the operation of all solid-state devices. A diode is a device that allows current in only one direction.

2.5.3 The Depletion Region

When the pn junction is formed, some of the conduction electrons near the junction drift across into the p region and recombine with holes near the junction, as shown in Fig. 2-7 (a). For each electron that crosses the junction and recombines with a hole, a pentavalent atom is left with a net positive charge in the n region near the junction. Also, when the electron recombines with a hole in the p region, a trivalent atom acquires a net negative charge. As a result, positive ions are found on the n side of the junction and negative ions are found on the p side of the junction. The existence of the positive and negative ions on opposite sides of the junction creates a *barrier potential*[46] (V_B) across the *depletion region*[47]. The barrier potential depends on temperature, but it is approximately 0.7 V for silicon and 0.3 V for germanium at room temperature. Since germanium diodes are rarely used, 0.7 V is normally the barrier potential found in most diode circuits.

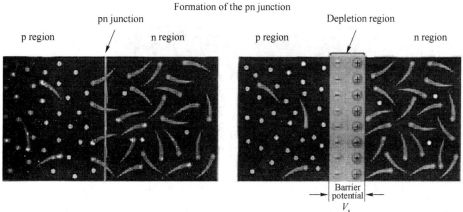

(a) At the instant of junction formation, free electrons in the n region near the pn junction begin to diffuse across the junction and fall into holes near the junction in the p region

(b) For every electron that diffuses across the junction and combines with a hole, a positive charge is left in the n region and a negative charge is created in the p region, forming a barrier potential. This action continues until the voltage of the barrier repels further diffusion

Fig. 2-7 Formation of the pn junction.

Conduction electrons in the n region must overcome both the attraction of the positive ions and the repulsion of the negative ions in order to migrate into the p region. After the ion layers build up, the area on both sides of the junction becomes essentially depleted of any conduction electrons or holes and is known as the depletion region. This condition is illustrated in Fig. 2-7 (b). Any further movement of charge across the boundary requires that the barrier potential be overcome.

2.6 Biasing the Semiconductor Diode

A single pn junction forms a semiconductor diode. There is no current across a pn junction at equilibrium. The primary usefulness of the semiconductor diode is its ability to allow current in only one direction as determined by the *bias*[48].

2.6.1 Forward Bias

The term bias in electronics refers to a fixed dc voltage that sets the operating conditions for a semiconductor device. Forward bias is the condition that permits current across a pn junction.

Fig. 2-8 shows the polarity required from a dc source to forward-bias the semiconductor diode. The negative side of a source is connected to the n region (at the cathode terminal), and the positive side of a source is connected to the p region (at the anode terminal). When the semiconductor diode is forward-biased, the anode is the more positive terminal and the cathode is the more negative terminal.

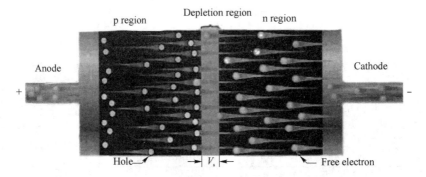

Fig. 2-8 Electron flow in a forward biased semiconductor diode.

This is how forward bias works: When a dc source is connected to forward-bias the diode, the negative side of the source pushes the conduction electrons in the n region toward the junction because of electrostatic repulsion. The positive side pushes the holes in the p region also toward the junction. When the external bias voltage is sufficient to overcome the barrier potential, electrons have enough energy to penetrate the depletion region and cross the junction, where they combine with the p region holes. As electrons leave the n region, more electrons flow in from the negative side of the source. Thus, current through the n region occurs by the movement of conduction electrons (majority carriers) toward the junction. When the conduction electrons enter the p region and combine with holes, they become valence electrons. Then they move as valence electrons from hole to hole toward the positive anode connection. The movement of these valence electrons essentially creates a movement of holes in the opposite direction. Thus, current in the p region occurs by the movement of holes (majority carriers) toward the junction.[②]

2.6.2 Reverse Bias

Reverse bias is the bias condition that prevents current across the pn junction. Fig. 2-9 shows the polarity required from a dc source to reverse-bias the semiconductor diode. The negative side of the source is connected to the p region, and the positive side to the n region. When the semiconductor diode is reverse-biased, the anode is the more negative terminal and the cathode is the more positive terminal.

This is how reverse bias works: The negative side of the source attracts holes in the p region away from the pn junction, while the positive side of the source attracts electrons away from the junction due to the attraction of opposite charges. As electrons and holes move away from the junction, the depletion region begins to widen; more positive ions are created in the n region, and more negative ions are created in the p region. The depletion region widens until the potential difference across it is equal to the external bias voltage, as shown in Fig. 2-9 (b). The depletion region effectively acts as an insulator between the layers of oppositely charged ions when the diode is reverse-biased.

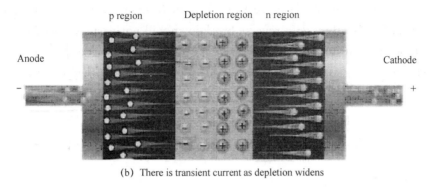

(b) There is transient current as depletion widens

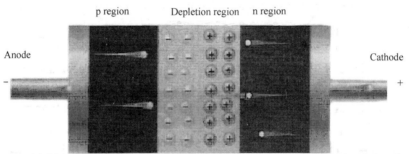

(c) Majority current ceases when barrier potential equals bias voltage. There is an extremely small reverse current due to minority carriers

Fig. 2-9 Reverse bias.

2.6.3 Peak Inverse Voltage (PIV)

When a diode is reverse-biased, it must be able to withstand the maximum value of reverse voltage that is applied or it will break down. The maximum rated voltage for a diode is designated as peak inverse voltage (PIV). The required PIV depends on the application; for most cases with ordinary diode, the PIV rating should be higher than the reverse voltage.

2.6.4 Reverse Breakdown

If the external reverse-bias voltage is increased to a large enough value, *avalanche breakdown*[49] occurs. Here is what happens: Assume that one minority conduction-band electron acquires enough energy from the external source to accelerate it toward the positive end of the diode. During its travel, it collides with an atom and imparts enough energy to knock a valence electron into the conduction band. There are now two conduction-band electrons. Each will collide with an atom, knocking two more valence electrons into the conduction band. There are now four conduction-band electrons, which, in turn, knock four more into the conduction band. This rapid multiplication of conduction-band electrons, known as an avalanche effect, results in a rapid buildup of reverse current.

Most diode circuits are not designed to operate in reverse breakdown, and the diode may be destroyed if it is. By itself, reverse breakdown will not harm a diode, but current limiting must be present to prevent excessive heating. One type of diode, the *zener diode*[50], is specially designed for reverse-breakdown operation if sufficient current limiting is provided.

2.7 Semiconductor Device-BJT and FET

As you recall from previous studies in this text, semiconductors have electrical properties somewhere between those of insulators and conductors. The use of semiconductor materials in electronic components is not new; some devices are as old as the electron tube. Two of the most widely known semiconductors in use today are the junction diode and transistor.

The single junction devices we have considered, including the PN homojunction diode, can be used to obtain rectifying current-voltage characteristics, and to form electronic switching circuits.

The transistor is a multifunction semiconductor device that, in conjunction with other circuit elements, is capable of current gain, voltage gain, and signal-power gain. The transistor is therefore referred to as an active device. The basic transistor action is the control of current at one terminal by voltage applied across two other terminals of the device.

Modern transistors are divided into two main categories: bipolar junction transistors (BJTs) and field effect transistors (FETs). Application of current in BJTs and voltage in FETs between the input and common terminals increases the conductivity between the common and output terminals, thereby controlling current flow between them. The transistor characteristics depend on their type.

2.7.1 Bipolar junction transistor

The BJT was the first type of transistor to be mass-produced. Bipolar transistors are so named because they conduct by using both majority and minority carriers. The three terminals of the BJT are named emitter, base and collector. Two p-n junctions exist inside a BJT: the base/emitter junction and base/collector junction[3]. The BJT is commonly described as a current-operated device because the collector/emitter current is controlled by the current flowing between base and emitter terminals. Unlike the FET, the BJT is a low input-impedance device. As the base/emitter voltage (V_{be}) is increased, the base/emitter current and hence the collector/emitter current (I_{ce}) increase exponentially (according to the Shockley diode model and the Ebers-Moll model). Because of this exponential relationship the BJT has a higher transconductance than the FET.

A Bipolar transistors can be made to conduct by light, since absorption of photons in the base region generates a photocurrent that acts as a base current; the collector current is approximately beta times the photocurrent. Devices designed for this purpose have a transparent window in the package and are called phototransistors.

BJT is configured as an NPN or PNP transistor and biased for conduction mode. It is a voltage-controlled current device.

2.7.2 Field-effect transistor

The FET, a voltage-amplifying device, is more compact and power efficient than BJT devices. The FET, sometimes called a unipolar transistor, uses either electrons (N-channel FET) or holes (P-channel FET) for conduction. Each is defined by its majority current carriers. The four terminals of the FET are named source, gate, drain, and body (substrate). On most FETs the body is connected to the source inside the package and this will be assumed for the following description.

*A voltage applied between the gate and source (body) controls the current flowing between the drain and source. As the gate/source voltage (V_{gs}) is increased the drain/source current (I_{ds}) increases roughly parabolically ($I_{ds} \propto V_{gs}^2$). In FETs the drain/source current flows through a conducting channel near the gate. This channel connects the drain region to the source region. The channel conductivity is varied by the electric field generated by the voltage applied between the gate/source terminals. In this way the current flowing between the drain and source is controlled.*④

FETs are divided into two families: junction FET (JFET) and insulated gate FET (IGFET).

The IGFET is more commonly known as metal-oxide-semiconductor FET (MOSFET), from their original construction as a layer of metal (the gate), a layer of oxide (the insulation), and a layer of semiconductor. The MOSFET is a device used to amplify or switch electronic signals. The basic principle of the device was first proposed by Julius Edgar Lilienfeld in 1925. A traditional metal-oxide-semiconductor (MOS) structure is obtained by growing a layer of silicon dioxide (SiO_2) on top of a silicon substrate and depositing a layer of metal or polycrystalline silicon. As the silicon dioxide is a dielectric material, its structure is equivalent to a planar capacitor, with one of the electrodes replaced by a semiconductor. The MOSFET includes a channel of n-type or p-type semiconductor material, and is accordingly called an NMOSFET or a PMOSFET (also commonly nMOS, pMOS). Though the bipolar junction transistor was at one time much more common, MOSFET is by far the most common transistor in both digital and analog circuit applications where, because of its relatively small size, thousands of devices can be fabricated in a single integrated circuit. The MOSFET is, without doubt, the core of integrated circuit design at the present time.

Unlike IGFETs, the JFET gate forms a pn diode with the channel which lies between the source and drain. Functionally, this makes the N-channel JFET the solid state equivalent of the vacuum tube triode which, similarly, forms a diode between its grid and cathode. Also, both devices operate in the depletion mode, they both have a high input impedance, and they both conduct current under the control of an input voltage.

Metal-semiconductor FETs (MESFETs) are JFETs in which the reverse biased pn junction is replaced by a metal-semiconductor Schottky-junction. These, and the HEMTs (high electron mobility transistors, or HFETs), in which a two-dimensional electron gas with very high carrier mobility is used for charge transport, are especially suitable for use at very high frequencies (microwave frequencies; several GHz).

Unlike bipolar transistors, FETs do not inherently amplify a photocurrent. Nevertheless, there are ways to use them, especially JFETs, as light-sensitive devices, by exploiting the photocurrents in channel-gate or channel-body junctions.

2.8 Semiconductor Applications

In the previous paragraphs, we mention just a few in the many different applications of semiconductor devices. The use of these devices has become so widespread that it would be impossible to list all their different applications. Instead, a broad coverage of their specific application is presented.

Semiconductor devices are all around us. They can be found in just about every commercial product we touch, from the family car to the pocket calculator. Semiconductor devices are contained in television sets, portable radios, stereo equipment, and much more.

Science and industry also rely heavily on semiconductor devices. Research laboratories use these devices in all sorts of electronic instruments to perform tests, measurements, and numerous other experimental tasks. Industrial control systems (such as those used to manufacture automobiles) and automatic telephone exchanges also use semiconductors. Even today heavy-duty versions of the solid-state rectifier diode are being use to convert large amounts of power for electric railroads. Of the many different applications for solid-state devices, space systems, computers, and data processing equipment are some of the largest consumers.

The various types of modem military equipment are literally loaded with semiconductor devices. Many radars, communication, and airborne equipment are transistorized. Data display systems, data processing units, computers, and aircraft guidance-control assemblies are also good examples of electronic equipments that use semiconductor devices. All of the specific applications of semiconductor devices would make a long impressive list. The fact is, semiconductors are being used extensively in commercial products, industry, and the military.

2.9 Semiconductor Competition

It should not be difficult to conclude, from what you already know, that semiconductor devices can and do perform all the conventional functions of rectification, amplification, oscillation, timing, switching, and sensing. Simply stated, these devices perform the same basic functions as the electron tube; but they perform more efficiently, economically, and for a longer period of time. Therefore, it should be no surprise to you to see these devices used in place of electron tubes. Keeping this in mind, we see that it is only natural and logical to compare semiconductor devices with electron tubes.

Physically, semiconductor devices are much smaller than tubes. For some commonly used tube sizes alongside semiconductor devices of similar capabilities, the reduction in size can be as great as 100 : 1 by weight and 1 000 : 1 by volume. It is easy to see that size reduction favors the semiconductor device. Therefore, whenever miniaturization is required or is convenient, transistors are favored over tubes. Bear in mind, however, that the extent of practical size reduction is a big factor; many things must be considered. Miniature electron tubes, for example, may be preferred in certain applications to transistors, thus keeping size reduction to a competitive area.

Power is also a two-sided story. For low-power applications, where efficiency is a significant factor, semiconductors have a decided advantage. This is true mainly because semiconductor devices perform very well with an extremely small amount of power; in addition, they require no filaments or heaters as in the case of the electron tube. For example, a computer operating with over 4 000 solid-state devices may require no more than 20 watts of power. However, the same number of tubes would require several kilowatts of power. For high-power applications, it is a different story - tubes have the upper hand. The high-power tube has no equivalent in any semiconductor device. This is because a tube can be designed to operate with over a thousand volts applied to its plate whereas the maximum allowable voltage for a transistor is limited to about 200 volts (usually 50 volts or less). A tube can also handle thousands of watts of power. The maximum power output for transistor generally ranges from 30 milliwatts to slightly over 100 watts.

When it comes to ruggedness and life expectancy, the tube is still in competition. Design and functional requirements usually dictate the choice of device. However, semiconductor devices are rugged and long-lived. They can be constructed to withstand extreme vibration and mechanical shock. They have been known to withstand impacts that would completely shatter an ordinary electron tube. Although some specially designed tubes render extensive service, the life expectancy of transistors is better than three to four times that of ordinary electronic tubes. There is no known failure mechanism (such as an open filament in a tube) to limit the semiconductor's life. However, semiconductor devices do have some limitations. They are usually affected more by temperature, humidity, and radiation than tubes are.

References

1. Donald A. Neamen. Semiconductor physics and devices: basic principles. 北京：清华大学出版社，McGraw-Hill Education (Asia) Co., 2003.

2. Thomas L. Floyd, David M. Buchla. 模拟电子技术基础（双语版）. 王燕萍译. 北京：清华大学出版社，2007.

3. http://www.tpub.com/index.htm.

New Words and Expressions

1. transistor [træn'zistə] n. 晶体管
2. integrated circuit 集成电路
3. conductivity [ˌkɔndʌk'tiviti] n. 传导性，传导率；这里为电导率
4. resistivity [ˌriːzis'tiviti] n. 抵抗力，电阻系数；这里为电阻率
5. conductor [kən'dʌktə] n. 导体
6. insulator ['insjuleitə] n. 绝缘体
7. impurity [im'pjuəriti] n. 杂质，混杂物
8. elemental semiconductor 元素半导体
9. compound semiconductor 化合物半导体
10. silicon ['silikən] n. 硅，硅元素
11. germanium [dʒəː'meiniəm] n. 锗
12. bipolar transistor 双极型晶体管
13. rectifier ['rektifaiə] n. 整流器
14. photodiode [ˌfəutən'daiəud] n. 光敏二极管，光电二极管
15. leakage current 漏电流（pn结在截止时流过的很微小的电流。理想pn结漏电流中还包括体内扩散电流与空间电荷区产生电流两部分，硅pn结空间电荷区产生电流，起支配作用。漏电流的大小与组成pn结的半导体材料禁带宽度呈指数关系，漏电流中还包括表面漏电流，表面漏电流的大小与pn结制作工艺密切相关）
16. amorphous [ə'mɔːfəs] adj. 无定型的
17. polycrystalline [ˌpɔli'kristəlain] adj. 多晶
18. grains [greinz] n. 晶粒
19. grain boundary 晶界
20. lattice ['lætis] n. 晶格，格子
21. unit cell 晶胞
22. equidistant [ˌiːkwi'distənt] adj. 距离相等的，等距的

23. body-centered cubic 体心立方
24. face-centered cubic 面心立方
25. diamond lattice 金刚石晶格
26. diagonal [daiˈægənl] adj. 对角线的,斜的,斜纹的;n. 对角线,斜纹织物
27. zincblende lattice 闪锌矿晶格
28. miller indices 密勒指数,指化为互质的晶面指数,用以表示晶面的方向
29. cartesian coordinates 笛卡儿坐标(表示点在空间中的位置,又称直角坐标,是法国数学家、哲学家笛卡儿发明并第一个使用的。它用数学的方法揭示二维图形或三维模型。这个坐标在计算机学中定义了显示模块的模拟位置)
30. shell [ʃel] n. 壳层(原子内带正电的密实部分集中于一个很小的核,带负电的电子分布于核外,中性原子的核外电子数等于原子序数Z。根据量子力学,原子内Z个电子在核外分布可处于各种可能的定态,这些定态就称为壳层)
31. metallic bonding 金属键
32. valence band 价带
33. conduction band 导带
34. luster [ˈlʌstə] n. 光彩,光泽;vi. 有光泽,发亮;vt. 使有光泽
35. covalent bonds 共价键
36. vacancy [ˈveikənsi] n. 空位
37. hole [həul] n. 空穴
38. electron-hole pair 电子空穴对
39. intrinsic [inˈtrinsik] adj. 本征的
40. pn junction pn 结
41. doping [ˈdəupiŋ] n. (半导体)掺杂(质),加添加剂[填料]
42. donor [ˈdəunə] n. 施主
43. majority carrier 多数载流子
44. minority carrier 少数载流子
45. acceptor [əkˈseptə(r)] n. 受主
46. barrier potential 势垒电位
47. depletion region 耗尽区
48. bias [ˈbaiəs] n. 偏压
49. avalanche breakdown 雪崩击穿
50. zener diode 齐纳二极管

Notes

① 无定型、多晶和单晶是固体的 3 种基本类型。每种类型的特征是用材料中有序化区域的大小加以判定的。有序化区域是指原子或者分子有规则几何排列或周期性的空间范畴。

② 正向偏置的工作原理如下:当直流电源将二极管正向偏置后,由于静电场的作用,电源的负端将 n 区中的导电电子推向 pn 结,而电源的正端也将 p 区中的空穴推向 pn 结。当

外加的偏置电压足以克服势垒电位时,电子就有足够的能量进入耗尽层并越过 pn 结,与 p 区中的空穴复合。当这些电子离开 n 区后,会有更多的电子从电源的负端流出。因此,导电电子(多数载流子)朝着 pn 结方向的移动产生了 n 区的电流。这些导电电子进入 p 区后与空穴复合,变成了价电子。然后,价电子会一个一个空穴地向阳极方向移动。价电子的移动实际上产生了空穴反方向的移动。所以,p 区中电流是由空穴(多数载流子)朝着 pn 结方向移动产生的。

③ 双极结型晶体管(BJT)是晶体管的一种形式,它是由掺杂半导体材料组成的一种三端子设备,用来放大或者开关。双极结型晶体管是第一种可批量生产的晶体管,由于其用多数载流子和少数载流子共同导电,所以称为双极晶体管。双极结型晶体管的三个端子分别为发射极、基极和集电极。双极结型晶体管中存在两种 pn 结:发射结和集电结。

④ 栅极和源极间施加电压可以控制漏极和源极之间的电流。随着栅源电压(V_{gs})的增加,漏源电流(I_{ds})呈抛物线型增长。在场效应管中,漏源电流流经栅极附近的导电沟道。沟道的导电性会随着施加在栅/源电极间的电压所产生的电场变化而变化。这样,就可以控制漏极和源极间的电流。

Electromagnetic Field and Electromagnetic Wave 第3章

PREVIEW

The electromagnetic (EM) interaction is one of the fundamental interactions of the physical world. It is the basic interaction in atoms and *molecules*[1]. It has been around since the birth of the universe; light is its most familiar form. In nature it manifests itself in sunshine, lightning, rainbows, and many other phenomena, so that its study is as old as the attempts to understand such common observations. Electric and magnetic fields are part of the spectrum of EM radiation which extends from static electric and magnetic fields, through radio frequency and infrared radiation, to X-rays. Radio waves, microwaves, visible light, and X-rays are all examples of EM waves that differ from each other in wavelength.

EM field theory is one of the best-established general theories that provides explanations and solutions to intricate optical and electrical engineering problems when other theories are no longer applicable. It is of fundamental importance to physicists and to electrical and computer engineers. It is indispensable in understanding the principle of *atom smashers*[2], cathode ray oscilloscopes, radar, satellite communication, television reception, remote sensing, *radio astronomy*[3], microwave devices, optical fiber communication, transients in transmission lines, EM compatibility problems, instrument-landing systems, electromechanical energy conversion, and so on.

3.1 The Concept of Electromagnetic Fields and Waves

EM field can be viewed as the combination of an electric field and a magnetic field. As we know, a static *charge*[4] gives rise to an effect that appears as a force acting on a charge body in the surrounding, within which an electric field is said to exist. Moving charges or electric currents lead to another kind of fields, which results in forces acting on magnets and conductors carrying currents, referred to as a magnetic field.

The electric field and the magnetic field are both the vector fields. If the magnitude and the location of the electric charge do not change with time, the electric field produced by the charge will also be constant over time. This kind of electric field is known as an electrostatic field. When the magnitude and the *velocity*[5] of an electric charge in motion are kept *constant*[6] so that the *resultant*[7] electric current is steady, the magnetic field produced will be time independent and known as a steady magnetic. If the charge and the current vary with time, the electric field and the magnetic field they produced will be function of time. It was found that time-varying electric field and magnetic field must co-exist and have definite relation to each other, leading to a time-varying EM field. The EM field extends indefinitely throughout space and describes the EM interaction.

EM wave (radiation) is a self-propagating wave in space with electric and magnetic components. It consists of *discrete*[8] packets of energy, which we call *photons*[9]. A photon consists of an *oscillating*[10] electric field component, E, and an oscillating magnetic field component, M. A moving charge gives rise to a magnetic field, and if the motion is changing (accelerated), then the magnetic field varies and in turn produces an electric field. These interacting electric and magnetic fields are at right angles to one another and also to the direction of *propagation*[11] of the energy. That is, the electric and magnetic fields are *orthogonal*[12] (perpendicular) to each other, and they are orthogonal to the direction of propagation of the photon. Thus, an EM wave is a *transverse wave*[13]. If the direction of the electric field is constant, the wave is said to be *polarized*[14]. EM radiation does not require a material medium and can travel through a *vacuum*[15]. *The electric and magnetic fields of a photon flip direction as the photon travels. We call the number of flips, or oscillations, that occur in one second the frequency, ν.*①

From a classical perspective, the EM field can be regarded as a smooth, continuous field, propagated in a wavelike manner; whereas, from a *quantum mechanical*[16] perspective, the field is seen as quantized, being composed of individual particles. Electric charges and currents are sources for EM fields. It should be pointed out that they are the only sources for producing EM fields. Up to now, no magnetic charge or magnetic current of significance has been found exist in nature. The way in which charges and currents interact with the EM field is described by Maxwell's equations.

3.2 History of Electromagnetic Wave

Electric and magnetic phenomena have been known for *millenia*[17]. The earliest examples were forces produced by static electricity and by *ferromagnetism*[18]. Of course there are other phenomena that we recognize today to be of EM origin, which have been observed since the beginning of time. For example, lighting is an electric discharge. Also, light consists of EM waves, in the quantum theory, photons. But before the scientific revolution it was not recognized that these varied phenomena have a common origin.

The *quantitative study*[19] of electricity and magnetism began with the scientific research of the French physicist Charles Augustin Coulomb. In 1787 Coulomb proposed a law of force for charges that, like Sir Isaac Newton's law of gravitation, varied inversely as the square of the distance. Using a sensitive *torsion balance*[20], he demonstrated its validity experimentally for forces of both repulsion and attraction. *Like the law of gravitation, Coulomb's law was based on the notion of "action at a distance", wherein bodies can interact instantaneously and directly with one another without the intervention of any intermediary.*②

At the beginning of the nineteenth century, the electrochemical cell was invented by Alessandro Volta, professor of natural philosophy at the University of Pavia in Italy. The cell created an *electromotive force*[21], which made the production of continuous currents possible.

In 1820 at the University of Copenhagen, Hans Christian Oersted, professor of physics, made the momentous discovery that an electric current in a wire could deflect a magnetic needle. This experiment illustrated the connection between electricity and magnetism. News of this discovery was communicated to the French Academy of Sciences two months later. These results sparked experiments across the globe as scientists attempted to find an explanation. The laws of force between current bearing wires were at once investigated by Andre-Marie Ampere and by Jean-Baptiste Biot and Felix Savart. The favoured explanation, which was provided by Ampere, was that central forces were the cause. Within six years the theory of steady currents was complete.

Subsequently, in 1831, the British scientist Michael Faraday demonstrated the *reciprocal effect*[22], in which a moving magnet in the vicinity of a coil of wire produced an electric current. This phenomenon, together with Oersted's experiment with the magnetic needle, led Faraday to conceive the notion of a magnetic field. A field produced by a current in a wire interacted with a magnet. Also, according to his law of induction, a time varying magnetic field incident on a wire would induce a voltage, thereby creating a current. Electric forces could similarly be expressed in terms of an electric field created by the presence of a charge.

By 1850 Faraday had completed much of his work but he did not *formulate*[23] his laws mathematically and the majority of scientists had failed to realize its significance. It was left to the Scottish physicist James Clerk Maxwell to establish the mathematical theory of electromagnetism based on the physical concepts of Faraday. In a series of papers published between 1856 and 1865, Maxwell restated the laws of Coulomb, Ampere, and Faraday in terms of Faraday's electric and magnetic fields. Maxwell thus unified the theories of electricity and magnetism, in the same sense that two hundred years earlier Newton had unified terrestrial and *celestial mechanics*[24] through his theory of universal gravitation.

As is typical of abstract mathematical reasoning, Maxwell saw in his equations a certain symmetry that suggested the need for an additional term, involving the time rate *of change of the electric field. With this generalization, Maxwell's equations also became consistent with the principle of conservation of charge.*③ Furthermore, Maxwell made the profound observation that his set of equations, thus modified, predicted the existence of EM waves. Therefore, disturbances in the EM field could propagate through space. Using the values of known experimental constants obtained solely from measurements of charges and currents, Maxwell *deduced*[25] that the speed of propagation was equal to speed of light. This quantity had been measured *astronomically*[26] by Olaf Romer in 1676 from the *eclipses*[27] of *Jupiter's*[28] satellites and determined experimentally from terrestrial measurements by H. L. Fizeau in 1849. He then asserted that light itself was an EM wave, thereby unifying optics with electromagnetism as well.

Maxwell's theory was not accepted by scientists immediately, in part because it had been derived from a *bewildering*[29] collection of mechanical analogies and difficult mathematical concepts. The form of Maxwell's equations as we are known today is due to the German physicist Heinrich Hertz. Hertz simplified them and eliminated unnecessary assumptions.

Hertz's interest in Maxwell's theory was occasioned by a prize offered by the Berlin Academy of Sciences in 1879 for research on the relation between polarization in insulators and *EM induction*[30]. By means of his experiments, Hertz discovered how to generate high frequency electrical oscillations. He was surprised to find that these oscillations could be detected at large distances from the apparatus. Up to that time, it had been generally assumed that electrical forces decreased rapidly with distance according to the Newtonian law. He therefore sought to test Maxwell's prediction of the existence of EM waves.

In 1888, Hertz set up standing EM waves using an oscillator and spark detector of his own design and made independent measurements of their wavelength and frequency. He found that their product was indeed the speed of light. *He also verified that these waves behaved according to all the laws of reflection, refraction, and polarization that applied to visible light, thus demonstrating that they differed from light only in wavelength and frequency.*④ "Certainly it is a fascinating idea," Hertz wrote, "that the processes in air that we have been investigating represent to us on a million-fold larger scale the same processes which go on in the neighborhood of a Fresnel mirror or between the glass plates used in exhibiting Newton's rings."

On this foundation, around the 19th century, Popov in Russia and Marconi in Italy invented the technology to transmit information using EM waves, paving the way for the subsequent development of modern wireless communications, broadcasting, radar, remote control, microwave sensing, wireless networks and local area networks, satellite positioning optical communications and other information technologies. The wide applications of these new technologies further enhance the development of EM theory.

The availability of high performance and high speed computers and large memory capacity not only made the calculations encountered in obtaining the solutions to many problems in EMs possible, but also gave rise to new methods to compute EM fields and waves. This gave birth to computational EMs, which is an important branch of modern EMs.

3.3 Basic Laws of Electromagnetic Theory

We know from experiments that charges, even though separated in vacuum, experience a mutual interaction. Recall the familiar *electrostatics*[31] demonstration in which a pith ball somehow senses the presence of a charged rod without actually touching it. As a possible explanation we might *speculate*[32] that each charge emits (and absorbs) a stream of undetected particles (virtual photons). The exchange of these particles among the charges may be regarded as the mode of interaction. Alternatively, we can take the classical approach and imagine instead that every charge is surrounded by something called an electric field. We then need only suppose that each charge interacts directly with the electric field in which it is immersed. Thus if a point charge q experiences a force F_E, the electric field E at the position of the charge is defined by $F_E = q \cdot E$. In addition, we observe that a moving charge may experience another force F_M, which is proportional to its velocity v. We are thus led to define yet another field, namely, the magnetic induction or just the magnetic field B, such that $F_M = q \cdot v \times B$. If force F_E and F_M occur concurrently, the charge is moving through a region pervaded by both electric and magnetic fields, whereupon $F = q \cdot E + q \cdot v \times B$.

As we'll see, electric fields are generated by both electric charges and time-varying magnetic fields. Similarly, magnetic fields are generated by electric currents and by time-varying electric fields. This interdependence of E and B is a key point in the description of light.

3.3.1 Faraday's Induction Law

"Convert magnetism into electricity" was the brief remark Michael Faraday jotted in his notebook in 1822, a challenge he set himself with an easy confidence that made it seem so attainable. After several years doing other research, Faraday returned to the problem of EM induction in 1831. His first apparatus made use of two coils mounted on a wooden spool, Fig. 3-1(a).

One, called the primary, was attached to a battery and a switch; the other, the secondary, was attached to a *galvanometer*[33]. He found that the galvanometer deflected in one direction just for a moment whenever the switch was closed, returning to zero almost immediately, despite the constant current still in the primary. Whenever the switch was opened, interrupting the primary current, the galvanometer in the secondary circuit momentarily swung in the opposite direction and then promptly returned to zero.

Using a ferromagnetic core to concentrate the "magnetic force", Faraday wound two coils around opposing sections of a soft iron ring, Fig. 3-1 (b). Now the effect was unmistakable-**a changing magnetic field generated a current.** Indeed, as he would continue to discover, change was the essential aspect of EM induction.

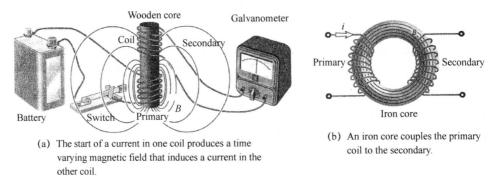

(a) The start of a current in one coil produces a time varying magnetic field that induces a current in the other coil.

(b) An iron core couples the primary coil to the secondary.

Fig. 3-1 The schematic diagram of the Faraday's apparatus to produce EM induction.

By thrusting a magnet into a coil, Faraday showed that there is a voltage-otherwise known as the induced electromotive force or emf-across the coil's terminals. (Electromotive force is a dreadful, outmoded term-it's not a force, but a voltage-so we'll avoid it and just use emf.) Furthermore, the amplitude of the emf depends on how rapidly the magnet is moved. The induced emf depends on the rate-of-change of B through the coil and not on B itself. A weak magnet moved rapidly can induce a greater emf than a strong magnet move slowly.

When the same changing B-field passes through two different wire loops, as in Fig. 3-2, the induced emf is larger across terminals of the larger loop.

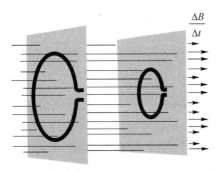

Fig. 3-2 A larger time-varying magnetic flux passes through the larger loop and induces a greater emf a cross its terminals.

In other words, here where the B-field is changing, **the induced emf is proportional to the area A of the loop penetrated perpendicularly by the field.** If the loop is successively tilted over, as is shown in Fig. 3-3, the area presented perpendicularly to the field ($A_\perp$) varies as $A\cos\theta$, and, when $\theta=90°$, the induced emf is zero because no amount of B-filed then penetrates the loop; when $\Delta B/\Delta t \neq 0$, emf $\propto A_\perp$. The converse also holds: **when the field is constant, the induced emf is proportional to the rate-of-change of the perpendicular area penetrated.** If a coil is twisted or rotated or even squashed while in a constant B-field so that the perpendicular area initially penetrated is altered, there will be an induced emf $\propto \Delta A_\perp/\Delta t$ and it will be proportional to B. In summary, when $A_\perp =$ constant, emf $\propto A_\perp \Delta B/\Delta t$ and, when $B =$ constant, emf $\propto B\Delta A_\perp/\Delta t$.

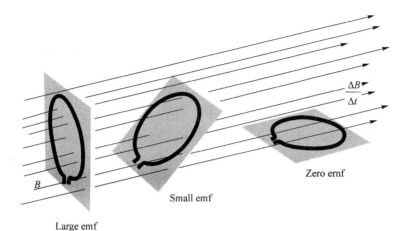

Large emf   Small emf   Zero emf

(a) The induced emf is proportional to the perpendicular area intercepted by the magnetic field.

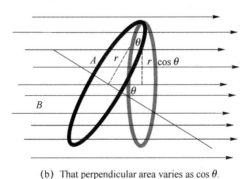

(b) That perpendicular area varies as cos θ.

Fig. 3-3 The relationship between the induced emf and the area intercepted by the magnetic field.

All of this suggests that the emf depends on the rate-of-change of both $A_\perp$ and B, that is, on the rate of charge of their product. This should bring to mind the notion of the flux of the field-the product of field and area where the penetration is perpendicular. Accordingly, the **flux of the magnetic field** through the wire loop is

$$\Phi_m = B_\perp A = BA_\perp = BA\cos\theta$$

More generally, if B varies in space as it's likely to, the flux of the magnetic field through any open area A bounded by the conducting loop (Fig. 3-4) is given by

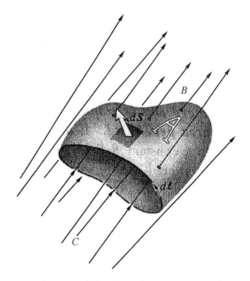

Fig. 3-4 **B**-field through an open area A.

$$\Phi_m = \iint_A \boldsymbol{B} \cdot d\boldsymbol{S} \qquad (3\text{-}1)$$

The induced emf, developed around the loop, is then

$$\text{emf} = -\frac{د\Phi_m}{dt} \tag{3-2}$$

We should not, however, get too involved with the image of wires and current and emf. Our present concern is with the electric and magnetic fields themselves.

In very general terms, an emf is a potential difference, and that's a potential-energy difference per unit charge. A potential-energy difference per unit charge corresponds to work done per unit charge, which is force per unit charge times distance, and that's electric field times distance. The emf exists only as a result of the presence of an electric field:

$$\text{emf} = \oint_C E \cdot dl \tag{3-3}$$

taken around the closed curve C, corresponding to the loop. Equating Eqs. (3-2) and (3-3), and making use of Eq. (3-1), we get

$$\oint_C E \cdot dl = -\frac{d}{dt}\iint_A \boldsymbol{B} \cdot d\boldsymbol{S} \tag{3-4}$$

We began this discussion by examining a conducting loop, and have arrived at Eq. (3-4); this expression, except for the path C, contains no reference to the physical loop. In fact, the path can be chosen arbitrarily and need not be within, or anywhere near, a conductor. The electric field in Eq. (3-4) arises not from the presence of electric charges but rather from the time-varying magnetic field. With no charges to act as sources or sinks, the field lines close on themselves, forming loops (Fig. 3-5).

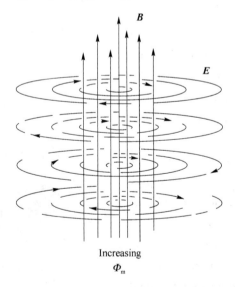

Fig. 3-5 A time-varying **B**-field. Surrounding each point where ϕ_m is changing, the **E**-field forms closed loops.

We are interested in EM waves traveling in space where are no wire loops, and the magnetic flux changes because **B** changes. The Induction Law (Eq. (3-4)) can then be rewritten as

$$\oint_C E \cdot dl = -\iint_A \frac{\partial B}{\partial t} \cdot dS \tag{3-5}$$

A partial derivative with respect to t is taken because B is usually also a function of the space variables. This expression in itself is rather fascinating, since it indicates that **a time-varying magnetic field will have an electric field associated with it.**

3.3.2 Gauss's Law-Electric

Another fundamental law of electromagnetism is named after the Germen mathematician Karl Friedrich Gauss (1777—1855). Gauss's Law is about the relationship between the flux of the electric field and the sources of that flux, charge. The ideas derive from fluid dynamic, where both the concepts of field and flux were introduced. The flow of a fluid, as represented by its velocity field, is depicted via *streamlines*[34], much as the electric field is pictured via field lines. Fig. 3-6 shows a portion of a moving fluid within which there is a region isolated by an imaginary closed surface.

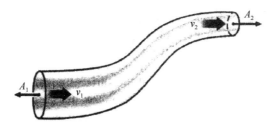

Fig. 3-6　A tube of fluid flow. Notice how the area vectors on the ends point outward.

The discharge rate, or volume flux (Av), is the volume of fluid flowing past a point in the tube per unit time. The volume flux through both end surfaces is equal in magnitude-what flows in per second flows out per second. The net fluid flux (into and out of the closed area) summed over all the surfaces equals zero. If, however, a small pipe is inserted into the region either sucking out fluid (a sink) or delivering fluid (a source), the net flux will then be nonzero.

To apply these ideas to the electric field, consider an imaginary closed area A placed in some arbitrary electric field, as depicted in Fig. 3-7.

The flux of electric field through A is taken to be

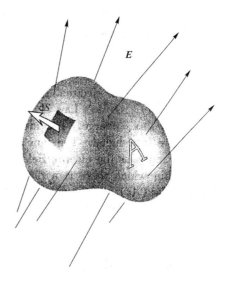

Fig. 3-7　**E**-field through a closed area A.

$$\Phi_E = \oiint_A E \cdot dS \tag{3-6}$$

The circled double integral serves as a reminder that the surface is closed. The vector dS is in the direction of an outward normal. **When there are no sources or sinks of the electric field within the region encompassed by the closed surface, the net flux through the surface equals zero**-that much is a general rule for all such fields.

In order to find out what would happen in the presence of internal sources and sinks, consider a *spherical*[35] surface of radius r centered on and surrounding a positive point-charge (q) in vacuum. The E-field is everywhere outwardly radial, and at any distance r it is entirely perpendicular to the surface: $E=E_\perp$ and so

$$\Phi_E = \oiint_A E_\perp \, dS = \oiint_A E \, dS$$

Moreover, since E is constant over the surface of the sphere, it can be taken out of the *integral*[36]:

$$\Phi_E = E \oiint_A dS = E 4\pi r^2$$

But we know from Coulomb's Law that the point-charge has an electric field given by

$$E = \frac{1}{4\pi\varepsilon_0} \frac{q}{r^2}$$

and so

$$\Phi_E = \frac{q}{\varepsilon_0}$$

This is the electric flux associated with a single point-charge q within the closed surface. Since all charge distributions are made up of point-charges, it's reasonable that the net flux due to a number of charges contained within any closed area is

$$\Phi_E = \frac{1}{\varepsilon_0} \sum q$$

Combining the two equations for Φ_E, we get **Gauss's Law**,

$$\oiint_A E \cdot dS = \frac{1}{\varepsilon_0} \sum q$$

In order to apply the *calculus*[37], it's useful to approximate the charge distribution as being continuous. Then if the volume enclosed by A is V and the charge distribution has a density ρ, Gauss's Law becomes

$$\oiint_A E \cdot dS = \frac{1}{\varepsilon_0} \iiint_V \rho \, dV \tag{3-7}$$

Electric Permittivity

For the special case of vacuum, the electric permittivity of free space is given by $\varepsilon_0 = 8.8542 \times 10^{-12} \, C^2/(N \cdot m^2)$. If the charge is embedded in some material medium its permittivity (ε) will appear in Eq. (3-7) instead of ε_0. One function of the permittivity in Eq. (3-7) is, of course, to balance out the units. There it's the medium-dependent proportionality constant between the device's capacitance and its geometric characteristics. Indeed ε is often measured by a procedure in which the material under study is placed within a capacitor. Conceptually, the permittivity embodies the electrical behavior of the medium; in a sense, it is a measure of the degree to which the material is permeated by the electric field in which it is immersed.

In the early days of the development of the subject, people in various areas worked in different systems of units, a state of affairs leading to some obvious difficulties. This necessitated the tabulation of numerical values for ε in each of the different systems, which was, at best, a waste of time. The same problem regarding densities was neatly avoided by using specific gravity. Thus it was advantageous to tabulate values not of ε but of a new related quantity that is independent of the system of units being used. Accordingly, we define that is K_E as $\varepsilon/\varepsilon_0$. This is the dielectric constant, and it is appropriately unitless. The permittivity of a material can be expressed in terms of ε_0 as

$$\varepsilon = K_E \varepsilon_0 \tag{3-8}$$

Our interest in K_E anticipates the fact that the permittivity is related to the speed of light in dielectric materials, such as glass, air, and quartz.

3.3.3 Gauss's Law-Magnetic

There is no known magnetic counterpart to the electric charge; that is, no isolated magnetic poles have ever been found, despite extensive searching, even in lunar soil samples. Unlike the electric field, the magnetic field **B** does not diverge from or converge toward some kind of magnetic charge (a monopole source or sink). Magnetic fields can be described in terms of current distributions. Indeed, we might envision an elementary magnet as a small current loop in which the lines of **B** are continuous and closed. Any closed surface in a region of magnetic field would accordingly have an equal number of lines of **B** entering and emerging from it (Fig. 3-8).

This situation arises from the absence of any monopoles within the enclosed volume. The flux of magnetic field ϕ_m through such a surface is zero, and we have the magnetic equivalent of Gauss's Law:

$$\Phi_m = \oiint_A \boldsymbol{B} \cdot \mathrm{d}\boldsymbol{S} = 0 \tag{3-9}$$

3.3.4 Ampere's Circuital Law

Another equation that will be of great interest is associated with Andre Marie Ampere (1775—1836). Known as the Circuital Law, its physical origins are a little obscure—it will take a bit of doing to justify it, but it's worth it. Accordingly, imagine a straight current-carrying wire in vacuum and the circular B-field surrounding it (Fig. 3-9).

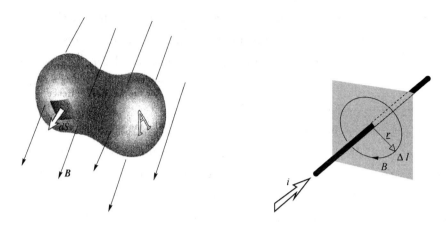

Fig. 3-8 **B**-field through a closed area A.   Fig. 3-9 The **B**-field surrounding a current-carrying wire.

We know from experiments that the magnetic field of a straight wire carrying a current i is $B=\mu i/2\pi r$. Now, suppose we put ourselves back in time to the nineteenth century when it was common to think of magnetic charge (q_m). Let's define this monopole charge so that it experiences a force when placed in a magnetic field B equal to $q_m B$ in the direction of B, just as an electric charge q_e experiences a force $q_e E$. Suppose we carry this north-seeking monopole around a closed circular path perpendicular to and centered on a current-carrying wire and determine the work done in the process. Since the direction of the force changes, because **B** changes direction, we will have to divide the circular path into tiny segments ($\Delta \ell$) and sum up the work done over each. Work is the component of the force parallel to the displacement times the displacement: $\Delta W = q_m B_{//} \Delta \ell$, and the total work done by the field is $\Sigma q_m B_{//} \Delta \ell$. In this case, **B** is everywhere tangent to the path, so that $B_{//}=B=\mu i/2\pi r$, which is constant around the circle. With both q_m and B constant, the summation becomes.

$$q_m \Sigma B_{//} \Delta \ell = q_m \Sigma B \Delta \ell = q_m B 2\pi r$$

Where $\Sigma \Delta \ell = 2\pi r$ is the circumference of the circular path.

If we substitute for B the equivalent current expression, which varies inversely with r, the radius cancels—the work is independent of the circular path taken. Since no work is done in traveling perpendicular to **B**, the work must be the same if we move q_m (out away from the wire or in toward it) along a radius, carrying it from one circular segment to another as we go around. Indeed, W is independent of path altogether—the work will be the same for any closed path encompassing the current. Putting in the current expression for B and canceling the "charge" q_m, we get the rather remarkable expression

$$\Sigma B_{//} \Delta \ell = \mu_0 i$$

which is to be summed over any closed path surrounding i. The magnetic charge has disappeared, which is nice, since we no longer expect to be able to perform this little thought experiment with a monopole. Still, the physics was consistent, and the equation should hold, monopoles or no. Moreover, if there are several current-carrying wires encompassed by the closed path, their fields will superimpose and add, yielding a net field. The equation is true for the separate fields and must be true as well for the field. Hence

$$\Sigma B_{//} \Delta \ell = \mu_0 \Sigma i$$

As $\Delta \ell \to 0$, the sum becomes an integral around a closed path:

$$\oint_C B \cdot d\ell = \mu_0 \sum i$$

Today this equation is known as **Ampere's Law**, though at one time it was commonly referred to as the "work rule". It relates a line integral of **B** tangent to a closed curve C, with the total current i passing within the confines of C.

When the current has a nonuniform cross section, Ampere Law is written in terms of the current density or current per unit area J, integrated over the area:

$$\oint_C B \cdot d\ell = \mu_0 \iint_A J \cdot dS \quad (3\text{-}10)$$

The open surface A is bounded by C (Fig. 3-10). The quantity μ_0 is called the **permeability of free space** and it's defined as $4\pi \times 10^{-7} \text{N} \cdot \text{S}^2/\text{C}^2$. When the current is imbedded in a material medium its permeability (μ) will appear in Eq. (3-10). As in Eq. (3-8),

$$\mu = K_m \mu_0 \quad (3\text{-}11)$$

with K_m being the dimensionless relative permeability.

Eq. (3-10), though often adequate, is not the whole truth. Ampere's Law is not particular about the area used, provided it's bounded by the curve C, which makes for an obvious problem when charging a

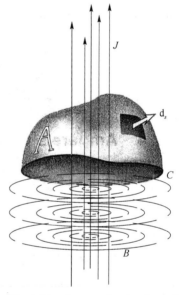

Fig. 3-10 Current density through an open area A.

capacitor, as shown in Fig. 3-11 (a). If flat area A_1 is used, a net current of i flows through it and there is a **B**-field along curve C. The right side of Eq. (3-10) is nonzero, so the left side is nonzero. But if area A_2 is used instead to encompass C, no net current passes through it and the field must now be zero, even though nothing physical has actually changed. Something is obviously wrong!

Moving charges are not the only source of a magnetic field. While charging or discharging a capacitor, one can measure a **B**-field in the region between its plates (Fig. 3-11(b)), which is indistinguishable form the field surrounding the leads, even though no electric current actually traverses the capacitor. Notice, however, that if A is the area of each plate and Q the charge on it,

$$E = \frac{Q}{\varepsilon A}$$

As the charge varies, the electric field changes, and taking the derivative if both sides yields

$$\varepsilon \frac{\partial E}{\partial t} = \frac{i}{A}$$

Which is effectively a **E** current density. James Clerk Maxwell hypothesized the existence of just such a mechanism, which he called the displacement current density, defined by

$$\boldsymbol{J}_D \equiv \varepsilon \frac{\partial \boldsymbol{E}}{\partial t} \tag{3-12}$$

The restatement of Ampere's Law as

$$\oint_C \boldsymbol{B} \cdot d\ell = \mu \iint_A (J + \varepsilon \frac{\partial E}{\partial t}) dS \tag{3-13}$$

was one of Maxwell's greatest contributions. It points out that even when $\boldsymbol{J}=0$, **a time-varying E-field will be accompanied by a B-field** (Fig. 3-7).

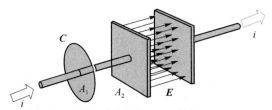

(a) Ampere's Law is indifferent to which area A_1 or A_2 is bounded by the path C. Yet a current passes through A_1 and not through A_2, and that means something is very wrong.

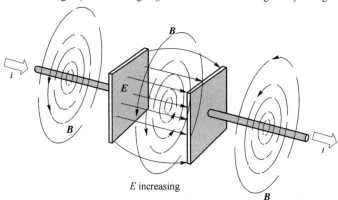

(b) **B**-field concomitant with a time-varying **E**-field in the gap of a capacitor.

Fig. 3-11 The change of Ampere's Law when a capacitor exists.

3.3.5 Maxwell's Equations

The set of integral expressions given by Eqs. (3-5), (3-7), (3-9), and (3-13) have come to be known as Maxwell's Equations. Remember that these are generalizations of experimental results. The simplest statement of Maxwell's Equations applies to the behavior of the electric and magnetic fields in free space, where $\varepsilon = \varepsilon_0$, $\mu = \mu_0$ and both ρ and $\boldsymbol{J}$ are zero. In that instance,

$$\oint_C E \cdot dl = -\iint_A \frac{\partial B}{\partial t} \cdot dS \tag{3-14}$$

$$\oint_C B \cdot dl = \mu_0 \varepsilon_0 \iint_A \frac{\partial E}{\partial t} \cdot dS \tag{3-15}$$

$$\oiint_A B \cdot dS = 0 \tag{3-16}$$

$$\oiint_A E \cdot dS = 0 \tag{3-17}$$

Observe that except for a multiplicative scalar, the electric and magnetic fields appear in the equations with a remarkable symmetry. However E affects B, B will in turn affect E. The mathematical symmetry implies a good deal of physical symmetry. The most significant outcome of this theory is the prediction of the existence of EM waves.

3.4 Properties of Electromagnetic Wave

The physics of EM radiation is *electrodynamics*[38], a subfield of electromagnetism. EM radiation exhibits both wave properties and particle properties at the same time (wave-particle duality). The wave characteristics are more apparent when EM radiation is measured over relatively large timescales and over large distances, and the particle characteristics are more evident when measuring small distances and timescales. Both characteristics have been confirmed in a large number of experiments.

There are experiments in which the wave and particle natures of EM waves appear in the same experiment, such as the diffraction of a single photon. When a single photon is sent through two slits, it passes through both of them interfering with itself, as waves do, yet is detected by a photomultiplier or other sensitive detector only once. Similar self-interference is observed when a single photon is sent into a *Michelson interferometer*[39] or other interferometers.

3.4.1 Wave Model

An important aspect of the nature of light is frequency. The frequency of a wave is its rate of oscillation and is measured in hertz, the SI unit of frequency, equal to one oscillation per second. Light usually has a spectrum of frequencies which sum together to form the resultant wave. Different frequencies undergo different angles of refraction.

A wave consists of successive *troughs* and *crests*[40], and the distance between two adjacent crests or troughs is called the wavelength. Waves of the EM spectrum vary in size, from very long radio waves the size of buildings to very short gamma rays smaller than atom nuclei. Frequency is inversely proportional to wavelength, according to the equation:

$$\nu = f \lambda \tag{3-18}$$

where v is the speed of the wave (c in a vacuum, or less in other media), f is the frequency and λ is the wavelength. As waves cross boundaries between different media, their speeds change but their frequencies remain constant.

Interference is the *superposition*[41] of two or more waves resulting in a new wave pattern. If the fields have components in the same direction, they constructively interfere, while opposite directions cause destructive interference. The energy in EM waves is sometimes called radiant energy.

3.4.2 Particle Model

Because energy of an EM wave is quantized, in the particle model of EM radiation, a wave consists of discrete packets of energy, or quanta, called photons. The frequency of the wave is proportional to the magnitude of the particle's energy. Moreover, because photons are emitted and absorbed by charged particles, they act as transporters of energy. The energy per photon can be calculated by Planck's equation:

$$E = hf \tag{3-19}$$

where E is the energy, h is Planck's constant.

As a photon is absorbed by an atom, it excites an electron, elevating it to a higher energy level. If the energy is great enough, so that the electron jumps to a high enough energy level, it may escape the positive pull of the nucleus and be liberated from the atom in a process called *photoionisation*[42]. Conversely, an electron that descends to a lower energy level in an atom emits a photon of light equal to the energy difference. Since the energy levels of electrons in atoms are discrete, each element emits and absorbs its own characteristic frequencies.

Together, these effects explain the absorption spectra of light. The dark bands in the spectrum are due to the atoms in the intervening medium absorbing different frequencies of the light. The composition of the medium through which the light travels determines the nature of the absorption spectrum. For instance, dark bands in the light emitted by a distant star are due to the atoms in the star's atmosphere. These bands correspond to the allowed energy levels in the atoms. A similar phenomenon occurs for emission. As the electrons descend to lower energy levels, a spectrum is emitted that represents the jumps between the energy levels of the electrons. This is manifested in the emission spectrum of *nebulae*[43]. Today, scientists use this phenomenon to observe what elements a certain star is composed of. It is also used in the determination of the distance of a star, using the so-called red shift.

3.4.3 Speed of Propagation

Any electric charge which accelerates, or any changing magnetic field, produces EM radiation. EM information about the charge travels at the speed of light. *Accurate treatment thus incorporates a concept known as retarded time (as opposed to advanced time, which is unphysical in light of causality), which adds to the expressions for the electrodynamic electric field and magnetic field.* [5] These extra terms are responsible for EM radiation. When any wire (or other conducting object such as an antenna) conducts alternating current, EM radiation is propagated at the same frequency as the electric current. Depending on the circumstances, it may behave as a wave or as particles. As a wave, it is characterized by a velocity (the speed of light), wavelength, and frequency.

One rule is always obeyed regardless of the circumstances: EM radiation in a vacuum always travels at the speed of light, relative to the observer, regardless of the observer's velocity. (This observation led to Albert Einstein's development of the theory of special relativity.)

In a medium (other than vacuum), velocity of propagation or refractive index are considered, depending on frequency and application. Both of these are ratios of the speed in a medium to speed in a vacuum.

3.5 Electromagnetic Spectrum and Applications

EM energy at a particular wavelength λ (in vacuum) has an associated frequency f and photon energy E. Thus, the EM spectrum may be expressed equally well in terms of any of these three quantities. They are related according to the equations:

$$E = hc/\lambda$$

So, high-frequency EM waves have a short wavelength and high energy; low-frequency waves have a long wavelength and low energy.

The EM spectrum is the range of all possible EM radiation. As shown in Fig. 3-12, the "EM spectrum" (usually just spectrum) of an object is the frequency range of EM radiation with wavelengths from thousands of kilometers down to fractions of the size of an atom. Generally, EM radiation is classified by wavelength into electrical energy, radio, microwave, terahertz, infrared, the visible region we perceive as light, ultraviolet, X-rays and gamma rays. It is commonly said that EM waves beyond these limits are uncommon, although this is not actually true. The short wavelength limit is likely to be the Planck length, and the long wavelength limit is the size of the universe itself, though in principle the spectrum is infinite.

1. Radio waves

Radio waves generally are utilized by antennas of appropriate size (according to the principle of resonance), with wavelengths ranging from hundreds of meters to about one millimeter. They are used for transmission of data, via modulation. Television, mobile phones, wireless networking and amateur radio all use radio waves. The use of the radio spectrum is regulated by many governments through frequency allocation.

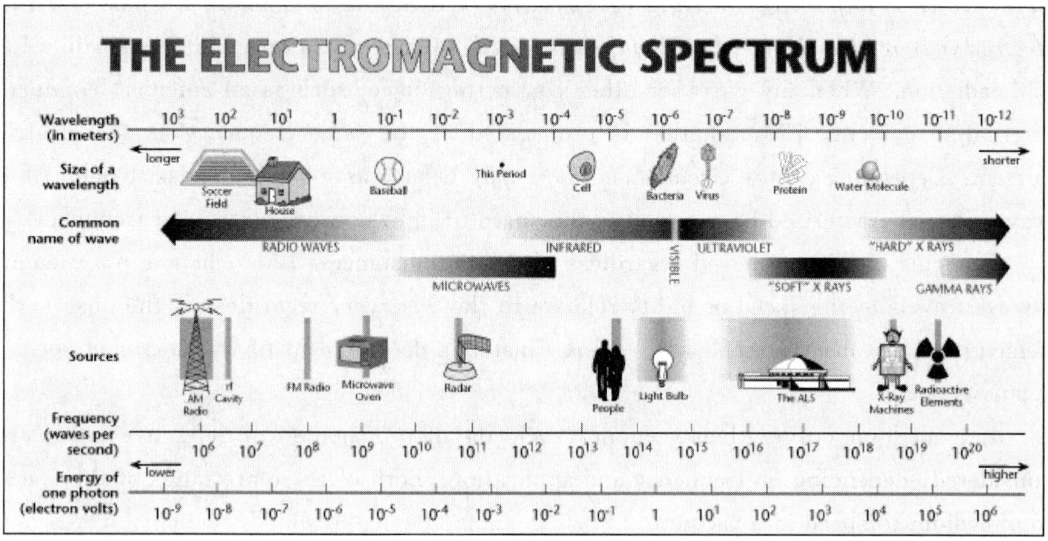

Fig. 3-12 EM spectrum

Radio waves can be made to carry information by varying a combination of the amplitude, frequency and phase of the wave within a frequency band. *When EM radiation impinges upon a conductor, it couples to the conductor, travels along it, and induces an electric current on the surface of that conductor by exciting the electrons of the conducting material*[⑥]. This effect (the skin effect) is used in antennas.

2. Microwaves

The super high frequency (SHF) and extremely high frequency (EHF) of microwaves come next up the frequency scale. Microwaves are waves which are typically short enough to employ tubular metal waveguides of reasonable diameter. Microwave energy is produced with klystron and magnetron tubes, and with solid state diodes such as Gunn and IMPATT devices. Microwaves are absorbed by molecules that have a dipole moment in liquids. In a microwave oven, this effect is used to heat food. Low-intensity microwave radiation is used in Wi-Fi, although this is at intensity levels unable to cause thermal heating.

Volumetric heating, as used by microwaves, transfer energy through the material electro-magnetically, not as a thermal heat flux. The benefit of this is a more uniform heating and reduced heating time; microwaves can heat material in less than 1% of the time of conventional heating methods.

When active, the average microwave oven is powerful enough to cause interference at close range with poorly shielded EM fields such as those found in mobile medical devices and cheap consumer electronics.

3. Terahertz radiation

Terahertz radiation is a region of the spectrum between far infrared and microwaves.

Until recently, the range was rarely studied and few sources existed for microwave energy at the high end of the band (sub-millimeter waves or so-called terahertz waves), but applications such as imaging and communications are now appearing. Scientists are also looking to apply terahertz technology in the armed forces, where high frequency waves might be directed at enemy troops to incapacitate their electronic equipment.

4. Infrared radiation

The infrared part of the EM spectrum covers the range from roughly 300 GHz (1 mm) to 400 THz (750 nm). It can be divided into three parts:

Far-infrared, from 300 GHz (1 mm) to 30 THz (10 μm). The lower part of this range may also be called microwaves. This radiation is typically absorbed by so-called rotational modes in gas-phase molecules, by molecular motions in liquids, and by phonons in solids. The water in the Earth's atmosphere absorbs so strongly in this range that it renders the atmosphere effectively opaque. However, there are certain wavelength ranges ("windows") within the opaque range which allow partial transmission, and can be used for astronomy. The wavelength range from approximately 200 μm up to a few mm is often referred to as "sub-millimeter" in astronomy, reserving far infrared for wavelengths below 200 μm.

Mid-infrared, from 30 to 120 THz (10 to 2.5 μm). Hot objects (black-body radiators) can radiate strongly in this range. It is absorbed by molecular vibrations, where the different atoms in a molecule vibrate around their equilibrium positions. This range is sometimes called the fingerprint region since the mid-infrared absorption spectrum of a compound is very specific for that compound.

Near-infrared, from 120 to 400 THz (2 500 to 750 nm). Physical processes that are relevant for this range are similar to those for visible light.

5. Visible radiation (light)

Above infrared in frequency comes visible light. This is the range in which the sun and stars similar to it emit most of their radiation. It is probably not a coincidence that the human eye is sensitive to the wavelengths that the sun emits most strongly. Visible light (and near-infrared light) is typically absorbed and emitted by electrons in molecules and atoms that move from one energy level to another. The light we see with our eyes is really a very small portion of the EM spectrum. A rainbow shows the optical (visible) part of the EM spectrum; infrared (if you could see it) would be located just beyond the red side of the rainbow with ultraviolet appearing just beyond the violet end.

EM radiation with a wavelength between 380 nm and 760 nm (790—400 terahertz) is detected by the human eye and perceived as visible light. Other wavelengths, especially near infrared (longer than 760 nm) and ultraviolet (shorter than 380 nm) are also sometimes referred to as light, especially when the visibility to humans is not relevant.

If radiation having a frequency in the visible region of the EM spectrum reflects off of an object, say, a bowl of fruit, and then strikes our eyes, this results in our visual perception of the scene. Our brain's visual system processes the multitude of reflected frequencies into different shades and hues, and through this not-entirely-understood psychophysical phenomenon, most people perceive a bowl of fruit.

At most wavelengths, however, the information carried by EM radiation is not directly detected by human senses. Natural sources produce EM radiation across the spectrum, and our technology can also manipulate a broad range of wavelengths. Optical fiber transmits light which, although not suitable for direct viewing, can carry data that can be translated into sound or an image. The coding used in such data is similar to that used with radio waves.

6. Ultraviolet light

Next in frequency comes ultraviolet (UV). This is radiation whose wavelength is shorter than the violet end of the visible spectrum, and longer than that of an x-ray.

Being very energetic, UV can break chemical bonds, making molecules unusually reactive or ionizing them (see photoelectric effect), in general changing their mutual behavior. Sunburn, for example, is caused by the disruptive effects of UV radiation on skin cells, which is the main cause of skin cancer, if the radiation irreparably damages the complex DNA molecules in the cells (UV radiation is a proven mutagen). The Sun emits a large amount of UV radiation, which could quickly turn Earth into a barren desert. However, most of it is absorbed by the atmosphere's ozone layer before reaching the surface.

7. X-rays

After UV come X-rays, which are also ionizing, but due to their higher energies they can also interact with matter by means of the *Compton effect*[44]. Hard X-rays have shorter wavelengths than soft X-rays. As they can pass through most substances, X-rays can be used to "see through" objects, most notably diagnostic x-ray images in medicine (a process known as radiography), as well as for high-energy physics and astronomy. Neutron stars and accretion disks around black holes emit X-rays, which enable us to study them. X-rays are given off by stars, and strongly by some types of nebulae.

8. Gamma rays

After hard X-rays come gamma rays, which were discovered by Paul Villard in 1900. These are the most energetic photons, having no defined lower limit to their wavelength. They are useful to astronomers in the study of high energy objects or regions, and find a use with physicists thanks to their penetrative ability and their production from radioisotopes. Gamma rays are also used for the irradiation of food and seed for *sterilization*[45], and in medicine they are used in radiation cancer therapy and some kinds of diagnostic imaging such as PET scans. The wavelength of gamma rays can be measured with high accuracy by means of Compton scattering.

Note that there are no precisely defined boundaries between the bands of the EM spectrum. Radiation of some types have a mixture of the properties of those in two regions of the spectrum. For example, red light resembles infrared radiation in that it can resonate some chemical bonds.

References

1. Eugene Hecht. Optics. 张存林改编. Beijing: High Education Press, 2004.
2. Robert R. G. Yang, Thomas T. Y. Wong. Electromagnetic Fields and Waves. Beijing: High Education Press, 2006.
3. Gerald L. Pollack, Daniel R. Stump. Electromagnetism. Beijing: High Education Press, 2005.
4. http://en.wikipedia.org/.

New Words and Expressions

1. molecule ['mɔlikjuːl] n. 分子
2. atom smashers 核粒子加速器
3. radio astronomy 电波(无线电)天文学
4. charge [tʃɑːdʒ] n. 电荷
5. velocity [vi'lɔsiti] n. 速度,速率
6. constant ['kɔnstənt] n. 常数,恒量
7. resultant [ri'zʌltənt] n. 合成矢量
8. discrete [dis'kriːt] a. 离散的,不连续的
9. photon ['fəutɔn] n. 光子
10. oscillate ['ɔsileit] v. 振荡
11. propagation [ˌprɔpə'geiʃən] n. (电磁辐射)传播
12. orthogonal [ɔː'ɔgənl] a. 直角的,直交的
13. transverse wave 横波(质点的振动方向与波的传播方向相互垂直的波。与纵波(longitudinal wave)相对应,纵波是质点的振动方向与传播方向一致的波)
14. polarize ['pəulәraiz] v. 极化(使……偏振化,使……两极分化)
15. vacuum ['vækjuəm] n. 真空,空间
16. quantum mechanics 量子力学(量子力学是研究微观粒子的运动规律的物理学分支学科,它主要研究原子、分子、凝聚态物质,以及原子核和基本粒子的结构、性质的基础理论,它与相对论一起构成了现代物理学的理论基础。量子力学的基本原理包括量子态的概念、运动方程、理论概念和观测物理量之间的对应规则和物理原理)
17. millennia [mi'leniə] n. 几千年(millennium 的复数形式)
18. ferromagnetism [ˌferəu'mægnitizəm] n. 铁磁性
19. quantitative study 定量研究
20. torsion balance 扭秤(利用扭力测量微力的一种仪器。库仑定律是库仑通过扭秤实验总结出来的,库仑扭秤在细金属丝的下端悬挂一根秤杆,它的一端有一个小球 A,另一端有一平衡体 P,在 A 旁放置一个同它一样大小的固定小球 B。为了研究带电体间的作用力,

先使 A 和 B 都带一定电荷,这时秤因 A 端受力而偏转。扭转悬丝上端的旋钮,使小球 A 回到原来的位置,平衡时悬丝的扭力矩等于电力施在 A 上的力矩。如果悬丝的扭转力矩同扭角间的关系已知,并测得秤杆的长度,就可以求出在此距离下 AB 之间的作用力。库仑扭秤实验在电学发展史上有重要的地位,它是人们对电现象的研究从定性阶段进入定量阶段的转折点)

  21. electromotive force 电动势
  22. reciprocal [ri'siprəkəl] *a.* 相互的,交互的,相反的,reciprocal effect 电磁感应
  23. formulate ['fɔːmjuleit] *v.* 用公式表示
  24. celestial mechanics 天体力学
  25. deduce [di'djuːs] *v.* 推论,演绎出
  26. astronomically [æstrə'nɒmik(ə)li] *adv.* 天文学地(天体地,宇航学地)
  27. eclipse [i'klips] *n.* 日蚀,月蚀
  28. Jupiter ['dʒuːpitə] *n.* 木星
  29. bewildering [bi'wilderiŋ] *a.* 令人困惑的,使人混乱的
  30. induction [in'dʌkʃən] *n.* 感应,感应现象
  31. electrostatic [i'lektrəu'stætik] *a.* 静电的,静电学的
  32. speculate ['spekjuˌleit] *v.* 深思,推测
  33. galvanometer [ˌgælvə'nɒmitə] *n.* 检流计
  34. streamline ['striːmlain] *a.* 流线型的
  35. spherical ['sferikəl] *a.* 球的,球面的,球状的
  36. integral ['intigrəl] *n.* [数学]积分
  37. calculus ['kælkjuləs] *n.* 微积分
  38. electrodynamics 电动力学(电动力学是研究电磁现象的经典动力学理论,它主要研究电磁场的基本属性、运动规律以及电磁场和带电物质的相互作用)
  39. Michelson interferometer 迈克尔逊干涉仪
  40. trough ['trɔːf] *n.* 波谷;crest [krest] *n.* 波峰
  41. superposition [ˌsjuːpəpə'ziʃən] *n.* 重叠,叠合,重合
  42. photoionisation [ˌfəutəuˌaiəni'zeiʃən] *n.* [物]光致电离,光化电离(作用)
  43. nebula ['nebjulə] *n.* 星云(nebulae 是其复数形式)
  44. Compton effect 康普顿效应(1923 年,美国物理学家康普顿在研究 X 射线通过实物物质发生散射的实验时,发现了一个新的现象,即散射光中除了有原波长的 X 光外,还产生了波长大于原波长的 X 光,其波长的增量随散射角的不同而变化。这种现象称为康普顿效应,康普顿效应第一次从实验上证实了爱因斯坦提出的关于光子具有动量的假设)
  45. sterilization [sterilai'zeiʃən] *n.* 消毒,灭菌

Notes

  ① 随着光子的运动,电场和磁场方向会发生反转,我们把每秒内发生反转的次数或振荡数称为频率,标为 ν。
  ② 如同万有引力定律,库仑定律也基于"超距作用"这一概念,处于一定范围的物体可

以立刻、直接地和其他物体发生作用,而不需要中介媒介。

③ 由于是典型的、抽象的数学推理,考虑到方程对称性,麦克斯韦在方程中加入一个含有电场变化速率的项。这一概括项使得麦克斯韦方程与电荷守恒原则取得一致。

④ 赫兹还证实这些波遵循可见光的反射定律、折射定律和偏振性,从而证实电磁波与可见光仅在波长和频率方面有所不同。

⑤ 这样精确的计算必须引入延迟时间的概念,并且在基于电动力学的电场和磁场表达式中加入这个概念。

⑥ 当电磁辐射撞到导体上时,电磁辐射与导体连接,沿着导体方向传播,并且通过激发导电物质的电子而在导体表面产生电流。

Fundamentals of Optics

第4章

PREVIEW

In general, the discussion about the principles of optics is restricted to those optical phenomena which may be treated in terms of Maxwell's *phenomenological theory*[1]. This includes all situations in which the atomistic structure of matter plays no decisive part.

A classical teaching text in optics deals with the basic two branches of the subject, one geometrical optics, the other physical optics.

Geometrical optics is that part of optics where the wave nature can be neglected. Physical optics is more inclusive: it is the branch of optics concerned with the wave properties of light, the superposition of waves (*interference*[2]), and the deviation of light from its rectilinear propagation by means other than geometrical optics (*diffraction*[3]). Physical optics also includes the concept of transformation, which is fundamental to optical data processing, pattern recognition and *holography*[4].

Optics is a field of science that is particularly lucid, logical, challenging, and beautiful. Most of our appreciation of the outside world—nature, art—comes to us through light. We will now proceed to discuss its many aspects: a brief history about optics, and contents and application of optics.

4.1 A Brief History about Optics

The physical principles underlying the optical phenomena with which we are concerned in the classical teaching texts in optics were substantially formulated before 1900. Since that year, optics, like the rest of physics, has undergone a thorough revolution by the discovery of the quantum of energy. While this discovery has profoundly affected our views about the nature of light, it has not made the earlier theories and techniques superfluous; rather, it has brought out their limitations and defined their range of validity. The extension of the older principles and methods and their applications to very many diverse situations has continued, and is continuing with undiminished intensity.[①]

In attempting to present in an orderly way the knowledge acquired over a period of several centuries in such a vast field it is impossible to follow the historical development, with its numerous false starts and detours. It is therefore deemed necessary to record separately, in this preliminary section, the main landmarks in the evolution of ideas concerning the nature of light.

4.1.1 The Views of the Antique Philosophers

The philosophers of antiquity speculated about the nature of light, being familiar with burning glasses[5], *with the rectilinear propagation*[6] *of light, and with refraction*[7] *and reflection*[8]. *The first systematic writings on optics of which we have any definite knowledge are due to the Greek philosophers and mathematicians*[②] [Empedocles (c. 490—430 BC), Euclid (c. 300 BC)].

4.1.2 Classical Optics

1. The nature of light

Amongst the founders of the new philosophy, Rene Descartes (1596—1650) may be singled out for mention as having formulated views on the nature of light on the basis of his *metaphysical*[9] ideas. Descartes considered light to be essentially a pressure transmitted through a perfectly elastic medium (the *aether*[10]) which fills all space, and he attributed the diversity of colors to rotary motions with different velocities of the particles in this medium. But it was only after Galileo Galilei (1564—1642) had, by his development of mechanics, demonstrated the power of the experimental method that optics was put on a firm foundation. The law of reflection was known to the Greeks; the law of refraction was discovered experimentally in 1621 by Willebrord Snell (Snellius, c. 1580—1626). In 1657 Pierre de Fermat (1601—1665) enunciated the celebrated Principle of Least Time in the form 'Nature always acts by the shortest course'.

2. General acceptance of the wave theory

The first phenomenon of interference, the colors exhibited by thin films now known as 'Newton's rings', was discovered independently by Robert Boyle (1627—1691) and Robert Hooke (1635—1703). Hooke also observed the presence of light in the geometrical shadow, the 'diffraction' of light but this phenomenon had been noted previously by Francesco Maria Grimaldi (1618—1663). The basic quality of color was revealed only when Isaac Newton (1642—1727) discovered in 1666 that white light could be split up into component colors by means of a *prism*[11], and found that each pure color is characterized by a specific *refrangibility*[12]. The difficulties which the wave theory encountered in connection with the rectilinear propagation of light and of *polarization*[13] (discovered by Huygens) seemed to Newton so decisive that he devoted himself to the development of an emission (or corpuscular) theory, according to which light is propagated from a *luminous*[14] body in the form of minute particles.

At the time of the publication of Newton's theory of color it was not known whether light was propagated instantaneously or not. The discovery of the finite speed of light was made in 1675 by Olaf Römer (1644—1710) from the observations of the eclipses of Jupiter's satellites.

The wave theory of light which, as we saw, had Hooke amongst its first champions was greatly improved and extended by Christian Huygens (1629—1695). He enunciated the principle, subsequently named after him, according to which every point of the 'aether' upon which the luminous disturbance falls may be regarded as the centre of a new disturbance propagated in the form of spherical waves; these secondary waves combine in such a manner that their envelope determines the wave-front at any later time. With the aid of this principle he succeeded in deriving the laws of reflection and refraction. He was also able to interpret the double refraction of *calc-spar*[15] [discovered in 1669 by Erasmus Bartholinus (1625—1698)] by assuming that in the crystal there is, in addition to a primary spherical wave, a secondary ellipsoidal wave. It was in the course of this investigation that Huygens made the fundamental discovery of polarization: each of the two rays arising from refraction by calc-spar may be extinguished by passing it through a second crystal of the same material if the latter crystal be rotated about the direction of the ray. It was, however, left to Newton to interpret these phenomena; he assumed that rays have 'sides'; and indeed this *'transversality'*[16] seemed to him an insuperable objection to the acceptance of the wave theory, since at that time scientists were familiar only with *longitudinal*[17] waves (from the propagation of sound).

*The rejection of the wave theory on the authority of Newton lead to its abeyance for nearly a century, but it still found an occasional supporter, such as the great mathematician Leonhard Euler (1707—1783).*③

It was not until the beginning of the nineteenth century that the decisive discoveries were made which led to general acceptance of the wave theory. The first step towards this was the enunciation in 1801 by Thomas Young (1773—1829) of the principle of interference and the explanation of the colors of *thin films*[18]. However, as Young's views were expressed largely in a qualitative manner, they did not gain general recognition.

*About this time, polarization of light by reflection was discovered by Etienne Louis Malus (1775—1812). Apparently, one evening in 1808, he observed the reflection of the sun from a window pane through a calc-spar crystal, and found that the two images obtained by double refraction varied in relative intensities as the crystal was rotated about the line of sight. However, Malus did not attempt an interpretation of this phenomenon, being of the opinion that current theories were incapable of providing an explanation.*④

In the meantime the emission theory had been developed further by Pierre Simon de Laplace (1749—1827) and Jean-Baptiste Biot (1774—1862). Its supporters proposed the subject of diffraction for the *prize question*[19] set by the Paris Academy for 1818, in the expectation that a treatment of this subject would lead to the crowning triumph of the emission theory. But their hopes were disappointed, for, in spite of strong opposition, the prize was awarded to Augustin Jean Fresnel (1788—1827), whose treatment was based on the wave theory, and was the first of a succession of investigations which, in the course of a few years, were to discredit the *corpuscular theory*[20] completely. The substance of his memoir consisted of a synthesis of Huygens' Envelope Construction with Young's Principle of Interference. This, as Fresnel showed, was sufficient to explain not only the "rectilinear propagation" of light but also the minute deviations from it—diffraction phenomena. Fresnel calculated the diffraction caused by straight edges, small apertures and screens; particularly impressive was the experimental confirmation by Arago of a prediction, deduced by Poisson from Fresnel's theory, that in the centre of the shadow of a small circular disc there should appear a bright spot.

In the same year (1818), Fresnel also investigated the important problem of the influence of the earth's motion on the propagation of light, the question being whether there was any difference between the light from stellar and terrestrial sources. Dominique Frangois Arago (1786—1853) found from experiment that (apart from *aberration*[21]) there was no difference. On the basis of these findings Fresnel developed his theory of the partial convection of the luminiferous aether by matter, a theory confirmed in 1851 by direct experiment carried out by Armand Hypolite Louis Fizeau (1819—1896). Together with Arago, Fresnel investigated the interference of polarized rays of light and found (in 1816) that two rays polarized at right angles to each other never interfere. This fact could not be reconciled with the assumption of longitudinal waves, which had hitherto been taken for granted. Young, who had heard of this discovery from Arago, found in 1817 the key to the solution when he assumed that the vibrations were transverse.

Fresnel at once grasped the full significance of this hypothesis, which he sought to put on a more secure dynamical basis and from which he drew numerous conclusions. For, since only longitudinal oscillations in a fluid are possible, the aether must behave like a solid body; but at that time a theory of elastic waves in solids had not yet been formulated. Instead of developing such a theory and deducing the optical consequences from it, Fresnel proceeded by inference, and sought to deduce the properties of the *luminiferous*[22] aether from the observations. The peculiar laws of light propagation in crystals were Fresnel's starting point; the elucidation of these laws and their reduction to a few simple assumptions about the nature of elementary waves represents one of the greatest achievements of natural science. In 1832, William Rowan Hamilton (1805—1865), who himself made important contributions to the development of optics, drew attention to an important deduction from Fresnel's construction, by predicting the so-called *conical refraction*[23], whose existence was confirmed experimentally shortly afterwards by Humphrey Lloyd J (1800—1881).

It was also Fresnel who (in 1821) gave the first indication of the cause of *dispersion*[24] taking into account the molecular structure of matter, a suggestion elaborated later by

Cauchy.

Dynamical models of the mechanism of aether vibrations led Fresnel to deduce the laws which now bear his name, governing the intensity and polarization of light rays produced by reflection and refraction.

Fresnel's work had put the wave theory on such a secure foundation that it seemed almost superfluous when in 1850 Foucault and Fizeau and Breguet undertook a crucial experiment first suggested by Arago. The corpuscular theory explains refraction in terms of the attraction of the light-corpuscles at the boundary towards the optically denser medium, and this implies a greater velocity in the denser medium; on the other hand the wave theory demands, according to Huygens' construction, that a smaller velocity obtains in the optically denser medium. The direct measurement of the velocity of light in air and water decided unambiguously in favor of the wave theory.

3. The development of the elastic aether theory

The decades that followed witnessed the development of the elastic aether theory. The first step was the formulation of a theory of the elasticity of solid bodies. Claude Louis Marie Henri Navier (1785—1836) developed such a theory, discerning that matter consists of countless particles (mass points, atoms) exerting on each other forces along the lines joining them. The now customary derivation of the equations of elasticity by means of the continuum concept is due to Augustine Louis Cauchy (1789—1857). Of other scientists who participated in the development of optical theory, mention must be made of Simeon Denis Poisson (1781—1840), George Green (1793—1841), James MacCullagh (1809—1847) and Franz Neumann (1798—1895). The various theories put forward by the authors mentioned above differ in regard to the assumed boundary conditions, which always conflicted in some way with the laws of mechanics.

An obvious objection to regarding the aether as an elastic solid is expressed in the following query: How is one to imagine planets travelling through such a medium at enormous speeds without any appreciable resistance? George Gabriel Stokes (1819—1903) thought that this objection could be met on the grounds that the planetary speeds are very small compared to the speeds of the aetherial particles in the vibrations constituting light; for it is known that bodies like pitch or sealing wax are capable of rapid vibrations but yield completely to stresses applied over a long period. Such controversies seem superfluous today since we no longer consider it necessary to have mechanical pictures of all natural phenomena.

A first step away from the concept of an elastic aether was taken by MacCullagh, who postulated a medium with properties not possessed by ordinary bodies. The latter store up energy when the volume elements change shape, but not during rotation. In MacCullagh's aether the inverse conditions prevail. The laws of propagation of waves in such a medium show a close similarity to Maxwell's equations of electromagnetic waves which are the basis of modern optics.

In spite of the many difficulties, the theory of an elastic aether persisted for a long time and most of the great physicists of the nineteenth century contributed to it. In addition to those already named, mention must be made of William Thomson (Lord Kelvin, 1824—1908), Carl Neumann (1832—1925), John William Strutt (Lord Rayleigh, 1842—1919), and Gustav Kirchhoff (1824—1887). During this period many optical problems were solved, but the foundations of optics remained in an unsatisfactory state.

4. Researches in electricity and magnetism

In the meantime researches in electricity and magnetism had developed almost independently of optics, culminating in the discoveries of Michael Faraday (1791—1867). James Clerk Maxwell (1831—1879) succeeded in summing up all previous experiences in this field in a system of equations, the most important consequence of which was to establish the possibility of electromagnetic waves, propagated with a velocity which could be calculated from the results of purely electrical measurements. Actually, some years earlier Rudolph Kohlrausch (1809—1858) and Wilhelm Weber (1804—1891) had carried out such measurements and the velocity turned out to be that of light. This led Maxwell to conjecture that light waves are electromagnetic waves; a conjecture verified by direct experiment in 1888 by Heinrich Hertz (1857—1894). In spite of this, Maxwell's electromagnetic theory had a long struggle to gain general acceptance. It seems to be a characteristic of the human mind that familiar concepts are abandoned only with the greatest reluctance, especially when a concrete picture of the phenomena has to be sacrificed. Maxwell himself, and his followers, tried for a long time to describe the electromagnetic field with the aid of mechanical models. It was only gradually, as Maxwell's concepts became more familiar, that the search for an 'explanation' of his equations in terms of mechanical models was abandoned; today there is no conceptual difficulty in regarding Maxwell's field as something which cannot be reduced to anything simpler.

*But even the electromagnetic theory of light has attained the limits of its serviceability. It is capable of explaining, in their main features, all phenomena connected with the propagation of light. However, it fails to elucidate the processes of emission and absorption, in which the finer features of the interaction between matter and the optical field are manifested.*⑤

4.1.3 Modern Optics

1. The discovery of certain regularities in spectra

The laws underlying these processes are the proper object of modern optics, indeed of modern physics. Their story begins with the discovery of certain regularities in *spectra*[25]. The first step was Josef Fraunhofer's (1787—1826) discovery (1814—1817) of the dark lines in the solar spectrum, since named after him; and their interpretation as absorption lines given in 1861 on the basis of experiments by Roger Wilhelm Bunsen (1811—1899) and Gustav Kirchhoff (1824—1887). The light of the continuous spectrum of the body of the sun, passing the cooler gases of the sun's atmosphere, loses by absorption just those wavelengths which are emitted by the gases. This discovery was the beginning of spectrum analysis, which is based on the recognition that every gaseous chemical element possesses a characteristic line spectrum. The investigation of these spectra has been a major object of physical research up to and including the present; and since light is its subject, and optical methods are employed, it is often considered as a part of optics. The problem of how light is produced or destroyed in atoms is, however, not exclusively of an optical nature, as it involves equally the mechanics of the atom itself; and the laws of spectral lines reveal not so much the nature of light as the structure of the emitting particles. Thus, from being a part of optics, *spectroscopy*[26] has gradually evolved into a separate discipline which provides the empirical foundations for atomic and molecular physics. This field is, however, beyond the scope of this book.

2. Planck's equation

Concerning methods, it has become apparent that classical mechanics is inadequate for a proper description of events occurring within the atom and must be replaced by the quantum theory, originated in 1900 by Max Planck (1858—1947). Its application to the atomic structure, led in 1913, to the explanation by Niels Bohr (1885—1962) of the simple laws of line spectra of gases. From these beginnings and from the ever increasing experimental material, modern quantum mechanics developed (Heisenberg, Born, Jordan, de Broglie, Schrödinger, Dirac). By its means considerable insight has been obtained into the structure of atoms and molecules.

However, our concept of the nature of light has also been greatly influenced by quantum theory. Even in its first form due to Planck there appears a proposition which is directly opposed to classical ideas, namely that an oscillating electric system does not impart its energy to the electromagnetic field in a continuous manner but in finite amounts, or 'quanta'[27] $\varepsilon = h\nu$, proportional to the frequency ν of the light, where $h = 6.55 \times 10^{-27}$ erg/s is Planck's constant. We may say that the occurrence of the constant h is the feature which distinguishes modern physics from the old.

It was only gradually that the paradoxical, almost irrational, character of Planck's equation $\varepsilon = h\nu$ was fully realized by physicists. This was brought about mainly by the work of Einstein and Bohr. On the basis of Planck's theory, Einstein (1879—1955) revived in 1905 the corpuscular theory of light in a new form by assuming that Planck's energy quanta exist as real light-particles, called "light quanta" or "*photons*"[28]. He thereby succeeded in explaining some phenomena which had been discovered more recently in connection with the transformation of light into corpuscular energy, phenomena which were inexplicable by the wave theory. Chief among these are the so-called *photoelectric*[29] effect and the fundamentals of *photochemistry*[30]. In phenomena of this type light does not impart to a detached particle an energy proportional to its intensity, as demanded by the wave theory, but behaves rather like a hail of small shots. The energy imparted to the secondary particles is independent of the intensity, and depends only on the frequency of the light (according to the law $\varepsilon = h\nu$). The number of observations confirming this property of light increased year by year and the situation arose that the simultaneous validity of both wave and corpuscular theories had to be recognized, the former being exemplified by the phenomena of interference, the latter by the photoelectric effect. It is only in more recent years that the development of quantum mechanics has led to a partial elucidation of this paradoxical state of affairs, but this has entailed giving up a fundamental principle of the older physics, namely the principle of *deterministic causality*[31].

3. The development of the lasers

The detailed theory of the interaction between field and matter required the extension of the methods of quantum mechanics (field quantization). For the electromagnetic radiation field this was first carried out by Dirac and these investigations form the basis of quantum optics. However, it was mainly the development of radically new light sources, the lasers, in the 1960s that led to the emergence of quantum optics as a new discipline. The invention of the laser provided new sources of very intense, coherent and highly directional light beams. Such sources are analogous to devices known as masers, developed a few years earlier, for generating and amplifying microwave radiation by conversion of atomic and molecular energy by the process of stimulated emission. Pioneering contributions which led to the invention of these devices were made notably by Basov, Prokhorov, Townes, Schawlow and Maiman. Apart from providing an important tool for research in quantum optics, the invention of the laser led to numerous applications and originated several new fields such as quantum-electronics, nonlinear optics, fiber optics and others.

4.1.4 Moving Bodies Optics

Another branch of optics, is the *optics of moving bodies*[32]. Like the quantum theory it has grown into a vast independent field of study. The first observed phenomenon in this field, recorded in 1728 by James Bradley (1692—1762), was the aberration of 'fixed stars', i.e. the observation of slightly different angular positions of the stars according to the motion of the earth relative to the direction of the light ray. Bradley correctly interpreted this phenomenon as being due to the finite velocity of light and thus was able to determine the velocity. We have already mentioned other phenomena belonging to optics of moving media: Fresnel was the first to enquire into the convection of light by moving bodies and to show that it behaved as if the luminiferous aether participated in the movement only with a fraction of the speed of the moving bodies; Fizeau then demonstrated this partial convection experimentally with the aid of flowing water. The effect of the motion of the light source or of the observer was investigated by Christian

Doppler (1803—1853) who formulated the well-known principle named after him. So long as the elastic theory of light held the field and the precision of measurements was sufficiently limited, Fresnel's ideas on partial convection sufficed for a satisfactory explanation of all the phenomena. But the electromagnetic theory of light encountered difficulties of a fundamental nature. Hertz was the first to attempt to generalize Maxwell's laws to moving bodies. His formulae were, however, in conflict with some electromagnetic and optical experiments. Of great importance was the theory of Hendrik Antoon Lorentz (1853—1928) who assumed an 'aether in a state of absolute rest' to be the carrier of the electromagnetic field and deduced the properties of material bodies from the interaction of elementary electric particles-the electrons. He was able to show that Fresnel's coefficient of convection could be obtained correctly from his theory and that in general all phenomena known at the time (1895) lent themselves to explanation by this hypothesis. But the enormous increase of precision in the determination of optical paths by means of the interferometer of Albert Abraham Michelson (1852—1931) led to a new anomaly: it proved impossible to demonstrate the existence of an "aether drift" required by the theory of the "stationary aether". The anomaly was resolved by Albert Einstein in 1905 in his special theory of relativity. The theory is founded on a critique of the concepts of time and space and leads to the abandonment of Euclidian geometry and the intuitive conception of simultaneity. Its further development into the so-called general theory of relativity led to a completely new conception of gravitational phenomena by a "geometrization" of the space-time manifold. The application of this theory involves the use of special mathematical and physical methods which, although relevant to optics in many cases, may easily be considered separately from it. The number of optical phenomena in which the motion of bodies (e. g. light sources) plays a significant part is rather small.

4.2 Contents of Optics

4.2.1 Rectilinear Propagation of Light

Look at sunlight that, on a misty morning, breaks through the dense foliage of tree. The light, made visible by the moisture in the air, travels along straight lines called rays. Rays follow the law of rectilinear propagation. But, why are the rays in Fig. 4-1 diverging? That is merely an illusion; in reality, the rays are parallel, just as railroad tracks are parallel extending to the horizon; they only seem to be converging.

1. Huygens' principle

Any space through which light travels is an optical medium. Most optical media have the same properties in all directions and are said to be *isotropic*[33]. Also, most optical media have these same properties throughout their mass and are said to be *homogeneous*[34].

When light starts out from a point source B (Fig. 4-2) in an isotropic homogeneous medium, it spreads out uniformly at the same speed in all directions; the position it is in at any given moment will be called light fronts or *wavefronts*[35]. In the case of the water ripples the disturbance is propagated in one plane only and the wavefronts are circular.

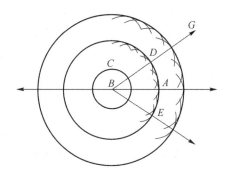

Fig. 4-1 Sunlight passing through the foliage of a tree.

Fig. 4-2 Huygens' construction for the propagation of light using wavefronts and wavelets.

Huygens usually considered to be the founder of the wave theory of light, assumed that any point on a wave surface acted as a new source from which spherical "secondary waves" or "*wavelets*[36]" spread out in a forward direction. The surface *DAE*, which touches or envelops all these wavelets, forms a new wavefront which is again a sphere with its center at *B*. This action can be repeated as long as the medium remains isotropic and homogeneous. Huygens refined this idea by assuming that the wavelets travel out in a forward direction only and that their effect is limited to that part which touches the enveloping new wavefront. This concept is known as **Huygens' principle** and, with developments by Fresnel and Kirchhoff is used to explain the effects of interference and diffraction. The basic construction of wavelets defining the new wavefront enables us to find the change in the form or the direction of the wavefront on passing to a new medium or on reflection at a surface.

From Fig. 4-2 it is clear that the path, such as *BDG*, traveled by any part of the disturbance, is a straight line perpendicular to the wavefront. For a large number of optical effects it is enough to assume that this is how light travels. Neither wavelets nor rays actually exist but both provide a useful way of dealing with the actions of light.

2. The pinhole camera

The action of a *pinhole camera*[37] shows that light travels in straight lines and therefore this device provides a verification of the law of rectilinear propagation of light. As its name suggests, the pinhole camera uses a small hole to form images. The light from each point on an illuminated object, on passing through a small aperture in an opaque screen, forms a narrow *pencil*[38] and, if the light is received on a second screen at some distance from and parallel to the first screen containing the aperture, each pencil produces a patch of light of the same shape as the aperture. Because the light travels in straight lines, the patches of light on the screen are in similar relative positions to those of the corresponding points on the object. The illuminated area of the screen is similar in shape to that of the original object but is turned upside down or inverted (Fig. 4-3(a)).

If the aperture is made small (a pinhole), the individual patches of light will overlap only to a small extent and a fairly well defined picture or image of the object is formed. As can be seen in Fig. 4-3(b), the size of the inverted image of any object will depend on the distances of object and image from the aperture. By using the mathematics of similar triangles again, we find that

$$\frac{h'}{h} = \frac{l'}{l} \qquad (4-1)$$

The degree of sharpness of the image formed by a pinhole can never be very good because if the diameter of the hole is made very small the effects of diffraction begin to blur the image. Also, the illumination of the image is very low compared with that of a camera having a lens, which will have a larger aperture allowing more light to pass through. The pinhole camera image is free from distortion and has large depth of focus; that is, the images of objects at greatly varying distance are all reasonably sharp at any screen position.

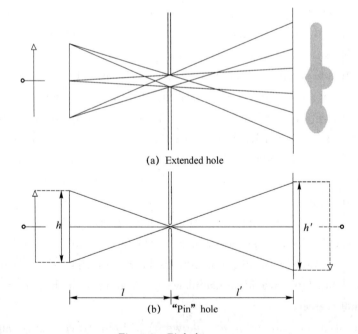

Fig. 4-3 Pinhole camera.

3. Shadows and eclipses

The formation of shadows is also explained by the law of rectilinear propagation of light. If the source of light is a point, the *shadow*[39] of any object will be sharp, neglecting the very small effects of diffraction. The size of a shadow cast onto a screen is calculated in just the same way as the size of the patch of light in Fig. 4-4 was calculated. Now we imagine EFHG to be an object rather than an aperture in a screen. The shadow it casts due to source B is $E'F'H'G'$. If the object is tilted, we must calculate the shadow size with a different value of A for each corner and the shadow will appear distorted. However, it remains the same shape as the object appears when viewed from the position of the source.

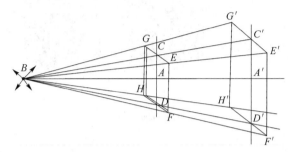

Fig. 4-4　The formation of shadows using a point source.

Usually, the light is coming from an extended source and we must consider the shadow as formed from different points on the source. In Fig. 4-5(a), B_1B_2 is an extended disk source, CD an opaque disk object and LP a screen. No light from the source can enter the space CDNM and on the screen there is a circular area of diameter MN in total shadow. This is called the *umbra*[40]. Surrounding the umbra is a space, CLM, DNP in partial shadow which is called the *penumbra*[41]. In the penumbra the illumination gradually increases from total darkness at the edge of the umbra to full illumination beyond the outer edge of the penumbra. For example, the point m is receiving light from the portion B_1b of the source. Because light travels in straight lines, the diameters of the umbra and penumbra may be found using similar triangles.

When the source is larger than the opaque object (Fig. 4-5(b)), the umbra is a cone having the object as its base. At a certain distance from the object, the umbra disappears and the shadow is completely penumbral, as shown. All shadows in sunlight are like this because nothing on earth is bigger than the sun.

In Fig. 4-5(b):

$$\frac{AO}{BO}=\frac{CD}{B_1B_2} \quad \text{or} \quad AO=CD\left(\frac{BO}{B_1B_2}\right) \tag{4-2}$$

As the sun is 1.4 million km in diameter and 150 million km away, it gives BO/B_1B_2 =107. All shadows due to sunlight of objects on the earth have an umbra which is 107 times larger than the object. The largest object close to the earth is the moon. This "object" is 3 500 km in diameter and 380 000 km from earth. These values are also approximately in the ration 1 to 107. Thus, when the moon passes between the sun and the earth, we have the situation represented by Fig. 4-5 (b) where B_1B_2 is the sun, CD is the moon, and the earth's surface is at O. This is called a *solar eclipse*[42]. An observer at O sees the moon just covering the sun and can then clearly see the *flares*[43] (*coronae*[44]) which are emitted from the sun's surface. When the earth passes between the moon and the sun we have a lunar eclipse. The moon passes into the earth's umbra but is still partly visible because the earth's atmosphere scatters sunlight into the umbral region.

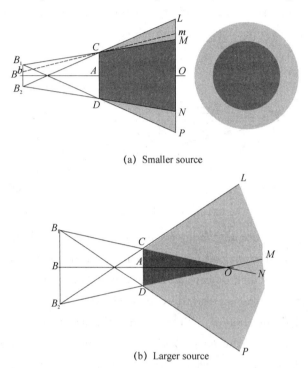

(a) Smaller source

(b) Larger source

Fig. 4-5 The formation of shadows using an extended source.

Shadows play an important part in the way we see solid objects. A distant white sphere, evenly *illuminated*[45], cannot be distinguished from a flat white disk. However, if the illumination gives some shadowing on the sphere, it is immediately seen as a solid object.

4.2.2 Reflection and Refraction

When light is incident on a surface between two media, part of the light is reflected, and part is refracted (Fig. 4-6). Reflection means that the light is returned to the first medium from which it came. Refraction means that on entering the second medium the light follows a direction different from its direction in the first medium.

The point where the light intersects the surface is the point of incidence. A line constructed at this point, perpendicular (normal) to the surface, is the surface normal. The angle subtended by the surface normal and the incident ray is the angle of incidence, $+I$ in Fig. 4-6. The angle subtended by the surface normal and the reflected ray is the angle of reflection, $-I$, and the angle subtended by the normal and the refracted ray is the angle of refraction, $+I'$. These angles are measured from the surface normal, toward the ray.

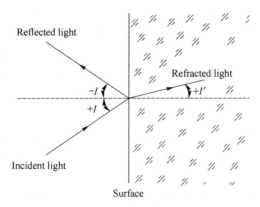

Fig. 4-6 Reflection and refraction of light at the surface between two media
(air to the left of the surface, glass to the right).

1. Reflection

When a surface is *polished*[46] nearly all the reflected light travels back in definite directions, as though coming from a source placed in some new position. The polished surface then acts as an aperture and limits the reflected beam. An observer in this reflected beam sees the image of the original source of the light without being aware of the reflecting surface if this is well polished. Such a reflection is said to be regular or *specular*[47]. Fig. 4-7 shows the effect on the ray directions and the beam of light. Once the position of the image of the object is found, the reflected rays can be drawn in by regarding the reflecting surface as an aperture.

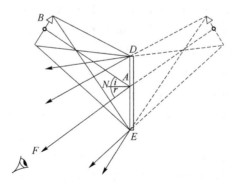

Fig. 4-7 Specular reflection.

When a surface is not polished, every irregularity of the surface will reflect light in a different direction and the light will not return as a definite beam. The surface itself will be visible from all directions, as the light is spreading out in all directions from each point on the surface. This type of reflection is said to be irregular or *diffuse*[48] and the light is diffused or *scattered*[49], although the actual reflection at each minute portion of the surface will be regular. All illuminated objects are visible because of the light irregularly reflected at their surfaces.

The amount of light reflected at a surface will vary greatly with different media. For example, light diffusely reflected from white, gray, and black paper will be about 80%, 25%, and 8% respectively of the incident light, the light arriving at the surface. Only a few materials have reflections greater than 90% and it is also quite difficult to obtain materials that reflect very little light. Special black paints have been formulated for use inside optical instruments where any scattered light must be absorbed as quickly as possible.

For specular reflection, a lot depends on the quality of polish. Mirrors made of steel do not reflect as much light as those made of silver. The best polished surfaces are obtained with glass and most mirrors are made by putting onto polished glass a thin layer of metal or other reflecting material. The ratio of reflected light to incident light is known as the reflectance of the mirror and values above 99% can be achieved. Polished surfaces are not perfectly smooth, because of the molecular structure of materials. However, once the irregularities are less than the wavelength of the incident light, the reflection becomes more and more specular. This means that quite rough surfaces can reflect heat radiation and radar waves. Even visible light can be reflected from unpolished surfaces if the incident light is nearly along the surface. A flat white sheet of paper can be seen to reflect specularly if the eye is placed at the edge of a flat sheet and looks across the sheet to objects beyond the other edge.

In the case of *transparent*[50] substances, such as glass, water, etc., the specular reflectance from a surface can be found using Fresnel's equations. It will depend not only on the angle at which the incident light meets the surface, but also on the refractive indices of the two media. For example, if some pieces of spectacle glass are placed in *glycerine*[51] or, better still, Canada *balsam*[52], media which have almost the same refractive index as the glass, almost no light is reflected at the surface of the glass and the pieces become nearly invisible. A similar effect is seen in the case of a grease spot on paper. The grease filling the pores of the paper has a refractive index more nearly that of the paper fibers than the air has, and so less light is reflected. Thus, the spot appears darker than the surrounding paper.

The light reflected by some materials is colored. This is because, of the various colors in white light, only some are reflected and the others are absorbed by the substance. Such reflection is said to be selective. A red object when illuminated with white light reflects only the red, the other colors passing into the material and being absorbed. If the red objects is illuminated with green light it appears black because there is no red light to reflect.

2. The law of reflection

In Fig. 4-7 a ray of light *BA* is incident on an optically smooth surface *DE*, and is regularly reflected to form the ray *AF*. This ray is one of a collection of rays leaving the object and being reflected along the whole length of the mirror surface DE to form the image which appears to be behind the mirror. In the geometry of the light ray BAF, BA and AF are straight lines while DE is a surface. This can cause confusion and the mathematics is easier to use (and to explain) if we deal with three straight lines. This can be the case if, instead of the surface itself, we use a line (AN) perpendicular to the surface at the point of incidence A. This line is called the normal to the surface at the point of incidence and is a unique line. No other line is perpendicular and no other surface through the point A has this line for its normal. The plane containing the incident ray BA and the normal AN is called the plane of incidence. The angle BAN which the incident ray makes with the normal is the angle of incidence, i. The light after reflection will travel along AF and the angle FAN is the angle of reflection, r.

The law of reflection may be stated as:

The incident and reflected rays and the normal to the surface lie in one plane and the incident and reflected rays make equal angles with the normal on opposite sides of it.

- Refraction

When a ray of light enters a new medium, its direction is usually changed. This apparent break in the ray path is called "refraction," from the same Latin word as fracture. The law of refraction, which describes the ray directions, is more complicated than the law of reflection. This means that, although the action of refraction of light rays at a polished surface gives an image of the object providing those rays, the image is clear only for narrow pencils of rays. In Fig. 4-8 the narrow ray bundles from A and B, after refraction, appear to be coming from A' and B', but the ray BC at a greatly different angle of incidence refracts to become CD, which does not appear to be coming from B'.

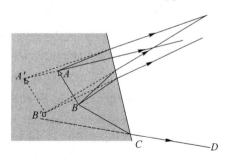

Fig. 4-8 Refraction at a plane surface: light traveling from lower index to higher index.

From the refraction of a single ray at a plane polished surface, we use a normal to the surface, as in the case of reflection. However, as in Fig. 4-9 shows, the normal must be shown right through the surface. The angle of incidence is shown as i and the angle of refraction as i'. We find that the relationship between these two angles depends on the difference in the velocity of the light in the two media. Foucault, in 1850, found by experiment that the speed of light in air was greater than in water. This result supported the wave theory of light suggested by Huygens and justifies our use of Huygens' construction to find the law of refraction. The action of all *lenses*[53] and prisms is entirely due to this change in velocity of light in different media.

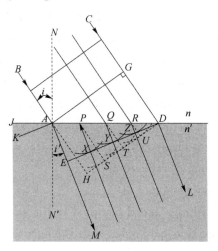

Fig. 4-9 Refraction at a plane surface-Huygens' principle.

3. The law of refraction

The new direction taken by light when it passes through the surface between two media of different refractive index can be found by applying Huygens' principle in a way similar to that used for the law of reflection. In Fig. 4-9, a parallel pencil of light BCDA is incident on the surface AD between two media of refractive index n and n'; n' is greater than n. AG is a plane wavefront, one edge of which has just reached the surface at A. If the surface had not been there, this wavefront would continue moving at velocity v and reach the position HD a short time later. As the incident wavefront meets the surface, each point on the surface, such as A, P, Q, R, and D, becomes in succession the center of wavelets traveling in the new medium. These wavelets travel more slowly in the second medium, at the velocity v', where $v'/v = n/n'$, according to the definition of refractive index. At this slower speed, by the time the light at G has traveled to D in the first medium, the radii of the wavelets in the second medium will be:

$$AE = AH\left(\frac{n}{n'}\right) \quad PX = PS\left(\frac{n}{n'}\right) \quad QY = QT\left(\frac{n}{n'}\right) \quad etc.$$

The envelope of all these wavelets will be the refracted wavefront ED. The refracted wavefront is still a plane surface and it is refracted towards the normal NN'. This is because the light traveled from a rare to a dense medium; n' is greater than n. If the light had moved from a dense to rare medium, we would take n' to be less than n, the new wavelets would have radii longer than in the first medium, and a similar diagram would show that the light is refracted away from the normal.

The angle BAN in Fig. 4-9 is the angle of incidence, i, and the angle MAN' is the angle of refraction, i'. From the definition of refractive index: $nDG = n'AE$, and so $nGD/AD = n'AE/AD$, which is

$$n\sin \angle DAG = n'\sin \angle ADE \tag{4-3}$$

If we rotate the line AG through 90° it lies on AB, because the wavefront is at right angles to the ray. If we rotate the line AD through 90° it lies on AN, because the normal is at right angles to the surface. Thus, it is shown that angel GAD is the same size as angle BAN, the angle of incidence, i.

If we draw the line AK parallel to DE, the new wavefront, we have angle ADE equal to angle JAK. Rotating AJ and AK through 90° shows that angle JAK is equal to the angle of refraction, i'.

Thus, from Equation (4-3), we have:

$$n\sin i = n'\sin i' \tag{4-4}$$

Sometimes this equation is expressed as:

$$\frac{\sin i}{\sin i'} = \frac{n'}{n} \tag{4-4a}$$

But this is a bad way to remember it—there is less chance of error with Equation (4-4). However, the law of refraction may still be stated as:

The incident and refracted rays and the normal to the surface at the point of incidence lie in the one plane on opposite sides of the normal and the ration of the sine of the angle of incidence to the sine of the angle of refraction is a constant for any two media for light of any one wavelength.

This law, which was first stated, but in a somewhat different form, by Willebrord Snell, is often known as Snell's law.

4.2.3 Interference and Diffraction

1. Interference

The term interference refers to the phenomenon that some parts of light under certain conditions, temporarily intensify or weaken each other (Fig. 4-10). Expression such as "*constructive*[54]" and "*destructive*[55]" interference should not be used because they seem to imply that somehow there could be a "destruction" of light. Certainly, this is not so. If less light reaches a given point, more light reaches some other point: interference merely causes a redistribution of the light.

2. Diffraction

When a point light source is casting a shadow on a screen, we expect the shadow to be sharp and well defined. But the edges of the shadow are blurred: A certain amount of the light is deflected into the shadow, and another portion is deflected outside the shadow forming brighter and darker fringes (Fig. 4-11). Such deviation of the light from the predictions of geometrical optics is diffraction.

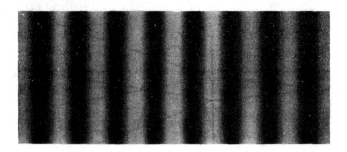

Fig. 4-10 Young's interference fringes.

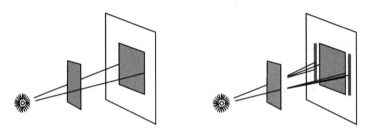

Fig. 4-11 Shadow in geometrical optics (left) and, more correctly, in wave optics (right).

4.3 Optics Systems

There exist so many types of optical systems that would be futile to even try to list them. Thus, instead of trying, we will limit ourselves to a discussion of a few representative groups of systems.

4.3.1 Telescopes

In the Galilean telescope, as in the astronomical telescope, the objective is positive, but in contrast to it, the eyepiece is negative. Still, the two focal points *coincide*[56]. In Fig. 4-12, top, F is both the second (right-hand) focal point of the first lens and the first (left-hand) focal point of the second lens. In Galileo's type (bottom), F is still the second focal point of the first lens and again the first (but now the right-hand) focal point of the (negative) second lens. Parallel light incident on the system is refracted toward F but before it reaches the focus, the light is intercepted by the negative lens and the emergent light is parallel again. The image, therefore, is seen at infinity. With accommodation, the image is seen at the distance of most distinct vision (not shown).

The distance between the lens is,

$$d = f_O + f_E \tag{4-5}$$

where the numerical values substituted for f_E must now be negative. The magnification is,

$$M_{\text{Telescope}} = -\frac{f_O}{f_E} \tag{4-6}$$

it is positive and the image upright. Telescopes of the Galilean type do not give much magnification (because the exit pupil lies to the left of the last lens and the eye cannot be brought there) but they are short, and hence are often used as *opera glasses*[57].

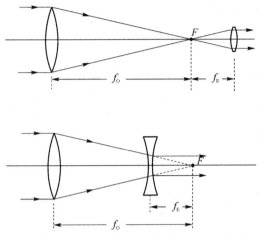

Fig. 4-12 Focal points coincide in both the astronomical telescope (top) and Galileo's telescope (bottom).

4.3.2 Retinal Acuity

Both interference and coherence play an important role in some *acuity*[58] measurements. That is especially true in cases of *cataract*[59], where, because of the turbidity of the *crystalline*[60] lens, conventional acuity measurements are not possible. Indeed, even with a cataractous lens blocking the way, fringes can be seen, as shown schematically in Fig. 4-13.

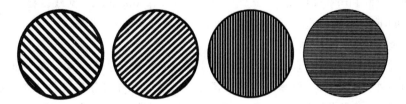

Fig. 4-13 Fringes of different spatial frequency and orientation as seen by the patient.

But, how can light go through a diffusing medium, and still form distinct fringes? Surely, no distinct image could form this way. The answer is that the lines seen by the patient do not pass as ready fringes through the eye; they are formed on the *retina*[61].

In practice, a beam of light is split into two and projected into the pupil of the eye. The two beams pass through the lens separate, side by side, but despite the turbidity of the lens they retain most of their spatial coherence and still can form fringes that are (nearly) as distinct as without the cataract.

References

1. Max Born, Emil Wolf. Principles of optics. seventh (expanded) edition. Cambridge University Press, 1999.

2. M. H. Freman, C. C. Hull. Optics. Eleventh Edition. Elsevier (Singapore) Pte Ltd, 2005.

3. G. Brooker. Modern Classical Optics. 北京:科学出版社,2009.

4. Jurgen R. Meyer-Arendt. Introduction to Classical and Modern Optics. Prentice-Hall International, Inc., 1972.

5. Francis A. Jenkins, Harvey E. White. Fundamentals of Optics. Fourth Edition. McGraw-Hill Kogakusha, Ltd., 1976.

New Words and Expressions

1. phenomenological [fi,nɔminə'lɔdʒikəl] *a.* 现象学的; phenomenological theory,唯象理论(杨振宁把物理学分为实验、唯象理论和理论架构三条路径。唯象理论是实验现象更概括的总结和提炼,但是无法用已有的科学理论体系做出解释,所以钱学森说唯象理论就是知其然而不知其所以然。唯象理论被称为前科学,因为它们也能被实践所证实。而理论架构是比唯象理论更基础的,它可以用数学和已有的科学体系进行解释)

2. interference [,intə'fiərəns] *n.* 干涉

3. diffraction [di'frækʃən] *n.* 衍射

4. holography [hə'lɔgrəfi] *n.* 全息照相术

5. burning glasses 取火镜,凸透镜的另一种叫法,因为可以用来取火

6. rectilinear [,rekti'liniə] *a.* 直线的;rectilinear propagation 直线传播

7. refraction [ri'frækʃən] *n.* 折射

8. reflection [ri'flekʃən] *n.* 反射

9. metaphysical [,metə'fizikəl] *a.* 形而上学的(形而上学是哲学术语。欧洲语言中的形而上学来自希腊语。这一词原是古希腊罗德岛的哲学教师安德罗尼柯给亚里士多德的一部著作起的名称,意思是"物理学之后"。形而上学也叫"第一哲学",如笛卡儿的《第一哲学沉思录》(Meditations on First Philosophy)也称为《形而上学沉思录》。亚里士多德把人类的知识分为三部分,用大树作比喻:第一部分,最基础的部分,也就是树根,是形而上学,它是一切知识的奠基;第二部分是物理学,好比树干;第三部分是其他自然科学,以树枝来比喻。中文译名"形而上学"取自《易经》中"形而上者谓之道,形而下者谓之器"一语)

10. aether ['i:θə] *n.* 以太(以太是古希腊哲学家设想出的一种物质,是一种假想出的电磁波的传播媒质,被认为无所不在。在古希腊,以太指的是青天或上层大气。在宇宙学中,有时又用以太来表示占据天体空间的物质。17世纪的笛卡儿是一个对科学思想的发展有重大影响的哲学家,他最先将以太引入科学,并赋予它某种力学性质)

11. prism ['prizəm] *n.* 棱镜

12. refrangibility [ri,frændʒi'biliti] *n.* 可折射性,可折射度

13. polarization [ˌpoulərai'zeiʃən] n. 偏振
14. luminous ['ljuːminəs] a. 发光的
15. calc-spar, n. 冰洲石,是方解石的一种(方解石是一种碳酸钙矿物,天然碳酸钙中最常见的就是它。敲击方解石可以得到很多方形碎块,故名方解。方解石的色彩因其中含有的杂质不同而变化,一般多为白色或无色。无色透明的方解石也叫冰洲石,这样的方解石有一个奇妙的特点,就是透过它可以看到物体呈双重影像。因此,冰洲石是重要的光学材料)
16. transversality [ˌtrænsvə'sæliti] n. 横向性
17. longitudinal [ˌlɔndʒi'tjuːdinl] a. 纵向的
18. film ['film] n. 膜;thin film,薄膜
19. prize question 指1818年巴黎科学院公布的有奖征文问题
20. corpuscular [kɔː'pʌskjuːlə] a. 微粒的;corpuscular theory,微粒理论(1638年,法国数学家皮埃尔·伽森荻提出物体是由大量坚硬粒子组成的。他在1660年出版的著作中表达了他对光的观点,认为光也是由大量坚硬粒子组成的。牛顿随后对于伽森荻的这种观点进行研究。他根据光的直线传播规律和光的偏振现象,最终于1675年提出假设,认为光是从光源发出的一种物质微粒,在均匀媒质中以一定的速度传播。微粒说很容易解释光的直进性和反射现象,因为粒子与光滑平面发生碰撞的反射定律与光的反射定律相同。然而微粒说在解释一束光射到两种介质分界面处会同时反射和折射,以及几束光交叉相遇后彼此毫不妨碍地继续向前传播等现象时,却发生了很大困难)
21. aberration [ˌæbə'reiʃən] n. 像差
22. luminiferous [ˌljuːmi'nifərəs] a. 发光的
23. conical ['kɔnikəl] a. 圆锥形的;conical refraction,锥形折射(这是当细光束入射到双轴晶体上所发生的一种现象)
24. dispersion [dis'pəːʃən] n. 色散
25. spectrum ['spektrəm] n. 光谱;spectra,spectrum 的复数
26. spectroscopy [spek'trɔskəpi] n. 光谱学
27. quantum ['kwɔntəm] n. 量子;quanta,quantum 的复数
28. photon ['foutɔn] n. 光子
29. photoelectric [ˌfoutoui'lektrik] a. 光电的
30. photochemistry [ˌfoutou'kemistri] n. 光化学
31. deterministic [diˌtəːmi'nistik] a. 决定论的;causality [kɔː'zæliti] n. 因果关系;deterministic causality,决定论因果律原理(决定论认为自然界和人类社会普遍存在客观规律和因果联系。决定论的直觉观念可以这样概括,即世界就像一部影片:正在放映的影片或者剧照是现在,影片已放映过的那些部分构成过去,尚未放映的那些部分构成未来。在影片中,未来和过去并存;在和过去完全相同的意义上,未来是确定的。尽管观众可能不知道未来,每一个未来事件原则上却毫无例外地可能是确然已知的,恰如过去一样,因为未来存在的意义与过去存在的意义相同。实际上,制片人——造物主——会知道未来。在这方面拉普拉斯有一个著名的想法"给予宇宙的初始条件,就能预测宇宙的一切未来"。因果律是指所有事物之间最重要、最直接(可以间接)的关系。表示任何一种现象或事物都必然有其原因,即"物有本末,事有终始"、"种瓜得瓜,种豆得豆"之意。一世的生命发展,可以由不同的

努力（几种不同的因），而得到不同的发展（不同的果）。俗云"事在人为"、"人定胜天"，就是这种因果看法的说辞。所以这里所谓的决定论因果原理是说爱因斯坦的狭义相对论依然保留了因果律的血统，延续了拉普拉斯决定论的香火）

32. optics of moving bodies 运动物体光学
33. isotropic [ˌaisou'trɔpik] a. 各向同性的（各向同性是指对于一种被测性质，在不同的化学结构方向上有相同的结果。均匀介质可以是各向同性，也可以是各向异性）
34. homogeneous [hɔ'mɔdʒinəs] a. 均匀的（均匀介质是指在参考限度内（一般要达到分子水平），考察对象的内部各处（注意是内部）具有相同的性质）
35. wavefront ['weivfrɔnt] n. 波前，波阵面
36. wavelet ['weilit] n. 子波，小波
37. pinhole ['pinhoul] n. 小孔；pinhole camera（无透镜的）针孔相机
38. pencil ['pensl] n. 光线锥 a pencil of light，一锥光，指一细束光（有时在英语中，一锥光也可写为 bundle of rays。光学设计中，在用计算机计算像差时常用后一种表达方式。几个 pencil 的光组合在一起叫做 beam）
39. shadow ['ʃædou] n. 影子，阴影
40. umbra ['ʌmbrə] n. 本影
41. penumbra [pi'nʌbrə] n. 半影
42. eclipse [i'klips] n. 食；solar eclipse 日食
43. flare [flæ] n. 太阳的耀斑
44. corona [kə'rounə] n. 日冕，coronae 是 corona 的复数形式
45. illuminate [i'lju:mineit] vt. 照明
46. polish ['pɔliʃ] vt. 抛光
47. specular ['spekjulə] a. 镜子的，像镜子一样的；specular reflection 镜面反射
48. diffuse [di'fju:z] a. 弥漫的，散开的；diffuse reflection 漫反射
49. scatter ['skætə] vt. 散射
50. transparent [træns'pɛərənt] a. 透明的
51. glycerine [ˌglisə'ri:n] n. 甘油
52. balsam ['bɔ:lsəm] n. 香脂；Canada balsam，加拿大树胶
53. lens [lenz] n. 透镜
54. constructive [kən'strʌktiv] a. 建设性的；constructive interference，相长干涉
55. destructive [dis'trʌktiv] a. 破坏性的；destructive interference，相消干涉
56. coincide [ˌkouin'said] vi. 恰好重合
57. opera glass 观剧用的小望远镜
58. acuity [ə'kjuiti] n. 敏锐；visual acuity 视力
59. cataract ['kætərəkt] n. 白内障
60. crystalline ['kristəlain] a. 结晶状的；crystalline lens（眼球的）水晶体
61. retina ['retinə] n. 视网膜

Notes

① 光学现象背后的物理原理,就这本书所涉及的那些来说,在 1900 年前已经大体上系统形成了。从那年以后,光学同物理学的其他部门一样,由于能量量子的发现而经历了一场彻底的革命。虽然这个发现曾深深地影响了我们对光之本性的见解,但是它并没有使早先的理论和技术失去作用;只不过是揭示了它们的能力限度,并确定了它们的有效范围。旧的原理和方法以及它们对许许多多不同情况的应用,一直不断扩大,而且现在还在继续扩大着,势头不减。

② 古代的哲学家已经熟悉火镜、光的直进、光的折射和反射,这引起他们对于光的本性的深思。就我们所知,头几本关于光学的系统著作是属于希腊的哲学家和数学家的。

③ 由于牛顿的权威,他对波动理论的摒弃使得这一理论停滞不前近一世纪之久。但是它仍然有个别的支持者,如大数学家欧拉。

④ 大约在这个时候,马吕斯(1775—1812)发现了反射光的偏振。事情似乎是这样,1808 年,一天傍晚,他通过冰洲石晶体观察落日从窗户玻璃上的反射,发现当把晶体绕视线转动时,双折射所产生的两个像的相对强度在改变。但是,马吕斯没有尝试对这个现象进行解释,他认为当时的理论都不能给予说明。

⑤ 但是,即使光的电磁理论,也已达到了它适用能力的极限。这个理论能够解释一切和光的传播有关的现象(就它们的主要特征而言)。然而,它不能说明光的发射过程和吸收过程。在这些过程中,物质和光波场相互作用的精细面貌被显现出来。

Fundamentals of Lasers 第5章

PREVIEW

The word laser is an acronym for *light amplification by stimulated emission of radiation*[1]. In 1916, Einstein predicted that the existence of *equilibrium*[2] between matter and electromagnetic radiation required that besides emission and absorption there must be a third process, now called stimulated emission. This prediction attracted little attention until 1954 when Townes and coworkers developed a microwave amplifier (master) using ammonia, NH_3. In 1958, Schawlow and Townes showed that the master principle could be extended into the visible region and in 1960, Maiman built the first laser using *ruby*[3] as the *active*[4] medium. From then on, laser development was nothing short of miraculous, giving optics new impetus and wide publicity.

5.1 Definition of Laser

Lasers are devices that generate or amplify coherent radiation at frequencies in the infrared, visible, or ultraviolet regions of the electromagnetic spectrum.[①] Lasers operate by using a general principle that was originally invented at microwave frequencies, where it was called microwave amplification by stimulated emission of radiation, or maser action. When extended to optical frequencies, this naturally becomes light amplification by stimulated emission of radiation, or laser action.

Here "light" must be understood broadly, since different kinds of lasers can amplify radiation at wavelengths ranging from the very long infrared region, merging with millimeter waves or microwaves, up through the visible region and extending now to the vacuum ultraviolet and even X-ray regions. Lasers come in a great variety of forms, using many different laser materials, many different atomic systems, and many different kinds of pumping or excitation techniques. The beams of radiation that lasers emit or amplify have remarkable properties of directionality, spectral purity, and intensity. These properties have already led to an enormous variety of applications, and others undoubtedly have yet to be discovered and developed.

5.2 A Brief History of Laser

Readers of H. G. Wells' novel *The War of the Worlds* might quite reasonably conclude that the first laser device to be operated on Earth was in fact brought here by Martian invaders a century ago, at least according to the description that:

"In some way they (the Martians) are able to generate an intense heat in a chamber of practically absolute nonconductivity … . This intense heat they project in a parallel beam against any object they choose, by means of a polished parabolic mirror of unknown composition… . However it is done, it is certain that a beam of heat is the essence of the matter. What is combustible flashes into flame at its touch, lead runs like water, it softens iron, cracks and melts glass, and when it falls upon water that explodes into steam."

(From *Pearson's* Magazine, 1897)

Those who have seen the effects produced by the beam from a modern multikilo-watt CO_2 laser will not be surprised at the recent discovery that the atmosphere of Mars consists primarily of carbon dioxide, and that natural laser action occurs in it!

Whether or not Martians operated CO_2 lasers in 1897, the first man-made stimulated emission device on Earth came in early 1954, when Charles H. Townes at Columbia University, assisted by J. P. Gordon and H. Zeiger, operated an ammonia beam maser, a microwave-frequency device that oscillated (very weakly) at approximately 24 GHz. This was closely followed by a similar development by N. G. Basov and A. M. Prokhorov in the Soviet Union. The Columbia group coined the name maser to represent microwave amplification by stimulated emission of radiation.

There was then much discussion and some experimental work in subsequent years on radio and microwave-frequency maser devices, using both molecular beams and magnetic resonance in solids, and also on theoretical developments toward an optical-frequency maser or laser. Perhaps the most important of these developments was when Nicolaas Bloembergen of Harvard University in 1956 suggested a continuous three-level *pumping*[5] scheme for obtaining a continuous *population inversion*[6] on one microwave resonance *transition*[7], by pumping with continuous microwave radiation on another transition.

Bloembergen's ideas were quickly verified in other laboratories, leading to a series of microwave *paramagnetic*[8] solid-state masers. These microwave masers were useful primarily as exceedingly low noise but rather complex and narrow-band microwave amplifiers. They are now largely obsolescent, except for a few highly specialized *radio-astronomy*[9] experiments or deep-space communications receivers.

The extension of microwave maser concepts to obtain maser or laser action at optical wavelengths was being considered by many scientific workers in the late 1950s. A widely cited and influential paper on the possibility of optical masers was published by Charles

Townes and A. L. Schawlow in 1958. Much recent attention has been given to a series of patent claims based on notebook entries recorded at about the same time by Gordon Gould, then a graduate student at Columbia.

The first experimentally successful optical maser or laser device of any kind, however, was the *flashlamp-pumped*[10] ruby laser at 694 nm in the deep red operated by Theodore H. Maiman at the Hughes Research Laboratories in 1960. The very important *helium-neon*[11] gas discharge laser also successfully operated later in the same year by Ali Javan and co-workers at the Bell Telephone Laboratories. This laser operated initially at 1.15 μm in the near infrared, but was extended a year later to the familiar helium-neon laser transition oscillating at 633 nm in the red.

An enormous number of other laser devices have of course since emerged, not only in the first few years following the initial demonstration of laser action, but steadily during the more than four decades since that time.[②] The variety of different types of lasers now available is enormous, with several hundred thousand different discrete wavelengths available, from perhaps close to a thousand different laser systems. Commercially important and widely used practical lasers are very much fewer, of course, but still numerous.

5.3 Principle of Laser Generation

5.3.1 Spontaneous and Stimulated Emission, Absorption

To describe the phenomenon of *spontaneous emission*[12] (Fig. 5-1), let us consider two energy levels, 1 and 2, of some atom or molecule of a given material with energies E_1 and E_2 ($E_1 < E_2$), respectively. In the following discussion, the two levels can be any two of an atom's infinite set of levels. It is convenient however to take level 1 as the ground level. Let us now assume that the atom is initially at level 2. Since $E_2 > E_1$, the atom tends to *decay*[13] to level 1. The corresponding energy difference $E_2 - E_1$ must therefore be released by the atom. When this energy is delivered in the form of an electromagnetic (em) wave, the process is called spontaneous (or radiative) emission. The frequency ν_0 of the radiated wave is then given by the well known expression:

$$\nu_0 = \frac{E_2 - E_1}{h} \tag{5-1}$$

where h is Planck's constant. Spontaneous emission is therefore characterized by the emission of a photon of energy $h\nu_0 = E_2 - E_1$ when the atom decays from level 2 to level 1 (Fig. 5-1(a)). Note that radiative emission is just one of two possible ways for the atom to decay. Decay can also occur in a nonradiative way. In this case the energy difference $E_2 - E_1$ is delivered in some form of energy other than em radiation (e.g., it may go into the *kinetic*[14] or internal energy of the surrounding atoms or molecules). This phenomenon is called nonradiative decay.

Let us now suppose that the atom is initially found in level 2 and an em wave of frequency $\nu = \nu_0$ (i. e. , equal to that of the spontaneously emitted wave) is incident on the material (Fig. 5-1(b)). Since this wave has the same frequency as the atomic frequency, there is a finite probability that this wave will force the atom to undergo the transition $2 \rightarrow 1$. In this case the energy difference $E_2 - E_1$ is delivered in the form of an em wave that adds to the incident wave. This is the phenomenon of stimulated emission. There is a fundamental difference between the spontaneous and stimulated emission processes. In the case of spontaneous emission, atoms emit an em wave that has no definite phase relation to that emitted by another atom. Furthermore the wave can be emitted in any direction. In the case of stimulated emission, since the process is forced by the incident em wave, the emission of any atom adds in phase to that of the incoming wave and in the same direction.

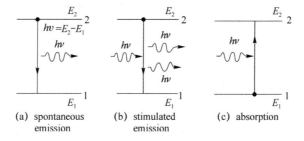

Fig. 5-1 Schematic illustration of the three processes

Let us now assume that the atom is initially lying in level 1 (Fig. 5-1 (c)). If this is the ground level, the atom remains in this level unless some external stimulus is applied. We assume that an em wave of frequency $\nu = \nu_0$ is incident on the material. In this case there is a finite probability that the atom will be raised to level 2. The energy difference $E_2 - E_1$ required by the atom to undergo the transition is obtained from the energy of the incident em wave. This is the absorption process.

To introduce probabilities for these emission and absorption phenomena, let N_i be the number of atoms (or molecules) per unit volume that at time t occupy a given energy level, i. From now on the quantity N_i is called the population of the level.

For the case of spontaneous emission, the probability that the process occurs is defined by stating that the rate of decay of the upper state population $(dN_2/dt)_{sp}$ *must be proportional to the population* N_2.③ We can therefore write

$$\left(\frac{dN_2}{dt}\right)_{sp} = -AN_2 \tag{5-2}$$

where the minus sign accounts for the fact that the time derivative is negative. The coefficient A, introduced in this way, is a positive constant called the rate of spontaneous emission or the Einstein A coefficient. (An expression for A was first obtained by Einstein from *thermodynamic*[15] considerations.) The quantity $\tau_{sp} = 1/A$ is the spontaneous emission (or radiative) lifetime. Similarly, for nonradiative decay, we can generally write

$$\left(\frac{dN_2}{dt}\right)_{nr} = -\frac{N_2}{\tau_{nr}} \quad (5\text{-}3)$$

where τ_{nr} is the nonradiative decay lifetime. Note that for spontaneous emission the numerical value of A (and τ_{sp}) depends only on the particular transition considered. For nonradiative decay, on the other hand, τ_{nr} depends not only on the transition but also on characteristics of the surrounding medium.

We can now proceed in a similar way for stimulated processes (emission or absorption). For stimulated emission we can write

$$\left(\frac{dN_2}{dt}\right)_{st} = -W_{21}N_2 \quad (5\text{-}4)$$

where $(dN_2/dt)_{st}$ is the rate at which transitions $2 \to 1$ occur as a result of stimulated emission and W_{21} is the rate of stimulated emission. As in the case of the A coefficient defined by Eq. (5-2), the coefficient W_{21} also has the dimension of (time)$^{-1}$. Unlike A, however, W_{21} depends not only on the particular transition but also on the intensity of the incident em wave. More precisely, for a plane wave, we can write

$$W_{21} = \sigma_{21}F \quad (5\text{-}5)$$

where F is the photon flux of the wave and σ_{21} is a quantity having the dimension of an area (the stimulated emission cross section) and depending on characteristics of the given transition.

As in Eq. (5-4), we can define an absorption rate W_{21} using the equation:

$$\left(\frac{dN_1}{dt}\right)_a = -W_{12}N_1 \quad (5\text{-}6)$$

where $(dN_1/dt)_a$ is the rate of transitions $1 \to 2$ due to absorption and N_1 is the population of level 1. As in Eq. (5-5), we can write

$$W_{12} = \sigma_{12}F \quad (5\text{-}7)$$

where σ_{12} is some characteristic area (the absorption cross section), which depends only on the particular transition.

In the preceding discussion the stimulated processes are characterized by the stimulated emission and absorption cross-sections σ_{21} and σ_{12}, respectively. Einstein showed at the beginning of the twentieth century that, if the two levels are *nondegenerate*[16], one has $W_{21} = W_{12}$ and thus $\sigma_{21} = \sigma_{12}$. If levels 1 and 2 are g_1-fold and g_2-fold degenerate, respectively, one then has:

$$g_2 W_{21} = g_1 W_{12} \quad (5\text{-}8)$$

that is

$$g_2 \sigma_{21} = g_1 \sigma_{12} \quad (5\text{-}9)$$

Note also that the fundamental processes of spontaneous emission, stimulated emission, and absorption can be described in terms of absorbed or emitted photons as follows (see Fig. 5-1): (a) In the spontaneous emission process, the atom decays from level 2 to level

1 through the emission of a photon. (b) In the stimulated emission process, the incident photon stimulates the transition 2→1, so that there are two photons (the stimulating one and the stimulated one). (c) In the absorption process, the incident photon is simply absorbed to produce transition 1→2. Thus each stimulated emission process creates a photon, whereas each absorption process annihilates a photon.

5.3.2 The Laser Idea

Consider two arbitrary energy levels 1 and 2 of a given material, and let N_1 and N_2 be their respective populations. If a plane wave with a photon flux F is traveling in the z-direction in the material (Fig. 5-2), the elemental change dF of this flux along the elemental length dz of the material is due to both stimulated absorption and emission processes occurring in the shaded region of Fig. 5-2. Let S be the cross-sectional area of the beam. The change in number between outgoing and incoming photons in the shaded volume per unit time is thus SdF. Since each stimulated process creates a photon whereas each absorption removes a photon, SdF must equal the difference between stimulated emission and absorption events occurring in the shaded volume per unit time. From Eqs. (5-4) and (5-6) we can write Sd$F = (W_{21}N_2 - W_{12}N_1)(Sdz)$, where Sdz is the volume of the shaded region. With the help of Eqs. (5-5), (5-7), and (5-9), we obtain

$$dF = \sigma_{21} F \left[N_2 - \left(\frac{g_2 N_1}{g_1} \right) \right] dz \tag{5-10}$$

Note that, in deriving Eq. (5-10), we did not consider radiative and nonradiative decays. In fact nonradiative decay does not add new photons, while photons created by radiative decay are emitted in any direction and thus give negligible contribution to the incoming photon flux F.

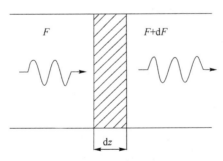

Fig. 5-2 Elemental change dF in the photon flux F for a plane em wave in traveling a distance dz through the material.

Equation (5-10) shows that the material behaves as an amplifier (i.e., dF/d$z > 0$) if $N_2 > g_2 N_1 / g_1$, while it behaves as an absorber if $N_2 < g_2 N_1 / g_1$. At thermal equilibrium populations are described by Boltzmann statistics. Then if N_1^e and N_2^e are the thermal equilibrium populations of the two levels:

$$\frac{N_2^e}{N_1^e} = \frac{g_2}{g_1} \exp -\left(\frac{E_2 - E_1}{kT}\right) \tag{5-11}$$

where k is Boltzmann's constant and T is the absolute temperature of the material. In thermal equilibrium we thus have $N_2^e < g_2 N_1^e / g_1$. According to Eq. (5-10) the material then acts as an absorber at frequency ν_0. This is what happens under ordinary conditions. However if a nonequilibrium condition is achieved for which $N_2 > g_2 N_1 / g_1$, then the material acts as an amplifier. In this case we say that there exists a population inversion in the material. This means that the population difference $N_2 - (g_2 N_1 / g_1)$ is opposite in sign to what exists under thermodynamic equilibrium $[N_2 - (g_2 N_1 / g_1) < 0]$. A material in which this population inversion is produced is referred to as an active medium.

If the transition frequency $\nu_0 = (E_2 - E_1)/kT$ falls in the microwave region, this type of amplifier is called a maser amplifier, an acronym for microwave amplification by stimulated emission of radiation. If the transition frequency falls in the optical region, the amplifier is called a laser amplifier, an acronym obtained from the preceding one with light substituted for microwave.

To make an oscillator from an amplifier, it is necessary to introduce suitable positive feedback.[4] In the microwave region this is done by placing the active material in a *resonant cavity*[17] having a resonance at frequency ν_0. In the case of a laser, feedback is often obtained by placing the active material between two highly reflecting mirrors, such as the plane parallel mirrors in Fig. 5-3. In this case a plane em wave traveling in a direction perpendicular to the mirrors bounces back and forth between the two mirrors, and is amplified on each passage through the active material. If one of the two mirrors (e. g. mirror 2) is partially transparent, a useful output beam is obtained from that mirror.

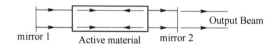

Fig. 5-3 Scheme of a laser.

It is important to realize that, for both masers and lasers, a certain *threshold*[18] condition must be reached. In the laser case, oscillation begins when the *gain*[19] of the active material compensates the losses in the laser (e. g., losses due to output coupling). According to Eq. (5-10) the gain per pass in the active material (i. e., the ratio between output and input photon flux) is $\exp\{\sigma[N_2 - (g_2 N_1/g_1)]l\}$, where we denote for simplicity $\sigma = \sigma_{21}$, and where l is the length of the active material. Let now R_1 and R_2 be the power reflectivities of the two mirrors (Fig. 5-3), respectively, and let L_i be the internal loss per pass in the laser cavity. If, at a given time, F is the photon flux in the cavity leaving mirror 1 and traveling toward mirror 2, then the photon flux F' leaving mirror 1 after one round trip is $F' = F\exp\{\sigma[N_2 - (g_2 N_1/g_1)]l\}(1-L_i)R_2 \times \exp\{\sigma[N_2 - (g_2 N_1/g_1)]l\}(1-L_i)R_1$. At thresh-threshold we must have $F' = F$ and therefore $R_1 R_2 (1-L_i)^2 \exp\{2\sigma[N_2 - (g_2 N_1/g_1)]l\} = 1$. This equation shows that threshold is reached when the population inversion $N = N_2 - (g_2 N_1/g_1)$ reaches a critical value, called the critical inversion, given by:

$$N_c = -\frac{\ln R_1 R_2 + 2\ln(1-L_i)}{2\sigma l} \tag{5-12}$$

Eq. (5-12) can be simplified if one defines

$$\gamma_1 = -\ln R_1 = -\ln(1-T_1) \tag{5-13a}$$

$$\gamma_2 = -\ln R_2 = -\ln(1-T_2) \tag{5-13b}$$

$$\gamma_i = -\ln(1-L_i) \tag{5-13c}$$

where T_1 and T_2 are mirror transmissions (for simplicity mirror absorption is neglected). The substitution of Eq. (5-13) into Eq. (5-12) gives

$$N_c = \frac{\gamma}{\sigma l} \tag{5-14}$$

where

$$\gamma = \gamma_i + \frac{(\gamma_1 + \gamma_2)}{2} \tag{5-15}$$

Note that the quantity γ_i defined by Eq. (5-13(c)), can be called the logarithmic internal loss of the cavity. In fact when $L_i \ll 1$, as usually occurs, one has $\gamma_i \cong L_i$. Similarly, since both T_1 and T_2 represent a loss for the cavity, γ_1 and γ_2, defined by Eqs. [(5-13a) and (5-13b)], can be called the logarithmic losses of the two cavity mirrors. Thus the quantity y defined by Eq. (5-15) can be called the single-pass loss of the cavity.

Once the critical inversion is reached, oscillation builds up from spontaneous emission. Photons spontaneously emitted along the cavity axis in fact initiate the amplification process. This is the basis of a laser oscillator, or laser, as it is more simply called. Note that, according to the meaning of the acronym laser, the term should be reserved for lasers emitting visible radiation. However, the same term is commonly applied to any device emitting stimulated radiation, whether in the far or near infrared, ultraviolet, or even in the X-ray region. To specify the kind of radiation emitted, one usually refers to infrared, visible, ultraviolet, or X-ray lasers, respectively.

5.3.3 Pumping Schemes

We now consider how to produce a population inversion in a given material. At first it may seem possible to achieve this through the interaction of the material with a sufficiently strong em wave, perhaps coming from a sufficiently intense lamp, at the frequency $\nu = \nu_0$. Since at thermal equilibrium $(N_1/g_1) > (N_2/g_2)$, absorption in fact predominates over stimulated emission. The incoming wave then produces more transitions $1 \to 2$ than transitions $2 \to 1$, so one would hope in this way to end up with a population inversion. We see immediately however that such a system would not work (at least in the steady state). When in fact $g_2 N_2 = g_1 N_1$, absorption and stimulated emission processes compensate one another, and, according to Eq. (5-10), the material becomes transparent. This situation is often referred to as two-level saturation.

With just two levels, 1 and 2, it is therefore impossible to produce a population inversion. We then question whether this is possible using more than two levels of the infinite set of levels of a given atomic system. As we shall see the answer in this case is positive, so we accordingly speak of a three-level or four-level laser, depending on the number of levels used (Fig. 5-4). In a three-level laser (Fig. 5-4(a)), atoms are in some way raised from level 1 (ground) to level 3. If the material is such that, after an atom is raised to level 3, it decays rapidly to level 2 (perhaps by a rapid nonradiative decay), then a population inversion can be obtained between levels 2 and 1. In a four-level laser (Fig. 5-4(b)), atoms are again raised from the ground level (for convenience we now call this level 0) to level 3. If the atom then decays rapidly to level 2 (e. g., again by rapid nonradiative decay), a population inversion can again be obtained between levels 2 and 1. Once oscillation starts in such a four-level laser however, atoms are transferred to level 1 through stimulated emission. For continuous wave (cw) operation, it is therefore necessary for the transition 1→0 also to be very rapid (this again usually occurs by rapid nonradiative decay).

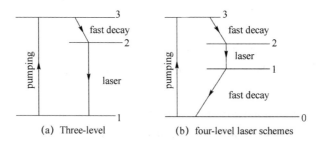

Fig. 5-4 Schematic illustration of three-and four-level laser.

We have just seen how to use three or four levels of a given material to produce population inversion. Whether a system works in a three- or four-level scheme (or whether it works at all) depends on whether preceding conditions are satisfied. We could of course ask why one should bother with a four-level scheme when a three-level scheme already seems to offer a suitable way of producing a population inversion. The answer is that one can, in general, produce a population inversion much more easily in a four-level than in a three-level laser. To see this, we begin by noting that the energy differences between the various levels shown in Fig. 5-4 are usually much greater than kT. According to Boltzmann statistics [see, e. g., Eq. (5-11)] we can then say that essentially all atoms are initially (i. e., at equilibrium) at the ground level. If we now let N_t represent the total atom density in the material, these atoms will initially all be in level 1, for the three-level case. Let us now begin raising atoms from level 1 to level 3. They then decay to level 2, and, if this decay is sufficiently rapid, level 3 remains more or less empty. Let us now assume for simplicity that the two levels are either nondegenerate (i. e., $g_1 = g_2 = 1$) or have the same degeneracy. Then, according to Eq. (5-10), absorption losses are compensated by the gain when $N_2 = N_1$. From this point on, any atom that is raised contributes to population inversion. In a four-level laser, however, since level 1 is also empty, any atom raised to level 2 immediately produces population inversion.

The preceding discussion shows that whenever possible we should seek a material that can be operated as a four-level rather than a three-level system. It is of course also possible to use more than four levels. It should also be noted that the term four-level laser is used for any laser whose lower laser level is essentially empty by virtue of being above the ground level by many kT. Then if levels 2 and 3 are the same level, we have a level scheme described as four-level in this sense, while having only three levels. Cases based on such a four-level scheme do exist.

Note that, more recently, the so-called quasi-three-level lasers have also become a very important laser category. In this case the ground level consists of many sublevels, the lower laser level being one of these sublevels. Therefore the scheme in Fig. 5-4(b) can still be applied to a quasi-three-level laser with the understanding that level 1 is a sublevel of the ground level and level 0 is the lowest sublevel of the ground level. If all ground-state sublevels are strongly coupled, perhaps by some rapid nonradiative decay process, then populations of these sublevels are always in thermal equilibrium. Let us further assume that the energy separation between levels 1 and 0 (see Fig. 5-4(b)) is comparable to kT. Then, according to Eq. (5-11), there is always some population present in the lower laser level and the laser system behaves in a way that is intermediate between a three- and a four-level laser.

The process by which atoms are raised from level 1 to level 3 (in a three-level scheme), from 0 to 3 (in a four-level scheme), or from the ground level to level 3 (in a quasi-three-level scheme) is known as pumping. There are several ways in which this process can be realized in practice, e.g., by some sort of lamp of sufficient intensity or by an electrical discharge in the active medium. We will not develop a more detailed discussion of the various pumping processes in this book. We note here, however, that, if the upper pump level is empty, the rate at which the upper laser level becomes populated by the pumping, $(dN_2/dt)_p$, can in general be written as $(dN_2/dt)_p = W_p N_g$ where W_p is a suitable rate describing the pumping process and N_g is the population of the ground level for either a three-or four-level laser while, for a quasi-three-level laser, it can be taken to be the total population of all ground state sublevels. In what follows, however, we will concentrate our discussion mostly on four level or quasi-three-level lasers. The most important case of three-level laser, in fact, is the Ruby laser, a historically important laser (it was the first laser ever made to operate) although no longer so widely used. For most four-level and quasi-three-level lasers in common use, the depletion of the ground level, due to the pumping process, can be neglected. One can then write $N_g = $ const and the previous equation can be written, more simply, as

$$(dN_2/dt)_p = R_p \tag{5-16}$$

where R_p may be called the pump rate per unit volume or, more briefly, the pump rate. To achieve the threshold condition, the pump rate must reach a threshold or critical value, R_{cp}.

5.4 Structure and Properties of Laser

5.4.1 Structure of Laser

1. Cavity configurations

The simplest type of a resonant cavity is a combination of two plane mirrors (Fig. 5-5, top). Such mirrors require precise *alignment*[20]. This configuration is very efficient because of its good filling but, because of difficult alignment and low stability, is rarely used today.

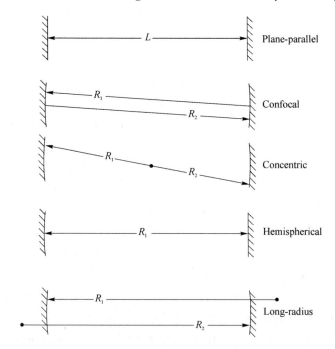

Fig. 5-5 Cavity configurations. L, distance between mirrors; R, radii of curvature.

A confocal *cavity*[21] has two *concave*[22] mirrors of the same radius of curvature, R, separated by a distance L that is equal to R, $L = R$. The focal length of the mirrors, therefore, is one-half of L and the focal points coincide in the center, hence the term "confocal." A confocal cavity is much easier to align than plane-parallel mirrors but the filling is poor; halfway between the mirrors, for instance, only a small fraction of the medium is utilized.

A *concentric cavity*[23] (also called spherical cavity) has two concave mirrors of the same radius, one-half of the distance between them, $L=2R$. Again, the filling is poor and alignment not easy.

A *hemispherical cavity*[24] is a hybrid between the plane-parallel and the confocal type. It has a concave mirror at one end and a plane mirror at the other. The plane mirror is placed at the center of curvature of the spherical mirror, thus $L=R_1$. Such a cavity is easier to align than those mentioned so far but again, the filling is poor and the output low.

A long-radius cavity has two concave mirrors, their radii of curvature significantly longer than the distance between them, $R_1=R_2>L$. This is a good compromise between the plane-parallel and the confocal variety; it is the type of cavity used most often in today's commercial lasers.

2. Mode structure

Assume for simplicity that the cavity is limited by two plane-parallel mirrors. Since the mirrors form a closed cavity, the standing-wave pattern inside the cavity has *nodes*[25], rather than *loops*[26], at both ends. If, as shown earlier in Fig. 5-5, top, L is the length of the cavity, the longest wavelength possible is $\lambda_1=2L$. The next shorter wavelength is $\lambda_2=L$, the next shorter wavelength $\lambda_3=\frac{2}{3}L$, and so on; thus,

$$\lambda=\frac{2}{q}L \qquad (5\text{-}17)$$

where q is the number of half-wavelengths, or axial modes, that fit into the cavity.

It is often better to write Eq. (5-17) in terms of frequency, ν. We take the relationship $v=\lambda\nu$, replace v by the velocity of light c, solve for ν, and substitute Eq. (5-17). That gives

$$\nu=q\frac{c}{2L} \qquad (5\text{-}18)$$

But a laser cavity must, by necessity, contain a medium (of index n) rather than free space. Hence, we replace the actual length of the cavity, L, by the optical path length, $S=Ln$, so that, instead of Eq. (5-18), we have

$$\nu=q\frac{c}{2S} \qquad (5\text{-}19)$$

which is the resonance condition for axial modes. A wave of frequency ν that travels along the axis of the cavity, therefore, forms within the cavity a series of standing waves, called stationary axial modes.

Now consider two consecutive modes (which differ by $q=1$). These modes have frequencies that, following Eq. (5-19), are separated by a frequency difference $\Delta\nu$,

$$\Delta\nu=\frac{c}{2S} \qquad (5\text{-}20)$$

Slightly different frequencies are closely, and evenly, spaced. Often several of them lie within the width of a single emission line. That means that the output of the laser then consists of a number of lines separated by $c/2S$, as shown in Fig. 5-6.

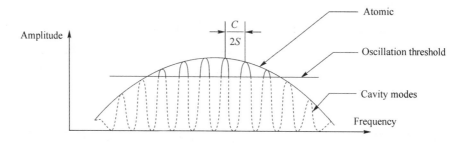

Fig. 5-6 Output of laser containing several resonance frequencies.

In addition to the axial modes we also have transverse modes[27], *called TEM, for transverse electromagnetic, modes. The TEM modes are generally few in number, and they are easy to see.*[5] Aim the laser at a distant screen and spread the beam out by a negative lens. Most of the light forms several bright patches, separated from one another by intervals called "*nodal lines*[28]." Within each patch, the phase of the light is the same, but between patches the phase is reversed. Fig. 5-7 shows several examples.

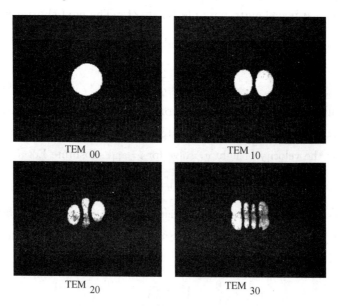

Fig. 5-7 Schematic representation of different TEM modes.

In the lowest possible transverse mode, TEM_{00}, there is no phase reversal across the beam (the beam is "uniphase"), the spatial coherence is the highest possible, and the beam can be focused to the smallest spot size and reach the highest power density. If, in addition, the laser also oscillates in the lowest possible axial mode, the cavity will select, and amplify, out of several resonant frequencies only one frequency. This results in the highest possible temporal coherence, that is, the light will be as monochromatic as light can be.

3. Beam shape

There are two parameters characteristic of a laser beam as it leaves the cavity. First, the beam has a certain profile, that is, a certain energy distribution across its diameter. With the laser operating in the TEM$_{00}$ mode, the energy has a *Gaussian distribution*[29]: at a given distance r from the axis, the irradiance I falls off exponentially,

$$I(r) = I_0 e^{-(2r/w)^2} \tag{5-21}$$

This distribution is completely described by the parameter w, the distance from the axis at which I has dropped to $1/e^2$ of I_0, the irradiance in the center (Fig. 5-8).

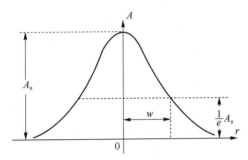

Fig. 5-8 Amplitude distribution across laser beam oscillation in the TEM$_{00}$ mode.

A beam retains its profile both inside and outside the cavity; the profile merely contracts or expands. For example, with a confocal cavity (two concave mirrors of the same radius of curvature) the beam has its least diameter, or beam waist, halfway between the mirrors. With a hemispherical cavity (concave-plane) the beam waist lies on the plane mirror.

The beam's radius, w, changes as a function of distance, z, from the waist, according to

$$w(z) = w_0 \sqrt{1 + \left(\frac{\lambda z}{\pi w_0^2}\right)^2} \tag{5-22}$$

where λ is the wavelength and w_0 the radius at the waist. For a confocal cavity this simplifies to

$$w_0 = \sqrt{\frac{L\lambda}{2\pi}} \tag{5-23}$$

where L is the distance between the mirrors.

Twice the radius w_0 is the diameter of the beam at the waist. The size of that diameter accounts for (part of) the divergence of the beam, simply because the shape of the beam outside the cavity is an extension of its shape inside, a relationship illustrated in Fig. 5-9.

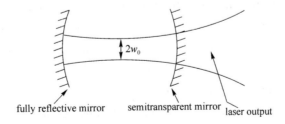

Fig. 5-9 Confocal cavity causes beam to contract to minimum beam diameter $2w_0$.

Farther away from the laser, in the far field where the beam's parameters can be considered linear functions of the distance, the beam's contour subtends with the axis an angle θ,

$$\theta = \frac{\lambda}{\pi w_0} \qquad (5\text{-}24)$$

This angle determines the "far-field half-angle divergence" illustrated in Fig. 5-10. Twice that angle is the full-angle divergence,

$$2\theta = \frac{4\lambda}{\pi d_0} \qquad (5\text{-}25)$$

an expression where we have replaced the radius at the waist by the diameter, d_0.

Not that the divergence of the beam is inversely proportional to d_0. With a small waist, the divergence is large. Conversely, for a well collimated beam (of small divergence), the waist must be large—as we have already seen from Fig. 5-9.

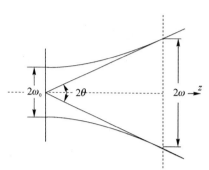

Fig. 5-10 Relationship between beam waist and divergence of a laser beam.

5.4.2 Properties of Laser Beams

Laser radiation is characterized by an extremely high degree of *monochromaticity*[30], coherence, directionality, and brightness. We can add a fifth property, viz., short duration, which refers to the capability of producing very short light pulses, a less fundamental but nevertheless very important property. We now consider these properties in some detail.

1. Monochromaticity

This property is due to the following two circumstances: (1) Only an em wave of frequency ν given by Eq. (5-1) can be amplified. (2) Since a two-mirror arrangement forms a resonant cavity, oscillation can occur only at the resonance frequencies of this cavity. The latter circumstance leads to an often much narrower laser linewidth (by as much as 10 orders of magnitude) than the usual linewidth of the transition $2 \rightarrow 1$, as observed in spontaneous emission.

2. Coherence

To first order, for any em wave, we can introduce two concepts of coherence, namely, spatial and temporal coherence. To define spatial coherence, let us consider two points P_1 and P_2 that, at time $t=0$, lie on the same wave front of some given em wave and let $E_1(t)$ and $E_2(t)$ be the corresponding electric fields at these two points. By definition the difference between phases of the two fields at time $t=0$ is zero. If this difference remains zero at any time $t>0$, we say that there is a perfect coherence between the two points. If such coherence occurs for any two points of the em wave front, we then say that the wave has *perfect spatial coherence*[31]. In practice, for any point P_1, point P_2 must lie within some finite area around P_1 to have a good phase correlation. In this case we say that the wave has *partial spatial coherence*[32], and, for any point P, we can introduce a suitably defined coherence area $S_c(P)$.

To define temporal coherence, we now consider the electric field of the em wave, at a given point P, at times t and $t+\tau$. If, for a given time delay τ, the phase difference between the two field remains the same for any time t, we say that there is a temporal coherence over a time τ. If this occurs for any value of τ, the em wave is said to have *perfect temporal coherence*[33]. If this occurs for a time delay τ such that $0 < \tau < \tau_0$, the wave is said to have *partial temporal coherence*[34], with a coherence time equal to τ_0. An example of an em wave with a coherence time equal to τ_0 is shown in Fig. 5-11. The figure shows a sinusoidal electric field undergoing phase jumps at time intervals equal to τ_0. We see that the concept of temporal coherence is, at least in this case, directly connected with that of monochromaticity. In fact, we will find in other books that any stationary em wave with coherence time τ_0 has a bandwidth $\Delta\nu \cong 1/\tau_0$. And we will also find that, for a nonstationary but repetitively reproducing beam (e. g., a repetitively Q-switched[35] or a *mode-locked*[36] laser beam), coherence time is not determined by the inverse of the oscillation bandwidth $\Delta\nu$ and may actually be much greater than $1/\Delta\nu$.

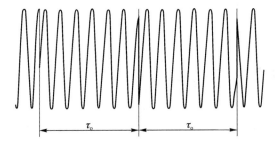

Fig. 5-11 Example of an em wave with a coherence time of approximately τ_0.

It is important to point out that the two concepts of temporal and spatial coherence are indeed independent of each other. In fact examples can be given of a wave with perfect spatial coherence but only limited temporal coherence (or vice versa). If the wave in Fig. 5-11 represents electric fields at points P_1 and P_2 considered earlier, spatial coherence between these two points would still be complete, although the wave has limited temporal coherence.

We conclude this section by emphasizing that the concepts of spatial and temporal coherence provide only a first-order description of the laser's coherence. We will find in other books in fact that, by virtue of differences between the corresponding higher order coherence properties, a laser beam is fundamentally different from an ordinary light source.

3. Directionality

This property is a direct consequence of the fact that the active medium is placed in a resonant cavity. For example, in the case of the plane parallel cavity shown in Fig. 5-12, only a wave propagating in a direction orthogonal to the mirrors (or in a direction very near to it) can be sustained in the cavity. To gain a deeper understanding of the directional properties of a laser beam (or in general of any em wave), it is convenient to consider separately the case of a beam with perfect spatial coherence and the case of partial spatial coherence.

We first consider the case of perfect spatial coherence. Even for this case a beam of finite aperture has unavoidable divergence due to diffraction. This can be understood with the help of Fig. 5-13, where a beam of uniform intensity and plane wave front is assumed to be incident on a screen S containing an aperture D. According to Huygens' principle the wave front at some plane P behind the screen can be obtained by the superposition of the elementary waves emitted by each point of the aperture. We thus see that, on account of the finite size D of the aperture, the beam has a finite divergence θ_d. Its value can be obtained from diffraction theory. For an arbitrary amplitude distribution, we obtain

$$\theta_d = \frac{\beta \lambda}{D} \tag{5-26}$$

where λ and D are the wavelength and the diameter of the beam, respectively. The factor β is a numerical coefficient of the order of unity whose value depends on the shape of the amplitude distribution and how both the divergence and the beam diameter are defined. A beam whose divergence can be expressed as in Eq. (5-26) is referred to as being diffraction-limited.

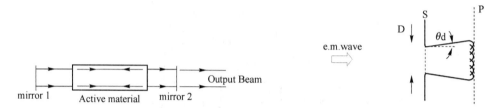

Fig. 5-12 Scheme of a laser.   Fig. 5-13 Divergence of a plane em wave due to diffraction.

If the wave has only partial spatial coherence, its divergence is greater than the minimum value set by diffraction. Indeed, for any point P' of the wave front, the Huygens argument in Fig. 5-13 can be applied only for points lying within the coherence area S_c around point P'. The coherence area thus acts as a limiting aperture for the coherent superposition of elementary wavelets. Thus, the beam divergence can now be written as:

$$\theta = \frac{\beta \lambda}{(S_c)^{1/2}} \tag{5-27}$$

where β is a numerical coefficient of the order of unity whose exact value depends on how both the divergence θ and coherence area S_c are defined.

We conclude this general discussion of the directional properties of em waves by pointing out that given suitable operating conditions, the output beam of a laser can be made diffraction limited.

4. Brightness

We define the brightness of a given source of em waves as the power emitted per unit surface area per unit solid angle. To be more praise let dS be the elemental surface area at point O of the source (Fig. 5-14(a)). The power dP emitted by dS into a solid angle dΩ around direction OO' can be written as:

$$dP = B\cos\theta dS d\Omega \tag{5-28}$$

where θ is the angle between OO' and the normal n to the surface. Note that the factor $\cos\theta$ occurs because the physically important quantity for emission along the OO' direction is the projection of dS on a plane orthogonal to the OO' direction, i.e., $\cos\theta dS$. The quantity B defined through Eq. (5-28) is called the source brightness at point O in the direction OO'. This quantity generally depends on polar coordinates θ and φ of the direction OO' and on point O. When B is a constant, the source is said to be *isotropic*[37] (or a *Lambertian source*[38]).

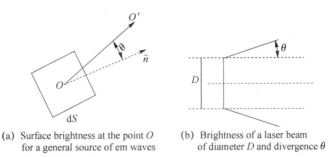

(a) Surface brightness at the point O for a general source of em waves

(b) Brightness of a laser beam of diameter D and divergence θ

Fig. 5-14 The comparison with the brightness of an em wave and a laser beam

Let us now consider a laser beam of power P, with a circular cross section of diameter D and with a divergence θ (Fig. 5-14b). Since θ is usually very small, we have $\cos\theta \cong 1$. Since the area of the beam is equal to $\pi D^2/4$ and the emission solid angle is $\pi\theta^2$, then, according to Eq. (5-28), we obtain the beam brightness as:

$$B = \frac{4P}{(\pi D\theta)^2} \qquad (5\text{-}29)$$

Note that, if the beam is diffraction limited, we have $\theta = \theta_d$, and, with the help of Eq. (5-26), we obtain from Eq. (5-29):

$$B = \left(\frac{2}{\beta\pi\lambda}\right)^2 P \qquad (5\text{-}30)$$

which is the maximum brightness for a beam of power P.

Brightness is the most important parameter of a laser beam and, in general, of any light source. To illustrate this point we first recall that, if we form an image of any light source through a given optical system and if we assume that the object and image are in the same medium (e.g., air), then the following property holds: The brightness of the image is always less than or equal to that of the source, the equality holding when the optical system provides lossless imaging of the light emitted by the source. To illustrate further the importance of brightness, let us consider the beam in Fig. 5-14(b), with divergence equal to θ, to be focused by a lens of focal length f. We are interested in calculating the peak intensity of the beam in the focal plane of the lens (Fig. 5-15(a)). To make this calculation we recall that the beam can be decomposed into a continuous set of plane waves with an angular spread of approximately θ around the propagation direction. Two such waves, making an angle θ', are indicated by solid and dashed lines, respectively, in Fig. 5-15(b). The two beams are each focused on a distinct spot in the focal plane, and, for a small angle θ', the two spots are transversely separated by a distance $r = f\theta'$. Since the angular spread of the plane waves that make up the beam in Fig. 5-15(a) equals the beam divergence θ, we conclude that the diameter d of the focal spot in Fig. 5-15(a) is approximately equal to $d = 2f\theta$. For an ideal lossless lens, the overall power in the focal plane equals the power P of the incoming wave. The peak intensity in the focal plane is thus $I_P = 4P/\pi d^2 = P/\pi(f\theta)^2$. In terms of beam brightness, according to Eq. (5-29), we then have $I_P = (\pi/4)B(D/f)^2$. Thus I_P increases with increasing beam diameter D. The maximum value of I_P is then attained when D is made equal to the lens diameter D_L. In this case we obtain

$$I_P = \left(\frac{\pi}{4}\right)(\text{N. A.})^2 B \qquad (5\text{-}31)$$

where N. A. $= \sin[\tan^{-1}(D_L/f)] \cong (D_L/f)$ is the lens numerical aperture. Equation(5-31) then shows that, for a given numerical aperture, the peak intensity in the focal plane of a lens depends only on beam brightness.

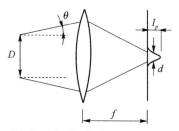 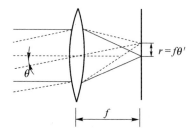

(a) Intensity distribution in the focal plane of a lens for a beam of divergence θ (b) Plane wave decomposition of the beam in (a)

Fig. 5-15 The peak intensity of the beam in the focal plane of the lens.

A laser beam of even moderate power (e. g., a few milliwatts) has a brightness several orders of magnitude greater than that of the brightest conventional sources. This is mainly due to the highly directional properties of the laser beam. According to Eq. (5-31) this means that the peak intensity produced in the focal plane of a lens can be several orders of magnitude greater for a laser beam compared to that of a conventional source. Thus the intensity of a focused laser beam can reach very large values, a feature exploited in many applications of lasers.

5. Short pulse duration

Without going into detail at this stage, we mention that, by means of a special technique called mode locking, it is possible to produce light pulses whose duration is roughly equal to the inverse of the linewidth of the laser transition $2 \rightarrow 1$. Thus, with gas lasers, whose linewidth is relatively narrow, the pulse width may be 0.1~1 ns. Such pulse durations are not regarded as particularly short, and indeed even some flash lamps can emit light pulses with a duration of somewhat less than 1 ns. On the other hand, the linewidth of some solid-state and liquid lasers can be $10^3 \sim 10^5$ times greater than that of a gas laser; in this case much shorter pulses may be generated (down to ~ 10 fs). This creates exciting new possibilities for laser research and applications.

Note that the property of short duration, which implies energy concentration in time, can in a sense be considered the counterpart of monochromaticity, which implies energy concentration in wavelength. However, short duration can perhaps be considered a less fundamental property than monochromaticity. In fact, while all lasers can in principle be made extremely monochromatic, only lasers with a broad linewidth, i. e. , solid-state and liquid lasers, may produce pulses of very short duration.

5.5 Lasers Types

The various laser types developed so far display a wide range of physical and operating parameters. Indeed, if lasers are characterized according to the physical state of the active material, we call them solid-state, liquid, or gas lasers. A rather special case is where the active material consists of free electrons at relativistic velocities passing through a spatially periodic magnetic field (free-electron lasers). If lasers are characterized by the wavelength of emitted radiation, one refers to infrared lasers, visible lasers, ultraviolet (uv) and x-ray lasers. The corresponding wavelength can range from ≈ 1 mm(i. e. , millimeter waves) to ≈ 1 nm (i. e. , to the upper limit of *hard X-rays*[39]). Wavelength span can thus be a factor $of \approx 10^6$ (recall that the visible range spans less than a factor 2, roughly from $400 \sim 700$ nm).

Output powers cover an even greater range of values. For cw lasers, typical powers range from a few mW, in lasers used for signal sources (e. g. , for optical communications or *bar code*[40] scanners), to tens of kW, in lasers used for material working, and to a few MW (≈ 5 MW so far), in lasers required in some military applications (e. g. , directed energy weapons). In pulsed lasers peak power can be much greater than in cw lasers, and it can reach values as high as 1 PW (10^{15} W)!

Again for pulsed lasers, the pulse duration can vary widely from the ms level typical of lasers operating in the so-called *free-running*[41] regime (i. e. , without any *Q-switching* or *mode-locking* element in the cavity) to about 10 fs(1 fs$=10^{-15}$ s) for some mode-locked lasers. Physical dimensions can also vary widely. In terms of cavity length for instance, the length can be as small as ~ 1 μm for the shortest lasers to some km value for the longest (e. g. , a 6.5 km long laser, which was set up in a cave for *geodetic*[42] studies).

This wide range of physical or operating parameters represents both a strength and a weakness. As far as applications are concerned, this wide range of parameters offers enormous potential in several fields of fundamental and applied sciences. On the other hand, in terms of markets, a large variation in terms of devices and systems can be an obstacle to mass production and its associated price reduction.

5.6 Application of Laser

Compare to radiation from other sources, laser radiation stands out in several ways. It is highly coherent, both spatially and temporally. It can be generated in the form of very short pulses, at high powers and, because of its high spatial coherence, at very high power densities. These are among the properties that make lasers the unique tool they are for a great many practical applications.

5.6.1 Industrial Applications

The high powers available from lasers have led to a great many industrial and medical applications, from more mundane tasks such as the machining of materials to the exotic, such as containing a *plasma*[43] and trying to release energy from *nuclear fusion*[44].

A well-known example of cutting with a laser beam appears in the James Bond movie Goldfinger, where the secret agent's nemesis cuts his way into the gold bullion depository at Fort Knox, using a laser mounted atop a personnel carrier. In the mind of the public, this episode has come to represent the wondrous capabilities of a laser. Today, some industrial lasers may be equal to the task of cutting through an armored door, but their principal use lies in a great variety of other applications.

1. Drilling

Drilling by laser is commonplace. Diamond, about the hardest material known, has been drilled before, but the process is tedious and time consuming. A laser does it quickly, producing traces of (black) graphite which facilitates absorption. Holes have been drilled also into teeth, paper clips, even into single human hairs.

2. Welding

Welding by laser meant earlier only welding on a *microscopic*[45] scale, such as in integrated circuits. But in recent years, as lasers have become much more powerful, even heavy steel plates have been welded. For example, steel plates 5cm thick can be fused using a 90 kW laser, at speeds higher than 2.5m per minute. Lasers are often guided by a computer programmed to move across the workpiece and perform various operations in sequence.

Because of their high directionality and high frequency, laser beams looked at first promising for communications. However, turbulence in the air severely limits the amount of information that can be transmitted, unless the beam is confined to a fiber waveguide. Optical radar, known as "lidar," for light detection and ranging, makes it possible to obtain echoes from clouds, haze, and atmospheric pollutants too small to be detected by conventional (microwave) radar.

Important among practical applications are precision measurements, including alignment and the measurement of distances, thicknesses, angles, and velocities. The distance to the moon, for example, has been determined to an accuracy better than 15cm.

5.6.2 Medical Applications

Laser effects on biological tissue are either thermal or nonlinear. Thermal effects depend on absorption, mainly in *pigments*[46] such as *melanin*[47] (as it occurs in the skin and the *iris*[48] and *choroid*[49] of the eye) and *hemoglobin*[50] (blood). Absorption causes a conversion of radiant energy into heat, increasing the temperature of the tissue and resulting in a *denaturation*[51] of proteins called *coagulation*[52]. With the process produced by light, it is called *photocoagulation*[53].

Nonlinear effects are entirely different. The rapid expansion of a plasma that is characteristic of a nonlinear effect produces a shock wave which mechanically (rather than thermally) causes a disruption of the tissue called *photodisruption*[54]. The difference between thermal and nonlinear effects can be shown by aiming a c.w. laser at the tip of a match and seeing it burst into flame. Firing a Q-switched laser (which because of its short pulse length has much higher power) at a match makes the tip crumble, without ignition.

Medical applications include the treatment of retinal detachment, where the focused beam causes small burns that on healing keep the retina back in place by the formation of *scar*[55] tissue. Similar is the treatment of *diabetic*[56] *retinopathy*[57], where local distentions of small blood vessels (*microaneurysms*[58]) and newly formed blood vessels (*neovascularization*[59]) are obliterated by coagulation. A cloudy posterior capsule, often left in place after removal of a cataract, can be opened quickly and without discomfort by *posterior capsulotomy*[60]. Lasers are used also in the treatment of *melanoblastoma*[61], a heavily pigmented tumor of the skin and the choroid of the eye that sometimes erupts into highly *malignant*[62] growth.

Both photocoagulation and photodisruption occur where the light is focused, rather than where the beam enters the eye. Therefore, the light can be aimed, without making any *incision*[63] at all, at the diseased part inside the eye, truly a *noninvasive*[64] kind of surgery.

References

1. Anthony E. Siegman. Lasers. The Maple-Vail Book Manufacturing Group, 1986.
2. Orazio Svelto. Principles of Lasers. fourth edition, Springer, 1998.
3. G. Cerullo, S. Longhi, M. Nisoli, S. Stagira, O. Svelto. Problems in Laser Physics. Kluwer Academic/Plenum Publishers, 2001.
4. M. Young. Optics and Lasers: An Engineering Physics Approach. Springer-Verlag Berlin Heidelberg, 1977.

New Words and Expressions

1. emission [iˈmiʃən] n. (光、热、电子、气味等的)发散;发出物;stimulate, vt. 激励,

stimulus 是其名词形式；radiation, n. 辐射（自然界中的一切物体，只要温度在绝对温度零度以上，就都以电磁波的形式时刻不停地向外传送热量。这种传送能量的方式称为辐射。物体通过辐射所放出的能量，称为辐射能，也简称辐射。light amplification by stimulated emission of radiation, 利用受激发射实现光放大）

2. equilibrium [ˌiːkwiˈlibriəm] n. 平衡

3. ruby [ˈruːbi] n. 红宝石

4. active [ˈæktiv] a. 活性的；active medium, 激活介质（在激光理论中，指处于集居数反转状态的物质）

5. pump [ˈpʌmp] vt. 用抽机抽（在激光理论中，一般说"抽运"或者"泵浦"，对应将粒子由低能级运送到高能级的动作）

6. population [ˌpɔpjuˈleiʃən] n. 在激光理论中称"集居数"或者"粒子数"，即物质内部处于各能级上的粒子个数。inversion, n. 反向，倒置（population inversion, 集居数反转、粒子数反转。当物质内部高能级上的粒子数密度高于低能级上的粒子数密度时，我们称物质处于集居数反转状态）

7. transition [trænˈsiʒən] n. 跃迁

8. paramagnetic [ˌpærəmægˈnetik] a. 顺磁的

9. radio [ˈreidiou] n. 无线电，射电；astronomy n. 天文学 radio-astronomy 射电天文学

10. flashlamp [ˈflæʃlæmp] n. 闪光灯 flashlamp-pumped 闪光灯泵浦

11. helium [ˈhiːljəm] n. 氦；neon n. 氖；helium-neon laser 氦氖激光器

12. spontaneous [spɔnˈteinjəs] a. 自发的 spontaneous emission 自发发射

13. decay [diˈkei] vi. 衰变；nonradiative decay 非辐射衰变

14. kinetic [kaiˈnetik] a. 运动的；kinetic energy, 动能

15. thermodynamic [ˈθəːmoudaiˈnæmik] a. 热力学的

16. nondegenerate [ˌnɔndiˈdʒenərit] a. 非简并的；degenerate a. 简并的；degenerate dimensions 简并度（量子力学中把能级可能有的所有微观状态称为该能级的简并度，用符号 g 表示。简并度也称为退化度或统计权重）

17. resonant [ˈrezənənt] a. 谐振的；resonant cavity 谐振腔

18. threshold [ˈθreʃhould] n. 阈值

19. gain [gein] n. 增益

20. alignment [əˈlainmənt] n. 调准

21. confocal [ˈkɔnˈfoukəl] a. 共焦的；confocal cavity 共焦腔（在谐振腔理论中，共焦腔是最重要和最具有代表性的一种稳定腔）

22. concave [ˈkɔnˈkeiv] a. 凹的

23. concentric [kɔnˈsentrik] a. 同一中心的；concentric cavity 共心腔

24. hemispherical [ˌhemisferikˈəl] a. 半球的；hemispherical cavity 半球面腔

25. node [noud] n. 波节

26. loop [luːp] n. 波腹

27. transverse [ˈtrænzvəːs] a. 横向的；transverse mode 横模

28. nodal line 节线

29. Gaussian distribution 高斯分布
30. monochromaticity [ˌmɔnəˌkroʊməˈtisiti] n. 单色性
31. perfect spatial coherence 完全空间相干
32. partial spatial coherence 部分空间相干
33. perfect temporal coherence 完全时间相干
34. partial temporal coherence 部分时间相干
35. Q-switched Q 开关
36. mode-locked 锁模
37. isotropic [ˌaisouˈtɔpik] a. 各向同性的
38. Lambertian source 朗伯光源（光亮度一般随观察方向而变，若一辐射体的光亮度是与方向无关的常量，则其发光强度与 cos θ 成正比(θ 是观察方向与光源法线的夹角)，此规律称为朗伯定律，这种辐射体称为朗伯辐射体或余弦辐射体。黑体是理想的余弦辐射体）
39. hard X-rays 硬 X 射线（即频率比较高的 X 射线，与 soft X-rays 相对应，后者是频率比较低的 X 射线）
40. bar code 条形码
41. free-running 自由运转
42. geodetic [ˌdʒiouˈdetik] a. 大地测量学的
43. plasma [ˈplæzmə] n. 等离子体
44. nuclear fusion 核聚变
45. microscopic [ˌmaikrəsˈkɔpik] a. 显微镜的，细微的
46. pigment [ˈpigmənt] n. 色素
47. melanin [ˈmelənin] n. 黑色素
48. iris [ˈaiəris] n. 虹膜
49. choroid [ˈkɔːrɔid] n. 脉络膜
50. hemoglobin [ˌhiːmouˈgloubin] n. 血红蛋白
51. denaturation [diːˌneitʃəˈreiʃən] n. 变性作用
52. coagulation [kouˌægjuˈleiʃən] n. 凝结
53. photocoagulation [ˈfoutoukouˌægjuˈleiʃən] n. 光致凝结（指利用强烈光能，如激光，产生瘢组织，用于治疗眼疾及生物实验等）
54. photodisruption [ˌfoutoudisˈrʌpʃən] n. 光致破裂
55. scar [skaː] n. 伤疤
56. diabetic [ˌdaiəˈbetik] a. 糖尿病的
57. retinopathy [ˌretiˈnɔpəθi] n. 视网膜病变
58. microaneurysm [ˈmaikrouˈænjuərizəm] n. 微小动脉瘤
59. neovascularization [ˌniːouˈvæskjulərizeiʃən] n. 血管新生
60. posterior capsulotomy 后囊膜切开术
61. melanoblastoma [ˈmelənəˈblæstoumə] n. 成黑素细胞瘤
62. malignant [məˈlignənt] a. 恶性的
63. incision [inˈsiʒən] n. 切开

64. noninvasive [nɔnˈinvæsiv] *a.* 无创的

Notes

① 激光器能够对位于电磁波谱中红外、可见光或紫外谱段内的相干辐射进行放大。

② 此后，出现了大量其他类型的激光器。这个此后，不仅是自第一台演示激光器出现以后的几年，而且是此后的四十多年的时间。

③ 在自发辐射的条件下，上能级集居数的变化率$(dN_2/dt)_{sp}$与上能级的集居数N_2成正比。

④ 要在激光放大器的基础上制作一台激光振荡器，必须引入合适的正反馈。

⑤ 除轴向模式以外，也存在称为 TEM 的横向模式，它是英文"横向电磁模式的缩写"。TEM 模式一般在数量上比较少，也很容易观察到。

第6章
Nonlinear Optics

PREVIEW

Laser technology has been developed for several decades. The progress of laser research has shown that our knowledge and understanding about the generation and control of coherent and intense optical radiation has reached a much higher level than before. Compared to various ordinary light sources, laser can provide intense coherent light beam with higher directionality, higher monochromaticity, higher brightness, and higher photon degeneracy. Employing the new and marvelous lasers sources, people have found a great number of interesting phenomena, which were unbelievable before the invention of the laser. We are now in the new epoch of the optics science.

Among these achievements, *nonlinear*[1] optics is a very attractive and wonderful branch. It has thoroughly changed the ideas existed in old optics science and has demonstrated many new unimaginable effects. Due to the interaction between laser radiation and matter, a great number of new effect and novel techniques have been discovered, such as the frequency of the light wave could be changed and *tuned*[2], the absorption constant and the refraction index of the medium would not be kept as constants, many higher energy states of the atoms and molecules could be detected by using laser beam with high intensity, the pulse duration of the laser beam could reach *femtosecond*[3] (10^{-15} second) and even shorter, *etc*. Studies in these new effects and the related novel techniques are the major issues of nonlinear.

6.1 Definition of Nonlinear Optics

Nonlinear optics is the study of phenomena that occur as a consequence of the modification of the optical properties of a material system by the presence of light.[①] Typically, only laser light is sufficiently intense to modify the optical properties of a material system. The nonlinear response can result in intensity-dependent variation of the propagation characteristics of the radiation fields or in the creation of radiation fields that propagate at new frequencies or in new directions. Nonlinear effects can take place in solids, liquids, gases, and plasmas, and may involve one or more electromagnetic fields as well as internal excitations of the medium. Most of the work done in the field has made use of the high powers available from lasers. The wavelength range of interest generally extends from the far-infrared to the vacuum ultraviolet, but some nonlinear interactions have been observed at wavelengths extending from the microwave to the X-ray ranges.

Nonlinear optics mainly deals with various new optics effects and novel phenomenon arising from the interactions of intense coherent optical radiation with matter.

Befoe 1960's, in the area of conventional optics many basic mathematical equations or formulae manifested a linear feature.

To show this linear feature of conventional optics, we can consider the following two examples.

First, in order to interpret the refraction, refraction, dispersion, scattering, as well as birefringence of light propagation in a medium, we should consider an important physical quantity, the electric polarization induced in the medium. In the regime of conventional optics, the electric polarization vector **P** is simply assumed to be linearly proportional to the electric field strength **E** of an applied optical wave, i.e.,

$$\boldsymbol{P} = \varepsilon_0 \chi \boldsymbol{E} \tag{6-1}$$

where ε_0 is the free-space *permittivity*[4], χ is the *susceptibility*[5] of a given medium. Based on this linear assumption, Maxwell's equations lead to a set of linear differential equations in which only the terms proportional to the first power of the field E are involved. As a result, there is no coupling between different light beams or between different monochromatic components when they pass through a medium. In other words, if there are several monochromatic optical waves with different frequencies passing through a medium simultaneously, no coherent radiation at any new frequency will be generated.

Second, in conventional optics, the attenuation of an optical beam propagating in an absorptive medium can be described as

$$\frac{dI}{dz} = -\alpha I \tag{6-2}$$

where I is the beam intensity, z is the variable along the propagation direction, and α is a constant for a given medium. The physical meaning of Eq. (6-2) is that the decrease of the beam intensity in a unit propagation length is linearly proportional to the local intensity itself. From Eq. (6-2) we obtain a well-known exponential attenuation expression

$$I(z) = I(0) \cdot e^{-\alpha z} \tag{6-3}$$

This expression implies that for a given propagation length of $z = l$, the transmitted intensity $I(l)$ is linearly proportional to the initial intensity of $I = I(0)$.

So far we have given two examples that manifest a simple linear feature as shown by Eqs. (6-1) and (6-2), respectively. These simple linear assumptions or conclusions given by the conventional optics were widely accepted, and verified by most experimental observation and measurements based in the use of ordinary light sources. However, these situations have been changed radically since the beginning of 1960's.

Shortly after the demonstration of the first laser device (a pulsed ruby laser) in 1960, it was found that these simple linear assumptions or conclusions described above were no longer adequate for circumstances in which an intense laser beam was incident on certain types of optical media. For the sake of clarity, we shall stay with our two examples and show why some higher-order approximations should be employed when an intense laser field interacts with an optical medium.

The first breakthrough was achieved in 1961 when a pulsed laser beam was sent into a *piezoelectric*[6] crystal sample. In this case researchers, for the first time in the history of optics, observed the second-harmonic generation (SHG[7]) at an optical frequency. Shortly after this discovery, several other coherent optical *frequency mixing*[8] effects (such as optical *sum-frequency generation*[9], optical *difference-frequency generation*[10], and optical third harmonic generation) were observed. The researchers realized that all these new effects could be reasonably explained if replaced the linear term on the right-hand side of Eq. (6-1) by a power series

$$\boldsymbol{P} = \varepsilon_0 [\chi^{(1)}\boldsymbol{E} + \chi^{(2)}\boldsymbol{E}\boldsymbol{E} + \chi^{(3)}\boldsymbol{E}\boldsymbol{E}\boldsymbol{E} + \cdots] \tag{6-4}$$

Here, $\chi^{(1)}, \chi^{(2)}$, and $\chi^{(3)}$ are the first-order (linear), second-order (nonlinear), and third-order (nonlinear) susceptibility and so on. They are material coefficients and in general are tensors. Substituting Eq. (6-4) into Maxwell's equations leads to a set of nonlinear differential equations that involve high-order-power terms of optical electric field strength; these terms are responsible for various observed coherent optical frequency-mixing effects.

In the same time period, researchers also found that the depletion behavior of an intense laser beam propagating in an absorptive optical medium did not follow the description indicated by Eq. (6-2) or Eq. (6-3). For instance, in a one-photon absorptive medium, if the intensity of the incident beam is high enough, the attenuation coefficient α is no longer a constant and may become a variable that depends on the incident intensity. Therefore, the exponential attenuation formula like Eq. (6-3) can not be applied and the linear relationship between $I(z=l)$ and $I(0)$ does not hold. In this case, either a saturable absorption or a reverse-saturable absorption effect may take place. Moreover, if there is a two-photon absorption process involved in the medium, the attenuation of an intense incident beam should be described as

$$\frac{dI}{dz} = -\alpha I - \beta I^2 \tag{6-5}$$

where β is the two-photon absorption coefficient, which could be viewed as a constant only if the saturation or reverse-saturation effect can be neglected. In more general cases, if we further extend our consideration to include multi-photon (three-photon or more) absorption processes, then Eq. (6-5) should be generalized to the following form:

$$\frac{dI}{dz} = -\alpha I - \beta I^2 - \gamma I^3 - \cdots \tag{6-6}$$

Here γ is the three-photon absorption coefficient and so on.

*Based on these comparisons described above, we can conclude that the main concern in conventional optics is the propagation and interaction with matter of the light from ordinary light sources, wherein the intensities of the light beams are so low that even a simple linear approximation is enough to give a good theoretical explanation for the related optical effects and phenomena.*② In this sense, the conventional optics may also be called "linear optics" or "optics of weak light". On the other hand, "nonlinear optics" mainly deals with the interaction of intense laser radiation with matter. In the latter case, the intensities of laser beams can be so high that a great number of new effects and novel phenomena can be observed, and some high-order nonlinear approximations have to be employed to explain these new effects and phenomena. In this sense, nonlinear optics may also be called "optics of intense light". In general, the contents of nonlinear optics are much more extensive than that of linear optics and, accordingly, the theories of the former are more complicated than that of the latter.

6.2 History of Nonlinear Optics

The formation of nonlinear optics originated in the early 1960's. The discovery of the optical second-harmonic generation by P. A. Franken in 1961 was commonly recognized as the first milestone of the formation of nonlinear optics. Shortly after that, several other optical frequency-mixing effects were sequentially demonstrated based on the use of laser radiation, which include the optical sum-frequency generation, optical third-harmonic generation, *optical rectification*[11], optical difference-frequency generation, and the *optical parametric amplification*[12] and oscillation. These experimental demonstrations not only verified the validity of nonlinear polarization theories but also provided an alternative approach to generate coherent optical radiation. During the same time period, another important event was the discovery of stimulated Raman scattering (SRS[13]), which can be recognized as the second milestone in the history of nonlinear optics. Later, researchers reported the observation of stimulated Brillouin scattering (SBS[14]), which arose from the interaction of an intense monochromatic optical field with the induced *hypersonic*[15] field in a scattering medium through the so-called optical *electrostriction*[16] mechanism. Since then, *the stimulated Brillouin scattering has become an efficient technique to generate or amplify the coherent optical radiation with a small frequency-shift or fine tenability.*③

Another major subject of nonlinear optics is related to the refractive-index change induced by an intense laser beam as well as the impact of this change on the laser beam itself. An important article focused on this issue was published in 1964 with a conceptual discussion and a semi-quantitative description of the self-focusing (self-trapping) behavior of an intense optical beam propagating in a nonlinear medium. Further studies of dynamic self-focusing processes for short laser pulses revealed special properties of the moving-focus as well as the new phenomena, self-phase modulation and spectral self-broadening. Now it is well known that the self-phase modulation and spectral self-broadening effects are among the basic mechanisms for generating ultra-short laser pulses and the continuum radiation with a super-broad spectral band.

Other kinds of nonlinear optical phenomena were also reported in the 1960's, the so-called transient coherent optical effects, include *photon echoes*[17], *self-induced transparency*[18], and *optical nutation*[19]. These effects are related to the *transient-response*[20] behavior of a resonant optical medium interacting with short optical pulses or a fast-switched optical field. Some of them are the optical analog of the corresponding effects in nuclear magnetic resonance studies. The studies of transient optical effect can provide a new approach to investigate the relaxation behavior of resonant transitions in absorptive media.

In addition, there are other two fundamental nonlinear optical effects. The optical saturable absorption effect in organic dye solutions and other materials were well studied and soon applied to the Q-switching and mode-locking of laser devices. The other effect is two-photon absorption (TPA). The earliest experimental demonstrations of TPA-induced fluorescence were achieved with the use of laser radiation. The initial research work of laser-based TPA and the related processes stimulated an extensive investigation on two-photon and multi-photon induced absorption, fluorescence, ionization and dissociation. Later, all these kinds of studies have formed the important part of nonlinear optics and laser spectroscopy.

From 1970 to 1990, accompanying with the great successes in laser science and technology, many new effects were exploited, including the optical bistability ($OBIS$[21]), *soliton*[22], *squeezed state*[23], *etc*. In the domain of laser technique, dramatic progresses in shortening the pulse duration further to femtosecond (fs) scale have greatly stimulated the researches of ultrafast processes in photophysics, photochemistry and photobiology. The applications of advanced laser techniques have led to the great successes in optical fiber communications, laser manufacturing of microstructures, *etc*.

Four-wave mixing (FWM) was found in the first decade of the laser epoch. The unique features of FWM are the recovery of the phase and the correction of the phase aberration, which are very attractive in many applications. A special technique is degenerate four-wave mixing ($DFWM$[24]), where two counter-propagating pump beams are used to generate a new beam in the opposite direction with the probe beam. This new beam has the complex conjugate relation with the probe beam. In such case, the phase aberration introduced by the propagation in atmosphere or other media could be effectively corrected, making DFWM to be very promising in the applications for the laser propagation in long-range distance, and the self-tracking system used for the laser fusion. A special configuration of FWM called coherent anti-Stokes Raman scattering ($CARS$[25])

was studied during this period. The unique advantage of CARS technique is that it could avoid the interference of the fluorescence in the measurement and improves greatly the signal to noise ratio.

The stimulated electronic Raman scattering ($SERS$[26]) is the stimulated process happening among the electronic states. SERS was widely studied in various metal vapors, such as Na, K, Rb and Cs. As the energy intervals between the excited states of these atoms are small, the generated SERS emissions are in the near infrared to middle infrared ranges, which are very useful in the research of large molecules and narrow gap semiconductors. In addition to SERS, the stimulated hyper Raman scattering was also observed. But the interest in this kind of research decreased gradually due to the fact it was hard to meet the demand of the applications with high conversion efficiency.

One of the most important discoveries in this period was the OBIS. In 1957, S. L. McCall et al. at the Bell laboratories observed optical bistable property in the sodium vapor inside a Fabry-Perot cavity. This character is caused by the combination of the resonant cavity and the nonlinear optical property of the medium. After the first observation, a great number of laboratories and universities carried out the research work and observed OBIS in a variety of materials. Different kinds of OBIS were soon discovered, such as absorptive OBIS, dispersive and hybrid OBIS. The great interest on this phenomenon was that it stimulated the human's imagination on manufacturing the optical computer. At the same time, the chaos phenomenon was also carefully studied.

In accordance with the development of the fiber communications, the nonlinear optical research of fibers demonstrated the observation of Stokes SRS, multi-order Stokes and anti-Stokes SRS in fibers. The research on the SRS process in fiber led to the invention of the fiber Raman laser. Even in this isotropic material, SHG in long fiber was generated. Self-phase modulation (SPM[27]) was found to broaden the spectral band of the laser beam propagating inside the fiber. It was realized later that SPM could be used to compensate a new kind of light called soliton.

The first soliton was observed by L. F. Mollenauer in 1980, seven years after the concept of soliton proposed by A. Hasegawa. Other scientists developed the theory of soliton and suggested the construction of soliton laser, which was built soon later. The success in fabricating the soliton laser has attracted much attention for its potential use in the optical communications, as it would decrease the noise and hopefully increase the volume of the date bit-rate.

The progress in quantum optics during these years was very encouraging. In 1985, R. E. Slusher at Bell laboratories reported the observation of a new state, called squeezed state, in sodium vapor by using non-degenerate four-wave mixing (NDFWM). The special feature of the squeezed state is that it can transfer the noise from one quadratic component to another quadratic component of the optical electric field, thus greatly reduces the noise in the squeezed component. This discovery was found potential in the research of the universe attraction force and in the low-noise optical communications.

For many nonlinear optical researches and applications, especially in those using SHG, SFG and optical parametric oscillation (OPO) effects, the nonlinear optical crystals with large second-order susceptibility are definitely required. For searching new efficient nonlinear optical crystals, it is important to calculate the second-order susceptibility of molecules and crystals. To solve this problem, C. T. Chen and his coworkers at the Chinese Academy of Sciences developed an anion radical theory, which was first successful applied to the calculation of the second-order susceptibilities of $NaNO_2$ and $LiNbO_3$. In 80s of the last century, they got the achievements in the elaborate design and the successful fabrication of new nonlinear optical crystals BBO and LBO, which improve greatly the quality of many nonlinear optical devices and laser systems.

Since 1990, the research in nonlinear optical field has been continuously developing both in theoretical and applicable aspects.

One of the most important progresses is the rapid development of the solid-state ultrashort laser systems, which provide the powerful tools that can be used to explore the ultrafast processes happening in the nature and to study the transient response of the novel materials. The crystals, such as Ti:sapphire, were found to have very broad fluorescence band and self mode-locking features, which make them to be the appropriate gain materials for constructing the ultrashort laser system. Based on the maturity of the solid-state fs laser techniques, the optical parametric amplification has been successfully used to generate the tunable fs laser pulses covering the near infrared, visible and even ultraviolet ranges. The development of fs laser systems also stimulates the research on the generation of the laser pulses with even shorter duration or shorter wavelength, including *attosecond*[28] pulses and soft X-ray pulses.

The research on the soliton has got big successes in recent years. Both the temporal and spatial solitons have been studied theoretically and experimentally. The various types of solitons, including bright soliton, dark soliton and grey soliton, have been generated and their interactions were studied. The temporal-spatial soliton was observed in the nonlinear optical crystals like $LiIO_3$. As the soliton can keep its temporal profile during the propagation in long distance, which is very important for the optical communication with huge data bit-rate, the soliton communication has been widely studied and the prototype communication system based on the soliton was constructed.

In accordance with the development of the optical communications, different optical devices with ultrafast response have been designed and fabricated, including the optical switching, optical modulator and detectors. *The design of the optical switching based on the photonic crystals and the combination of the cascade second-order processes with semiconductor quantum wells*[29] *have been proposed and studied experimentally.*① All these researches will certainly improve the qualities of the optical component and increase the data bit-rate for the optical communication.

During this period, there are still many research work and progresses on the pulse compression, the quantum optics, the time-resolved spectroscopic, *etc*.

The developments in the past nearly sixty years have proved that nonlinear optics is a so exciting and fruitful research brand, which provides big progress in study the materials and systems in various scientific fields. It can be expected that continuous development of nonlinear optics will bring new achievement and successes for the science and technology.

6.3 Features of Interaction of Intense Light with Matter

Regarding the interaction of light radiation with matter, the total number of newly discovered effects and phenomena after the advent of lasers is even larger than that before the invention of lasers. One may ask why so many new things can be found in a so short time period (only five to six decades). To answer this question, we should consider the essential differences between the light beams from laser devices and that from ordinary light sources. Only based on these differences, we can realize how powerful the laser radiation could be when it interacts with matter.

As mentioned in Chapter five, the laser radiation is generated based in stimulated emission from a population inversion system, whereas the ordinary light is based on spontaneous emission from conventional light sources. Consequently, these two emission mechanisms lead to a great difference in the parameters used to describe the properties of light radiation.

The following are the common parameters to characterize a quasi-directional and quasi-monochromatic light field.

(1) **Intensity** is defined as

$$I = \frac{P}{S} \tag{6-7}$$

where P is the total light power (in units of watt) and S is the cross section of the light beam (in units of m² or cm²). The unit of the intensity is W/m² or W/cm².

(2) **Spectral intensity** is defined as

$$I(\nu) = \frac{P}{S \Delta \nu} \tag{6-8}$$

where $\Delta \nu$ is the spectral width of the light radiation (in units of hertz). The unit of the spectral intensity is W/(cm² · Hz).

(3) **Brightness** is defined as

$$B = \frac{P}{S\Omega} = \frac{I}{\Omega} \tag{6-9}$$

where Ω is the divergent solid angle of the light beam (in unit of steradian). The unit of the brightness is W/(cm² · sr).

(4) **Spectral brightness** is defined as

$$B(\nu) = \frac{P}{S\Omega \Delta \nu} = \frac{I(\nu)}{\Omega} \tag{6-10}$$

The unit of the brightness is W/(cm² sr Hz).

(5) **Photon degeneracy** is defined as the average photon number contained in a single mode of optical field. This parameter is the basic quantity to describe the photon field in quantum electrodynamics and can be determined in the following way. For a quasi-directional and quasi-monochromatic light radiation the total photon number passing through a given beam section of S within a given time interval of Δt is

$$F = \frac{P \Delta t}{h \nu} \tag{6-11}$$

where $h\nu$ is the energy of a single photon, h is Planck constant, ν is the frequency of light. On the other hand, the mode number (or phase-sell number) associated with the above F photons is given by

$$N = \frac{\Delta t}{\delta t} \cdot \frac{S}{\delta S} = \frac{\Delta t}{(1/\Delta \nu)} \cdot \frac{S}{(\lambda^2/\Omega)} \tag{6-12}$$

Here $\delta t = 1/\Delta \nu$ is the longitudinal coherent time of the optical radiation, $\Delta \nu$ is the spectral width, $\delta S = \lambda^2/\Omega$ is the coherent section of the light beam, Ω is the solid angle of beam divergence. Assuming the light beam is nonpolarized, there should be two independent polarization states; thus the photon degeneracy $\bar{n}$ can be finally determined by

$$\bar{n}(\nu) = \frac{F}{2N} = \frac{P}{(2h\nu/\lambda^2) S \Omega \Delta \nu} \tag{6-13}$$

The photon degeneracy is a dimensionless quantity. From Eqs. (6-7) to (6-10) one can see that the light intensity represents the power density, the spectral intensity represents the power density within a unit spectral interval, the brightness represents the power density within a unit solid angle, and the spectral brightness represents the power density within a unit solid angle and a unit spectral interval, respectively. In addition, comparing Eq. (6-10) with Eq. (6-13) one can see that there is only a difference of factor $(2h\nu/\lambda^2)^{-1}$ between the spectral brightness $B(\nu)$ and the photon degeneracy $\bar{n}(\nu)$; therefore, they can be viewed as two equivalent quantities. According to conventional optics, the brightness of a light beam cannot be increased by passing it through any kinds of optical imaging or transmission systems. It can also be expressed in terms of quantum statistics that the total number of modes for a given photon ensemble cannot be compressed by any ordinary optical systems; therefore, the photon degeneracy cannot be increased by any types of ordinary optical devices. However, these two equivalent conclusions are no longer valid for lasers and nonlinear optical devices. It is well known that the brightness or photon degeneracy of a weak optical signal can be dramatically increased based on the coherent amplification through a lasing medium, a stimulated scattering medium, or an optical parametric amplifier system. For a laser oscillator system, the number of the total lasing modes can be greatly restricted by choosing appropriate cavity configurations and mode selection techniques. As a result, the photo degeneracy of the output laser beam can be extremely high.

According to the electromagnetic theory of light, on the other hand, the spectral intensity of a quasi-parallel laser beam is equal to the magnitude of the *Poynting's vector*[30] of a monochromatic plane electromagnetic wave, i. e,

$$I(\nu) = \frac{1}{2}\varepsilon_0 c n_0 |E(\nu)|^2 \qquad (6\text{-}14)$$

where c is the speed of light in vacuum, n_0 is the linear refractive index of the medium, and $E(\nu)$ is the electric field strength of the monochromatic plane wave. From Eqs. (6-8) and (6-14) one can see that the values of $I(\nu)$ and $E(\nu)$ can be significantly increased when the beam size of the light radiation is compressed by using a reverse beam-expander or a focusing optical system, which are often employed in the experimental studies of nonlinear optics.

In Table 6-1, we list the typical parameters of light radiation from the strongest ordinary light source (the sun) and from laser devices. From this table one can see that the spectral brightness as well as the photon degeneracy of the radiation from high peak-power laser devices can be 10^{15} to 10^{19}- times greater than that of the radiation from an ordinary light source (like the sun).

Table 6-1 Characteristics of radiation from ordinary light source and lasers.

Parameters	Sun	Gas Lasers	Solid Lasers	Q-Switched or Mode-Locked Lasers
Monochromaticity $(\Delta\nu/\nu)$	White light	$10^{-8} \sim 10^{-13}$	$10^{-3} \sim 10^{-8}$	$10^{-2} \sim 10^{-6}$
Directionality Ω/sr	6.8×10^{-5} (on the earth)	$10^{-5} \sim 10^{-7}$	$10^{-8} \sim 10^{-13}$	$10^{-6} \sim 10^{-8}$
Brightness /W·(cm^2·sr)$^{-1}$	$\sim 10^3$	$10^4 \sim 10^8$	$10^7 \sim 10^{11}$	$10^{12} \sim 10^{17}$
Spectral Brightness /W(cm^2·sr·Hz)$^{-1}$	$\sim 10^{-12}$	$10^{-2} \sim 10^2$	$10 \sim 10^3$	$10^4 \sim 10^7$
Photon Degeneracy	$\leqslant 10^{-2}$	$10^8 \sim 10^{12}$	$10^{11} \sim 10^{13}$	$10^{14} \sim 10^{17}$

In addition, the values of $I(\nu)$ and $E(\nu)$ of a laser beam can be further increased by using an optical focusing system as described above. In the sense of radiation potentials in interacting with matter and creating various nonlinear responses, the differences between ordinary light and laser light are mostly similar to the differences between conventional weapons and strategic nuclear weapons. Therefore, we can say that the light from ordinary light sources is a weak optical radiation characterized by $\bar{n} \ll 1$ and can only create an extremely low electric field strength. Based on this reason, all the nonlinear terms in the expression of the polarization (see Eq. (6-4)) can be neglected. In contrast, the laser radiation is an intense coherent light characterized by $\bar{n} \gg 1$ and can provide a much stronger optical-frequency electric filed, which can even be comparable with the internal electric field of the atom or molecule. In such a case, the nonlinear terms of the polarization expression cannot be entirely neglected and may play a vital role for various nonlinear optical effects. Based on quantum statistics, a light radiation with $\bar{n} \ll 1$ manifests the feature of a shot noise field when it interacts with matter; whereas a radiation with $\bar{n} \gg 1$ manifests the feature of a coherent wave field when it interacts with matter. That is an alternative insight to understand why so many nonlinear optical effects (especially the coherent wave mixing effects in nonlinear media) can be observed only by using laser radiation but not ordinary optical radiation.

In summary, on the one hand, the parameters of laser radiation (such as power, beam divergence, pulse duration, wavelength, spectral width, polarization status, etc.) can be well controlled or modified based on existing laser techniques. On the other hand, there is a great variety of nonlinear optical media, which can be various materials (inorganic, organic, biological, etc.), in different physical states (solid, liquid, gas, plasma, liquid crystal, etc.), and with different reaction centers (molecules, atoms, ions, atomic nuclei, electrons, color centers, phonons, excitons, plasmons[31], etc.). So that, it is not surprising that so many new effects and novel phenomena in nonlinear optics have been found within only four to five decades since the 1960's. These effects and phenomena are related to the intense light induced opto-optical, opto-electric, opto-magnetic, opto-acoustic, opto-thermal, opto-mechanical, opto-chemical, and opto-biological interactions in optical media. Generally speaking, all these kinds of interactions can be used to develop various new techniques that may provide many advantages, such as high efficiency, high resonant selectivity, high spectral resolution, high temporal resolution, high spatial resolution, and high sensitivity.

6.4 Theory Framework of Nonlinear Optics

Basically, two major theoretical approaches can be employed in nonlinear optics as well as in laser physics. The first is the semi-classical theory, and the second is the quantum electrodynamical theory. The most essential feature of the semi-classical theory is that the media composed of atoms or molecules are described by the theory of quantum mechanics, while the light radiation is described by the classical Maxwell's theory. The key issue of semi-classical theory in nonlinear optics is to give the expressions of macroscopic nonlinear electric polarization for optical media. For this purpose, the density matrix method, which is a special approach based on both quantum mechanics and statistical physics, is used to derive the expressions for various orders of electric susceptibilities as $\chi^{(1)}$, $\chi^{(2)}$, $\chi^{(3)}$, $\cdots$, and the expressions for various orders of polarization components as $P^{(1)}$, $P^{(2)}$, $P^{(3)}$, $\cdots$ and so on. Substituting the appropriate nonlinear polarization components into the generalized wave equations, we are able, in principle, to predict many possible nonlinear optical responses of the medium for a given condition of the input intense optical field(s).

In contrast, the quantum theory of radiation in the regime of quantum electrodynamics treats the medium and optical field as a combined and quantized system. In other words, both the medium and the optical field should be described in the way of quantum mechanics. As a result, the wave function of the combined system is expressed as the product of the *eigen function*[32] of a molecular system and the eigen function of a quantized photon field. In this case, the key issue is to determine the probability of state change of the combined system due to interaction between the photon field and the medium. Usually, *the state changes of the combined system are related to the transition of molecular system from its initial eigen state to the final state and the simultaneous changes of the photon numbers among different photon mode.*[5]

It should be pointed that there is no major contradiction or inconsistency between the results and conclusions given by these two theoretical approaches. In fact, they can give the same quantitative results in many cases, such as the cross section of Raman scattering as well as the cross section of two-photon absorption. Nevertheless, these two theoretical approaches have their own usefulness and shortcomings. In this sense, these two different theoretical regimes are parallel and complementary to each other in the scope of nonlinear optics.

The most successful example of the semi-classical theory in nonlinear optics is the derivation of quantitative expressions for various orders of nonlinear susceptibilities of optical media. A semi-classical theoretical approach can be employed to explain all those nonlinear optical effects and phenomena, such as various coherent optical wave-mixing effects. Nevertheless, there are some limitations inherently associated with the semi-classical theory. First, this theory cannot distinguish the difference between the stimulated and the spontaneous processes of radiation, scattering, and parametric photon emission. In order to describe the spontaneous processes, the correspondence principle has to be invoked in the semi-classical regime. For example, Einstein's coefficient relation has to be used to describe the difference between the probabilities of spontaneous emission and stimulated emission. Second, some important physical facts (such as transition relaxation and spectral linewidth) can only be considered by introducing a phenomenological damping factor into the equation of density matrix. Finally, there are a number of nonlinear optical effects (such as stimulated Raman scattering, SBS, CARS process, two-photon absorption, third-harmonic generation, as well as induced refractive index change), all of them can be described with a nominal third-order nonlinear susceptibility $\chi^{(3)}$. In these cases, however, the nonlinear polarization theory can not reveal the essential difference in origins and mechanisms of those entirely different effects. As a result of that failure, sometimes one may find confusion and terminological ambiguity in classification and description of some nonlinear optical processes within the regime of semi-classical theory.

In quantum electrodynamics, the quantum theory of radiation is a more rigorous theoretical approach that, in principle, can be perfectly used to explain or describe any kinds of effects and phenomena related to the interaction of radiation field with matter in both qualitative and quantitative ways. There are many well-known examples that have shown the advantage of the quantum theory of radiation over the semi-classical theory. First, the relationship between stimulated emission (or scattering) and spontaneous emission (or scattering) can be naturally derived without the need of using the correspondence principle. Second, the selection rule, life-time of state, and spectral linewidth can be quantitatively determined for a given molecular system. Third, the conversation of energy and momentum between the photon field and molecular system can be logically applied to various nonlinear optical processes without the need of using the so-called Manley-Rowe relation (for conservation of energy) and the phase-matching requirement (for conversation of momentum). Finally, the most important feature of the quantum theory of radiation is that a concept of virtual energy level can be introduced, which represents an intermediate quantum state occupied by the combined system of the photon field and the medium. Based on the concept of virtual energy level or intermediate state, the principles and mechanisms of most major nonlinear optical effects can be consistently interpreted and, in many cases, clearly illustrated by an energy-level diagram involving the transitions via virtual energy levels. On the other hand, however, the mathematics derivation in the regime of quantum electrodynamics is rather lengthy and cumbersome specific issues. Therefore, in practice the all-quantum derivations of the related formulae are only applied in those cases where the semi-classical approach is obviously poorly or failed. Various nonlinear optical effects and phenomena described by these two theoretical approaches are described in section 6.5.

6.5 Descriptions of Nonlinear Optical Processes

In the present section, we present brief qualitative descriptions of a number of nonlinear optical processes. In addition, for those processes that can occur in a lossless medium, we indicate how they can be described in terms of the nonlinear contributions to the polarization described by Eq. (6-4). Our motivation is to provide an indication of the variety of nonlinear optical phenomena that can occur. In this section we also introduce some notational conventions and some of the basic concepts of nonlinear optics.

6.5.1 Second-Harmonic Generation

As an example of a nonlinear optical interaction, let us consider the process of second-harmonic generation, which is illustrated schematically in Fig. 6-1.

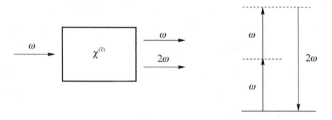

(a) Geometry of SHG (b) Energy-level diagram describing SHG

Fig. 6-1 Second-harmonic generation.

Here a laser beam whose electric field strength is represented as

$$\widetilde{E}(t) = E e^{-i\omega t} + \text{c. c.} \tag{6-15}$$

is incident upon a crystal for which the second-order susceptibility $\chi^{(2)}$ is nonzero. The nonlinear polarization that is created in such a crystal is given according to Eq. (6-4) as $\widetilde{P}^{(2)}(t) = \varepsilon_0 \chi^{(2)} \widetilde{E}^2(t)$ or explicitly as

$$\widetilde{P}^{(2)}(t) = 2\varepsilon_0 \chi^{(2)} EE^* + (\varepsilon_0 \chi^{(2)} E^2 e^{-i2\omega t} + \text{c. c.}). \tag{6-16}$$

We see that the second-order polarization consists of a contribution at zero frequency (the first term) and a contribution at frequency 2ω (the second term).

The wave equation in nonlinear optical media can be expressed as

$$\nabla^2 \widetilde{E} - \frac{n^2}{c^2} \frac{\partial^2 \widetilde{E}}{\partial t^2} = \frac{1}{\varepsilon_0 c^2} \frac{\partial^2 \widetilde{P}^{\text{NL}}}{\partial t^2} \tag{6-17}$$

According to Eq. (6-17), this latter contribution can lead to the generation of radiation at the second-harmonic frequency. Note that the first contribution in Eq. (6-16) does not lead to the generation of electromagnetic radiation (because its second time derivative vanishes); it leads to a process known as optical rectification, in which a static electric field is created across the nonlinear crystal.

Under proper experimental conditions, the process of second-harmonic generation can be so efficient that nearly all of the power in the incident beam at frequency ω is converted to radiation at the second-harmonic frequency 2ω. One common use of second-harmonic generation is to convert the output of a fixed-frequency laser to a different spectral region. For example, the Nd:YAG laser operates in the near infrared at a wavelength of 1.06 μm. Second-harmonic generation is routinely used to convert the wavelength of the radiation to 0.53 μm, in the middle of the visible spectrum.

Second-harmonic generation can be visualized by considering the interaction in terms of the exchange of photons between the various frequency components of the field. According to this picture, which is illustrated in part (b) of Fig. 6-1, two photons of frequency ω are destroyed, and a photon of frequency 2ω is simultaneously created in a single quantum-mechanical process. The solid line in the figure represents the atomic ground state, and the dashed lines represent what are known as virtual levels. These levels are not energy eigen levels of the free atom but rather represent the combined energy of one of the energy eigen states of the atom and of one or more photons of the radiation field.

6.5.2 Frequency Mixing Generation

Let us next consider the circumstance in which the optical field incident upon a second-order nonlinear optical medium consists of two distinct frequency components, which we represent in the form

$$\tilde{E}(t) = E_1 e^{-i\omega_1 t} + E_2 e^{-i\omega_2 t} + \text{c.c.} \tag{6-18}$$

Then, assuming as in Eq. (6-4) that the second-order contribution to the nonlinear polarization is of the form

$$\tilde{P}^{(2)}(t) = \varepsilon_0 \chi^{(2)} \tilde{E}(t)^2 \tag{6-19}$$

we find that the nonlinear polarization is given by

$$\tilde{P}^{(2)}(t) = \varepsilon_0 \chi^{(2)} [E_1^2 e^{-2i\omega_1 t} + E_2^2 e^{-2i\omega_2 t} + 2E_1 E_2 e^{-i(\omega_1+\omega_2)t} + 2E_1 E_2^* e^{-i(\omega_1-\omega_2)t} + \text{c.c.}]$$
$$+ 2\varepsilon_0 \chi^{(2)} [E_1 E_1^* + E_2 E_2^*] \tag{6-20}$$

It is convenient to express this result using the notation

$$\tilde{P}^{(2)}(t) = \sum_n P(\omega_n) e^{-i\omega_n t} \tag{6-21}$$

where the summation extends over positive and negative frequencies ω_n. The complex amplitudes of the various frequency components of the nonlinear polarization are hence given by

$$\begin{aligned}
P(2\omega_1) &= \varepsilon_0 \chi^{(2)} E_1^2 \quad \text{(SHG)} \\
P(2\omega_2) &= \varepsilon_0 \chi^{(2)} E_2^2 \quad \text{(SHG)} \\
P(\omega_1+\omega_2) &= 2\varepsilon_0 \chi^{(2)} E_1 E_2 \quad \text{(SFG)} \\
P(\omega_1-\omega_2) &= 2\varepsilon_0 \chi^{(2)} E_1 E_2^* \quad \text{(DFG)} \\
P(0) &= 2\varepsilon_0 \chi^{(2)} (E_1 E_1^* + E_2 E_2^*) E_1 E_2^* \quad \text{(OR)}
\end{aligned} \tag{6-22}$$

Here we have labeled each expression by the name of the physical process that it describes, such as second-harmonic generation (SHG), sum-frequency generation (SFG), difference-frequency generation (DFG), and optical rectification (OR). Note that, in accordance with our complex notation, there is also a response at the negative of each of the nonzero frequencies just given:

$$\begin{aligned}
P(-2\omega_1) &= \varepsilon_0 \chi^{(2)} E_1^{*2} & P(-2\omega_2) &= \varepsilon_0 \chi^{(2)} E_2^{*2} \\
P(-\omega_1-\omega_2) &= 2\varepsilon_0 \chi^{(2)} E_1^* E_2^* & P(\omega_2-\omega_1) &= 2\varepsilon_0 \chi^{(2)} E_2 E_1^*
\end{aligned} \tag{6-23}$$

However, since each of these quantities is simply the complex conjugate of one of the quantities given in Eq. (6-22), it is not necessary to take explicit account of both the positive and negative frequency components.

We see from Eq. (6-22) that four different nonzero frequency components are present in the nonlinear polarization. However, typically no more than one of these frequency components will be present with any appreciable intensity in the radiation generated by the nonlinear optical interaction. The reason for this behavior is that the nonlinear polarization can efficiently produce an output signal only if a certain phase-matching condition is satisfied, and usually this condition cannot be satisfied for more than one frequency component of the nonlinear polarization. Operationally, one often chooses which frequency component will be radiated by properly selecting the polarization of the input radiation and the orientation of the nonlinear crystal.

6.5.3 Sum-Frequency Generation

Let us now consider the process of sum-frequency generation, which is illustrated in Fig. 6-2. According to Eq. (6-22), the complex amplitude of the nonlinear polarization describing this process is given by the expression

$$P(\omega_1+\omega_2)=2\varepsilon_0\chi^{(2)}E_1E_2$$

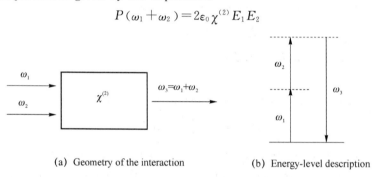

(a) Geometry of the interaction (b) Energy-level description

Fig. 6-2 Sum-frequency generation.

In many ways the process of sum-frequency generation is analogous to that of second-harmonic generation, except that in sum-frequency generation the two input waves are at different frequencies. *One application of sum-frequency generation is to produce tunable radiation in the ultraviolet spectral region by choosing one of the input waves to be the output of a fixed-frequency visible laser and the other to be the output of a frequency-tunable visible laser.*[6]

6.5.4 Difference-Frequency Generation

The process of difference-frequency generation is described by a nonlinear polarization of the form

$$P(\omega_1-\omega_2)=2\varepsilon_0\chi^{(2)}E_1E_2^*$$

and is illustrated in Fig. 2-3. Here the frequency of the generated wave is the difference of those of the applied fields. Difference-frequency generation can be used to produce tunable infrared radiation by mixing the output of a frequency-tunable visible laser with that of a fixed-frequency visible laser.

Superficially, difference-frequency generation and sum-frequency generation appear to be very similar processes. However, an important difference between the two processes can be deduced from the description of difference-frequency generation in terms of a photon energy-level diagram (part (b) of Fig. 6-3). We see that conservation of energy requires that for every photon that is created at the difference frequency $\omega_3 = \omega_1 - \omega_2$, a photon at the higher input frequency (ω_1) must be destroyed and a photon at the lower input frequency (ω_2) must be created. Thus, the lower frequency input field is amplified by the process of difference-frequency generation. For this reason, the process of difference-frequency generation is also known as optical parametric amplification. According to the photon energy-level description of difference-frequency generation, the atom first absorbs a photon of frequency ω_1 and jumps to the highest virtual level. This level decays by a two-photon emission process that is stimulated by the presence of the ω_2 field, which is already present. Two-photon emission can occur even if the ω_2 field is not applied. The generated fields in such a case are very much weaker, since they are created by spontaneous two-photon emission from a virtual level. This process is known as parametric fluorescence.

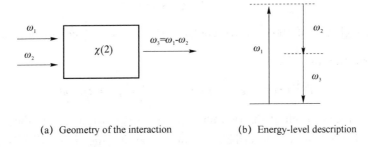

(a) Geometry of the interaction (b) Energy-level description

Fig. 6-3 Difference-frequency generation.

6.5.5 Optical Parametric Oscillation

We have just seen that in the process of difference-frequency generation the presence of radiation at frequency ω_2 or ω_3 can stimulate the emission of additional photons at these frequencies. If the nonlinear crystal used in this process is placed inside an optical resonator, as shown in Fig. 6-4, the ω_2 and/or ω_3 fields can build up to large values.

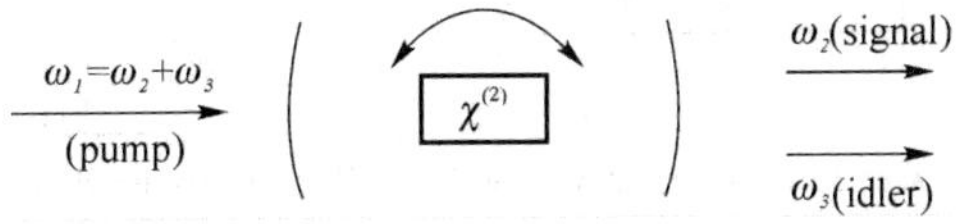

Fig. 6-4 The optical parametric oscillator. The cavity end mirrors have high reflectivities at frequencies ω_2 and/or ω_3. The output frequencies can be tuned by means of the orientation of the crystal.

Such a device is known as an optical parametric oscillator. Optical parametric oscillators are frequently used at infrared wavelengths, where other sources of tunable radiation are not readily available. Such a device is tunable because any frequency ω_2 that is smaller than ω_1 can satisfy the condition $\omega_2 + \omega_3 = \omega_1$ for some frequency ω_3. In practice, one controls the output frequency of an optical parametric oscillator by adjusting the phase-matching condition. The applied field frequency ω_1 is often called the pump frequency, the desired output frequency is called the signal frequency, and the other, unwanted, output frequency is called the idler frequency.

6.5.6 Third-Order Nonlinear Optical Processes

We next consider the third-order contribution to the nonlinear polarization

$$\widetilde{P}^{(3)}(t) = \varepsilon_0 \chi^{(3)} \widetilde{E}(t)^3 \qquad (6\text{-}24)$$

For the general case in which the field $\widetilde{E}(t)$ is made up of several different frequency components, the expression for $\widetilde{P}^{(3)}(t)$ is very complicated. For this reason, we first consider the simple case in which the applied field is monochromatic and is given by

$$\widetilde{E}(t) = \varepsilon \cos \omega t \qquad (6\text{-}25)$$

Then, through use of the identity $\cos^3 \omega t = \frac{1}{4} \cos 3\omega t + \frac{3}{4} \cos \omega t$, we can express the nonlinear polarization as

$$\widetilde{P}^{(3)}(t) = \frac{1}{4} \varepsilon_0 \chi^{(3)} \varepsilon^3 \cos 3\omega t + \frac{3}{4} \varepsilon_0 \chi^{(3)} \varepsilon^3 \cos \omega t \qquad (6\text{-}26)$$

The significance of each of the two terms in this expression is described briefly below. The first term in Eq. (6-26) describes a response at frequency 3ω that is created by an applied field at frequency ω. This term leads to the process of third-harmonic generation, which is illustrated in Fig. 6-5. According to the photon description of this process, shown in part (b) of the figure, three photons of frequency ω are destroyed and one photon of frequency 3ω is created in the microscopic description of this process.

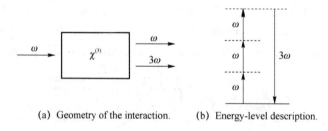

(a) Geometry of the interaction.　　(b) Energy-level description.

Fig. 6-5　Third-harmonic generation.

6.5.7 Intensity-Dependent Refractive Index

The second term in Eq. (6-26) describes a nonlinear contribution to the polarization at the frequency of the incident field; this term hence leads to a nonlinear contribution to the refractive index experienced by a wave at frequency ω. The refractive index in the presence of this type of nonlinearity can be represented as

$$n = n_0 + n_2 I \qquad (6\text{-}27)$$

where n_0 is the usual (i.e., linear or low-intensity) refractive index, where

$$n_2 = \frac{3}{2n_0^2 \varepsilon_0 c}\chi^{(3)} \qquad (6\text{-}28)$$

is an optical constant that characterizes the strength of the optical nonlinearity, and where $I = \frac{1}{2}n_0 \varepsilon_0 c \varepsilon^2$ is the intensity of the incident wave.

Self-Focusing is one of the processes that can occur as a result of the intensity dependent refractive index is self-focusing, which is illustrated in Fig. 6-6. This process can occur when a beam of light having a nonuniform transverse intensity distribution propagates through a material for which n_2 is positive. Under these conditions, the material effectively acts as a positive lens, which causes the rays to curve toward each other. This process is of great practical importance because the intensity at the focal spot of the self-focused beam is usually sufficiently high to lead to optical damage of the material.

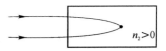

Fig. 6-6 Self-focusing of light.

6.5.8 Third-Order Interactions

Let us next examine the form of the nonlinear polarization

$$\tilde{P}^{(3)}(t) = \varepsilon_0 \chi^{(3)} \tilde{E}^3(t) \qquad (6\text{-}29)$$

induced by an applied field that consists of three frequency components:

$$\tilde{E}(t) = E_1 e^{-i\omega_1 t} + E_2 e^{-i\omega_2 t} + E_3 e^{-i\omega_3 t} + c.c. \qquad (6\text{-}30)$$

When we calculate $\tilde{E}^3(t)$, we find that the resulting expression contains 44 different frequency components, if we consider positive and negative frequencies to be distinct. Explicitly, these frequencies are

$\omega_1, \omega_2, \omega_3, 3\omega_1, 3\omega_2, 3\omega_3, (\omega_1+\omega_2+\omega_3), (\omega_1+\omega_2-\omega_3), (\omega_1+\omega_3-\omega_2), (\omega_2+\omega_3-\omega_1),$
$(2\omega_1 \pm \omega_2), (2\omega_1 \pm \omega_3), (2\omega_2 \pm \omega_1), (2\omega_2 \pm \omega_3), (2\omega_3 \pm \omega_1), (2\omega_3 \pm \omega_2)$ and the negative of each. Again representing the nonlinear polarization as

$$\tilde{P}^{(3)}(t) = \sum_n P(\omega_n) e^{-i\omega_n t} \qquad (6\text{-}31)$$

we can write the complex amplitudes of the nonlinear polarization for each of the positive frequencies as

$$P(\omega_1) = \varepsilon_0 \chi^{(3)} (3 E_1 E_1^* + 6 E_2 E_2^* + 6 E_3 E_3^*) E_1$$

$$P(\omega_2) = \varepsilon_0 \chi^{(3)} (6 E_1 E_1^* + 3 E_2 E_2^* + 6 E_3 E_3^*) E_2$$

$$P(\omega_3) = \varepsilon_0 \chi^{(3)} (6 E_1 E_1^* + 6 E_2 E_2^* + 3 E_3 E_3^*) E_3$$

$$P(3\omega_1) = \varepsilon_0 \chi^{(3)} E_1^3, \; P(3\omega_2) = \varepsilon_0 \chi^{(3)} E_2^3, \; P(3\omega_3) = \varepsilon_0 \chi^{(3)} E_3^3$$

$$P(\omega_1 + \omega_2 + \omega_3) = 6\varepsilon_0 \chi^{(3)} E_1 E_2 E_3$$

$$P(\omega_1 + \omega_2 - \omega_3) = 6\varepsilon_0 \chi^{(3)} E_1 E_2 E_3^*$$

$$P(\omega_1 + \omega_3 - \omega_2) = 6\varepsilon_0 \chi^{(3)} E_1 E_3 E_2^*$$

$$P(\omega_2+\omega_3-\omega_1)=6\varepsilon_0\chi^{(3)}E_2E_3E_1^*$$

$$P(2\omega_1+\omega_2)=3\varepsilon_0\chi^{(3)}E_1^2E_2, P(2\omega_1+\omega_3)=3\varepsilon_0\chi^{(3)}E_1^2E_3$$

$$P(2\omega_2+\omega_1)=3\varepsilon_0\chi^{(3)}E_2^2E_1, P(2\omega_2+\omega_3)=3\varepsilon_0\chi^{(3)}E_2^2E_3$$

$$P(2\omega_3+\omega_1)=3\varepsilon_0\chi^{(3)}E_3^2E_1, P(2\omega_3+\omega_2)=3\varepsilon_0\chi^{(3)}E_3^2E_2$$

$$P(2\omega_1-\omega_2)=3\varepsilon_0\chi^{(3)}E_1^2E_2^*, P(2\omega_1-\omega_3)=3\varepsilon_0\chi^{(3)}E_1^2E_3^*$$

$$P(2\omega_2-\omega_1)=3\varepsilon_0\chi^{(3)}E_2^2E_1^*, P(2\omega_2-\omega_3)=3\varepsilon_0\chi^{(3)}E_2^2E_3^*$$

$$P(2\omega_3-\omega_1)=3\varepsilon_0\chi^{(3)}E_3^2E_1^*, P(2\omega_3-\omega_2)=3\varepsilon_0\chi^{(3)}E_3^2E_2^* \quad (6\text{-}32)$$

We have displayed these expressions in complete detail because it is very instructive to study their form. In each case the frequency argument of P is equal to the sum of the frequencies associated with the field amplitudes appearing on the right-hand side of the equation, if we adopt the convention that a negative frequency is to be associated with a field amplitude that appears as a complex conjugate. Also, the numerical factor (1, 3, or 6) that appears in each term on the right-hand side of each equation is equal to the number of distinct permutations of the field frequencies that contribute to that term. Some of the nonlinear optical mixing processes described by Eq. (6-32) are illustrated in Fig. 6-7.

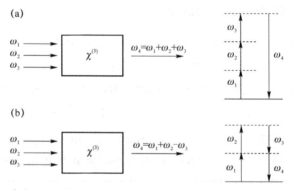

Fig. 6-7 Two of the possible mixing processes described by Eq. (6-32) that can occur when three input waves interact in a medium characterized by a $\chi^{(3)}$ susceptibility.

6.5.9 Parametric versus Nonparametric Processes

All of the processes described thus far in this chapter are examples of what are known as parametric processes. The origin of this terminology is obscure, but the word parametric has come to denote a process in which the initial and final quantum-mechanical states of the system are identical. Consequently, in a parametric process population can be removed from the ground state only for those brief intervals of time when it resides in a virtual level. According to the uncertainty principle, population can reside in a virtual level for a time interval of the order of $\hbar/\delta E$, where δE is the energy difference between the virtual level and the nearest real level. Conversely, processes that do involve the transfer of population from one real level to another are known as nonparametric processes. The processes that we describe in the remainder of the present section are all examples of nonparametric processes.

One difference between parametric and nonparametric processes is that parametric processes can always be described by a real susceptibility; conversely, nonparametric processes are described by a complex susceptibility by means of a procedure described in the following section. Another difference is that photon energy is always conserved in a parametric process; photon energy need not be conserved in a nonparametric process, because energy can be transferred to or from the material medium. For this reason, photon energy level diagrams of the sort shown in Figs. 6-1, 6-2, 6-3, 6-5, and 6-7 to describe parametric processes play a less definitive role in describing nonparametric processes.

As a simple example of the distinction between parametric and nonparametric processes, we consider the case of the usual (linear) index of refraction. The real part of the refractive index describes a response that occurs as a consequence of parametric processes, whereas the imaginary part occurs as a consequence of nonparametric processes. This conclusion holds because the imaginary part of the refractive index describes the absorption of radiation, which results from the transfer of population from the atomic ground state to an excited state.

6.5.10 Saturable Absorption

One example of a nonparametric nonlinear optical process is saturable absorption. Many material systems have the property that their absorption coefficient decreases when measured using high laser intensity. Often the dependence of the measured absorption coefficient α on the intensity I of the incident laser radiation is given by the expression

$$\alpha = \frac{\alpha_0}{1 + I/I_s} \tag{6-33}$$

where α_0 is the low-intensity absorption coefficient, and I_s is a parameter known as the saturation intensity.

One consequence of saturable absorption is optical bistability. One way of constructing a bistable optical device is to place a saturable absorber inside a Fabry—Perot resonator, as illustrated in Fig. 6-8. As the input intensity is increased, the field inside the cavity also increases, lowering the absorption that the field experiences and thus increasing the field intensity still further. If the intensity of the incident field is subsequently lowered, the field inside the cavity tends to remain large because the absorption of the material system has already been reduced. A plot of the input-versus-output characteristics thus looks qualitatively like that shown in Fig. 6-9. Note that over some range of input intensities more than one output intensity is possible.

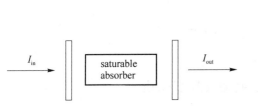

Fig. 6-8 Bistable optical device.

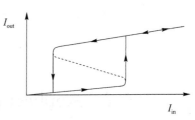

Fig. 6-9 Typical input-versus-output characteristics of a bistable optical device.

6.5.11 Two-Photon Absorption

In the process of two-photon absorption, which is illustrated in Fig. 6-10, an atom makes a transition from its ground state to an excited state by the simultaneous absorption of two laser photons. The absorption cross section σ describing this process increases linearly with laser intensity according to the relation

$$\sigma = \sigma^{(2)} I \qquad (6\text{-}34)$$

Fig. 6-10 Two-photon absorption.

where $\sigma^{(2)}$ is a coefficient that describes strength of the two-photon absorption process. (Recall that in conventional, linear optics the absorption cross section σ is a constant.) Consequently, the atomic transition rate R due to two-photon absorption scales as the square of the laser intensity. To justify this conclusion, we note that $R = \sigma I / \hbar \omega$, and consequently that

$$R = \frac{\sigma^{(2)} I^2}{\hbar \omega} \qquad (6\text{-}35)$$

Two-photon absorption is a useful spectroscopic tool for determining the positions of energy levels that are not connected to the atomic ground state by a one-photon transition.

6.5.12 Stimulated Raman Scattering

In stimulated Raman scattering, which is illustrated in Fig. 6-11, a photon of frequency ω is annihilated and a photon at the Stokes shifted frequency $\omega_s = \omega - \omega_v$ is created, leaving the molecule (or atom) in an excited state with energy $\hbar \omega_v$. The excitation energy is referred to as ω_v because stimulated Raman scattering was first studied in molecular systems, where $\hbar \omega_v$ corresponds to a vibrational energy. The efficiency of this process can be quite large, with often 10% or more of the power of the incident light being converted to the Stokes frequency. In contrast, the efficiency of normal or spontaneous Raman scattering is typically many orders of magnitude smaller.

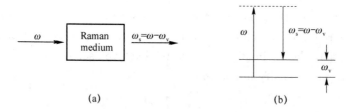

Fig. 6-11 Stimulated Raman scattering.

6.6 Application and Outlook

The field of nonlinear optics has grown enormously in recent years since its advent in the early 1960s, soon after the invention of the laser. Nowadays, nonlinear optics has evolved into many different branches, depending on the form of the material used for studying the nonlinear phenomena. The growth of research in nonlinear optics is closely linked to the rapid technological advances that have occurred in related fields, such as ultrafast phenomena, fiber optics, and optical communications. Nonlinear-optics activities range from the fundamental studies related to the interaction between matter and radiation to the development of the devices, components, and systems of tremendous commercial interest for widespread technologies such as optical telecommunications, medicine, and biology.

The application of nonlinear optics that has experienced the most dramatic technological development and economic impact in recent years is definitely related to the design of modern optical communication systems. On the one hand, the nonlinear response of optical fibers leads to impairments in the signal transmission quality in long-haul fiber-optics links. For example, the input power in a fiber is limited by the onset of stimulated Brillouin or Raman scattering. On the other hand, fiber nonlinearity can be exploited to advantage for counteracting the dispersive pulse broadening through the concept of optical solitons, or for compensating fiber losses through the use of stimulated Raman scattering. Currently, hot topics that are included in this issue include the interaction among solitons that belong to different wavelength-multiplexed channels, the coupling of nonlinearity, and polarization-mode dispersion, and the interplay between Raman scattering and solitons. Many designs about parametric and Raman-amplification techniques provide wide-band amplification in addition or as an alternative to the use of erbium-doped fiber amplifiers (EDFAs).

Since the nearly instantaneous response of optical fibers permitting single-channel bit rates as high as 1 Tbit/s, the present bottleneck to the channel capacity is set by the limited speed of electronics required for modulation and switching of the information. This issue motivates the research and development of nonlinear optical devices for all-optical data processing and wavelength conversion, such as supercontinuum generation in microstructure fibers, all-optical packet switching and nonlinear coupling in waveguides and resonators, signal processing and spatial soliton propagation in semiconductor microrings and in photorefractive materials. The availability of wavelength conversion functionality will be of great relevance in future all-optical networks. The conversion methods depend on the nonlinear optical material, range from second-harmonic generation (SHG) to quasi-phase matching in optical wave-guides to semiconductor optical amplifiers and highly nonlinear fibers.

The future always belongs to the younger generation. Since the field continues to attract bright students, it may be expected that unexpected new developments will occur. Generally, history is highly nonlinear, and the course of revolutions and the rise and fall of empires is difficult to predict. The future course of nonlinear optics is also unpredictable.

Future technological development should be based on current science. All-optical picosecond switching and quantum logic with entangled states has been demonstrated. Entangled states of two photons are produced, for example, by parametric down conversion of coherent beam or by entangled polarization of two photons emitted in an S-state to S-state transition. Entangled one photon—one atom states have been achieved by Haroche *et al* in 1999.

One may envision ultrafast optical supercomputers based on these developments. Two-dimensional (2-D) and three-dimensional (3-D) photonic bandgap materials may be helpful in the manipulation of light beams in all-optical or integrated optical-electronic switching devices.

Three-dimensional holographic information storage has been around for several decades but has yet to achieve large-scale applications. The optical storage of compact disks could be extended to several layers in the perpendicular direction. Fluorescence from centers activated by absorption of two photons from different beams or submicroscopic damage spots from strongly focused femtosecond pulses could, in principle, lead to high-density storage of bits of information.

In 1979, Tajima and Dawson proposed the acceleration of relativistic electrons in the wake field of space charges in the plasmas created by laser pulses with large spatial and temporal gradients. The technological development of powerful femtosecond pulse generators may lead to a new type of electron accelerator. Such devices would be much more compact and presumably cheaper than an extension of the current linear accelerator. High-power femtosecond laser pulses can propagate in the atmosphere over considerable distances. A computational model, which includes self-focusing, multi-photon ionization, the formation of plasma blobs with large spatial and temporal gradients, and the diffraction of light by these plasma blobs, describes the formation of a dynamic, turbulent light guide.

As to future science, our predictions are limited to extensions of currently active areas. Short X-ray pulses have already been obtained by femtosecond excitation of small targets. Perhaps attosecond spectroscopy will reveal the actual motion of electrons in atoms, molecules, and nanoparticles. Clearly, much more work remains to be done in the realm of relativistic plasmas at flux densities exceeding 10^{20} W/cm^2.

It is confirmed and accepted that the soliton communication system can carry the data for more than 40 Gbit/s and would be a realistic and efficient optical communication system in near future.

The field of nonlinear optics is alive and well and has grown much beyond our expectations of four or five decades ago. We believe it will continue to exceed my current expectations in the future.

References

1. M. Born and E. Wolf. Principles of Optics, 6th ed. Pergamon Oxford, 1980.
2. K. Sh. Ho, S. H. Liu, G. S. He. Physics of Nonlinear Optics. World Scientific Publishing Company, 2000.
3. R. W. Boyd. Nonlinear Optics. 3th ed. Academic Press, 2008.
4. S. X. Qian, R. Y. Zhu. Nonlinear Optics. Shanghai: Fudan University Press, 2005.

New Words and Expressions

1. nonlinear [ˈnɔnˈliniə] *adj.* 非线性的
2. tuned [tjuːnd] *adj.* 调谐的，已调谐的
3. femtosecond [ˈfemtəuˌsekənd] *n.* 飞秒(也叫毫微微秒，简称 fs，是标衡时间长短的一种计量单位。1 飞秒只有 1 秒的一千万亿分之一，即 10^{-15} 秒)
4. permittivity [ˌpəːmiˈtiviti] *n.* [电]介电常数；电容率
5. susceptibility [səˌseptəˈbiliti] *n.* 极化率；磁化系数
6. piezoelectric [paiˌiːzəuiˈlektrik] *adj.* 压电的
7. second-harmonic generation (SHG) 二次谐波产生；倍频(一种非线性的光学过程，过程中光子和一种非线性的材料相作用，然后生成具有两倍能量的新的光子，也叫 frequency doubling，因为光子的频率增加一倍，波长减小一半)
8. frequency mixing 混频(不同频率 ω_1、ω_2 的二束光或多束光在非线性介质中叠加，得到 $\omega_1+\omega_2$ 的和频光波或 $\omega_1-\omega_2$ 的差频光波，这种现象称光的混频，利用混频可以获得需要波长的相干光)
9. sum-frequency generation (SFG) 和频产生
10. difference-frequency generation (DFG) 差频产生
11. optical rectification 光学整流(E^2 项的存在将引起介质的恒定极化项，产生恒定的极化电荷和相应的电势差，电势差与光强成正比而与频率无关，类似于交流电经整流管整流后得到直流电压)
12. optical parametric amplification (OPA) 光参量放大(光参量放大过程是三波在非线性介质中的耦合作用，通常是将一个强的泵浦光和一个弱的信号光同时入射到非线性晶体中，在满足相位匹配条件时，它们相互耦合产生一个差频光(空闲光)，同时弱的信号光在此过程被放大，这就是所谓的光参量放大)
13. stimulated Raman scattering (SRS) 受激拉曼散射(普通光源产生的拉曼散射是自发拉曼散射，散射光是不相干的。当入射采用很强的激光时，由于激光辐射与物质分子的强烈作用，使散射过程具有受激辐射的性质，称受激拉曼散射。所产生的拉曼散射光具有很高的相干性，其强度也比自发拉曼散射光强得多。利用受激拉曼散射可获得多种新波长的相干辐射，并为深入研究强光与物质相互作用的规律提供手段)
14. stimulated Brillouin scattering (SBS) 受激布里渊散射，又称为声子散射(phonon scattering)(受激布里渊散射主要是由于入射光功率很高，由光波产生的电磁伸缩效应在物

质内激起超声波,入射光受超声波散射而产生的。散射光具有发散角小、线宽窄等受激发射的特性。也可以把这种受激散射过程看成光子场与声子场之间的相干散射过程。可以利用受激布里渊散射研究材料的声学特性和弹性力学特性)

15. hypersonic [ˌhaipə(ː)ˈsɔnik] adj. 极超音速的,远超过音速的
16. electrostriction [iˌlektrəuˈstrikʃən] n. 电致伸缩(在外电场作用下电介质所产生的与场强二次方成正比的应变,称为电致伸缩。这种效应是由电场中电介质的极化所引起,并可以发生在所有的电介质中。其特征是应变的正负与外电场方向无关)
17. photon echoes 光子回波
18. self-induced transparency 自感应透明(弱光下介质的吸收系数(见光的吸收)与光强无关,但对很强的激光,介质的吸收系数与光强有依赖关系,某些本来不透明的介质在强光作用下吸收系数会变为零,好像是透明的,这种现象就称为自感应透明)
19. optical nutation 光学章动(章动:地球天极就黄道极而言的小的周期性转动,在一定的条件下,体系在光场的作用下,体系的激发程度将会随时间作振荡,这种振荡行为称为光学章动。光学章动现象,是指以一个前沿上升时间极短的方形激光长脉冲入射到共振介质中,介质对入射光并不是简单地呈现出平稳吸收(吸收介质)或放大(增益介质),而是经历一段有限的弛豫振荡式的反应,而后才过渡到稳定的状态(设入射方脉冲激光持续时间足够长))
20. transient-response 瞬态响应
21. optical bistability (OBIS) 光学双稳态(光在二能级原子系统共振吸收时,出现两个稳定透射状态的光学现象。光学双稳器件有可能应用在高速光通信、光学图像处理、光存储、光学限幅器以及光学逻辑元件等方面)
22. soliton [ˈsɔlitən] n. 光弧子,孤立子,孤波(就是一种能在光纤中传播的长时间保持形态、幅度和速度不变的光脉冲。利用光弧子特性可以实现超长距离、超大容量的光通信)
23. squeezed state 压缩态
24. degenerate four-wave mixing (DFWM) 简并四波混频
25. coherent anti-Stokes Raman scattering (CARS) 相干反斯托克斯拉曼散射
26. stimulated electronic Raman scattering (SERS) 受激电子拉曼散射
27. self-phase modulation (SPM) 自相位调制
28. attosecond 原秒,阿秒
29. quantum well 量子阱
30. poynting's vector 坡印廷矢量
31. plasmon [ˈplæzˌmən] n. 等离振子;等离子体激元(即等离子体中各种形式的波的量子(可看成准粒子))
32. eigen function 本征函数

Notes

① 非线性光学是研究在光的作用下材料的光学特性发生改变的一门科学。
② 基于上述的比较,我们可以得出结论:常规光学的主要关注点是光的传播和光与物

质相互作用，这些来自于普通光源的光束强度如此低以至于用简单的线性近似就足以对相关的光学效应和光学现象给出很好的理论解释。

③ 受激布里渊散射已经成为产生或放大相干光的一种有效方法，这种方法频移小、稳定性高。

④ 提出了基于光子晶体光开关的设计和级联二阶过程与量子阱的组合并进行了实验研究。

⑤ 合体系状态的变化与分子体系从初始本征态到终态的跃迁和不同光子模之间光子数的变化有关。

⑥ 和频的一个应用就是在紫外光谱区产生可调谐的辐射，可通过频率固定以及频率可调的两个可见激光的输出来实现。

Integrated Circuit Fabrication

第7章

PREVIEW

Our world is full of integrated circuits (ICs). You can find many of them in computers. For example, most people have probably heard about the *microprocessor*[1]. The microprocessor is an integrated circuit that processes all information in the computer. It keeps track of what keys are pressed and if the mouse has been moved. It counts numbers and runs programs, games and the operating system. Integrated circuits are also found in almost every modern electrical device such as cars, television sets, CD players, mobile phones, *etc*.

IC technology is the enabling technology for a whole host of innovative devices and systems that have changed the way we live. ICs are much smaller and consume less power than the *discrete*[2] components used to build electronic systems. Integration allows us to build systems with many more transistors, allowing much more computing power to be applied to solve a problem. IC is also much easier to design and manufacture and is more reliable than discrete system; that makes it possible to develop systems that is more efficient than *general-purpose*[3] computers for the task at hand.

7.1 The Concept of Integrated Circuit

The integrated circuit is a direct result of the development of various processing techniques needed to fabricate the transistor and interconnect lines on the single chip (shown in Fig. 7-1). It is called an integrated circuit because the components, circuits, and base material are all made together, or integrated, out of a single piece of silicon, as opposed to a discrete circuit in which the components are made separately from different materials and assembled later. Although the function is similar to a circuit made with separate components, the internal structure of the components are different in an integrated circuit. The transistors, resistors, and capacitors are formed very small, and in high density on a foundation of silicon. They are formed by a variation of printing technology. ICs range in complexity from simple logic modules and amplifiers to complete microcomputers containing millions of elements.

Fig. 7-1　Photomicrographs of ICs.

In an integrated circuit, electronic components such as resistors, capacitors, diodes, and transistors are formed directly onto the surface of a silicon crystal. There are two kinds of component structures. *Passive*[4] components such as resistors and capacitors conduct electrical current regardless of how the component is connected. IC resistors are passive components. They can have unwanted resistance known as parasitic resistance. IC capacitor structures can also have unintentional capacitance.

Active[5] components, such as diodes and transistors can be used to control the direction of current flow.

The most important device for advanced integrated circuits is the MOSFET (metal-oxide-semiconductor field-effect transistor), which was reported by Kahng and ATalla in 1960. Although present-day MOSFETs have been scaled down to the *deep-submicron*[6] regime, the choice of silicon and thermally grown *silicon dioxide*[7] remains the most important combination of materials. The MOSFET and related integrated circuits now constitute about 90% of the semiconductor device market.

For many years, nMOS transistors have been the choice of most IC manufacturers. *Complementary-symmetry*[8] metal—oxide)—semiconductor (CMOS), with both nMOS and pMOS transistors in the same IC, has been the most popular device technology since the early 1980s.

7.2　History of Integrated Circuit

The first integrated circuits were created in the late 1950s in response to a demand from the military for miniaturized electronics to be used in missile control systems. At that time, transistors and printed circuit boards were the state-of-the-art electronic technology. Although transistors made many new electronic applications possible, engineers were still unable to make a small enough package for the large number of components and circuits required in complex devices like sophisticated control systems and handheld programmable calculators. Several companies were in competition to produce a breakthrough in miniaturized electronics. In September 1958, a *rudimentary*[9] integrated circuit fabricated in germanium was demonstrated by Jack Kilby of Texas Instruments. It contained one bipolar transistor, three resistors, and one capacitor, all made in germanium and connected by wire bonding: a hybrid circuit. At about the same time, *monolithic*[10] IC by fabricating all devices in a single semiconductor substrate and connecting the devices by aluminum metallization was made using a planar technology by Robert Noyce of Fairchild Semiconductor. The first monolithic IC of a flip-flop circuit contains six devices. The aluminum interconnection lines were obtained by etching evaporated aluminum layer over the entire oxide surface using the lithographic technique. In fact, when the integrated circuit was finally patented in 1959, the patent was awarded jointly to two individuals working separately at the two different companies. These inventions laid to foundation for the rapid growth of the microelectronics industry.

The first circuit used bipolar transistor. Practical Metal Oxide Semiconductor (MOS) transistors were then developed in the mid-1960s. The MOS technologies, especially CMOS, have become a major focus for IC design and development. Silicon is the main semiconductor material. Gallium arsenide and other compound semiconductors are used for applications requiring very high frequency devices and for optical devices.

Since the invention of the first IC in 1959, circuit design has become more sophisticated, and the integrated circuits become more complex. The number of components and circuits that could be incorporated into a single chip doubled every year for several years.

The first microcomputer chip, often called a microprocessor, was developed by Intel Corporation in 1969. It went into commercial production in 1971 as the Intel 4004. Intel 4004 was made by Hoff et al., who put the entire central processing unit (CPU) of a simple computer on one chip. It was a four-bit micro-processor, with a chip size of 3 mm by 4 mm, and it contained 2300 MOSFETs. It was fabricated by a p-channel *polysilicon*[11] gate process using an 8 μm design rule. This microprocessor performed as well as those in \$300 000 IBM computers of the early 1960s: each of which needed a CPU the size of a large desk. This was a major breakthrough for the semiconductor industry.

From then, Intel introduced their 8088 chip, 80286, 80386, and 80486 in succession. In the late 1980s and early 1990s, the designations 286, 386, and 486 were well known to computer users as reflecting increasing levels of computing power and speed. Intel's Pentium chip is the latest in this series and reflects an even higher level. The Intel released the Intel® Core™ 2 Quad processor contained 5.8 hundred million transistors and a 128 Gbit/s dynamic random access memory (DRAM) in 2009. Intel® Core™ 2 Quad processor is built on 45 nm Intel® Core™ microarchitecture enabling faster, cooler, and quieter desktop PC and workstation experiences.

Since the beginning of the microelectronics era, the smallest *linewidth*[12] (or the minimum feature length) of an integrated circuit has been reduced at a rate of about 13% per year. At this rate, the minimum feature length will shrink to about 25 nm in year 2015. Devices miniaturization results in reduced unit cost per circuit function.

7.3 Integrated Circuit Fabrication

Semiconductor device fabrication is the process used to create chips, the integrated circuits that are present in everyday electrical and electronic devices. It is a multiple-step sequence of photographic and chemical processing steps during which electronic circuits are gradually created on a *wafer*[13] made of pure semiconducting material. Silicon is the most commonly used semiconductor material today, along with various compound semiconductors.

The entire manufacturing process from start to packaged chips ready for shipment takes six to eight weeks and is performed in highly specialized facilities referred to as *fabs*[14].

As shown in Fig. 7-2, the fabrication of integrated circuits consists basically of the following five process steps:

(1) Wafer preparation: silicon is purified and prepared into wafers;

(2) Wafer fabrication: microchips are fabricated in a wafer fab by either a merchant chip supplier, captive chip producer or foundry;

(3) Wafer test: Each individual *die*[15] is probed and electrically tested to sort for good or bad chips;

(4) Assembly and packaging: Each individual die is assembled into its electronic package;

(5) Final test: Each packaged IC undergoes final electrical test.

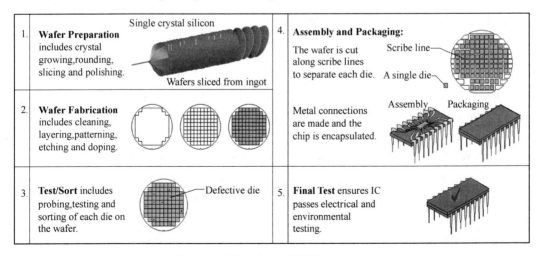

Fig. 7-2 The stages of IC fabrication.

7.3.1 Integrated Circuit Design

IC design is a subset of electrical engineering, encompassing the particular logic and circuit design techniques required to design ICs. ICs consist of miniaturized electronic components built into an electrical network on a monolithic semiconductor substrate by photolithography.

IC design can be divided into the broad categories of digital and analog IC design. Digital IC design is used to produce components such as microprocessors, FPGAs, memories (RAM, ROM, and flash) and digital *ASICs*[16]. Digital design focuses on logical correctness, maximizing circuit density, and placing circuits so that clock and timing signals are routed efficiently. Analog IC design also has specializations in power IC design and *RF*[17] IC design. Analog IC design is used in the design of op-amps, linear regulators, phase locked loops, *oscillators*[18] and active filters. Analog design is more concerned with the physics of the semiconductor devices such as gain, matching, power dissipation, and resistance. Fidelity of analog signal amplification and filtering is usually critical and as a result, analog ICs use larger area active devices than digital designs and are usually less dense in circuitry.

Some integrated circuits can be considered standard, off-the-shelf items. Once designed, there is no further design work required. Examples of standard ICs would include voltage regulators, amplifiers, analog switches, and analog-to-digital or digital-to-analog converters. These ICs are usually sold to other companies who incorporate them into printed circuit boards for various electronic products. Other integrated circuits are unique and require extensive design work. An example would be a new microprocessor for computers. This design work may require research and development of new materials and new manufacturing techniques to achieve the final design.

7.3.2 The Manufacturing Process

Today, planar technology is used extensively for IC fabrication. The manufacturing steps include oxidation, etching, photolithography, diffusion, ion implantation, and metallization. First we will introduce the substrate preparation.

1. Crystal Growth and Wafer Fabrication

Pure silicon is the basis for most integrated circuits. It provides the base, or substrate for the entire chip and is chemically doped to provide the N and P regions that make up the integrated circuit components. The starting materials, silicon dioxide for a silicon wafer are chemically processed to form a high purity polycrystalline semiconductor from which single crystals are grown. The single-crystal *ingots*[19] are shaped to define the diameter of material and are sawed into wafers. These wafers are etched and polished to provide smooth surface upon which devices will be made. The basic technique for silicon crystal growth from the melt, which is material in liquid form, is the *Czochralski*[20] technique. A substantial percentage (>90%) of silicon crystals for the semiconductor industry are prepared by the Czochralski technique, and so is virtually all the silicon used for fabricating integrated circuit.

The starting material for silicon is a relatively pure form of sand called quartzite. This is placed in a furnace with various forms of carbon. Although a number of reactions take place in the furnace, the overall reaction is

$$SiC + SiO_2 \rightarrow Si + SiO \uparrow + CO \uparrow \qquad (7\text{-}1)$$

This process produces metallurgical-grade silicon with a purity of about 98%. Next, the silicon is pulverized and treated with hydrogen chloride (HCl) at 300 ℃ to form *trichlorosilane*[21].

$$Si + 3HCl \rightarrow SiHCl_3 \uparrow + H_2 \uparrow \qquad (7\text{-}2)$$

The trichlorosilane is a liquid at room temperature. Fractional distillation of the liquid removes the unwanted impurities. The purified $SiHCl_3$ is then used in a hydrogen reduction reaction to prepare the *electronic-grade silicon* (EGS) [22]:

$$SiHCl_3 + H_2 \rightarrow Si + 3HCl \uparrow \qquad (7\text{-}3)$$

This reaction takes place in a reactor containing a resistance-heated silicon rod, which serves as the nucleation point for the deposition of silicon. EGS, a polycrystalline material of high purity, is the raw material used to prepare device-quality, single-crystal silicon. Pure EGS generally has only a few parts per million of impurities.

The Czochralski technique uses an apparatus called a *crystal puller*[23]. A simplified version of this device is shown in Fig. 7-3. The puller has three main components: (a) a furnace, which includes a fused-silicon crucible, a graphite susceptor, a rotation mechanism, a heating element, and a power supply; (b) a crystal-pulling mechanism, which include a seed holder and a rotation mechanism; (c) an ambient control, which includes a gas source, a flow control, and an exhaust system. In addition, the puller has an overall microprocessor-based control system to control process parameters such as temperature, crystal diameter, pull rate, and rotation speeds, as well as to permit programmed process steps. Various sensors and feedback loops allow the control system to respond automatically, reducing operator intervention.

In the crystal-growing process, EGS is placed in the crucible, and furnace is heated above the melting temperature of silicon. A suitably oriented seed crystal is suspended over the crucible in a seed holder. The seed is inserted into he melt. Part of it melts, but the tip of the remaining seed crystal still touches the liquid surface. It is then slowly withdrawn. Progressive freezing at the solid-liquid interface yields a large, single crystal. A typical pull rate is a few millimeters per minute. For large-diameter silicon ingots, an external magnetic field is applied to the basic Czochralski puller. The purpose of the external magnetic field is to control the concentration of defects, impurities, and oxygen.

In crystal growth, a known amount of dopant is added to the melt to obtain the desired doping concentration in the grown crystal. Dopant impurity atoms such as boron or phosphorus can be added to the molten intrinsic silicon in precise amounts in order to dope the silicon, thus changing it into n-type or p-type extrinsic silicon.

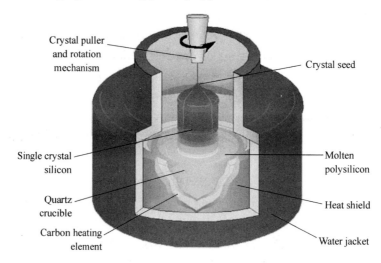

Fig. 7-3 Basic Czochralski (CZ) crystal growing apparatus.

As a crystal is pulled from the melt, the doping concentration incorporated into the crystal (solid) is usually different from the doping concentration of the melt (liquid) at the interface. The ratio of these two concentrations is defined as the *equilibrium segregation coefficient*[24], k_0:

$$k_0 = \frac{C_s}{C_l} \tag{7-4}$$

where C_s and C_l are, respectively, the equilibrium concentrations of the dopant in the solid and liquid near the interface. For the commonly used *dopants*[25] for silicon, the values of k_0 are below 1, which means that during growth the dopants are rejected into the melt. Consequently, the melt becomes progressively enriched with the dopants as the crystal grows.

The typical stages of wafer fabrication are shown in Fig. 7-4. *After a crystal is grown, the first shaping operation is to remove the seed and the other end of the ingot, which is last to solidify. The next operation is to grind the surface so that the diameter of the material is defined. After that, one or more flat regions are ground along the length of ingot. These regions, or flats, mark the specific crystal orientation of the ingot and the conductivity type of the material. The largest flat, the primary flat, allows a mechanical locator in automatic processing equipment to position the wafer and to orient the devices relative to the crystal. Other smaller flats, called secondary flats, are ground to identify the orientation and conductivity type of the crystal.*①

The ingot is then ready to be sliced by diamond saw into wafers. Slicing determines four wafer parameters: surface orientation (e.g., <111> or <100>); thickness (e.g., 0.5~0.7 mm, depending on wafer diameter); taper, which are the wafer thickness variations from one end to another; and bow, which is the surface curvature of the wafer, measured from the center of the wafer to its edge.

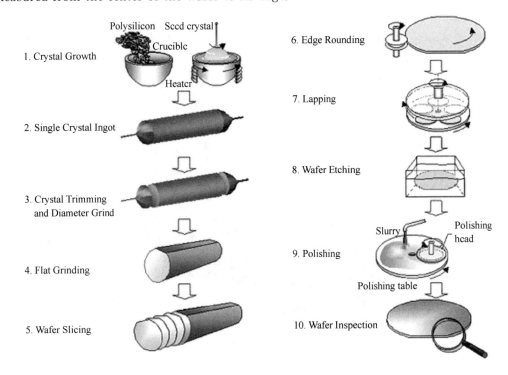

Fig. 7-4 The stages of wafer fabrication.

After slicing, both sides of the wafer are lapped using a mixture of Al_2O_3 and *glycerine*[26] to produce a typical flatness uniformity within 2 μm. The lapping operation usually leaves the surface and edges of the wafer damaged and contaminated. The damaged and contaminated regions can be removed by chemical etching. The next step of wafer shaping is polishing. Its purpose is to provide a smooth surface where device features can be defined by photolithographic process. The final steps are wafer evaluation and packaging.

A real crystal (such as a silicon wafer) differs from the ideal crystal in important ways. It is finite; thus, surface atoms are incompletely bonded. Furthermore, it has defects, which strongly influence the electrical, mechanical, and optical properties of the semiconductor. There are four categories of defects: point defects, line defects, area defects, and volume defects.

Modern semiconductor manufacturing is performed in a *clean room*[27] (Fig. 7-5), isolated from the outside environment and contaminants.

The need for such a clean room arises because dust particles in the air can settle on semiconductor wafers and lithographic masks and can cause defects in the devices, which result in circuit failure. For example, a dust particle on a semiconductor surface can disrupt the single-crystal growth of an *epitaxial*[28] film, causing the formation of dislocations. A dust particle incorporated into the gate oxide can result in enhanced conductivity and cause device failure due to low breakdown voltage. The situation is even more critical in the lithographic area. When dust particles adhere to the surface of a *photomask*[29], they behave as opaque patterns on the mask. And these patterns will be transferred to the underlying layer along with the circuit patterns on the mask.

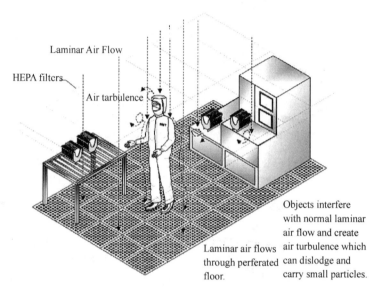

Fig. 7-5 Contamination control in wafer fabs.

In a clean room, the total number of dust particles per unit volume must be tightly controlled, along with the temperature and humidity. Because the number of dust particle increases as particle size decreases, a more stringent control of the clean room environment is required when the minimum feature lengths of ICs are reduced to the deep submicron range.

2. Photolithography

Photolithography is the process of transferring patterns of geometric shapes on a mask to a thin layer of photosensitive material (called photoresist[30]*) covering the surface of a semiconductor wafer. These patterns define the various regions in an integrated circuit, such as the implantation regions, the contact windows, and the bonding-pad areas. The resist patterns defined by the photolithography process are not permanent elements of the final device, but only replicas of circuit features. To produce circuit features, these resist patterns must be transferred once more into the underlying layers comprising the device. Pattern transfer is accomplished by an etching process that selectively removes unmasked portions of a layer.*②

The vast majority of lithographic equipment for IC fabrication is optical equipment using *ultraviolet*[31] light (wavelength = 0.2~0.4 μm). This section considers the exposure tools, masks and resist for optical lithography. It also considers the pattern transfer process, which serves as a basis for other lithographic systems.

(1) Exposure Tools

The pattern transfer process is accomplished by using a lithographic exposure tool. The performance of an exposure tool is determined by three parameters: resolution, registration, and throughput. Resolution is the minimum feature dimension that can be transferred with high fidelity to a resist film on a semiconductor wafer. Registration is a measure of how accurately patterns on successive masks can be aligned with respect to previously defined patterns on the wafer. Throughput is the number of wafers that can be exposed per hour for a given mask level.

(2) Masks

Masks used for IC manufacturing are usually reduction *reticles*[32]. The first step in mask making is to use a computer-aided design (CAD) system in which designers can completely describe the circuit patterns electrically. The digital data produced by the CAD system then drives a pattern generator, which is an electron beam lithographic system that transfers the patterns directly to electron-sensitized mask. The mask consists of a fused-silica substrate covered with a chromium layer. The circuit pattern is first transferred to the electron sensitized layer, which is transferred once more into the underlying chromium layer for the finished mask.

The patterns on a mask represent one level of an IC design. The composite layout is broken into mask levels that correspond to the IC process sequence, such as the isolation region on one level, the gate region on another, and so on. Typically, 15 to 20 different mask levels are required for a complete IC process cycle.

One of the major concerns about masks is defect density. Mask defects can be introduced during the manufacture of the mask or during subsequent lithographic processes. Even a small mask-defect density has a profound effect on the final IC yield. Yield is defined as the ratio of good chips per wafer to the total number of chips per wafer. As a first-order approximation, the yield Y for a given masking level can be expressed as

$$Y \cong e^{-D_0 A_0} \tag{7-5}$$

where D_0 is the average number of "fatal" defects per unit area, and A_0 is the defect-sensitive area (or "critical area") of the IC chip. If D_0 remains the same for all mask levels, then the final yield becomes

$$Y \equiv e^{-ND_0 A_0} \tag{7-6}$$

(3) Photoresist

Photoresist is a radiation-sensitive compound that can be classified as *positive*[33] or *negative*[34], depending on how it responds to radiation. For positive resists, the exposed regions become more soluble and are thus more easily removed in the *development*[35] process. The result is that the patterns formed in the positive resist are the same as those on the mask. For negative resists, the exposed regions become less soluble, and the patterns formed in the negative resist are the reverse of the mask patterns.

Positive photoresists consist of three components: a photosensitive compound, a base resin, and an organic solvent. Prior to exposure, the photosensitive compound is insoluble in the developer solution. After exposure, the photosensitive compound absorbs radiation in the exposed pattern areas, changes its chemical structure, and becomes soluble in the developer solution. After development, the exposed areas are removed.

Negative photoresists are polymers combined with a photosensitive compound. After exposure, the photosensitive compound absorbs the optical energy and converts it into chemical energy to initiate a polymer cross-linking reaction. This reaction causes cross linking of the polymer molecules. The cross-linked polymer has a higher molecular weight and becomes insoluble in the developer solution. After development, the unexposed areas are removed. One major drawback of a negative photoresist is that in the development process, the whole resist mass swells by absorbing developer solvent. This swelling action limits the resolution of negative photoresist.

(4) Pattern Transfer

Photolithography produces three-*dimensional*[36] patterns on the wafer surface using a photoresist and exposure to light. Currently, photolithography is based on optical lithography. Negative lithography uses negative resists, where the image in the resist is the negative of the pattern found on the reticle. Positive lithography uses positive resist, where the image formed in the resist is the same pattern formed in the reticle. Advanced lithography in sub-micron wafer fabs is done primarily with positive resist.

From Fig. 7-6, we can see that modern photolithography consists of an ultraviolet light source, optical system, a reticle with a die pattern, an alignment system, and a wafer covered with a light-sensitive photoresist.

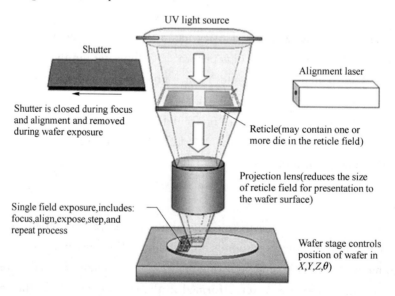

Fig. 7-6 Lithography process from mask design to wafer printing.

Wafer steppers and step-and-scan systems have three basic purposes: ① focus and align the wafer to the reticle, ② reproduce a reticle image on the wafer through exposure of the resist, and ③ meet wafer throughput objectives. A general trend is the shorter the wavelength of the exposing light, the better resolution of the feature.

There are four steps of photolithography showed as follows:

① Post-Exposure Bake: A thermal post-exposure bake (PEB) is done for all chemically amplified deep UV resists to cause an acid-catalyzed reaction. This reaction makes the exposed resist soluble in the developer solution. The PEB is also done for i-line resists to reduce the standing waves effect.

② Develop: Photoresist development uses a liquid chemical developer to dissolve the soluble regions of the resist. Minimal chemical reaction is required for negative resist development. Positive resist development involves chemical reaction. The most common developer today for positive-tone i-line resist is TMAH. Standard TMAH developer formulations are common in the industry. The most common development techniques are continuous spray and puddle. Critical parameters for development are temperature, time, volume, wafer chuck, normality, rinse and exhaust flow.

③ Hard Bake: A post-development thermal hard bake is done to evaporate any residual solvent and to harden the resist.

④ Develop Inspect: A post-development inspection is done to find defects in the resist prior to the following operation (etch or ion implant).

(5) Next-generation lithographic methods

Subwavelength[37] lithography is a recent trend where the patterned images have critical dimensions that are significantly less than the exposure wavelength (e. g., a 248 nm exposure wavelength is used to pattern a 0.18 micron CD on the wafer surface).

Next generation lithography is divided into four main research areas:

① Extreme UV (EUV): Extreme UV employs optical lithography with a laser-produced plasma source to produce UV wavelengths of about 13 nm. There are many challenges to bring EUV into production.

② Scattering with Angular Limitation Projection Electron Beam Lithography (SCALPEL): SCALPEL uses an established electron beam source to image a wafer pattern. This technology uses a 4X mask and does not require expensive optics.

③ Ion projection lithography (IPL): Ion projection lithography (IPL) uses ion beams to expose resists, either through a mask or by serially writing on the resist. Very high resolution is achievable.

④ X-ray: X-ray lithography is an established technology for patterning, used by one major IC manufacturer to produce microprocessors on 200 mm wafers in the 1990s. The short X-ray wavelengths (down to 10 nm) produce high resolution, but the required mask is difficult to build.

The lithographic methods discussed above have 100 nm or better resolution. Each method has its limitations: the diffraction effect in optical lithography, the proximity effect in electron beam lithography. Mask fabrication complexities in X-ray lithography, difficulty in mask blank production for EUV lithography, and stochastic space charge in ion beam lithography.

For IC fabrication, many mask levels are involved. However, it is not necessary to use the same lithographic method for all levels. A mix-and-match approach can take advantage of the unique features of each lithographic process to improve resolution and to maximize throughput. For example, a 4:1 EUV method can be used for the most critical mask levels, whereas a 4:1 or 5:1 optical system can be used for the rest.

Currently, the vast majority of lithographic equipment is optical systems. The primary factor limiting resolution in optical lithography is diffraction. However, because of advancements in excimer lasers and photoresist chemistry, optical lithography will remain the mainstream technology, at least to the 100 nm generation.

At the present time, no obvious successor to optical lithography can be identified unambiguously. However, a mix-and-match approach can take advantage of the unique features of each lithography process to improve resolution and to maximize throughput.

3. Oxidation

Many different kinds of thin films are used to fabricate integrated circuits, including thermal oxides, dielectric layers, polycrystalline silicon and metal films. For MOSFET, the first important thin film from the thermal oxide group is the gate oxide layer, under which a conducting channel can be formed between the source and the drain. A related layer is the field oxide, which provides isolation from other device. Both gate and field oxide generally are grown by a thermal oxidation process because only thermal oxidation can provide the highest-quality oxides having the lowest interface trap densities. Semiconductors can be oxidized by various methods, such as thermal oxidation, electrochemical anodization, and plasma-enhanced chemical vapor deposition (PECVD), but thermal oxidation is by far the most important for silicon devices. It is a key process in modern silicon IC technology.

Thermal oxide is grown by a chemical reaction between silicon and oxygen. This is done with dry oxidation or wet oxidation. The following chemical reactions describe the thermal oxidation of silicon in oxygen (dry oxidation) or water vapor (wet oxidation):

$$Si + O_2 \rightarrow SiO_2 \qquad (7\text{-}7)$$

$$Si + 2H_2O(gas) \rightarrow SiO_2 + 2H_2 \uparrow \qquad (7\text{-}8)$$

Oxides used for masking are usually grown by wet oxidation. A typical growth cycle consists of a sequence of dry-wet-dry oxidations. Most of the growth in such a sequence occurs in the wet phase, since the SiO_2 growth rate is much higher when water is used as the oxidant. Dry oxidation, however, results in a higher-quality oxide that is dense and has a higher breakdown voltage. It is for these reasons that the shin gate oxides in MOS device are usually formed using dry oxidation.

The process of thermal oxidation is shown in Fig. 7-7. Silicon dioxide grows by consuming silicon. The thickness of silicon consumed is 0.46 of the total oxide thickness. The growth of the oxidation layer is controlled and limited by the movement of oxygen through the oxide at the oxide-silicon interface. This oxide-silicon interface has an incomplete oxidation of silicon that causes an undesirable charge build-up that must be controlled. Use of a chlorine-containing gas during the oxidation process can neutralize the charge accumulation at the interface.

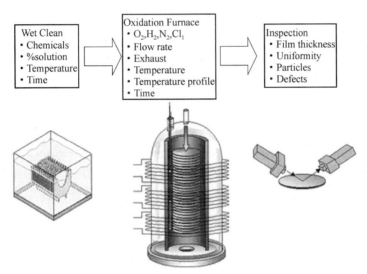

Fig. 7-7 The oxidation of silicon.

Factors that affect oxide growth are: heavily doped silicon has increased oxidation, the (111) crystal oxidizes faster in the linear stage than the (100) crystal, increased pressure causes increased growth, and plasma can enhance oxidation.

Silicon dioxide is a high-quality insulator that can be thermally grown on silicon wafers. It can also serve as a barrier layer during impurity diffusion or implantation, and it is a key component of MOS devices in a circuit. These factors have contributed significantly to silicon's current status as the dominant semiconductor material in use today.

4. Deposition

A thin film is a thin, solid layer of a material created on a substrate. Some properties of an acceptable thin film for wafer fabrication are good step coverage, ability to fill high aspect ratio gaps, good thickness uniformity, high purity and density, excellent adhesion. Film deposition is generally categorized as a chemical process (chemical vapor deposition or plating) or a physical process (sputtering, evaporation or spin-on methods).

Chemical vapor deposition (CVD) is also known as vapor-phase epitaxy (VPE). CVD is a process whereby an epitaxial layer is formed by a chemical reaction between gaseous compound. All material for the thin film is supplied by an external source. CVD reactors can be generally classified as atmospheric pressure CVD (APCVD), low pressure CVD (LPCVD) or plasma-assisted CVD. The plasma-assisted CVD is either plasma-enhanced CVD (PECVD) or high-density plasma CVD (HDPCVD).

The first type of CVD reactor used in the semiconductor industry was atmospheric pressure CVD (APCVD). APCVD generally operates in the mass-transport limited regime, which requires a system design for optimal reactant gas flow to every wafer. An example of an APCVD deposition with *TEOS-ozone*[38] application is SiO_2 deposition with TEOS-ozone.

A common CVD reactor is low pressure CVD (LPCVD). This reactor operates in the reaction-rate limited regime. An LPCVD reactor is often hot-wall, which leads to particle deposits on the reactor wall. This requires frequent reactor cleaning. Examples of LPCVD applications are the deposition of SiO_2 and doped polysilicon. For the deposition of SiO_2:

$$SiH_4 + O_2 \xrightarrow{450\ ^\circ C} SiO_2 + 2H_2 \uparrow \qquad (7\text{-}9)$$

*CVD silicon dioxide cannot replace thermally grown oxides, because the best electrical properties are obtained with thermally grown films. CVD oxides are used instead to complement thermal oxides. A layer of undoped silicon dioxide is used to insulate multilevel metallization, to mask ion implantation and diffusion, and to increase the thickness of thermally grown field oxides.*③

Plasma-assisted CVD equipment relies on plasma energy. The two types of plasma processes in CVD are plasma-enhanced CVD (PECVD, shown in Fig. 7-8) and high-density plasma CVD (HDPCVD). For fine-geometry devices, HDPCVD is used because of its superior gap-fill properties.

5. Metallization

Wafer metallization is the deposition of a thin film of conductive metal onto the wafer surface. Requirements for a successful metal material are: ①high conductivity, ②good adhesion, ③ readily deposited, ④ high-resolution patterning and planarization, ⑤reliability, ⑥resistance to corrosion and ⑦resistance to mechanical stress.

Metals and metal *alloys*[39] used in wafer fabrication are: aluminum, aluminum-copper alloys, copper, barrier metals, silicides and metal plugs. Aluminum is the traditional interconnect metal. Aluminum-copper alloys are used to reduce electromigration. Copper is the ideal interconnect metal. Its benefits are: ①reduction in resistivity, ②reduction in power consumption, ③tighter packing density, ④superior resistance to electromigration and ⑤fewer process steps. A barrier metal is a thin layer of deposited metal that prevents intermixing of the materials above and below the barrier. Refractory metals react with silicon to form a silicide. A silicide is a metal compound that is thermally stable and has low electrical resistivity at the silicon/refractory metal interface. A silicide structure (self-aligned silicide) attains properly aligned source, drain and polysilicon gate in transistors. Metal plugs fill the via connections between two conductive layers.

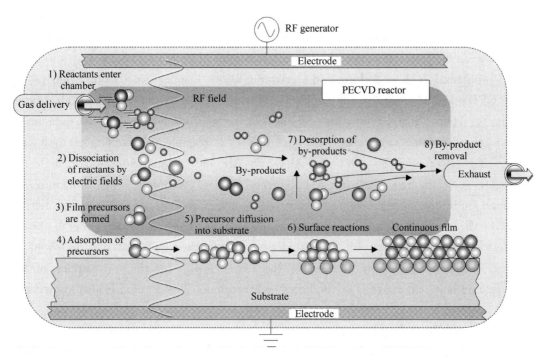

Fig. 7-8 Schematic of CVD transport and reaction steps.

Evaporation occurs when a source material is heated above its melting point in an evacuated chamber. The evaporated atoms then travel at high velocity in straight-line trajectories. The source can be melted by resistance heating, by RF heating, or with a focused electron beam.

Fig. 7-9 shows the traditional (aluminum) metallization and the new dual damascene (copper) metallization processes.

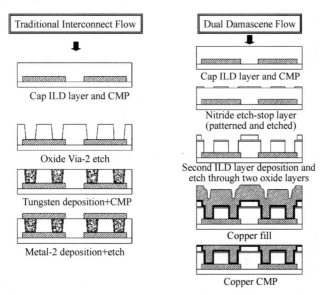

Fig. 7-9 Traditional (aluminum) metallization and the new dual damascene (copper) metallization.

The Al film can be deposited by PVD or CVD. Since aluminum and its alloys have low resistivities, these metal satisfy the low resistance requirements. Aluminum also adheres well to silicon dioxide. However, the use of aluminum in IC with shallow junctions often creates problems, such as spiking and electromigration. Copper can also be deposited by PVD, CVD, and electrochemical methods. However, the use of Cu as an alternative material to Al in ULSI circuits has drawbacks, such as its tendency to corrode under standard chip manufacturing conditions, its lack of a feasible dry etching method or a stable self-passivating oxide similar to Al_2O_3 on Al, and its poor adhesion to dielectric materials, such as SiO_2 and low-k polymers. Several techniques for fabrication of multilevel Cu interconnects have been reported. The first method is a conventional method to pattern the metal lines, followed by electric deposition. The second method is to pattern the dielectric layer first and fill copper metal into trenches. This step is followed by chemical mechanical polishing to remove the excess metal on the top surface of the dielectric and leave Cu material in the holes and trenches. This method is also known as a damascene process.

For the dual damascene process, the vias and trenches in the dielectric are defined using two lithography and reactive ion etching (RIE) steps before depositing the Cu metal. Then a Cu chemical mechanical polishing process is used to remove the excess metal on the top surface, leaving the planarized wiring and via imbedded in the insulation. One special benefit of the dual damascene technique is that the via plug is now of the same material as the metal line and the risk of via electromigration failure is reduced.

6. Etching

As discussed above, lithography is the process of transferring patterns to photoresist covering the surface of a semiconductor wafer. To produce circuit features, these resist patterns must be transferred into the underlying layers comprising the devices. The pattern transfer is accomplished by an etching process that selectively removes unmasked portions of a layer.

Etching is the process of selectively removing unneeded material from the wafer surface, using either chemical or physical means. Dry etching exposes the wafer to a plasma that interacts physically or chemically (or both) to remove the surface material. Wet etching uses liquid chemicals to chemically remove the wafer surface material.

Dry etching is the primary etching method in advanced wafer fabrication. The etching profile is anisotropic with good control. The main disadvantage to dry etching is poor selectivity to the underlying layer, which requires effective endpoint control.

Three main dry etching applications are: ①dielectric, ②silicon, and ③metal.

Oxide is a common dielectric dry etching application, and is typically based on *fluorocarbon*[40] chemistry. High selectivity is required for the underlying material. Silicon dry etching is commonly done for polysilicon gate formation or silicon trench etching (for device isolation or capacitors structures). Silicon etching chemistry has traditionally been fluorine-based, but this has changed due to poor selectivity. Chlorine or bromine are common silicon etching chemistries today. Metal dry etching is done for aluminum alloy etching for interconnect wiring. A chlorine-based etching chemistry is often used. Tungsten metal is also dry etched.

Wet etching has been largely replaced by dry etching. Wet chemical strips are still used to remove layers, such as photoresist or a silicon nitride mask. Wet etching is particularly suitable for blanket etching.

The challenges for future etching technology are high etching selectivity, better dimensioned control, low aspect ratio-dependent etching, and low plasma-induced damage. Low-pressure, high density plasma reactors are necessary to meet requirements. As processing evolves from 200 mm to 300 mm and even large diameter wafers, continued improvements are required for etching uniformity across the wafer.

7. Impurity Doping

Impurity doping is the introduction of controlled amounts of impurity dopants into semiconductors. The practical use of impurity doping mainly has been to change the electrical properties of the semiconductor material.

The early doping method was thermal diffusion. In this method the dopant atoms are placed on or near the surface of the wafer by deposition from the gas phase of dopant or by using doped oxide sources. The doping concentration decreases monotonically from the surface, and the profile of the dopant distribution is determined mainly by the temperature and diffusion time.

Diffusion of impurities is typically done by placing semiconductor wafers in a carefully controlled, high-temperature quartz-tube furnace and passing a gas mixture that contains the desired dopant through it. The temperature usually ranges between 800 ℃ and 1 200 ℃ for silicon. The number of dopant atoms that diffuse into the semiconductor is related to the partial pressure of the dopant impurity in the gas mixture.

For diffusion in silicon, boron is the most popular dopant for introducing a p-type impurity, whereas arsenic and phosphorus are used extensively as n-type dopants. These three elements are highly soluble in silicon. These dopants can be introduced in several ways, including solid sources, liquid sources and gaseous sources. However, liquid sources are most commonly used. An example of the chemical reaction for phosphorus diffusion using a liquid source is:

$$4POCl_3 + 3O_2 \rightarrow 2P_2O_5 + 6Cl_2 \uparrow \tag{7-10}$$

The P_2O_5 forms a glass-on-silicon wafer and is then reduced to phosphorus by silicon,

$$2P_2O_5 + 5Si \rightarrow 4P + 5SiO_2 \tag{7-11}$$

The phosphorus is released and diffuses into the silicon, and Cl_2 is vented.

There are also some doping processes in the wafer fab. The control of the dopant profile in the doped region requires the control of both depth and concentration, which is best achieved with ion implantation.

Ion implantation is a physical process. It is preferred over diffusion because of its excellent control over doping concentration and depth. An ion implanter creates positively-charged ions that are formed into a beam, accelerated in a voltage field, and implanted into the wafer. The important ion implant parameters are dose and range. Dose (Q) is the number of implanted ions per unit area of wafer surface, with units of atoms/cm^2. Range is the total distance an ion travels in the silicon during ion implantation. The beam current is a key variable for defining the quantity (or dose) of ions implanted. The implanter energy is the key variable for defining the ion implant depth (range).

8. Electrical Testing

Manufacturing is defined as the process by which raw materials are converted into finished products. *However, before finished ICs can be put to their intended use in various commercial electronic systems and products, several other key processes must take place. These include electrical testing and packaging. Testing is necessary to yield high-quality products. Quality requires conformance of all products to a set of specifications and the reduction of specifications and the reduction of any variability in the manufacturing process. Maintaining quality often involves the use of statistical process control. A designed experiment is an extremely useful tool for discovering key variables that influence quality characteristics. Statistical experimental design is a powerful approach for systematically varying controllable process conditions and determining their impact on output parameters that measure quality.*①

Electrical test is the measurement of electrical parameters on ICs at the wafer level to verify conformance to specifications. There are five different electrical tests:

① IC design verification,

② in-line parametric test (also known as wafer electrical test, or WET),

③ wafer sort (probe),

④ burn-in reliability,

⑤ final test.

Tests number 2 & 3 are wafer-level electrical tests.

The in-line parametric test (also known as a DC test) is performed early in the process, usually after the first metal layer has been deposited and etched. A parametric test is done on test structures located on the wafer. This test will identify process problems, establish wafer pass/fail criteria, collect data, assess special tests and obtain wafer level reliability data.

In-line parametric tests are usually done on test structures, also known as process control monitors (PCMs). Test structures are commonly located in the scribe line region and are used to test a wide range of parameters (e.g., leakage current, critical dimensions, threshold voltage, resistance, *etc.*).

In-line parametric data is collected on a sample basis and interpreted by engineers to improve the fab process. An assessment of wafer level reliability can also be done to predict device quality.

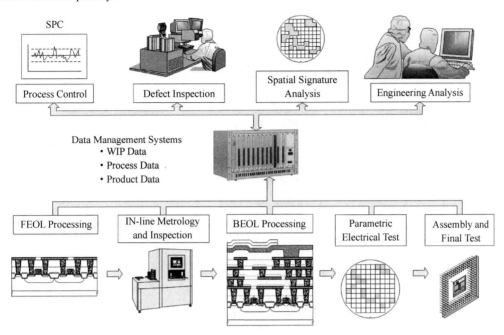

Fig. 7-10 Yield management in a wafer fab.

The four test subsystems for in-line parametric testers are: probe card interface, wafer positioning, tester instrumentation and a computer for system control. Probe card interfaces between the tester and the device under test (DUT). The wafer positioning system (prober) aligns the wafer for contact with the probe card. The instrumentation in automated test equipment (ATE) measures *sub-picoamp*[41] current and picofarad-level capacitance.

Wafer sort is done at the end of wafer fabrication to electrically test each die on the wafer. The objectives of wafer sort are: chip functionality, chip sorting, fab yield response and test coverage.

The procedure for performing wafer sort is similar to in-line parametric test, except now every die on the wafer is tested. The electrical test is a functional test. Wafers are assigned a bincode number after wafer sort to categorize the test results.

The three types of wafer sort tests are: ①DC tests, ②output checks, and ③functional tests.

Fabrication and design issues that affect wafer yield are larger wafer diameters, increased die size, increase in number of process steps, shrinking feature sizes, process maturity and crystal defects.

9. Assembly and Packaging

Chips that pass the wafer sort test undergo final assembly and packaging. IC final assembly separates each good die from the wafer and attaches the die to a metal lead frame or substrate. IC packaging encloses the die in a protective package. IC packaging has four functions: protection from the environment/handling, signal interconnections, physical support and heat dissipation. There are two packaging levels: 1st level packaging involves the IC, whereas 2nd level packaging is placing the IC on a circuit board. There are numerous packaging design constraints, showed in Fig. 7-11.

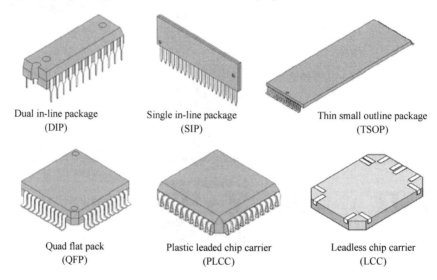

Fig. 7-11 Typical IC packages.

Traditional IC packaging materials are plastic packaging and ceramic packaging.

Plastic packaging uses an epoxy polymer to encapsulate the wirebonded die and leadframe. This technology has many different types of plastic packages.

Ceramic packaging is used for state-of-the-art IC packages that require either maximum reliability or high-power. The two main types of ceramic packaging are either a refractory (high temperature) ceramic or ceramic DIP (CERDIP) technology. Both have a hermetic seal (sealed against moisture).

7.4 Application

The impact of integrated circuits on our lives has been enormous. ICs have become the principal components of almost all electronic devices. These miniature circuits have demonstrated low cost, high reliability, low power requirements, and high processing speeds compared to the vacuum tubes and transistors which preceded them. Integrated circuit microcomputers are now used as controllers in equipment such as machine tools, vehicle operating systems, and other applications where hydraulic, pneumatic, or mechanical controls were previously used. Because IC microcomputers are smaller and more versatile than previous control mechanisms, they allow the equipment to respond to a wider range of input and produce a wider range of output. They can also be reprogrammed without having to redesign the control circuitry. Integrated circuit microcomputers are so inexpensive they are even found in children's electronic toys.

7.5 The Future

We are able to design and fabricate in large quantities circuits with several hundred million transistors. We are already in the age of deep-submicron VLSI: the typical fabrication process transistors that are much smaller the one micron in size. As we move toward even smaller transistors and even more transistors per chip, several type of challenges must be faced.

The first challenge is interconnect. In the early days of the VLSI era, wires were recognized to be important because they occupied valuable chip area, but properly designed wiring did not pose a bottleneck to performance. Today, wires cannot be ignored: the delay through a wire can easily be longer than the delay through the gate driving it. And because parasitic components of wires are so significant, crosstalk between signals on wires can cause major problems as well. Proper design methodologies and careful analysis are keys to taming the problems introduced by interconnect.

Another challenge is power consumption. Power consumption is a concern on every large chip because of the large amount of activity generated by so many transistors. Excessive power consumption can make a chip so hot that it becomes unreliable. Careful analysis of power consumption at all stages of design is essential for keeping power consumption within acceptable limits.

And we must certainly face the challenge of design complexity as we start to be able to create complete systems-on-silicon. In about ten years, we will be able to fabricate chips with ten billion transistors: a huge design task at all levels of abstraction, ranging from layout and circuit to architecture.

It is difficult to tell with any certainty what the future holds for the integrated circuit. The next major leap in the advancement of electronic devices, if such a leap is to come, may involve an entirely new circuit technology. Better devices than the very best microprocessor have always been known to be possible. The human brain, for example, processes information much more efficiently than any computer, and some futurists have speculated that the next generation of processor circuits will be biological, rather than mineral. At this point, such matters are the stuff of fiction. There are no immediate signs that the integrated circuit is in any danger of extinction.

References

1. D. Kahng, M. M. Atalla. Silicon-silicon dioxide surface. IRE Device Research Conference, 1960.

2. J. S. Kilby. Invention of the integrated circuit. IEEE Trans. Electron Device, 1976: 648.

3. R. N. Noyce. Semiconductor device-and-lead structure. U. S. Patent: 2981877.

4. Gary S. May, Simon M. Sze. Fundamentals of semiconductor fabrication. NY: John Wiley & Sons, Inc. , 2003.

5. Michael Quick, Julian Serda. Semiconductor manufacturing technology. NJ: Prentice Hall, 2006.

6. James D. Plummer, Michael D. Deal, Peter B. Griffin. Silicon VLSI technology fundamentals. Practice and modeling. NJ: Prentice Hall, 2003.

New Word and Expressions

1. microprocessor [maikrəʊ'prəʊsesə(r)] n. 微处理器
2. discrete [dis'kri:t] adj. 离散的,分离的
3. general-purpose ['dʒenərəl'pɜːpəs] adj. 通用的,多方面的,多用途的
4. passive ['pæsiv] adj. 无源的 passive device 无源器件
5. active ['æktiv] adj. 有源的 active device 有源器件
6. deep-submicron 深亚微米
7. dioxide [dai'ɔksaid] n. 二氧化物
8. complementary-symmetry 互补对称的
9. rudimentary [ruːdi'mentəri] adj. 根本的,原始的,未发展的
10. monolithic [ˌmɔnə'liθik] n. 单片电路,单片集成电路
11. polysilicon [ˌpɔli'silikən] n. 多晶态硅,多晶硅
12. linewidth ['lainwidθ] n. 线宽(指集成电路版图设计中连线的最小宽度)
13. wafer ['weifə] n. 晶圆,整片的硅片
14. fab n. 半导体的制备工厂
15. die [dai] n. 一般指封装中的硅片(一片晶圆可以制成几十到上千的硅片)
16. ASIC (Application Specific Integrated Circuits) 专用集成电路
17. RF (radio frequency) 无线电频率(表示可以辐射到空间的电磁频率)
18. oscillator ['ɔsileitə] n. 振荡器,振动器
19. ngot ['iŋɡət] n. 晶锭
20. Czochralski 指的是切克劳斯基法,就是我们常说的直拉法(CZ法生长出的单晶硅,用在生产低功率的集成电路元件,CZ法容易生产出大尺寸的单晶硅棒)
21. trichlorosilane [ˌtraiˌklɔːrə'tɔljui] n. 三氯硅烷
22. EGS (electronic-grade silicon) 电子级硅(纯度在 99.999 9 % 以上,通常用来制作器件级单晶硅的生料)
23. crystal puller 拉晶机(用来生产晶锭)
24. equilibrium segregation coefficient 平衡分凝系数
25. dopant ['dəupənt] n. 杂质,掺杂物
26. glycerine ['ɡlisəriːn] n. 甘油

27. clean room 超净间
28. epitaxial [ˌepi'tæksiəl] adj. 取向外生的,外延的
29. photomask ['fəutəumɑːsk] n. 光掩膜版
30. photoresist [ˌfəutəuri'zist] n. 光致抗蚀剂
31. ultraviolet ['ʌltrə'vaiəlit] adj. n. 紫外的,紫外线辐射的,紫外线辐射
32. reticle ['retikl] n. 十字线,用于各层掩膜版的对准
33. positive ['pɔzətiv] adj. 积极的,正的,阳的
34. negative ['negətiv] n. adj. 否定的,消极的,负的
35. development [di'veləpmənt] n. 显影
36. three-dimensional [θriːdimenʃənəl] adj. 三维的,三度的,立体的
37. subwavelength 亚波长
38. TEOS-ozone 臭氧/正硅酸乙酯（一种CVD技术）
39. alloy ['ælɔi] n. 合金; vt. 成为合金
40. fluorocarbon [ˌflu(ː)ərə'kɑːbən] n. 碳氟化合物
41. sub-picoamp 亚皮安

Notes

① 晶体生长出来以后，第一步整形加工时去掉籽晶和之后固化的锭尾，下一步加工时外圆研磨以确定晶锭的直径。这一切完成以后，沿晶锭的纵向磨出一个或者几个小平面，这些区域或者平面标志出晶锭的晶向和导电类型。最大的平面为主平面，在自动化工艺设备中用它对晶片机械定位，还可以为晶体相关器件确定晶向。其他较小的平面为次平面，用来识别材料的晶向和导电类型。

② 光刻就是将掩膜上的几何图形转移到覆盖在半导体晶片表面的对光照敏薄膜材料上去的工艺过程。这些图形确定集成电路中的各个区域,诸如注入区、接触窗口和压焊区等。由光刻工艺确定的抗蚀剂图形并不是最后器件的构成部件，仅是电路图形的印模，为了制备出实际电路图形，还必须再一次把抗蚀剂图形转移到下面组成器件的材料层上。也就是使用能够对非掩膜部分进行选择性去除的刻蚀工艺来完成图形的转移。

③ 化学汽相淀积二氧化硅薄膜并不能代替热生长二氧化硅，因为热生长二氧化硅薄膜具有最佳的电学性质，化学汽相淀积二氧化硅薄膜和热生长二氧化硅薄膜是互为补充的。未掺杂的二氧化硅薄膜可以用作多层金属化之间的绝缘膜和离子注入或扩散的掩膜，或者用来增加热生长氧化物的厚度。

④ 在IC成品能够应用到众多商业电子系统和产品之前，有几个关键工艺必须完成，包括电学测试和封装。测试是出产高质量产品所必需的，所谓质量是要求所有产品符合一组性能规范，并且减少制造工艺中的任何差异。保持质量通常涉及统计过程控制的应用，一项设计好的试验对于探索影响质量特性规范的关键变量来说是非常有益处的工具。在系统的改变工艺条件并确定其对检测质量的输出参数的影响方面，统计试验设计是一种强有力的方法。

Optical Communications

第 8 章

PREVIEW

The objective of any communication system is the transfer of information from one point to another. This information transfer most often is accomplished by *superimposing*[1] the information onto an electromagnetic wave. The modulated *carrier*[2] is then transmitted to the destination, where the electromagnetic wave is received and the information recovered. Such systems are often designated by the location of the carried frequency in the electromagnetic spectrum (Fig. 8-1). In radio systems the electromagnetic carrier wave is selected with a frequency from the radio frequency (RF) portion of the spectrum. Microwave or millimeter systems have carrier frequencies from those portions of the spectrum. In an optical communication system, the carrier is selected from the optical region, which includes the infrared, visible, and ultraviolet frequencies.

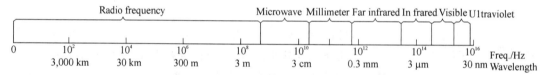

Fig. 8-1 The electromagnetic spectrum.

The principal advantage in communication with optical frequencies is the potential increase in information and power that can be transmitted. In any communication system the amount of information transmitted is directly related to the bandwidth of the modulated carrier, which is generally limited to a fixed portion of the carrier frequency itself. Thus, increasing the carrier frequency theoretically increases the available transmission bandwidth, and therefore the information capacity of the overall system. This means frequencies in the optical range will have a usable bandwidth about 10^5 times of a carrier in the RF range. *This available improvement is extremely inviting to a communication engineer vitally concerned with transmitting large amounts of information. In addition, the ability to concentrate available transmitter power within the transmitted electromagnetic wave also increases with carrier frequency. Thus, using higher carrier frequencies increases the capability of the system to achieve higher power* densities, which generally leads to improved performance. For both of these reasons optical communications has emerged as a field of special technological interest.[①]

Unfortunately, communication with optical carrier frequencies has several major difficulties. Since optical frequencies are accompanied by extremely small wavelengths, optical component design requires essentially its own technology, completely different from design techniques associated with RF, microwave, and millimeter devices.[②] The development of satisfactory optical components has been a primary impairment to optical communication in the past. A significant advance was made by the advent of the laser, a relatively high-powered optical carrier source available in both the infrared and visible frequency range. Further progress was made by development of wide band optical modulators and efficient detectors.

Another serious drawback to optical communications is the effect of the propagation path on the optical wave. This is because optical wavelengths are commensurate with molecule and particle sizes, and propagation effects are generated that are uncommon to radio and microwave frequencies. Furthermore, these effects tend to be *stochastic*[3] and time varying in nature, which hinders accurate propagation modeling.

8.1 The System Model

The block diagram of a typical optical communication system is shown in Fig. 8-2. The diagram is composed of standard communication blocks, endemic to any communication system. A source producing some type of information is to be transmitted to some remote destination. This source has its output modulated onto an optical carrier. This carrier is then transmitted as an optical light field, or beam, through the optical channel. At the receiver the field is optically collected and processed, generally in the presence of all interference and inherent background radiation.

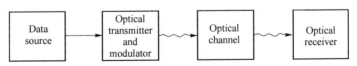

Fig. 8-2 Optical communication system block diagram.

The modulation of the source information onto the optical carrier can be in the form of frequency modulation (FM), phase modulation (PM), or possibly amplitude modulation (AM), each of which can be theoretically implemented at any carrier frequency in the electromagnetic range. In addition, however, several other less conventional modulation schemes are also often utilized with optical sources. These include intensity modulation (IM), in which information is used to modulate the intensity of he optical carrier, and polarization modulation (PLM), in which spatial characteristics of the optical field are modulated.

The optical receiver in Fig. 8-2 collects the incident optical field and processes it to recover the transmitted information. A typical optical receiver can be represented by the three basic blocks shown in Fig. 8-3, consisting of an optical receiving lens system, an optical photodetector, and postdetection processor. The lens system filters and focuses the received field onto the photodetector, where the optical signal is converted to an electronic signal. The processor performs the necessary amplification and filtering operations to recover the desired information from the detector output.

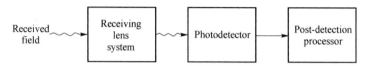

Fig. 8-3 The optical receiver.

Optical receivers can be divided into two basic types—power detecting receivers and *heterodyning*[4] receiver. Power detecting receivers have the front end system shown in Fig. 8-4(a). The lens system and photodetector operate to detect the instantaneous power in the collected field as it arrivers at the receiver. Heterodyning receivers have the front end system shown in Fig. 8-4(b). A locally generated optical field is electromagnetically mixed through a front end mirror, and the combined wave is photodetected. Heterodyning receivers are more difficult to implement and require close *tolerances*[5] on the spatial coherence of the two optical fields being mixed. For this reason, heterodyned receivers are often called (spatially) coherent receivers.

Since the receiver front end essentially an optical receiving antenna, it can be described most simply by its effective receiver area and field of view. The receiver area is the collecting area presented to the impinging field, and, ideally, corresponds to its physical area. Often, however, receiver losses are accounted for by defining an effective receiver area which is less than its actual size. The field of view of a receiver antenna defines the various directions of arrival of electromagnetic waves that the photodetector will observe.

The receiver front end, in addition to focusing the optical field onto the photodetector, also provides some degree of filtering, as shown in Fig. 8-4. These filters are employed to photodetection to reduce the amount of undesired background radiation.

Photodetectors convert the focused optical field into electrical signal for processing. Although there are several types of detectors available all behave according to quantum mechanical principles, utilizing photosensitive materials to produce current or voltage responses to changes in impinging optical filed power.

The detection of optical fields is hampered by the various noise sources present throughout the receiver. The most predominant in long-distance communication is the interference radiation that is collected at the receiver lens along with the desired optical field. The background effect can be essentially eliminated over short distances where direct-coupled fiberoptic waveguides can be used for the transmission path. A second noise source is the circuit and electronic noise generated in the processing operations. Lastly, the photodetector itself, not being a purely ideal device, produces internal interference during the photodetection operation. This generally takes the form of a detector "dark current"—an output response being produced ever when no impinging field is applied to the input. Each of these noise sources must be properly accounted for in any receiver analysis.

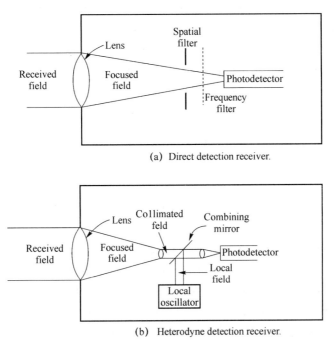

Fig. 8-4 The front end system of the two kinds of optical receivers.

8.2 Optical Transmitters

The optical transmitter in Fig. 8-2 can be essentially subdivided into a *cascade*[6] connection of an optical source, a modulator, and an optical antenna, as shown in Fig. 8-5. Optical sources (laser, photodiodes, light bulbs[7]) produce optical electromagnetic fields while having provisions for modulating data waveforms onto its output. Depending on the source, the modulation may be impressed during the generation of light, or after the

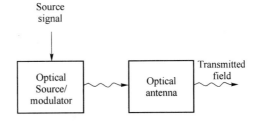

Fig. 8-5 The optical modulator/transmitter.

light has been generated.

The optical antenna is a lens system that focuses the modulated source output into an optical beam (electromagnetic field) for transmission. Any type of electromagnetic transmitting antenna is described basically by its radiation pattern, the latter describing the power density transmitted in each direction. These patterns can be summarized by their gain and beam angle. The gain of an antenna is related to the maximum power density of the radiation pattern. Formally, the antenna gain G_a is defined as

$$G_a = \frac{\text{maximum power density of the radiation pattern}}{\text{power density due to an isotropic antenna}} \qquad (8\text{-}1)$$

An isotropic antenna is one that transmits electromagnetic energy uniformly in all directions.

The antenna beam angle Ω_a is defined as the solid angle in *steradians*[8], measured from the antenna, into which the maximum power density must be concentrated in order to have the same total power. Thus,

$$G_a \left(\frac{P}{4\pi}\right) \Omega_a = P \qquad (8\text{-}2)$$

or

$$\Omega_a = \frac{4\pi}{G_a} \text{sr} \qquad (8\text{-}3)$$

The beam therefore indicates the solid angle into which most of the transmitted power appears to flow, and is inversely related to the antenna gain. Often this solid beam angle is described by its planar angle beam width (the projection of the solid angle onto a plane through its center, as shown in Fig. 8-6. For a circular lens antenna of diameter d, transmitting an electromagnetic wave of wavelength λ, the antenna planar beamwidth θ_a and gain G_a are given approximately by

$$\theta_a \simeq \frac{\lambda}{d} \qquad (8\text{-}4)$$

$$G_a = \left(\frac{4d}{\lambda}\right)^2 \qquad (8\text{-}5)$$

Fig. 8-7 shows a plot of these parameters as a function of diameter for several optical frequencies.

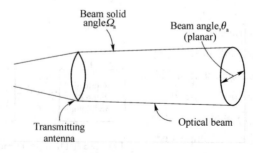

Fig. 8-6　Transmitting antenna system.

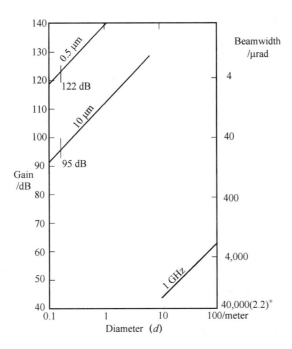

Fig. 8-7 Antenna gain and beam width versus diameter.

8.3 The Transmitted Optical Field

Since the transmitted optical field is an electromagnetic wave it is described at any spatial point by solutions to Maxwell's equations. Let ξ represent a point of a selected coordinate system in which the field source is located at the origin, as shown in Fig. 8-8. At any time t, the electrical field is described at ξ by

$$\text{electric field} = \text{Real}\{f(t,\xi)\} \quad \text{V/length} \tag{8-6}$$

where Real{ } means "real part of" and $f(t,\xi)$ is referred to as the complex field. At each such point ξ, the field has an intensity given by

$$I(t,\xi) = \frac{1}{2}\left(\frac{1}{Z_w}\right)|f(t,\xi)|^2 \quad \text{W/area} \tag{8-7}$$

where Z_w is the wave *impedance*[9]. The instantaneous power of the field over an arbitrary area A at time t is given by the surface integral of the intensity over the area,

$$P_A(t) = \int_A I(t,\xi)(\boldsymbol{i} \cdot \mathrm{d}\boldsymbol{a}) \tag{8-8}$$

where the integration is over all ξ in A, and the dot product indicates the directional cosine between the unit vector $\boldsymbol{i}$ in the direction of power flow and $\mathrm{d}\boldsymbol{a}$, the normal vector to the surface area at ξ (Fig. 8-8).

If the source producing the field in Fig. 8-8 is a point source operating in a free space medium, the filed propagates as a plane wave in directions specified by the antenna gain pattern. At a point ξ, the complex field of a plane wave can be written as

$$f(t,\xi)=E(t,\xi)\exp\left[j\left(\omega t-\frac{2\pi}{\lambda}|\xi|\right)\right] \tag{8-9}$$

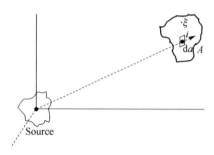

Fig. 8-8　Transmission geometry.

where $|\xi|$ is the distance to the point ξ, $E(t,\xi)$ is the instantaneous field amplitude vector at ξ, and ω, t are the wave radian frequency and wavelength respectively. The amplitude vector E describes the field polarization in a plane (x, y) normal to the direction of propagation. This can be expanded as

$$E(t,\xi)=E_x(t,\xi)1_x+E_y(t,\xi)1_y \tag{8-10}$$

where $E_x(t,\xi)$ and $E_y(t,\xi)$ are the complex polarization components, and 1_x, 1_y are unit coordinate vectors in the (x, y) plane. The polarization components determine the polarization state of the plane wave. If $|E_x(t,\xi)|=|E_y(t,\xi)|$ and are 90° out phase, the field is circularly polarized. If both are in phase or one is zero, the field is linearly polarized. For a point ξ located within the transmitting antenna beamwidth, the linearly polarized field can be simplified to

$$f(t,\xi)=a(t,\xi)\exp[j\omega t] \tag{8-11}$$

where

$$a(t,\xi)=\frac{C}{|\xi|}E(t)\exp\left[\frac{-j2\pi|\xi|}{\lambda}\right] \tag{8-12}$$

and

$$C=\left[\frac{G_a}{4\pi}\right]^{1/2} \tag{8-13}$$

Here $E(t)$ is the transmitted field amplitude *variation*[10] of the point source and G_a is the antenna gain. The exponential term in Eq. (8-12) accounts for the time delay in propagating the distance $|\xi|$. The complex field in Eq. (8-11) has the intensity given by Eq. (8-7),

$$I(t,\xi)=\frac{C^2}{2Z_w|\xi|^2}|E(t)|^2 \tag{8-14}$$

It is convenient to define

$$P_s(t)=\frac{|E(t)|^2}{2Z_w} \tag{8-15}$$

as the transmitted source power function and rewrite (8-14) as simply

$$I(t,\xi)=\frac{G_a}{4\pi|\xi|^2}P_s(t) \tag{8-16}$$

Thus, for a plane wave, the instantaneous field intensity at a point ξ depends directly on the transmitted field power and antenna gain, and varies indirectly with the square of the distance to ξ. The function $a(t,\xi)$ in Eq. (8-11) is called the complex envelope of the plane wave field at ξ. If $a(t,\xi)$ does not depend on t, the field is said to be monochromatic field, and the electric field in Eq. (8-11) corresponds to a pure sine wave in time at any ξ. If $a(t,\xi)$ has time variation with a narrow frequency band relative to the carrier frequency ω, the field is said to be quasi monochromatic. Any time variation in the complex envelope $a(t,\xi)$ must be due to the amplitude function $E(t)$ in Eq. (8-12). Thus, any type of modulation imposed on the optical carrier at the transmitter must be exhibited in the complex amplitude $E(t)$.

We are often interested in determining the plane wave field power over an area A, due to a remote point source. This can be obtained directly from Eq. (8-8). Consider the area A in Fig. 8-9 containing points r of a planar coordinate system having its origin at the center of A. Let a point source a distance L away transmit a plane wave in the direction of a ray vector z through the origin of A, as shown. If we assume $L \gg |r|$, then all points in A are essentially a distance L away from the source. Neglecting the propagation delay, the field at a point r in A due to the point source can be written

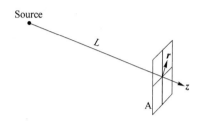

Fig. 8-9   Rotated transmission geometry.

$$f(t,r) = a(t)\exp[j(\omega t - z \cdot r)] \qquad (8\text{-}17)$$

where

$$a(t) = \left[\frac{G_a}{4\pi L^2}\right]^{\frac{1}{2}} E(t)$$

and the vector z has magnitude $2\pi/\lambda$. The dot product accounts for the phase variation over the surface of A. The power over A is then given by Eq. (8-18):

$$P_A(t) = \frac{1}{2Z_w}\int_A |a(t)|^2 \left(\frac{z}{|z|}\cdot da\right) = \frac{G_a P_s(t)}{4\pi L^2}\int_A \left(\frac{z}{|z|}\cdot da\right) \qquad (8\text{-}18)$$

If the area A is normal to the direction of arrival of the plane wave, $z/|z| \cdot da = da$, and

$$P_A(t) = \frac{G_a A}{4\pi L^2} P_s(t) \qquad (8\text{-}19)$$

where A is the integrated area of A. Thus the power collected over the normal area A, due to a plane wave from a remote point source, is directly proportional to the area A. The factor

$$L_P = \frac{1}{4\pi L^2} \qquad (8\text{-}20)$$

is called the free space propagation loss in transmitting power over a distance L.

Let us extend Eq. (8-17) to the case of several point sources. Suppose each is approximately a distance L away, each transmitting toward A from a different direction z_i, with the same carrier frequency ω (Fig. 8-10(a)). The field at r in A now becomes the combined fields from each point,

$$f(t,r) = a(t,r)e^{j\omega t} \qquad (8\text{-}21)$$

where now

$$a(t,r) = \sum_i a_i(t) e^{-j(z_i \cdot r)} \qquad (8\text{-}22)$$

Here $\{a_i(t)\}$ are the complex field envelope variations, and the sum is over all source points. Thus each point r receives the superposition of the individual plane wave.

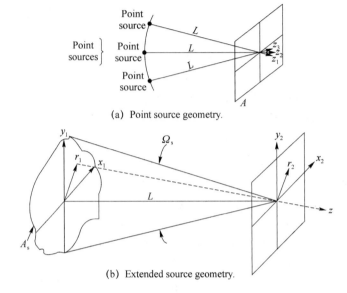

(a) Point source geometry.

(b) Extended source geometry.

Fig. 8-10 Extended source geometry.

Eq. (8-22) suggests an extension to an integral over an extended source amplitude function. Let $F_s(t,r)$ describe the source field envelope at time t and point r_1 in the source plane a distance L away from the receiver plane, as shown in Fig. 8-10(b). The resulting field that will be produced at point r_2 in the receiver plane is obtained by use of *Fresnel-Kirchhoff*[11] diffraction

$$f_r(t,r_2) = \frac{\exp\left[\frac{j\pi}{\lambda L}|r_2|^2 + j\left(\frac{2\pi L}{\lambda}\right)\right]}{j\lambda L} \cdot$$

$$\int_{A_s} F_s(t,r_1) \exp\left(j\frac{\pi}{\lambda L}|r_1|^2\right) \exp\left[-j\frac{2\pi}{\lambda l}(x_1 x_2 + y_1 y_2)\right] dr_1 \qquad (8\text{-}23)$$

where (x,y) are the coordinates of the corresponding points r_1 and r_2, and A_s is the area of the source. Thus a source amplitude function produces a receiver field at a distance L according to Eq. (8-23). When $L\lambda \gg |r_1|^2$, it is convenient to deal with the source angular spectrum rather than its amplitude function. The angular spectrum describes the source amplitude along ray lines z emitted from the source plane and passing through the center of the receiver, as shown in Fig. 8-10(b). If we consider a ray z with arrival angles (θ_x, θ_y) with respect to the normal to the receiver area, we can then define the source angular spectrum $B_s(t,z)$ as the source amplitude in the direction of arrival of z. Thus, $B_s(t,z)$ is obtained by evaluating $F_s(t,r_1)$ at the point $r_1 = (L\theta_x, L\theta_y)$. If in addition we let $|z| = \frac{2\pi}{\lambda}$, then Eq. (8.23) can be rewritten as

$$f_r(t,r_2) = \frac{\exp\left[\frac{j\pi}{\lambda L}|r_2|^2 + j\frac{2\pi L}{\lambda}\right]}{j\frac{\lambda}{L}} \iint_{\Omega_s} B_s(t,z) e^{-jz \cdot r_2} d\theta_x d\theta_y \qquad (8\text{-}24)$$

where Ω_s is the solid angle subtended by the source area A_s. When compared with Eq. (8-22), (8-24) appears as an integration over a continuum of point source, with $B_s(t,z)$ describing the source emission from A_s in the direction of $-z$.

In later analysis of optical fields, it is often convenient to consider *orthogonal*[12] expansions of the complex envelope into *orthonormal*[13] functions. That is, we consider the field over a spatial area A and a time interval $(0, T)$, and expand the field envelope within these regions as an infinite series:

$$a(t,r) = \sum_{i=1}^{\infty} a_i \phi_i(t,r) \qquad 0 \leqslant t \leqslant T, r \in A \qquad (8\text{-}25)$$

where

$$a_i = \int_A \int_0^T a(t,r) \phi_i^*(t,r) dt dr \qquad (8\text{-}26)$$

Here $\{a_i\}$ are the complex expansion coefficients, and $\{\phi_i(t,r)\}$ represents a complete set of complex orthonormal basis functions over A and $(0, T)$. That is,

$$\int_A \int_T \phi_i(t,r) \phi_j^*(t,r) dt dr = \begin{cases} 1, & i=j \\ 0, & i \neq j \end{cases} \qquad (8\text{-}27)$$

where the asterisk denotes complex conjugate. The equality in Eq. (8-25) is in a squared integrable sense, and the convergence of the sum on the right to the envelope function on the left requires only a bounded energy constraint on the radiation field.[③] The advantage of an expansion of this form is primarily for mathematical convenience, although such expansions often yield physical insight into the related optical processing. It is natural to consider the function $\{\phi_i(t,r)\}$ as defining the "modes" of the field over the area A and interval $(0, T)$. The coefficients $\{a_i\}$ then become the modal coefficients, describing the envelope in each mode. Since different orthonormal sets are available, mode descriptions of a given field are not necessarily unique, each corresponding to a different expansion set.

8.4 Stochastic Fields

In optical system modeling we are often forced to deal with stochastic, or random, fields. Such fields arise when dealing with transmission effects which cause random variations to occur in the transmitted beam. These random variations lead to statistical fluctuations in the received field intensity which can only be analyzed after associating proper statistics with the field itself.

The complex envelope of a stochastic field must be considered random at each point t

and r describing the field over a designated area. As such, random fields completely described by their probability densities. Stochastic field analysis is often confined to second-order statistics associated with the field, in particular, its coherence function, in the regard the time-space (mutual) coherence function of a stochastic field $f(t,r)$ at points (t_1,r_1) and (t_2,r_2) is formally defined as

$$R_f(t_1,r_1;t_2,r_2)=E[f(t_1,r_1)f^*(t_2,r_2)] \tag{8-28}$$

where E is the expectation operator over the joint field densities at the points involved. The mean squared value of the field at (t, r) then follows as $R_f(t,r;t,r)$, and can be evaluated directly from the coherence function at any t and r.

Stochastic fields are often described by their inherent coherence properties. A stochastic field is said to be temporally stationary if the time dependence in its coherence function depends only on the time difference t_1-t_2. The field is spatially homogeneous if the spatial dependence in the coherence function depends only on the spatial distance (r_1-r_2). A field is completely homogeneous if it is both temporally stationary and spatially homogeneous. A stochastic field is said to be coherence-separable if its coherence function factors as

$$R_f(t_1,r_1;t_2,r_2)=R_t(t_1,t_2)R_s(r_1,r_2) \tag{8-29}$$

The factor $R_s(r_1,r_2)$ is called the spatial coherence function while $R_t(t_1,t_2)$ is called the temporal correlation of the field. The function $R_s(r,r)$ is called the field irradiance function. Often the spatial coherence function is normalized as

$$\widetilde{R}_s(r_1,r_2)=\frac{R_s(r_1,r_2)}{[R_s(r_1,r_1)R_s(r_2,r_2)]^{\frac{1}{2}}} \tag{8-30}$$

The normalized space coherence function is therefore bounded in magnitude by 1. A field that is coherence-separable and homogeneous is said to be spectrally pure, and its coherence function can always be written as $R_t(\tau)\widetilde{R}_s(\rho)$ where $\tau=t_1-t_2$ and $\rho=r_1-r_2$. Spectrally pure fields therefore have $\widetilde{R}_s(0)=1$ and a mean squared value of $R_t(0)$ at all r. The Fourier transform of $R_t(\tau)$ is called the intensity spectrum of the field.

A stochastic field is space coherent over an area A_0 if $\widetilde{R}_s(r_1,r_2)=1$ for all r_1,r_2 in A_0.

Stochastic field envelopes also have infinite series expansions into orthonormal functions as in Eq. (8-25), except the coefficients in Eq. (8-26) are now random variables. The convergence of the sum is now in a mean squared sense, and requires bounded average energy in the field over the expansion area and time interval. Again, any set of complete orthonormal functions can be used for the expansion. If the coefficients $\{a_i\}$ are uncorrelated variables, the expansion is called a *Karhunen-Loeve*[14] (KL) expansion. A KL expansion will occur if the orthonormal functions $\phi_i(t,r)$ are such that they each satisfy the integral equation

$$\int_A\int_0^T R_f(t_1,r_1;t_2,r_2)\phi_i(t_2,r_2)\mathrm{d}t_2\mathrm{d}r_2 = \gamma_i\phi_i(t_1,r_1) \tag{8-31}$$

for some set of constants $\{\gamma_i\}$. The members of the set $\{\phi_i(t,r)\}$ satisfying this equation are called *eigenfunctions*[15], and the $\{\gamma_i\}$ are its *eigenvalues*[16]. It can be shown that the eigenvalues are also the mean squared value of the corresponding random coefficients $\{a_i\}$.

8.5 The Optical Channel

When designing a communication system the properties of the propagation path from transmitter to receiver must be taken into account. Proper characterization of this path is equivalent to defining the communication channel in Fig. 8-2. Electromagnetic propagation can be roughly divided into guided and unguided transmissions. In an unguided channel the source transmits the field freely into a medium with no attempt to control its propagation other than by its antenna gain pattern. The principal example of an unguided channel is the so-called space channel in which the medium involved may be free space, the atmosphere, or the ocean. In a guided channel, a waveguide is used to confine the wave propagation from transmitter to receiver. The primary example of a guided system in the optical region is the fiberoptic channel.

8.5.1 The Unguided (Space) Channel

The operating characteristics of the space channel depend primarily on the properties of the medium involved. The simplest type of unguided channel is the free space channel, in which the medium involved between transmitter and receiver is free space. This would characterized propagation paths outside the Earth's atmosphere, or perhaps in a short-range, controlled-laboratory. The principal effect is the propagation loss in Eq. (8-20). The transmission is distortion free, and the object of system design is merely to overcome the loss factor by sufficient size transmitters and receivers.

When the propagating medium is not free space, additional effects must be included in the channel model. This is because when propagating through a nonfree space environment, an electromagnetic wave undergoes effects tending to alter the structure of the wave. These alterations depend on the frequency of the wave, and are due primarily to interactions with inhomogeneities and foreign particles comprising the medium. One can expect these effects to predominate whenever the particle size is comparable to or greater than the wavelength of the field. For this reason atmospheric distortion may be quite severe in the optical range, where wavelengths are commensurate with matter as small as molecules. Thus the nonfree space channel presents a major communication hurdle that must be of concern to system designers. Particles in the transmission path primarily cause field absorption and scattering, although the degree of each will depend on the type of channel. If the absorption is severe, little communication can be accomplished, even with sophisticated techniques. On the other hand, if the field is merely distorted, with little additional power loss, application of communication theoretic techniques can sometimes be applied to recover a sufficient portion of the field modulation so as to maintain a satisfactory communication link.

Absorption and scattering in a space channel manifest themselves in the electromagnetic field through both amplitude and spatial effects. Amplitude effects are exhibited in the time variation of the field, and primarily involve power loss, power fluctuations, and frequency filtering. Spatial effects appear as variations in the beam direction or as distortion effects across the beam front. In particular, they exhibit effects over points of a receiving surface, and limit the extent to which a transmitted beam can be collected coherently. Since the particle structure of the channel tends to be random in nature amplitude and spatial fluctuations tend to be stochastic in nature and can only be described statistically, sometimes only by their coherence properties.

8.5.2 The Guided (Fiberoptic) Channel

In a guided channel the optical beam is confined to a closed path, or "pipe", from transmitter to receiver. Such optical channels have application whenever hard wire lines can be used, such as Earth-based systems, or short- range internal intercommunications. Besides having the inherent bandwidth of the optical beam, the guided channel has the advantage of ① being completely shielded from background and electromagnetic interference, ②immunity from turbulence, ③complete control of the propagating beam by the periodic insertion of refocusing and amplification devices, and ④ interfacing neatly with the rapidly developing field of integrated optics. ④

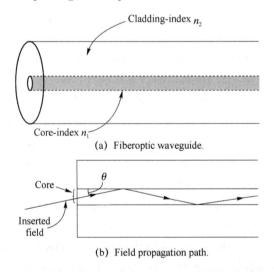

Fig. 8-11 The guided channel model.

Although optical waveguides can be constructed similar to microwave guides (hollow, metallic pipes), the modern techniques use *encased*[17] glass fibers for lower loss. The waves propagate in a *cylindrical*[18] glass core, which is surrounded by a dielectric, called a cladding (Fig. 8-11(a)). The core is made to have a slightly higher refractive index than *the cladding*[19]. Optical beams are transmitted into the core by inserting them at an angle θ (Fig. 8-11(b)). The beam will propagate if the angle θ satisfies

$$\theta \leqslant \cos^{-1}\left(\frac{n_2}{n_1}\right) \tag{8-32}$$

where n_1 and n_2 are the refractive indices of the core and cladding respectively. Beam directions having steeper angles are absorbed in the cladding and do not propagate. If $n_1 \approx n_2$, then θ will be small, and only small *grazing*[20] angles are allowed to propagate. These smaller have less boundary absorption, and therefore less loss during propagation. The only field attenuation results from absorption by the impurities in the core.

Mathematically, the electromagnetic filed within a waveguide can be described by the same field equations as for free space, except boundary conditions must be satisfied at the guide walls. Thus, guided fields can be represented by orthonormal expansions, just as in Eq. (8-25). Again the individual terms of the expansions define the modes of the propagating field, as in the space channel. However, in free space the modes tend to be plane waves that separate spatially, whereas in guides the modes essentially superimpose as waves with orthogonal field vectors. (These field vectors correspond to the various types of transverse electric fields similar to those found in microwaveguides.) These additional terms are generated by nonperfect boundary conditions which create cross coupling. Physically this corresponds to imperfections in the core walls, especially at bends and interconnections. Even though a single field mode is inserted into the guide, additional modes are therefore almost unavoidable. These additional modes will each have slightly different grazing angles, and will propagate if they satisfy Eq. (8-32). We therefore see that the cladding is an important part of the fiberoptic guide. In addition to supporting and shielding the glass core, it allows for careful control of the dielectric index n_2. By proper construction, this will control the grazing angle θ which, in addition to reducing the loss, can limit the number of modes (number of terms in the field expansion) that will propagate. The approximate number of modes D_s of wavelength λ that propagate in a core of diameter d is given by

$$D_s \cong \left(\frac{2\pi d}{\lambda}\right)^2 (n_1^2 - n_2^2) \tag{8-33}$$

As n_2 is made closer to n_1, the number of modes (propagating field patterns) is reduced. Only a single mode will propagate if the core is narrow enough and if $n_2 \approx n_1$, that is, if

$$d \approx \frac{\lambda}{2\pi (n_1^2 - n_2^2)^{\frac{1}{2}}} \tag{8-34}$$

Typically, claddings can be constructed with indices within several percent of n_1, and Eq. (8-34) therefore requires a core diameter on the order of a few microns. This obviously presents a nontrivial fabrication problem in fiberoptic construction.

From a communication point of view, having many modes propagate is generally disadvantageous. This is due to the delay dispersion among the modes and the associated power division. Since each mode propagates at a slightly different angle, they propagate at different velocities, and are therefore delayed with respect to each other. If the delay dispersion is sufficient, the fields interfere. For a power detection receiver at the end of the guide, a dispersion of t_d sec limits the system coherence bandwidth. Improved methods of fiber construction can often be used to reduce the dispersion.

8.6 The Detected Optical Field

The objective of the receiving optical antenna in Fig. 8-3 is to collect the received field for the photodetecting surface. The receiver therefore responds to the instantaneous field over the receiver area. A detailed optical antenna system is shown in Fig. 8-12. The receiving lens is located in the aperture plane, having a receiver area A_r and focal length f_c. The lens focuses the received field onto the focal plane located a distance f_c behind the lens. The focused field appears as a diffraction pattern in the focal plane. The photosensitive optical detector, with area A_d, is located in the field plane, and responds to the portion of the diffracted field on its surface.

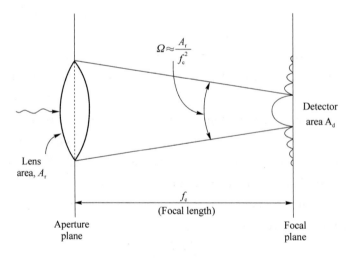

Fig. 8-12 Receiver optical system.

We often must determine the amount of transmitted field power collected over the received area A_r. Let the source be a point source transmitting a normal plane wave at a distance L from the receiver, with a transmitter gain G_a in the receiver direction. For a free space channel, the instantaneous power collected over A_r is given directly by Eq. (8-19):

$$p_r(t) = G_a L_p A_r P(t) = \frac{G_a p(t)}{4\pi L^2} A_r \tag{8-35}$$

For the nonfree space channel, absorption and scatter effects L_t must be included. The received power must then be modified to

$$P_r(t) = (G_a L_p L_t A_r) P(t) \tag{8-36}$$

where L_t accounts for these channel effects. In dealing with instantaneous power, on a slowly varying channel, L_t is treated as a random gain associated with the channel, and appears as a multiplicative random variable. As such, it introduces an average channel gain, with an additive power variance.

Often we must accurately describe the field wave itself at the detector, rather than simply its power value at the receiver lens. This requires us to account for the conversion of the received field in the aperture plane to the diffracted field in the focal plane. Thus if $f_r(t, r)$ is the received field over the aperture lens, and if $f_r(t, r)$ is the diffracted field in the focal plane, then the two are related by

$$f_d(t,u,v) = \frac{\exp\left[j\frac{\pi}{\lambda f_c}(u^2+v^2)\right]}{j\lambda f_c} \int_{A_r} f_r(t,x,y)\exp\left[-j\frac{2\pi}{\lambda f_c}(xu+yv)\right]dxdy \quad (8-37)$$

where $r=(x,y)$ are the field coordinates in the aperture plane and (u, v) are the field coordinates in the focal plane, as shown in Fig. 8-13. Eq. 8-37 describes the manner in which the received and focal plane fields are related. Note that $f_d(t, r)$ is also related to the two-dimensional Fourier transform of $f_r(t, r)$. That is, if we denote

$$F_r(t,\omega_1,\omega_2) = \int_{A_r} f_r(t,x,y)\exp[-j(x\omega_1+y\omega_2)]dxdy \quad (8-38)$$

as the two-dimensional transform, then

$$f_d(t,u,v) = \frac{\left[j\frac{\pi}{\lambda f_c}(u^2+v^2)\right]}{j\lambda f_c} F_r\left(t,\frac{2\pi u}{\lambda f_c},\frac{2\pi v}{\lambda f_c}\right) \quad (8-39)$$

Thus diffraction patterns in optical receivers can be generated by simply resorting to transform theory. In communication analyses, this is an extremely useful result, since it means much of our receiver analysis reduces to straightforward linear system theory.

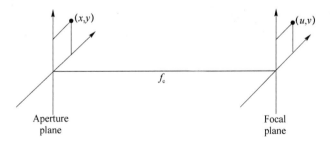

Fig. 8-13 Receiver optical system coordinates.

Consider a normal monochromatic plane wave over the receiver area A_r. From our discussion in Section 8.3 the received field is then

$$f_r(t,x,y) = \begin{cases} a_0 e^{j\omega t} & x,y \in A_r \\ 0 & \text{elsewhere} \end{cases} \quad (8-40)$$

The resulting diffraction pattern in the focal plane is then obtained directly from Eq. (8-37). Its magnitude becomes

$$|f_d(t,u,v)| = \frac{a_0}{\lambda f_c}\left|\int_{A_r}\exp\left[-j\frac{2\pi}{\lambda f_c}(xu+yv)\right]dxdy\right| \quad (8\text{-}41)$$

If the aperture lens area is assumed rectangular with dimensions (d, b), the limits of integration in (8-41) become $|x|\leqslant\frac{d}{2}$, $|y|\leqslant\frac{b}{2}$, and the result integrates to

$$|f_d(t,u,v)| = a_0\left(\frac{bd}{\lambda f_c}\right)\left|\frac{\sin\frac{\pi du}{\lambda f_c}}{\frac{\pi du}{\lambda f_c}}\cdot\frac{\sin\frac{\pi bv}{\lambda f_c}}{\frac{\pi bv}{\lambda f_c}}\right| \quad (8\text{-}42)$$

The result for the u coordinate is sketched in Fig. 8-14(a). A similar plot exists along the v coordinate. If a circular lens of diameter d is used, the transform in Eq. (8-41) can be evaluated by converting to polar coordinates. This yields

$$|f_d(t,u,v)| = \left(\frac{a_0}{\lambda f_c}\right)2\pi\left|\int_0^d rJ_0\left(\frac{\pi r\rho}{\lambda f_c}\right)dr\right|$$
$$= a_0\left(\frac{\pi d^2}{4\lambda f_c}\right)\left|\frac{2J_1\left(\pi\frac{d\rho}{\lambda f_c}\right)}{\left(\pi\frac{d\rho}{\lambda f_c}\right)}\right| \quad (8\text{-}43)$$

where $\rho=(u^2+v^2)^{\frac{1}{2}}$ and $J_0(x)$ and $J_1(x)$ are Bessel functions. This diffraction pattern is also sketched in Fig. 8-14(b), as a function of the circular radial distance (and is the familiar "Airy disc" in optical diffraction theory). Note that in both cases, Eq. (8-42) and (8-43), the diffracted pattern occupies an area of approximately $(\lambda f_c)^2/A_r$ (i. e. , the area *encompassed*[21] by the largest *hump*[22]) in the focal plane. Since this area is quite small at optical wavelengths, the detector area is generally many times larger than plane wave diffraction patterns.

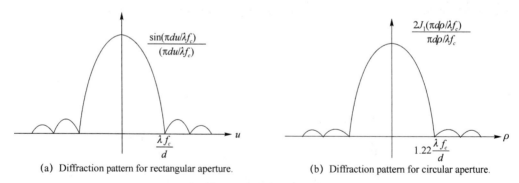

(a) Diffraction pattern for rectangular aperture.   (b) Diffraction pattern for circular aperture.

Fig. 8-14 Diffraction patterns.

If the plane wave arrives off the normal, as in Fig. 8-15(a), the received field over the receiver lens is now described by

$$f_r(t,x,y) = (a_0 e^{j\omega t})e^{-j\mathbf{z}\cdot\mathbf{r}}$$
$$= (a_0 e^{j\omega t})\exp\left[-j\frac{2\pi}{\lambda}(x\sin\theta_x+y\sin\theta_y)\right] \quad (8\text{-}44)$$

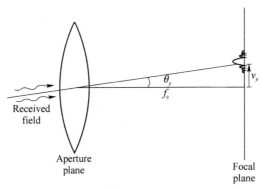

(a) Off-axis reception

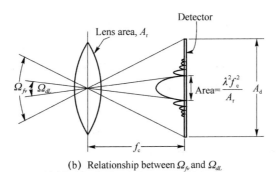

(b) Relationship between Ω_{fv} and Ω_{dl}

Fig. 8-15   Fields on the lens and detector.

where θ_x, θ_y are the arrival angles from the normal. From transform theory, the resulting diffraction pattern magnitude is now

$$|f_d(t,u,v)| = \left(\frac{a_0}{\lambda f_c}\right)\left|F_r\left[t,\frac{2\pi}{\lambda f_c}(u-u_x),\frac{2\pi}{\lambda f_c}(v-v_y)\right]\right| \tag{8-45}$$

where $u_x = f_c \sin \theta_x$ and $v_y = f_c \sin \theta_y$. Thus, off-angle incident plane waves generate position-shifted diffraction patterns in the focal plane. If the arrival angle is too large, the pattern is shifted off the detector surface area, and the field is not detected. This allows for a formal definition of receiver field of view as the solid angle, looking out from the receiver, within which all arriving plane waves must occur in order to project their diffraction pattern onto the detector. By standard geometric analysis in Fig. 8-15(b) we see that

$$\Omega_{fv} \approx \frac{A_d}{f_c^2} \tag{8-46}$$

where f_c is the focal length, A_d the detector area, and the approximation assumes that small angles are involved. In addition, we note that all arriving plane waves that superimpose their diffraction patterns are in essence indistinguishable in terms of direction of arrival. Thus the absolute minimal field of view that we can distinguish is that set of arrival angles whose patterns superimpose. This minimal field of view is limited only by the receiver optics (diffraction pattern) and is called the diffraction limited field of view of the receiver. Denoting this as Ω_{dL} we see from Fig. 8-15(b) that

$$\Omega_{dL} \cong \frac{\frac{(\lambda f_c)^2}{A_r}}{f_c^2} = \frac{\lambda^2}{A_r} \tag{8-47}$$

Thus, the diffraction limited field of view depends on the receiver area. In practice, of course, detectors cannot easily be constructed whose area yields a receiver field of view equal to the diffraction limited field of view. That is, $\Omega_{fv} \gg \Omega_{dL}$, and the receiver field of view is generally many times its diffraction limited angle. However, Eq. (8-47) does point out the inherent spatial resolution of an optical system (since λ is on the order of microns) as opposed to an FR antenna having centimeter wavelengths.

When the received field is not a plane wave, then we must resort to two-dimensional transform theory to determine the focal plane field. Consider an extended source at a distance L with an arbitrary amplitude spectrum $F_s(t,r)$ producing at the receiver aperture plane the field $f_s(t,x,y)$, according to Eq. (8-23). The lens focuses the portion of this on its surface onto the focal plane. If we define the lens pupil function

$$G(x,y) = \begin{cases} 1, & (x,y) \in A_r \\ 0 & \text{elsewhere} \end{cases} \tag{8-48}$$

then the field at the receiver lens due to the source is

$$f_r(t,x,y) = G(x,y)f_s(t,x,y) \tag{8-49}$$

The focal plane field is then obtained by substituting Eq. (8-49) into Eq. (8-37). However, it also can be written using the complex convolution of the transforms of each term in Eq. (8-49). The inverse Fourier transform of $f_s(t,x,y)$ is related to the source spectrum $F_s(t,x,y)$. If we let $g(u,v)$ be the Fourier transform of the pupil function $G(x,y)$, then the focal plane field magnitude becomes

$$|f_d(t,-u,-v)| = \frac{L}{f_c} \left| \int_{A_s} F_s(t,L\lambda x,L\lambda y) g\left(\frac{u}{\lambda f_c} - x, \frac{v}{\lambda f_c} - y\right) dx dy \right| \tag{8-50}$$

Thus the optical receiver reproduces the source amplitude function in the focal plane through its convolution with the function g. Since $g(u,v)$ is the transform of $G(x,y)$ in Eq. (8-48), it is related to the diffraction pattern produced by a normal plane wave over the receiver lens, and therefore is similar to Eq. (8-42) or Eq. (8-43). Another interpretation can be made by considering the case when $F_s(t,x,y) = \delta(x)\delta(y)$, corresponding to a monochromatic point source at $x=0, y=0$. Eq. (8-50) then yields $|f_d| = g\left(\frac{u}{\lambda f_c}, \frac{v}{\lambda f_c}\right) \cdot \frac{1}{\lambda^2 L f_c}$. This can be interpreted as the focal plane field resulting from a point source at distance L centered in front of the lens. The function $g(u,v)$ therefore indicates the manner in which the receiver optics "spreads" the point in the focal plane, and is often called the point spread function of the receiver. Hence, extended sources are focused as convolutions of source amplitude and point spread functions. Similar interpretations can also be associated with the reception of stochastic fields in random media.

At important point in our later discussions involves the application of Parceval's theorem to the integrated receiver and detector fields. This will yield the equality

$$\int_{A_d} |f_d(t,r)|^2 dr = \left(\frac{1}{2\pi}\right)^2 \int_{-\infty}^{\infty}\int |F_r(r,\omega_1,\omega_2)|^2 d\omega_1 d\omega_2 \quad (8-51)$$

$$= \int_{A_r} |f_r(t,r)|^2 dr$$

Since the *integrands*[23] are the field intensities we see that the integrals are proportional to the power collected over the receiver and detector areas. This means the power collected over the detector area due to the focal plane field is equal to the power collected over the receiver surface due to the received field. Hence, power is preserved in focusing the received field onto the detector (provided the detector is large enough to encompass the entire focused field). This means detector power levels can be computed directly at the receiver lens without the necessity of computing the actual diffracted field.

If the received field has an orthonormal expansion as in Eq. (8-25),

$$f_r(t,r) = \sum_i f_i \phi_i(t,r); \quad 0 \leqslant t \leqslant T, \quad r \in A_r \quad (8-52)$$

then the detector field has the associated expansion

$$f_d(t,r) = \sum_i f_i \hat{\phi}_i(t,r); \quad 0 \leqslant t \leqslant T, \quad r \in A_d \quad (8-53)$$

where

$$\hat{\phi}_i(t,u,v) \equiv \frac{\exp\left[j\frac{\pi}{\lambda f_c}(u^2+v^2)\right]}{j\lambda f_c} \int_{A_r} \phi_i(t,x,y) \exp\left[-j\frac{2\pi}{\lambda f_c}(xu+yv)\right] dx dy \quad (8-54)$$

The detector functions $\{\hat{\phi}_i\}$ are the diffracted versions of the received functions $\{\phi_i\}$, and therefore are related to its Fourier transform. By use of Parceval's theorem, we can easily show that these detector functions are themselves orthonormal. Hence, Eq. (8-53) itself represents an orthonormal expansion of the detected field over A_d having the same coefficients as the receiver field expansion. This means the detector field expansion can be derived from the received field expansion by using the same coefficients and modifying the orthonormal functions according to Eq. (8-54). Note that since the orthonormal functions are different, the associated field intensity will be distributed differently at the detector from that at the receiver lens, even though its power (integral) has been preserved. The principal point here is that the optical field can be expanded gather at the receiver area or at the detector area with a straightforward conversion between the two. The former is obviously more convenient when discussing the received field, whereas the latter is better suited for analysis at the detector surface. If the fields are random, the fact that the coefficients are preserved means that a Karhunen-Loeve expansion at the receiver is transformed directly into a KL expansion at the detector with the same eigenvalues.

8.7 Background Radiation

In addition to the desired signal power, a receiving system viewing an atmospheric background also collects unexpected background radiation falling within the spatial and frequency ranges of the detector. This collected background radiation is processed along with the desired signal background, and presents a basic degradation to the overall system performance. Of particular importance is the actual amount of background radiation power that is collected. The determination of the power, however, requires an accurate model for the source of this radiation. The accepted model is to consider the background to be generated from uniformly radiating sources. These sources divide into two basic types—① the diffuse sky background, assumed to occupy the whole hemisphere, and therefore is always present in any antenna field of view, and ② discrete, or point, sources, such as stars, planets, sun, and the like, that are more localized but more intense, and may or may not be in the antenna field of view. The analysis methods of background noise radiators are described in relative books, readers interested may look up in them, we will not introduce detailedly.

8.8 Photodetection

Photodetection of the light field represents the sky operation in the receiver, converting the collected field to a current or voltage waveform for subsequent post detecting processing. For optimal design of this latter processor it is important that the system designer be cognizant of the characteristics of the photodetecting element. This becomes particularly significant when the actual statistics of the detector waveform are necessary for optimal design procedures.

An optical photodetector has the basic structure shown in Fig. 8-16. A photosensitive material responds to incident light over its surface by releasing free electrons from its inner surface. These electrons are susceptible to an electric force field that pulls the released electrons to a collecting *anode*[24].

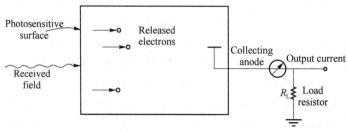

Fig. 8-16 Photodetector model.

If photomultiplication is desired, a series of *dynode*[25] surfaces are used, each one responding to incident electrons by releasing more electrons to the next dynode. As each dynode releases more electrons than it collects, a form of electron multiplication occurs, the overall effect to produce an inherent gain in the detector operation. The flow of electrons from photosensitive surface to final anode is manifested at the output terminals as an output current. Thus each electron movement is exhibited as a current contribution to the detector output, and the cumulation of such effects represents the observed output current. This current is converted to a voltage by passing through a detector load resistor. Since the conversion of optical field to electron follow and the reproduction of electrons by anode impingement, are both probabilistic in nature, the photodetector output always evolves as a random process in time. The overall effect is to induce an inherent randomness to the photodetection operation when responding to any optical filed, whether stochastic or not. This detector randomness must be properly accounted for in system models.

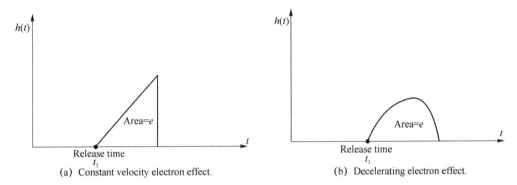

Fig. 8-17 Current response function.

The photodetected output current process is described mathematically by the superposition of the individual current effects of each released electron. As a single electron moves from the photosensitive material to the final collecting anode, it produces a current response function $h(t)$. (This is the time response observed in an ideal ammeter connected to the output, when an electron is released at $t=0$.) Physically, each electron moves for a short time period, ideally coming to rest at the anode. Hence its current response $h(t)$ will also be of a finite time duration, existing only while the electron is in motion. The actual shape of $h(t)$ depends on the electron velocity during transition. Specifically, $h(t)$ is the rate of movement of charge. Thus an electron moving at constant velocity to the anode produces the response function in Fig. 8-17(a), whereas a decelerating electron is described by Fig. 8-17(b). In all cases however, the area under the response function is a fixed constant, since the integral of $h(t)$ is the change in electric charge during electron motion. Thus,

$$\int_0^\infty h(t)\mathrm{d}t = \text{charge of a single electron}$$

$$= e = 1.6 \times 10^{-19} \text{ coulombs} \qquad (8\text{-}55)$$

In a photomultiplier, the release of an electron produces the movement of many other electrons to the collecting anode. If the photomultiplier is ideal, exactly G_m electrons are collected for each photoemissive electron released, and (8-55) becomes

$$G_m \int_0^\infty h(t)\,dt = G_m e \tag{8-56}$$

Thus the effective charge is increased by the factor G_m, the latter called the gain of the photomultiplier. In nonideal photomultiplication, the number of collected electrons, G_m, for each released electron, is itself random, and Eq. (8-56) must be analyzed with G_m as a random variable.

An electron released at a later time, say t_m, produces the response function $h(t-t_m)$. If the optical field is impressed at time $t=0$, the total cumulative response at time t is the combined response of all electrons released during the interval $(0, t)$. This produces the output current function

$$x(t) = \sum_{m=1}^{k(0,t)} h(t - t_m) \tag{8-57}$$

where t_m is the time of release of the jth electron and $k(0, t)$ is the number of electrons released during the time interval $(0, t)$. Note that only electrons released prior to time t contribute to the output at time t. The number $k(0, t)$ is often called the "count" of the electrons, and $k(0, t)$, considered as function of t, is often called the counting process of the photodetection operation. Since photodetection is statistical in nature, the location times $\{t_m\}$ and the electron count $k(0, t)$ are random variables when used to model the optical detector output. Thus, Eq. (8-57) represents a sum of a random number of randomly located response functions $h(t)$. Such processes are called shot noise processes, and have been used to model more general types of burstlike noise phenomena, such as shot noise in vacuum tubes. The function $h(t)$ are constrained by the electron transit behavior, as stated before.

Since the $\{t_m\}$ are random variables, and the count $k(0,t)$ is a random count process in time, the current $x(t)$ in Eq. (8-57) is itself generated as a somewhat complicated random process. Clearly, any analysis to determine its inherent statistics requires specification of the statistics of the location times and counting process. Note that the output $x(t)$ does not explicitly contain the received field in any obvious way—yet we expect the photodetector to exhibit the properties of the received field. Thus we would expect the optical field to be embedded within the counting process in some manner.

The relationship of he received electromagnetic field and the number of released electrons is governed by the interaction between the radiation field and electrons of the photosensitive material. There are two accepted ways to treat this relationship. In the purely quantum treatment, the field is quantized into photons, the average number of which is related to the field energy. Each field photon gives rise to an electron with probability η. *The electrons released are therefore a statistical measurement of the photon occupancy in the field, and electron counting is often called photon, or photoelectron, counting.* ⑤ The alternate treatment is the *semiclassical*[26] approach, which is actually a consequence of the quantum treatment. This model treats the field classically (i. e., as a wave) and prescribes a probabilistic relation to account for its interaction with the atomic structure of the detector surface. A complete description of the emission and absorption of light by an atom well beyond our interest here, we will not say it anymore.

Our discussion has been limited to a single photodetector in the focal plane, which produces an output shot noise process in response to the total diffracted field at the receiver. The natural extension from a single photodetector is to a collection of smaller photodetectors placed side by side in the focal plane, as show in Fig. 8-18, with each detector producing its own output. Such a combination of detectors is called a photodetector array. Detector arrays are characterized by the parallel set of response functions from each of its elements. Since off-axis arriving plane waves concentrate their diffraction patterns at different points in the focal plane, each detector of the array detects a different angle of the receiver field of view. Thus arrays effectively spatially "sample" the field of view simultaneously, producing separate response processes from each sample in parallel. Detector arrays, therefore, give the optical receiver a form of diversity reception. As the array size is increased the degree of diversity is increased at the expense of added parallel processing. The availability of a high degree of parallel diversity processing in a single receiver makes the optical detector array a theoretically powerful device in optical communications.

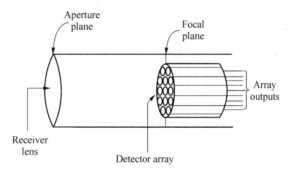

Fig. 8-18 Receiver with focal plane detector array.

8.9 Optical Intersatellite Links

Intersatellite links (ISLs) can be established between two geostationary spacecrafts (GEOs), between a low earth orbiting (LEO) spacecraft and a GEO, or between a deep space probe and a GEO or LEO. The main traffic to be carried by a GEO-GEO link would be telecommunications (e. g. telephony, business, user data or TV). These intersatellite links would allow network interconnectivity or provide new services in a more favourable manner. For a LEO-LEO link, transmission of data collected at the LEO seems to be the most attractive application. This data relay service would improve the collection of earth observation data and be of great importance for the future space station.

These links can be established either at RF frequencies or at optical frequencies. The main advantage of using optical frequencies is the high antenna gain of optical ISL. Other advantages of optical systems are the large available bandwidth and ease of suppression of external interference due to the extremely narrow bandwidth. Additionally, optical frequencies are suitable for applications outside the earth's atmosphere which would have a strong absorption for nearly all optical frequencies. For data transmission between a deep space probe and an earth orbiting spacecraft, the data rate achievable would be higher, and the required deep space (optical) antenna diameter lower, than for today's microwave systems if communication systems operating at optical frequencies were to be used.

Optical communication systems for space applications have been considered since the early 1970s. At that time the two potential systems were based on CO_2 lasers, operating at 10.6 μm, and flashlamp pumped Nd:YAG lasers operating at 1.06 μm. The CO_2 laser communications system was investigated in the U.S.A. and Europe. The system studied in Europe has reached an advanced state of development. Optical phase-locked-loops and optical *Costas loops*[27] operating at 10μm have been realized. The CO_2 laser communications system is very similar to the well-known phase modulated microwave systems, using phase modulation of the optical carrier. The receiver consists of an optical PLL for carrier recovery and demodulation. A laboratory breadboard of the CO_2 laser communications system is being completed.

The rapid progress made with terrestrial optical fibre communications systems, and especially the improvements achieved in the development of reliable and powerful semiconductor laser diodes, offers the possibility of using solid state technology for optical intersatellite links. Frequencies corresponding to wavelengths of around 800 and 1 300/1 500 nm are available. Optical communications with semiconductor laser diodes was identified as a promising candidate for the European data relay satellite (DRS). But system feasibility has still to be demonstrated, so significant development effort is necessary before the flight hardware is produced. Within its Payload and Spacecraft Development and Experimentation program (PSDE) the European Space Agency (ESA), has started to develop an optical payload based on today's technology for a planned in-orbit demonstration starting in 1993. In the U.S.A. the development of an optical terminal for space-to-ground and space-to-space links is under way. This terminal will be flow on *ACTS*[28]. The Japanese also are working on an optical terminal for space-to-ground and space-to-space links, to be flown on *ETCS*Ⅵ[29].

References

1. Robert M. Gagliardi, Sherman Karp. Optical Communications. A Wiley-Interscience Publication, 1975.

2. Timothy Pratt, Charles Bostian, Jeremy Allnutt. Satellite Communications. Second Edition, Publishing House of Electronics Industry, 2003.

3. Dennis Roddy. Satellite Communications. Third Edition, Tsinghua University Press, 2003.

4. M. Wittig, G. Oppenhauser. Performance of Optical Intersatellite Links. International Journal of Satellite Communications. 1988, 6: 153-162.

New Words and Expressions

1. superimpose ['sju:pərim'pouz] vt. 把……放在另一物的上面，这里指调制
2. carrier ['kæriə] n. 载波
3. stochastic [stə'kæstik] adj. 随机的
4. heterodyne ['hetərədain] n. 外差法
5. tolerance ['tɔlərəns] n. 容差
6. cascade [kæs'keid] adj. 级联的，串联的
7. bulb [bʌlb] n. 电灯泡
8. steradians [stri'reidiən] n. 球面度
9. impedance [im'pi:dəns] n. 阻抗
10. variation [ˌvɛəri'eiʃən] n. 变分
11. Fresnel-Kirchhoff 菲涅耳-基尔霍夫（菲涅耳是法国土木工程兼物理学家，基尔霍夫是德国物理学家、化学家、天文学家）
12. orthogonal [ɔː'θɔgəl] adj. 互相垂直的
13. orthonormal [ɔːθou'nɔːməl] adj. 标准正交的
14. Karhunen-Loeve, 卡亨南-赖佛变换
15. eigenfunction ['aigənfʌŋkʃən] n. 特征函数
16. eigenvalue ['aigənvælju:] n. 特征值
17. encase [in'keis] vt. 包装
18. cylindrical [si'lindrik(ə)l] adj. 圆柱形的
19. cladding ['klædiŋ] n. 包层
20. graze [greiz] vt. 掠过，擦过
21. encompass [in'kʌmpəs] vt. 包围，包含
22. hump [hʌmp] n. 顶点，峰值
23. integrand ['intigrænd] n. 被积函数
24. anode ['ænoud] n. 阳极，正极
25. dynode ['dainoud] n. 倍增器电极，打拿极

26. semiclassical [ˌsemiˈklɑːsikəl] *adj.* 半经典的

27. Costas loop 有时也称为科斯塔斯环,或同相正交环,是一种用于提取载波的方法

28. ACTS 即 advanced communications technology satellite,美国宇航局的先进通信技术卫星

29. ETCS 即 European Train Control System,欧洲列车控制系统

Notes

① 这个能力的进展,对那些极度关心传输大量信息的通信工程师而言,非常诱人。此外,所发射的电磁波中,有效发射功率的集总能力也随载频的增加而增加。因此,利用较高频率的载频,能增加系统的容量和获得较高的功率密度,通常这就改善了性能。由于这两个原因,光通信已作为人们在技术上特别感兴趣的一个领域出现了。

② 光通信有很多困难,因为与光频伴随而来的就是波长甚短。光部件要求自己特有的工艺,它完全不同于射频、微波和毫米波器件所相应的设计工艺。

③ 其中注星号者为复共轭。式(8-25)意味着函数均方可积,并且等式右边的和式收敛于等式左边的包络函数,这仅对辐射场要求一个有界限约束的能量。

④ 在导行信道中,光束从发射机到接收机都被限制在一个闭合的通路,即"管子"之中。凡可以应用金属导线的线路,如地面系统的通信或短程内部使用的通信,这些信道都可以应用光信道。除了光束特有的带宽之外,导行信道还有下列优点:①完全屏蔽背景和电磁干扰;②免除了扰动;③由于可以周期地插入再聚焦和放大设备而能够完全控制光束的传播;④与迅速发展的集成光学平稳对接。

⑤ 接收到的电磁场与所释放的电子数之间的关系是由辐射场与光敏材料之间的相互作用决定的。处理这种相互作用关系的方法有两种。一种是纯量子处理方法。在这种方法中,是将场量化为光子。而光子的平均值就代表场的能量。每个场光子导致一个电子发射的概率为 η。这样,所释放的电子就能统计地描述场中的光子占有率。电子计数也就常称为光子计数或光电子计数。

第9章
Holographic Data Storage

PREVIEW

With its omnipresent computers, all connected via the Internet, the Information Age has led to an explosion of information available to users. The decreasing cost of storing data, and the increasing storage capacities of the same small device footprint, has been key enablers of this revolution. While current storage needs are being met, storage technologies must continue to improve in order to keep pace with the rapidly increasing demand.

To meet the current demand in market, devices with large storage capacity are introduced. Compact Disks (CDs) are capable of storing more than 700 MB to 800 MB of information, Digital Versatile Disc (DVD) offer storage space for more than 15 GB of information, common hard disks used in PCs provide data storage space in form of 80, 160, 200, 500, 1 000 GB etc sizes.

*However, both magnetic and conventional optical data storage technologies, where individual bits are stored as distinct magnetic or optical changes on the surface of a recording medium, are approaching physical limits beyond which individual bits may be too small or too difficult to store.*① These devices can't satisfy the demand in future. Storing information throughout the volume of a medium—not just on its surface—offers an intriguing high-capacity alternative. *Holography*[1] breaks through the density limits of conventional storage by going beyond recording only on the surface, to recording through the full depth of the medium.

In addition to high storage density, holographic data storage promises fast *access times*[2], because the laser beams can be moved rapidly without inertia, unlike the actuators in disk drives. With the inherent parallelism of its *pagewise storage and retrieval*[3], a very large compound data rate can be reached by having a large number of relatively slow, and therefore low-cost, parallel channels.

Combining high storage densities, fast transfer rates, with durable, reliable, low cost media, make holography poised to become a compelling choice for next-generation storage and content distribution needs.

9.1 The Concept of Holography

In all conventional imaging technologies, such as *photography*[4], a picture of a three-dimensional scene is recorded on a *photosensitive*[5] surface by a lens or, more simply, by a *pinhole*[6] in an opaque screen. What is recorded is merely the intensity distribution in the original scene. As a result, all information on the *relative phases*[7] of the light waves from different points or, in other words, information about the relative optical paths to different parts of the scene is lost.

The unique characteristic of holography is the idea of recording the complete wave field, that is to say, both the phase information and the *amplitude*[8] of the light waves scattered by an object. Since all recording media respond only to the intensity, it is necessary to convert the phase information into variations of intensity. This can be done by holography.

Holography (from the Greek word "holos" meaning "whole" and "graphos" meaning "message") is a technique that allows the light scattered from an object to be recorded and later reconstructed so that it appears as if the object is in the same position relative to the recording medium as it was when recorded. The image changes as the position and orientation of the viewing system changes in exactly the same way as if the object were still present, thus making the recorded image appears three dimensional.[②]

A *hologram*[9] is a record of the interaction of two beams of coherent light, in the form of microscopic pattern of *interference fringes*[10]. A hologram contains information on both the phase and the amplitude of the object wave so it does indeed record the "whole message" of an object. Because they cannot be copied by ordinary means, holograms are widely used to prevent counterfeiting of documents such as credit cards, driver's licenses, and admission tickets.

Although a hologram is a visual image of a physical object, it is quite different from a photograph. For instance, when an object is photographed, each portion of the photo contains an image of the corresponding portion of the original object. Each section of a hologram, however, contains a complete image of the original object, viewed from a vantage point that corresponds to the section's position on the hologram. Thus, if the transparent plate containing a transmission hologram is broken, each piece will still be able to project the entire image, albeit from a different point of view. Using a piece from near the top of the holographic plate will produce an image as seen from above, while using a piece from near the bottom of the plate will create the impression of looking upward toward the object.

9.2 History of Holographic Data Storage

The first hologram was made in 1947 by Dennis Gabor, a Hungarian-born scientist who was working at the Imperial College of London. Gabor was attempting to refine the design of an electron *microscope*[11]. He devised a new technique, which he decided to test with a filtered light beam before trying it with an electron beam. Gabor made a transmission hologram by carefully filtering his light source. Garbor's two papers (A new microscopic principle and microscopy by reconstructed *wavefronts*[12]) for which he was subsequently to be awarded a Nobel prize in 1971, were published respectively in 1948 and 1949. He also received patent GB685286 on the invention. Gabor's holography was limited to film transparencies using a mercury arc lamp as the light source. His holograms contained distortions and an extraneous *twin image*[13].

Gabor's first paper on holography evoked immediate response from scientists worldwide. Among those who made important contributions to the development of the technique were G. L. Rogers, A. B. Baez, H. El-Sum, P. Kirkpatrick and M. E. Haine. In these early years, the mercury arc lamp was the most coherent light source available for making holograms. Because of the low coherency of this light, it was not possible to produce holograms of any depth, thus restricting further research. Despite equipment limitations, these researchers identified many of the properties of holography and further elaborated on Gabor's theory. Most important, they extended their understanding of the process and its potential influence to another generation of scientists.

This barrier was overcome in 1962 with the invention of the laser, Emmett Leith and Juris Upatnieks at the University of Michigan decided to duplicate Gabor's technique using the laser and an "*off-axis*"[14] technique borrowed from their work in the development of side-reading radar. They recognized from their work that holography could be used as a 3-D visual medium. The result was the first laser transmission hologram of 3-D objects (a toy train and bird).

At almost the same time, another major advance in holography was reported by Denisyuk [1962, 1963, 1965]. In his technique, which has some similarities to Lippmann's technique of colour photography, the *object*[15] and *reference*[16] beams are incident on the photographic *emulsion*[17] from opposite sides. *As a result, the interference fringes recorded are actually layers, almost parallel to the surface of the emulsion and about half a wavelength apart.*③ Such holograms, when illuminated with white light from a point source, reflect a sufficiently narrow wavelength band to reconstruct an image of acceptable quality, similar to that normally obtained with *monochromatic*[18] illumination.

These advances set off an explosive growth of activity, and optical holography soon found a very large of scientific applications. They included high-resolution imaging of *aerosols*[19], imaging through diffusing and aberrating media, multiple imaging, image *deblurring*[20], pattern recognition, computer-generated holograms, and the production and correction of optical element. Perhaps the most significant of these applications was holographic storage.

The idea of holographic storage was first proposed in 1963 by Pieter J. Van Heerden at Polaroid who predicted that a volume V of holographic recording medium can store about V/λ^3 bits of information (where λ is the wavelength of light used in the holographic storage device). This yields 6 terabits of information in a cube-of-sugar-like, 1 cm³ storage volume, using green light of wavelength 550 nanometers. The theoretical limits for the storage density of this technique are approximately tens of *terabits*[21] (1 terabit = 1024 gigabits = 128 gigabytes) per cubic centimeter.

In 1969, Kogelnik first developed the coupled-wave theory for volume holograms, predicting *diffraction efficiency*[22] and *Bragg selectivity*[23] for thick gratings. Later analysis examined the theory applied to the regime between thick and thin holograms. Using the Bragg selectivity inherent to volume holography, multiple holograms can be stored and recovered independently in the same volume by changing the propagation properties of the reference beam. As a result, the information storage capacity is greatly increased by volume holography.

Despite this attractive potential and fairly impressive early progress, research into holographic data storage died out in the mid-1970s. Because the lack of cheap parts and the advancement of magnetic and semiconductor memories, the application of holographic data storage was placed on hold.

With the components needed for such a technology has become widely available and cheaper, interest in volume-holographic data storage was rekindled and research for holographic memory systems has been reactivated in the early 1990s. Hardware advances carried out independent of holography have made holographic storage more achievable. These include such improvements as complementary metal-oxide semiconductor (CMOS) sensor technology, development of *spatial light modulators*[24] (SLM) using *ferroelectric*[25] liquid crystals and mirror arrays, and reduction in the cost and size of shorter wavelength green lasers. Yet the biggest challenge has been to find the right material for the recording medium.

Holographic data storage in photorefractive materials has been recognized by Chen et al. in 1968, one year after the discovery of the photorefractive phenomenon in *lithium niobate*[26] ($LiNbO_3$) by Ashkin et al. From this starting point a multitude of demonstration platforms have been built, including full-running prototypes. In 1991, scientists at RCA Laboratories demonstrated the technology by recording 500 holograms in an iron-doped

LiNbO$_3$ crystal, and 550 holograms of high-resolution images in a light-sensitive polymer material. The most remarkable US projects in this field have been funded by DARPA, NSIC, AFRL and AFOSR and were realised by a consortium of specialized American universities combined with industrial and military sources. PRISM (Photorefractive Information Storage Materials) started in 1994 and the HDSS (Holographic data storage system) program in 1995. The resulting demonstration platforms, e. g. the well-known DEMON I, II and III (DEMONstration) clearly showed the high technological objectives and potential impact of this technology. The main convincing results, beside the proofs of principle, were the achievement of a data density of 250 Gbit/inch^2 (≈ 40 Gbit/cm^2) in DEMON II and a bit-error-rate of less than 1×10^{-12} retrieved from single crystals of LiNbO$_3$ doped with iron. However, the project was stymied by limitations from storage materials available at the time.

From about 1994 to the present, lots of research groups at universities, corporations and government labs began to study on the holographic storage system. Over twenty companies involved in developing holographic storage such as IBM, InPhase, GE, Holoplex, Polaroid spinoff Aprilis and Optware. IBM researchers evaluated the engineering tradeoffs between the performance specifications of a practical system, as affected by the fundamental material, device, and optical physics in 2000. In 2005, companies such as Optware and Maxell have produced a 120 mm disc that uses a holographic layer to store data to a potential 3. 9 TB, which they plan to market under the name Holographic Versatile Disc. In the same year, InPhase Technologies produced the world's first commercial holographic drive and media, and published a white paper reporting an achievement of 500 Gbit/inch^2 in 2006. GE Global Research demonstrated their own holographic storage material that could allow for discs that utilize similar read mechanisms as those found on Blue-Ray Disc players in 2009. This holographic storage material can support 500 gigabytes of data storage capacity in a standard DVD-sized disc. GE's micro-holographic storage technology allows for 100 DVDs worth of data to be stored on a single disc.

The first products are likely to be expensive, and only feasible for large organizations with unusual needs for storage. However, with technologies improved, holographic storage would be available and affordable for the average consumer within the next few years.

9.3 Principle of Holographic Data Storage

In holographic data storage, an entire page of information is stored at once as an optical interference pattern within a thick, photosensitive optical material (see Fig. 9-1).

This is done by *intersecting*[27] two coherent laser beams within the storage material.

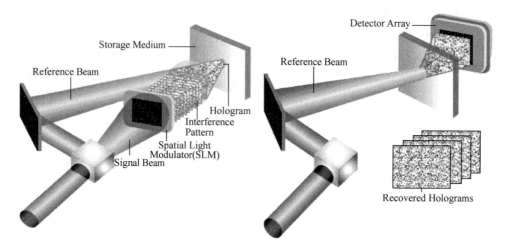

Fig. 9-1 Elementary sketch map of volume holographic storage.

The first, called the object beam (O beam), contains the information to be stored; the second, called the reference beam (R beam), is designed to be simple to reproduce—for example, a simple *collimated*[28] beam with a planar wavefront. The resulting optical interference pattern causes chemical and/or physical changes in the photosensitive medium: A replica of the interference pattern is stored as a change in the absorption, refractive index, or thickness of the photosensitive medium. *When the stored interference grating is illuminated with one of the two waves that was used during recording, some of this incident light is diffracted by the stored grating in such a fashion that the other wave is reconstructed.*④ Illuminating the stored grating with the reference wave reconstructs the object wave, and vice versa. Interestingly, a backward-propagating or *phase-conjugate*[29] reference wave, illuminating the stored grating from the "back" side, reconstructs an object wave that also propagates backward toward its original source.

A large number of these interference gratings or patterns can be superimposed in the same thick piece of media and can be accessed independently, as long as they are distinguishable by the direction or the spacing of the gratings. Such separation can be accomplished by changing the angle between the object and reference wave or by changing the laser wavelength. Any particular data page can then be read out independently by illuminating the stored gratings with the reference wave that was used to store that page. Because of the thickness of the hologram, this reference wave is diffracted by the interference patterns in such a fashion that only the desired object beam is significantly reconstructed and imaged on an electronic camera.

9.4 Theory about Formation and Reconstruction of a Hologram

The process of producing a holographic reconstruction is explained below purely in terms of interference and diffraction. Two different theories are generally used to study the diffraction of light from volume holograms. In the weak grating regime, which means higher-order scattering by the hologram is negligible, the first Born's approximation often used to predict the diffraction efficiency of a volume hologram. However, in the strong grating regime, the Born's approximation breaks down and coupled wave theory must be applied.

9.4.1 Volume Grating and Bragg Diffraction

Assuming the O beam and the R beam are plane waves, the two beams interfere with one another to form an interference pattern, a structure of equidistant family of planes called *volume grating*[30] inside the recording medium, as shown in Fig. 9-2.

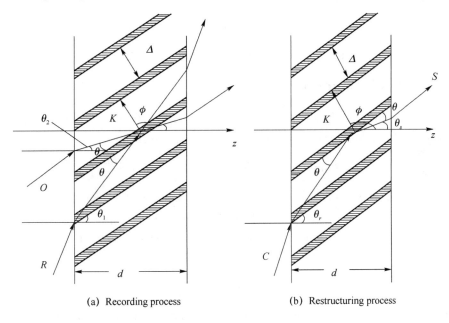

(a) Recording process   (b) Restructuring process

Fig. 9-2 The theory of recording and restructuring process of holographic storage.

θ_1 and θ_2 is the intersecting angle of the z-axis and the O beam and the R beam, respectively in medium. The fringe planes are located at the angle *bisector*[31] of the intersecting angle. The intersecting angle between the fringe plane and the two beams can be expressed as

$$\theta = (\theta_1 - \theta_2)/2 \qquad (9\text{-}1)$$

In order to maximize the total amplitude of diffraction waves, according to the theory of three dimensional grating diffraction, the relationship between the wavelength of the recording beam (λ), the fringe planes and the period of the grating (Λ) must be satisfied with the Bragg condition:

$$2\Lambda \sin \theta = \lambda \qquad (9\text{-}2)$$

where θ is the Bragg angle.

The period of the grating in medium is given by

$$\Lambda = \frac{\lambda}{2\sin \theta} \qquad (9\text{-}3)$$

Assuming the wave vectors of O beam and the R beam are k_o and k_r, respectively, a hologram consisting of a single grating k_g can be recorded

$$k_g = k_o - k_r \qquad (9\text{-}4)$$

where $k_g = \frac{2\pi}{\Lambda}$.

The hologram can be reconstructed by a plane read-out wave with Bragg matched at any wavelength $\lambda' < 2\Lambda$, where λ' presents a wavelength different from that of the recording beam. When the hologram is reconstructed at different wavelength, the incident angle of the readout beam θ' should be adapted to the corresponding Bragg angle, which is represented by

$$\theta' = \arcsin\left(\frac{k}{k'}\sin \theta\right) \qquad (9\text{-}5)$$

where θ' is the intersecting angle of the two recording beams.

9.4.2 Born's approximation

Under the first *Born's approximation*[32], the diffracted optical field from a transmission volume hologram as shown in Fig. 9-3 is given by

$$E_D \propto \mathrm{sinc}\left[\frac{L(k_P + k_G - k_D) \cdot \hat{z}}{2\pi}\right] = \mathrm{sinc}\left(\frac{L\Delta k_z}{2\pi}\right) \qquad (9\text{-}6)$$

where k_P, k_G, k_D are the incident wave *vector*[33], grating vector, and the diffracted wave vector respectively. L is the hologram thickness. Δk_z equals $k_P + k_G - k_D$. The diffraction efficiency, which is defined as the portion of incident intensity diffracted by the hologram, is therefore

$$\eta \propto \mathrm{sinc}^2\left(\frac{L\Delta k_z}{2\pi}\right) \qquad (9\text{-}7)$$

When $k_P + k_G = k_D$, i.e. $\Delta k_z = 0$, we get the maximum diffraction efficiency. This is the so-called *Bragg matching*[34] condition. In the wave-vector space (k-sphere) diagram, this means k_P, k_G, and k_D form a closed triangle as shown in Fig. 9-3. We call the quantity Δk_z the *Bragg mismatch*[35] factor, which can be caused by angular or wavelength detuning from the Bragg matching condition.

When the Bragg mismatch is due to the angular detuning $\Delta\theta$, the diffraction efficiency of a transmission volume hologram is given by

$$\eta \propto \sin c^2\left[\left(\frac{2L\sin \theta}{\lambda}\right)\Delta\theta\right] \qquad (9\text{-}8)$$

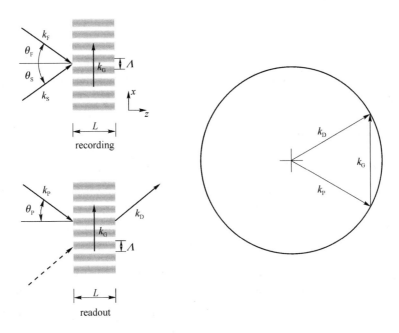

Fig. 9-3 (left) Recording and readout of a transmission volume hologram, and (right) the corresponding wave-vector space diagram.

where λ is the wavelength in the medium and θ is the Bragg-matched incident angle in the medium.

The angular spacing between the central peak and the first null of the sinc function is referred to as the angle Bragg selectivity, and is given by

$$\Delta\theta_B = \frac{\lambda}{2L\sin\theta} \tag{9-9}$$

When the Bragg mismatch comes from the wavelength detuning $\Delta\lambda$, the diffraction efficiency is

$$\eta \propto \mathrm{sinc}^2\left(\frac{2L\sin^2\theta}{\lambda^2\cos\theta}\Delta\lambda\right) \tag{9-10}$$

And the corresponding wavelength Bragg selectivity is given by

$$\Delta\lambda_B = \frac{\lambda^2\cos\theta}{2L\sin^2\theta} \tag{9-11}$$

In the case of a simple Bragg reflector the wavelength selectivity $\Delta\lambda$ can be roughly estimated by $\Delta\lambda/\lambda \approx \Lambda/L$. The assumption is just that the grating is not too strong, i.e., that the full length of the grating is used for light diffraction. Considering that because of the Bragg condition the simple relation $\Lambda = \lambda/(2n)$ holds, where n is the refractive index of the material at this wavelength, one sees that for typical values ($\lambda=500$ nm, $L=1$ cm, $n=1.5$) one gets $\Delta\lambda/\lambda \approx 10^{-5}$ showing the extraordinary wavelength selectivity of such volume holograms.

In the case of a simple grating in the transmission geometry the angular selectivity $\Delta\theta$ can be estimated as well: $\Delta\theta \approx \Lambda/L$. Using again typical numbers ($\lambda=500$ nm, $L=1$ cm,

$\theta=45°$) one ends up with $\Delta\theta \approx 4 \times 10^{-5}$ rad $= 0.002°$ showing the impressive angular selectivity of volume holograms.

Due to the highly spatial and wavelength Bragg selectivity, the basic advantage of volume hologram is that a large number of holograms can be stored and read out selectively in the same volume.

9.4.3 Coupled Wave Theory

The preceding theories for thin holograms cannot apply when the diffraction efficiency becomes high, because for high diffraction efficiencies the illuminating wave will be strongly depleted as it passes through the grating.[5] In some way one must take into account the fact that at some point within the grating there will be two mutually coherent waves of comparable magnitude traveling together. Such an account is the basis of the coupled wave theory, so aptly applied to the problem of diffraction from thick holograms by Kogelnik. This elegant analysis gives closed form results for the angular and wavelength sensitivities for all of the possible hologram types: transmission and reflection, amplitude or phase, with and without loss, and with *slanted*[36] or unslanted fringe planes. The equations also give, of course, the maximum diffraction efficiency achievable when the grating is illuminated at the Bragg angle and the fringe planes are unslanted. The equations are the result of a theory that assumes that the gratings are relatively thick so that there are only two waves in the medium to be considered, that is, that the Bragg effects are rather strong. Nevertheless, the equations are surprisingly accurate over a very large range of Q-values, including values considerably less than 10.

For a complete treatment of the theory one should refer to Ref. 1. Here we will only outline briefly the underlying ideas of the theory and give the principal results.

The coupled wave theory assumes that there are only two waves present in the grating: the illuminating reference wave R and the diffracted object wave O. It is assumed that the Bragg condition is approximately satisfied by these two waves and that all other orders strongly violate the Bragg condition and hence are not present. The equations that are derived express the coherent interaction between the waves R and O.

Fig. 9-1(b) defines the grating assumed by Kogelnik for his analysis. The z-axis is perpendicular to the surfaces of the medium, the x-axis is in the plane of incidence and parallel to the medium boundaries, and the y-axis is perpendicular to the page. The fringe planes are oriented perpendicularly to the plane of incidence and slanted respect to the medium boundaries at an angle ϕ. The grating vector k is oriented perpendicularly to the fringe planes. The same average dielectric constant is assumed for the region inside and outside the grating boundaries. The angle of incidence for the illuminating wave R in the medium is θ. The Bragg angle is θ_0. It is assumed that the fringes are sinusoidal variations of the index of refraction or of the absorption constant, or both for the case of mixed gratings. The assumed equations are therefore

$$n_0 = n + n_1 \cos(k \cdot r) \qquad (9\text{-}12)$$

and

$$\alpha_0 = \alpha + \alpha_1 \cos(k \cdot r) \qquad (9\text{-}13)$$

where n and α are the average values of the index and absorption constant, respectively. The slant of the fringe planes is described by the constants C_R and C_S, which are given by

$$C_R = \cos\theta \qquad (9\text{-}14)$$

$$C_S = \cos\theta - \frac{k}{\beta}\cos\phi \qquad (9\text{-}15)$$

where $\beta = \frac{2\pi n}{\lambda}$, and λ is the free space wavelength.

When the Bragg condition is satisfied we have

$$\cos(\phi - \theta) = K/2\beta \qquad (9\text{-}16)$$

and

$$C_R = \cos\theta_0 \qquad (9\text{-}17)$$

$$C_S = -\cos(2\phi - \theta_0) \qquad (9\text{-}18)$$

In the case where the Bragg condition is not satisfied, either by a deviation $\Delta\theta$ from the Bragg angle θ_0 or by a deviation $\Delta\lambda$ from the correct wavelength λ_0, where both $\Delta\theta$ and $\Delta\lambda$ are assumed to be small, Kogelnik introduces a *dephasing*[37] measure ϑ. This parameter is a measure of the rate at which the illuminating wave and the diffracted wave get out of phase, resulting in a destructive interaction between them. The dephasing measure is given by

$$\vartheta = \Delta\theta \cdot k \cdot \sin(\varphi - \theta_0) - \frac{\Delta\lambda k^2}{4\pi n} \qquad (9\text{-}19)$$

where

$$\Delta\theta = \theta - \theta_0 \qquad (9\text{-}20)$$

and

$$\Delta\lambda = \lambda - \lambda_0 \qquad (9\text{-}21)$$

The coupled wave equations that result from this theory are

$$C_R R' + \alpha R = -ikS \qquad (9\text{-}22)$$

$$C_S S' + (\alpha + i\delta)S = -ikR \qquad (9\text{-}23)$$

where k is the constant defined by

$$k = \frac{\pi n_1}{\lambda} - \frac{i\alpha_1}{2} \qquad (9\text{-}24)$$

and the primes denote differentiation with respect to z, and $i = \sqrt{-1}$. The physical interpretation of these equations as described by Kogelnik is as follows:

As the illuminating and diffracted waves travel through the grating in the z direction their amplitudes are changing. These changes are caused by the absorption of the medium as described by the terms α_R and α_S, or by the coupling of the waves through the terms kR and kS. When the Bragg condition is not satisfied, the dephasing measure δ is nonzero and the two waves become out of phase and interact destructively.

The solutions to these equations take on various forms depending on the type of hologram (grating) considered. When transmission holograms are considered, we say the fringe planes are unslanted when they are perpendicular to the surface. This condition is described by $C_R = C_S = \cos\Theta$ since $\varphi = \pi/2$ in this case. If the Bragg condition is also satisfied, then of course $\Theta = \Theta_0$. For reflection holograms, on the other hand, no slant means that the fringe planes are parallel to the surface, so $\varphi = 0$. If the Bragg condition also holds, then $C_R = -C_S = \cos\Theta_0$.

1. Transmission Holograms

For a pure phase, transmission hologram the absorption constant $\alpha_0 = 0$ and the solution of the coupled wave equations leads to a diffraction efficiency, for the general case of slanted fringes and Bragg condition not satisfied, given by

$$\eta = \sin^2(v^2 + \zeta^2)^{1/2}/(1 + \zeta^2/v^2) \tag{9-25}$$

$$v = \frac{\pi n_1 d}{\lambda (C_R C_S)^{1/2}} \tag{9-26}$$

$$\zeta = \vartheta d/(2C_S) = \Delta\Theta k d \sin(\varphi - \Theta_0)/(2C_S) = -\Delta\lambda k^2 d/(8\pi n C_S) \tag{9-27}$$

In the case for which there is no slant and the Bragg condition is satisfied, the formula reduces to the well-known equation.

$$\eta = \sin^2 \frac{\pi n_1 d}{\lambda \cos \Theta_0} \tag{9-28}$$

2. Reflection Holograms

The general equation for the diffraction efficiency of a pure phase reflection hologram with slanted fringe planes and non-Bragg illumination is

$$\eta = [1 + (1 - \xi^2/v^2)/\sin h^2(v^2 - \xi^2)^{1/2}] \tag{9-29}$$

$$v = i\pi n_1 d/[\lambda(C_R C_S)^{1/2}] \tag{9-30}$$

$$\xi = -\vartheta d/(2C_S) = \Delta\Theta K d \sin(\Theta_0 - \varphi)/(2C_S) = \Delta\lambda K^2 d/(8\pi n C_S) \tag{9-31}$$

Note that v is real since C_S is negative. For an unslanted grating and Bragg incidence, the diffraction efficiency can be expressed as

$$\eta = \tanh^2[\pi n_1 d/(\lambda \cos \Theta_0)] \tag{9-32}$$

9.5 Hardware for Holographic Data Storage

Fig. 9-1 shows the most important hardware components in a holographic storage system: the SLM used to imprint data on the object beam, two lenses for imaging the data onto a matched detector array, a storage material for recording volume holograms, and a reference beam intersecting the object beam in the material. What is not shown in Fig. 9-1 is the laser source, beam-forming optics for collimating the laser beam, *beamsplitters*[38] for dividing the laser beam into two parts, stages for aligning the SLM and detector array, shutters for blocking the two beams when needed, and waveplates for controlling polarization. Assuming that holograms will be angle-multiplexed (superimposed yet accessed independently within the same volume by changing the incidence angle of the reference beam), a beam-steering system directs the reference beam to the storage material. Wavelength multiplexing has some advantages over angle multiplexing, but the fast *tunable laser*[39] sources at visible wavelengths that would be needed do not yet exist.

The optical system shown in Fig. 9-1, with two lenses separated by the sum of their focal lengths, is called the "4-f" configuration, since the SLM and detector array turn out to be four focal lengths apart. Other imaging systems such as the Fresnel configuration (where a single lens satisfies the imaging condition between SLM and detector array) can also be used, but the 4-f system allows the high numerical apertures (large ray angles) needed for high density. In addition, since each lens takes a spatial *Fourier transform*[40] in two dimensions, the hologram stores the Fourier transform of the SLM data, which is then Fourier-transformed again upon readout by the second lens. This has several advantages: Point defects on the storage material do not lead to lost bits, but result in a slight loss in signal-to-noise ratio at all pixels; and the storage material can be removed and replaced in an offset position, yet the data can still be reconstructed correctly. In addition, the Fourier transform properties of the 4-f system lead to the parallel optical search capabilities offered by holographic associative retrieval. The disadvantages of the Fourier transform geometry come from the uneven distribution of intensity in the shared focal plane of the two lenses, which we discuss in the axicon section below.

9.6 Coding and Signal Processing

In a data-storage system, the goal of *coding and signal processing*[41] is to reduce the *Bit Error Rate*[42] (BER) to a sufficiently low level while achieving such important figures of merit as high density and high data rate. This is accomplished by stressing the physical components of the system well beyond the point at which the channel is error-free, and then introducing coding and signal processing schemes to reduce the BER to levels acceptable to users. Although the system retrieves raw data from the storage device with many errors (a high raw BER), the coding and signal processing ensures that the user data are delivered with an acceptably low level of error (a low user BER).

Coding and signal processing can involve several qualitatively distinct elements. The cycle of user data from input to output can include interleaving, *error-correction-code*[43] (ECC) and modulation encoding, signal preprocessing, data storage in the holographic system, hologram retrieval, signal postprocessing, binary detection, and *decoding*[44] of the interleaved ECC.

The ECC encoder adds redundancy to the data in order to provide protection from various noise sources. The ECC-encoded data are then passed on to a modulation encoder which adapts the data to the channel: It manipulates the data into a form less likely to be corrupted by channel errors and more easily detected at the channel output. The modulated data are then input to the SLM and stored in the recording medium. On the retrieving side, the CCD returns pseudo-analog data values (typically camera count values of eight bits) which must be transformed back into digital data (typically one bit per pixel). The first step in this process is a postprocessing step, called equalization, which attempts to undo distortions created in the recording process, still in the *pseudo-analog*[45] domain. Then the array of pseudo-analog values is converted to an array of binary digital data via a detection scheme. The array of digital data is then passed first to the modulation decoder, which performs the inverse operation to modulation encoding, and then to the ECC decoder.

9.6.1 Binary Detection

The simplest detection scheme is threshold detection, in which a threshold T is chosen: Any CCD pixel with intensity above T is declared a 1, while those below T are assigned to class 0. However, it is not at all obvious how to choose a threshold, especially in the presence of spatial variations in intensity, and so threshold detection may perform poorly. The following is an alternative.

Within a sufficiently small region of the detector array, there is not much variation in pixel intensity. If the page is divided into several such small regions, and within each region the data patterns are balanced (i. e., have an equal number of 0 s and 1 s), detection can be accomplished without using a threshold. For instance, in sorting detection, letting N denote the number of pixels in a region, one declares the $N/2$ pixels with highest intensity to be 1 s and those remaining to be 0 s. This balanced condition can be guaranteed by a modulation code which encodes arbitrary data patterns into codewords represented as balanced arrays. Thus, sorting detection combined with balanced modulation coding provides a means to obviate the inaccuracies inherent in threshold detection.

9.6.2 Interpixel Interference

Interpixel[46] interference is the phenomenon in which intensity at one particular pixel contaminates data at nearby pixels. Physically, this arises from optical diffraction or aberrations in the imaging system. The extent of interpixel interference can be quantified by the point-spread function, sometimes called a PSF filter. If the channel is linear and the PSF filter is known, the interpixel interference can be represented as a convolution with the original (encoded) data pattern and then "undone" in the equalization step via a filter inverse to the PSF filter (appropriately called deconvolution).

Deconvolution[47] has the advantage that it incurs no capacity overhead (code rate of 100%). However, it suffers from mismatch in the channel model (the physics of the intensity detection makes the channel nonlinear), inaccuracies in estimation of the PSF, and enhancement of random noise. An alternative approach to combating interpixel interference is to forbid certain patterns of high spatial frequency via a modulation code.

A code that forbids a pattern of high spatial frequency (or, more generally, a collection of such patterns of rapidly varying 0 and 1 pixels) is called a low-pass code. Such codes constrain the allowed pages to have limited high spatial frequency content. A general scheme for designing such codes is that via a strip encoding method in which each data page is encoded, from top to bottom, in narrow horizontal pixel strips. The constraint is satisfied both along the strip and between neighboring strips.

9.6.3 Error Correction

In contrast to modulation codes, which introduce a distributed redundancy in order to improve binary detection of pseudo-analog intensities, error correction incorporates explicit redundancy in order to identify decoded bit errors. An ECC code receives a sequence of decoded data (containing both user and redundant bits) with an unacceptably high raw BER, and uses the redundant bits to correct errors in the user bits and reduce the output user BER to a tolerable level (typically, less than 10^{-12}). The simplest and best-known error-correction scheme is parity checking, in which bit errors are identified because they change the number of 1s in a given block from odd to even, for instance. Most of the work on ECC for holographic storage has focused on more powerful *ReedSolomon (RS) codes*[48]. These codes have been used successfully in a wide variety of applications for two reasons: 1) They have very strong error-correction power relative to the required redundancy, and 2) their algebraic structure facilitates the design and implementation of fast, low-complexity decoding algorithms. As a result, there are many commercially available RS chips.

In a straightforward implementation of an ECC, such as an RS code, each byte would be written into a small array (say 2 times 4 for 8-bit bytes), and the bytes in a codeword would simply be rastered across the page. There might be approximately 250 bytes per codeword. If the errors were independent from pixel to pixel and identically distributed across the page, this would work well. However, experimental evidence shows that the errors are neither independent nor identically distributed. For example, interpixel interference can cause an error event to affect a localized cluster of pixels, perhaps larger than a single byte. And imperfections in the physical components can cause the raw BER to vary dramatically across the page (typically, the raw BER is significantly higher near the edges of the page).

Assume for simplicity that ECC can correct at most two byte errors per codeword. If the codewords are interleaved so that any *cluster error*[49] can contaminate at most two bytes in each codeword, the cluster error will not defeat the error-correcting power of the code.

Interleaving schemes such as this have been studied extensively for one-dimensional applications (for which cluster errors are known as burst errors). However, relatively little work has been done on interleaving schemes for multidimensional applications such as holographic recording. One recent exception is a class of sophisticated interleaving schemes for correcting multidimensional cluster errors developed.

For certain sources of error, it is reasonable to assume that the raw-BER distribution is fixed from hologram to hologram. Thus, the raw-BER distribution across the page can be accurately estimated from test patterns. Using this information, codewords can then be interleaved in such a way that not too many pixels with high raw BER can lie in the same codeword (thereby lowering the probability of decoder failure or miscorrection). This technique, known as matched interleaving, can yield a significant improvement in user BER.

9.6.4 Predistortion

The techniques we have described above are variations on existing coding and signal-processing methods from conventional data-storage technologies. In addition, a novel preprocessing technique unique to holographic data storage has been developed at IBM Almaden. This technique, called "predistortion", works by individually manipulating the recording exposure of each pixel on the SLM, either through control of exposure time or by relative pixel transmission (analog brightness level on the SLM). Deterministic variations among the ON pixels, such as those created by fixed-pattern noise, nonuniformity in the illuminated object beam, and even interpixel *crosstalk*[50], can be suppressed (thus decreasing BER). Many of the spatial variations to be removed are present in an image transmitted with low power from the SLM directly to the detector array. Once the particular pattern of nonuniform brightness levels is obtained, the recording exposure for each pixel is simply calculated from the ratio between its current brightness value and the desired pixel brightness.

At low density, raw-BER improvements of more than 15 orders of magnitude are possible. More significantly, at high density, interpixel crosstalk (which is deterministic once each data page is encoded) can be suppressed and raw BER improved from 10^{-4} to 10^{-12}. Another use of the predistortion technique is to increase the contrast between the 1 and 0 pixel states provided by the SLM. By using interferometric subtraction while recording the hologram, the amount of light received at the 0 detector pixels can be reduced.

9.6.5 Gray Scale

The previous sections have shown that the coding introduced to maintain acceptable BER comes with an unavoidable overhead cost, resulting in somewhat less than one bit per pixel. The predistortion technique described in the previous section makes it possible to record data pages containing gray scale. Since IBM researches record and detect more than two brightness levels per pixel, it is possible to have more than one bit of data per pixel. To encode and decode these gray-scale data pages, several local-threshold methods and balanced modulation codes were developed.

If pixels take one of g brightness levels, each pixel can convey $\log_2 g$ bits of data. The total amount of stored information per page has increased, so gray-scale encoding appears to produce a straightforward improvement in both capacity and readout rate. However, gray scale also divides the system's signal-to-noise ratio (SNR) into $g-1$ parts, one for each transition between brightness levels. Because total SNR depends on the number of holograms, dividing the SNR for gray scale (while requiring the same error rate) leads to a reduction in the number of holograms that can be stored. The gain in bits per pixel must then outweigh this reduction in stored holograms to increase the total capacity in bits.

9.6.6 Capacity Estimation

To quantify the overall storage capacity of different gray-scale encoding options, an experimental capacity-estimation technique was developed by IBM. In general, as the raw BER of the system increases, the number of holograms, M, increases slowly. In order to maintain a low user BER (say, 10^{-12}) as this raw-BER operating point increases, the *redundancy*[51] of the ECC code must increase. Thus, while the number of holograms increases, the ECC code rate decreases. These two opposing trends create an "optimal" raw BER, at which the user capacity is maximized. For the Reed-Solomon ECC codes, this optimal raw BER is approximately 10^{-3}. By computing these maximum capacities for binary data pages and gray-scale data pages from $g=2$ to $g=6$, we were able to show that gray-scale holographic data pages provide an advantage over binary encoding in both capacity and readout rate. The use of three gray levels offered a 30% increase in both capacity and readout rate over conventional binary data pages.

9.7 Associative Retrieval

The data to be stored are imprinted onto the object beam with SLM; typically, this is a liquid crystal panel similar to those on laptop computers or in modern camcorder viewfinders. To retrieve data without error, the object beam must contain a high-quality imaging system—one capable of directing this complex optical wavefront through the recording medium, where the wavefront is stored and then later retrieved, and then onto a pixelated camera chip. The image of the data page at the camera must be as close as possible to perfect. Any optical aberrations in the imaging system or misfocus of the detector array would spread energy from one pixel to its neighbors.

Optical distortions[52] (where pixels on a square grid at the SLM are not imaged to a square grid) or errors in magnification will move a pixel of the image off its intended receiver, and either of these problems (blur or shift) will introduce errors in the retrieved data. To avoid having the imaging system dominate the overall system performance, near-perfect optics would appear to be unavoidable, which of course would be expensive. However, the above-mentioned readout of phase-conjugated holograms provides a partial solution to this problem. Here the reconstructed data page propagates backward through the same optics that was used during the recording, which compensates for most shortcomings of the imaging system. However, the detector and the SLM must still be properly aligned.

A rather unique feature of holographic data storage is *associative retrieval*[53]: Imprinting a partial or search data pattern on the object beam and illuminating the stored holograms reconstructs all of the reference beams that were used to store data. *The intensity that is diffracted by each of the stored interference gratings into the corresponding reconstructed reference beam is proportional to the similarity between the search pattern and the content of that particular data page.*⑥ By determining, for example, which reference beam has the highest intensity and then reading the corresponding data page with this reference beam, the closest match to the search pattern can be found without initially knowing its address.

Volume holographic data storage conventionally implies that data imprinted on an object beam will be stored volumetrically [Fig. 9-4(a)], to be read out at some later time by illumination with an addressing reference beam [Fig. 9-4(b)]. However, the same hologram (the interference pattern between a reference beam and a data-bearing object beam) can also be illuminated by the object beam [Fig. 9-4(c)]. This reconstructs all of the angle-multiplexed reference beams that were used to record data pages into the volume. The amount of power diffracted into each "output" beam is proportional to the 2D cross-correlation between the input data page (being displayed on the SLM) and the stored data page (previously recorded with that particular reference beam). Each set of output beams can be focused onto a detector array, so that each beam forms its own correlation "peak." Because both the input and output lenses perform a two-dimensional Fourier transform in spatial coordinates, the optical system is essentially multiplying the Fourier transforms of the search page and each data page and then taking the Fourier transform of this product (thus implementing the convolution theorem optically). Because of the volume nature of the hologram, only a single slice through the 2D correlation function is produced (the other dimension has been "used" already, providing the ability to correlate against multiple templates simultaneously).

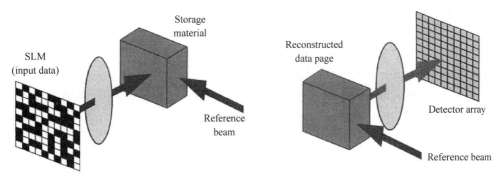

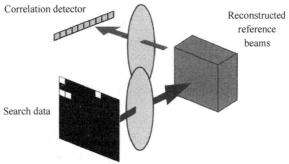

(a) Two coherent beams, one carrying a page of information, interfere within a photosensitive material to record a hologram.

(b) Illumination the hologram with the reference beam reconstructs a weak copy of the original information-bearing beam for capture with a detector array.

(c) Illuminating multiple stored hologram with a new page of search information reconstructs all of the reference beams, computing in parallel the correlation between the search data and each of the stored pages.

Fig. 9-4 Holographic data storage system.

The center of each correlation peak represents the 2D inner product (the simple overlap) between the input page being presented to the system and the associated stored page. If the patterns which compose these pages correspond to the various data fields of a database, and each stored page represents a data record, the optical correlation process has just simultaneously compared the entire database against the search argument. This parallelism gives content-addressable holographic data storage an inherent speed advantage over a conventional serial search, especially for large databases. For instance, if an *unindexed*[54] conventional "retrieve-from-disk-and-compare" software-based database is limited only by sustained hard-disk readout rate (25 Mbit/s), a search over one million 1 KB records would take ~40 s. In comparison, with off-the-shelf, video-rate SLM and CCD technology, an appropriately designed holographic system could search the same records in ~30 ms — a 1 200× improvement. Custom components could enable 1 000 or more parallel searches per second.

For this optical correlation process to represent a database search, the spatial patterns of bright (ON) pixels on the holographic data pages must somehow represent the digital data from fixed-length database fields. The SLM is divided into separate regions, each dedicated to a particular fixed-length field of the database. For example, a two-bit data field might be encoded by four blocks of pixels at a particular point within the SLM page. Such an encoding implements an exact search through the database. By thresholding the detected optical signal (essentially an analog quantity), any matching records are identified. Thresholding becomes commensurately more difficult, however, when many fields are being searched simultaneously. And when the threshold does not work correctly, completely unrelated records are identified as matches because near matches between pixel block patterns do not represent near matches in encoded data value.

More compact data representations can be realized by combining both *fuzzy*[55] and exact search encodings. The higher-order bits would be encoded compactly with binary-type encoding, while the low-order bits remained available for fuzzy searching. This trades search flexibility for more capacity (in terms of fields per database record).

With the fuzzy coding techniques, volume holographic content-addressable data storage is an attractive method for rapidly searching vast databases with complex queries. Areas of current investigation include implementing system architectures which support many thousands of simultaneously searched records, and quantifying the capacity reliability tradeoffs.

9.8 Recording Materials

Thus far, we have discussed the effects of the hardware, and of coding and signal processing, on the performance of holographic data storage systems. Desirable parameters described so far include storage capacity, data input and output rates, stability of stored data, and device compactness, all of which must be delivered at a specified (very low) user BER. To a large extent, the possibility of delivering such a system is limited by the properties of the materials available as storage media. The connections between materials properties and system performance are complex, and many tradeoffs are possible in adapting a given material to yield the best results. Here we attempt to outline in a general way the desirable properties for a holographic storage medium.

Properties of foremost importance for holographic storage media can be broadly characterized as "optical quality", "recording properties", and "stability". These directly affect the data density and capacity that can be achieved, the data rates for input and output, and the BER.

As mentioned above, for highest density at low BER, the imaging of the input data from the SLM to the detector must be nearly perfect, so that each data pixel is read cleanly by the detector. The recording medium itself is part of the imaging system and must exhibit the same high degree of perfection. Furthermore, if the medium is moved to access different areas with the readout beam, this motion must not compromise the imaging performance. Thus, very high standards of *optical homogeneity*[56] and fabrication must be maintained over the full area of the storage medium. With sufficient materials development effort and care in fabrication, the necessary optical quality has been achieved for both inorganic photorefractive crystals and organic photopolymer media. As discussed above, phase-conjugate readout could ultimately relax these requirements.

A more microscopic aspect of optical quality is intrinsic light scattering of the material. The detector noise floor produced by scattering of the readout beam imposes a fundamental minimum on the efficiency of a stored data hologram, and thus on the storage density and rate of data readout.

Because holography is a volume storage method, the capacity of a holographic storage system tends to increase as the thickness of the medium increases, since greater thickness implies the ability to store more independent diffraction gratings with higher selectivity in reading out individual data pages without crosstalk from other pages stored in the same volume. For the storage densities necessary to make holography a competitive storage technology, a media thickness of at least a few millimeters is highly desirable. In some cases, particularly for organic materials, it has proven difficult to maintain the necessary optical quality while scaling up the thickness, while in other cases thickness is limited by the physics and chemistry of the recording process.

Holographic recording properties are characterized in terms of *sensitivity*[57] and *dynamic range*[58]. Sensitivity refers to the extent of refractive index modulation produced per unit exposure (energy per unit area). Diffraction efficiency (and thus the readout signal) is proportional to the square of the index modulation times the thickness. Thus, recording sensitivity is commonly expressed in terms of the square root of diffraction efficiency, η:

$$S = \frac{\sqrt{\eta}}{Ilt} \tag{9-33}$$

where I is the total intensity, l is the medium thickness, and t is the exposure time; this form of sensitivity is usually given in units of cm/J. Since not all materials used are the same thickness, it is a more useful comparison to define a modified sensitivity given by the usual sensitivity times the thickness:

$$S' = S \times l \tag{9-34}$$

This quantity has units of cm^2/J and can be thought of as the inverse of the writing fluence required to produce a standard signal level. The unprimed variable, S, might be used to convey the potential properties of a storage material, given that the particular sample under test is extremely thin; in contrast, S' quantifies the ability of a specific sample to respond to a recording exposure.

For high output data rate, one must read holograms with many pixels per page in a reasonably short time. To read a megapixel hologram in about 1 ms with reasonable laser power and to have enough signal at the detector for low error rate, a diffraction efficiency around $\eta = 3\times 10^{-5}$ is required. To write such a hologram in 1 ms, to achieve input and output data rates of 1 Gbit/s, the sensitivity for this example must be at least $S' = 20 \text{ cm}^2/\text{J}$.

The term dynamic range refers to the total response of the medium when it is divided up among many holograms multiplexed in a common volume of material; it is often parameterized as a quantity known as $M\#$ (pronounced "M-number"), where

$$M\# = \sum \eta^{1/2} \tag{9-35}$$

and the sum is over the M holograms in one location. The $M\#$ also describes the scaling of diffraction efficiency as M is increased, i.e.,

$$\eta = (M\#/M)^2 \tag{9-36}$$

Dynamic range has a strong impact on the data storage density that can be achieved. For example, to reach a density of 100 bit/μm^2 (64 Gbit/inch^2) with megapixel data pages, a target diffraction efficiency of 3×10^{-5}, and area at the medium of 0.1 cm^2 would require $M\# = 5$, a value that is barely achievable with known recording materials under exposure conditions appropriate for recording high-fidelity data holograms.

Stability is a desirable property for any data storage system. In the case of holographic storage, the response of the recording medium, which converts the optical interference pattern to a refractive index pattern (the hologram), is generally linear in light intensity and lacks the response threshold found in *bistable*[59] storage media such as magnetic films. In the case of write-once-read-many (WORM) media such as photopolymers, the material response is irreversible; once the material has been fully exposed, further optical irradiation produces no further response, and the data can be interrogated by the readout beam without erasing it or distorting it. Much basic research in holographic storage has been performed using photorefractive crystals as storage media. Of these crystals, Fe-doped lithium niobate has been the workhorse. Its sensitivity is sufficient for demonstration purposes, but lacks a factor of 100 for practical application. Since photorefractives are reversible materials, they suggest the possibility of a rewritable holographic storage medium. However, because they are linear and reversible, they are subject to erasure during readout. Several schemes have been investigated for stabilizing or "fixing" the recording so that the data can be read without erasure. One scheme that does this without compromising the ability to erase the data, known as two-color recording, has received a good deal of attention recently. Recording is enabled by simultaneous irradiation of the crystal by a gating beam of different wavelength than the usual object and reference beams. In the absence of the gating wavelength, the data can be read without causing erasure. More details are given in the next section.

Stability in the dark over long periods is also an issue; organic photopolymer materials are often subject to *aging processes*[60] caused by residual reactive species left in the material after recording or by stresses built up in the material during recording. Erasure may occur because of residual thermal diffusion of the molecules which record the hologram. Index modulation in photorefractives results from a space charge that is built up by the optical excitation and migration of mobile charge carriers. Stability in the dark depends on the trapping of these carriers with trap energies that are not thermally accessible at room temperature.

9.9 Two-color or Photon-gated Holography

Two main schemes for providing nondestructive readout have been proposed, both in lithium niobate, although the concepts are applicable to a broader range of materials.

The first was thermal fixing, in which a copy of the stored index gratings is made by thermally activating proton diffusion, creating an optically stable complementary proton grating. Because of the long times required for thermal fixing and the need to fix large blocks of data at a time, thermally fixed media somewhat resemble reusable WORM materials.

Another class of fixing process uses two wavelengths of light. One approach uses two different wavelengths of light for recording and reading, but for storage applications this suffers from increased crosstalk and restrictions on the spatial frequencies that can be recorded. The most promising two-color scheme is "photon-gated"[61] recording in photorefractive materials, in which charge generation occurs via a two-step process. Coherent object and reference beams at a wavelength λ_1 record information in the presence of gating light at a wavelength λ_2. The gating light can be incoherent or broadband, such as a white-light source or LED. Reading is done at λ_1 in the absence of gating light. Depending on the specific implementation, either the gating light acts to sensitize the material, in which case it is desirable for the sensitivity to decay after the writing cycle, or the gating light ionizes centers in which a temporary grating can be written at the wavelength λ_1. Fig. 9-5 shows a schematic of energy levels comparing the two-color and one-color schemes for a photorefractive material with localized centers in the bandgap. A very important and unique figure of merit for photon-gated holography is the gating ratio, the ratio between the sensitivity of the material in the presence and absence of gating light.

As we know, the most important photorefractive properties for two-color holographic data storage are the gating ratio (measuring the degree of nonvolatility), sensitivity, $M\#$ or dynamic range, dark decay, and optical quality. Two-color, photon-gated holography provides a promising solution to the long-standing problem of destructive readout in read/write digital holographic storage. In lithium niobate, optimization of the sensitivity requires control over stoichiometry (or doping), degree of reduction, temperature, gating wavelength, and gating intensity. Two-color materials differ fundamentally from one-color materials in that the dynamic range or $M\#$ can be increased by using higher writing intensity, and the sensitivity can be increased with higher gating intensity. Another route to increasing the $M\#$ would be to find a material which exhibits a two-color erase process. Substantial progress has been made in recent years in the field of two-color holography, and further progress can be expected on this complex and challenging problem.

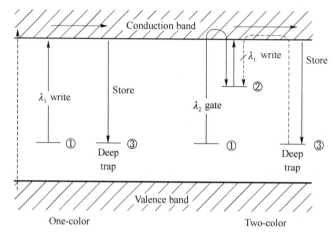

Fig. 9-5　Schematic level diagram of the one-color and two-color photorefractive effects. In stoichiometric lithium niobate, level is attributed to a Nb bipolaron state or Fe^{2+}/Fe^{3+} state, level 2 to a Nb_{Li} antisite polaron, and level 3 to an Fe^{3+} trap. The single center model for one-color recording is appropriate for low-power continuous-wave writing.

Outlook

Holographic data storage has several characteristics that are unlike those of any other existing storage technologies. Most exciting, of course, is the potential for data densities and data transfer rates exceeding those of magnetic data storage. In addition, as in all other optical data storage methods, the density increases rapidly with decreasing laser wavelength. In contrast to surface storage techniques such as CD-ROM, where the density is inversely proportional to the square of the wavelength, holography is a volumetric technique, making its density proportional to one over the third power of the wavelength. In principle, laser beams can be moved with no mechanical components, allowing access times of the order of 10 μs, faster than any conventional disk drive will ever be able to randomly access data. As in other optical recording schemes, and in contrast to magnetic recording, the distances between the "head" and the media are very large, and media can be easily removable. In addition, holographic data storage has shown the capability of rapid parallel search through the stored data via associative retrieval.

On the other hand, holographic data storage currently suffers from the relatively high component and integration costs faced by any emerging technology. In contrast, magnetic hard drives, also known as direct access storage devices (DASD), are well established, with a broad knowledge base, infrastructure, and market acceptance. Are there any scenarios conceivable for holographic data storage, where its unique combination of technical characteristics could come to bear and overcome the thresholds faced by any new storage technology?

Four conceivable product scenarios are shown in Fig. 9-6. The first two scenarios use read/write media, while the latter two are designed for WORM materials, which are much easier to develop but must support data retention times as long as tens of years. The first scenario takes advantage of rapid optical access to a stationary block of media, resulting in a random-access time of the order of 10 μs. The capacity is limited to about 25 GB by the size of the block of media that can be addressed by simple, inexpensive optics. Such a device could bridge the gap between conventional semiconductor memory and DASD, providing a nonvolatile holographic cache with an access time that is between DASD and dynamic random-access memory (DRAM).

Using the same optical components but replacing the stationary block of media with a rotating disk results in performance characteristics similar to those of a disk drive, albeit with terabytes (10^{12} bytes) of capacity per platter [Fig. 9-6 (b)]. In the CD-ROM type of embodiment [Fig. 9-6 (c)], holographic data storage takes advantage of the fact that single-exposure full-disk replication has been demonstrated. The player for the holographic ROM is conceptually very simple: The photodiode from a conventional ROM player is replaced by a CMOS camera chip, and the reconstructed data page is then imaged with suitable optics onto that camera.

Combining one of the DASD-type R/W heads and possibly a number of CD-ROM-type readers, a robotic picker, and sufficient tiles of media, a data warehouse with petabyte (10^{15} bytes) capacity in a standard 19-inch rack is conceivable [Fig. 9-6 (d)]. While the access time to any of the stored files is determined by the robotic picker and will be of the order of tens of seconds, the aggregate sustained data rate could be enormous. In this scenario, the relatively high component cost of a read/write holographic engine is amortized over a large volume of cheap media to obtain competitive cost per gigabyte.

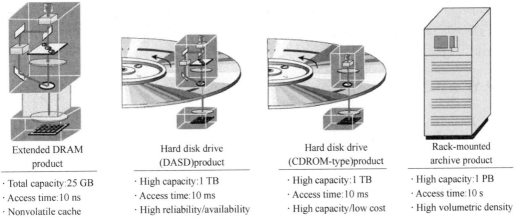

Fig. 9-6　Four scenarios highlighting the properties of holographic data storage: an all-solid-state memory module, which takes advantage of the potential for short access times; two rotating-disk geometries, with either erasable or WORM-type media; and, finally, a data warehouse with removable media. With its high volumetric density, holographic data storage has the potential to affect all types of data storage.

Will one of these scenarios with data stored in holograms and become reality in the foreseeable future? In collaboration and competition with a large number of scientists from around the globe, we continue to study the technical feasibility of holographic storage and memory devices with parameters that are relevant for real-world applications. Whether this research will one day lead to products depends on the insights that we gain into these technical issues and how well holography can compete with established techniques in the marketplace.

References

1. Herwig Kogelnik. Coupled Wave Theory for thick Hologram Grating. The Bell System Technical Journal, 1969, 48 (9): 2909-2947.
2. J. Ashley, M.-P. Bernal, and G. W. Burr, et al. Holographic data storage. IBM J. RES. DEVELOP., 2000, 44(3): 341-368.
3. H. Coufal, D. Psaltis, G. T. Sincerbox. Holographic Data Storage. Berlin: Springer-Verlag, 2000: 27-28.
4. D. Gabor. A New Microscopic Principle. Nature, 1948, 161(4098): 777-778.
5. E. N. Leith, J. Upatnieks. Reconstructed Wavefronts and Communication Theory. J. Opt. Soc. Am.. 1962, 52(10): 1123-1130.
6. P. J. Van Heerden. Theory of Optical Information Storage in Solids. Appl. Opt., 1963, 2(4): 393-400.
7. F. H. Mok, M. C. Tackitt, H. M. Stoll. Storage of 500 High-resolution Holograms in a $LiNbO_3$ Crystal. Opt. Lett., 1991, 16(8): 605-607.
8. http://en.wikipedia.org/.
9. Zhaopeng Xu. Study on Growth and Holographic Properties of Cerium-Ferrum Series Co-Doped Lithium Niobate. (Doctoral Thesis). Harbin: Harbin Institute of Technology, 2006.

New Words and Expressions

1. Holography [hə'lɔgrəfi] n. 全息摄影术；全息术
2. access time 存取时间，访问时间
3. pagewise storage and retrieval 页面存储和检索
4. photography [fə'tɔgrəfi] n. 摄影，摄影术
5. photosensitive [ˌfəutəu'sensitiv] adj. [物] 光敏感的，感光性的
6. pinhole ['pinhəul] 针孔，小孔
7. phase [feiz] n. 相，相位；vt. 定相，调整相位
8. amplitude ['æmplitjuːd] n. 振幅
9. hologram ['hɔləugræm] n. 全息图；全息摄影
10. interference fringe 干扰条纹

11. microscope ['maɪkrəskəʊp] n. 显微镜
12. wavefront /'weivfrʌnt/ 波阵面
13. twin image 孪生像
14. off-axis 离轴
15. object light 物光
16. reference light 参考光
17. emulsion [i'mʌlʃən] n. 乳状液，[医]乳剂，[摄]感光乳剂
18. monochromatic ['mɔnəukrəu'mætik] adj. [物]单色的，单频的
19. aerosol ['ɛərəsɔ] n. 气溶胶；浮质
20. deblur [di'blɜː] vt. 使变清晰；去模糊
21. terabit ['terəbit] n. [计]兆兆位(量度信息单位)
22. diffraction efficiency 衍射效率
23. Bragg selectivity 布拉格选择性
24. spatial light modulator 空间光调制器(是一类能将信息加载于一维或两维的光学数据场上，以便有效地利用光的固有速度、并行性和互连能力的器件)
25. ferroelectric [ˌferəui'lektrik] n. [电]铁电物质；adj. 铁电的
26. lithium niobate 铌酸锂
27. intersect [ˌintə'sekt] vt. 横断；vi. (直线)相交，交叉
28. collimate ['kɔlimeit] v. 校准
29. phase-conjugate 相位共轭(将信号光与闲频光写为复振幅形式，二者如果只看相位的话，仅符号相反(与复数的共轭类似)，因此称为相位共轭。相位共轭波的特性是与原始波有相同的频率，且其空间复振幅为原始波的空间复振幅的复共轭。能对光波实现相位复共轭作用的光学系统称相位共轭镜。从点光源发散的发散光束经共轭镜反射后，形成一会聚共轭光束，此光束精确地沿入射光的路径返回到原始点光源处。由于具有这种性质，所以当后向共轭波再次通过相位畸变介质，可以使相位畸变得到补偿，因此有广泛应用)
30. grating ['greitiŋ] n. 光栅，摩擦，摩擦声
31. bisector [baɪ'sektə(r)] n. (数学)二等分线，平分线
32. Born's approximation 博恩近似值
33. vector ['vektə] n. [数]向量，矢量
34. Bragg matching 布拉格匹配
35. Bragg mismatch 布拉格失配
36. slant [slɑːnt] v. (使)倾斜，歪向；n. 倾斜
37. dephasing [di:'feiziŋ] 移相，失相
38. beamsplitter [bi:m'splitə] n. 分光器，分光镜，射束分离器
39. tunable laser 可调谐激光(器)
40. Fourier transform 傅里叶变换
41. coding and signal processing 译码及信号处理
42. Bit Error Rate 误码率
43. error-correction-code 纠错码

44. decoding [diˈkəudiŋ] 译码，解码
45. pseudo-analog 伪随机模拟
46. interpixel 像素间
47. deconvolution [ˌdiːkɔnvəˈluːʃən] n. [计]去卷积，反褶积
48. ReedSolomon (RS) code 里德所罗门码（是基于块的纠错码，是一种用于数字通信和存储中的应用程序）
49. cluster error 集群误差
50. crosstalk [ˈkrɔsˌtɔːk] 串扰
51. redundancy [riˈdʌndənsi] n. 冗余
52. optical distortion 光学畸变
53. associative retrieval 关联检索
54. unindexed [ˌʌnˈindekst] adj. 没有索引的，未编入索引的
55. fuzzy [ˈfʌzi] adj. 模糊的，失真的
56. optical homogeneity 光学均匀性
57. sensitivity [ˈsensiˈtiviti] n. 灵敏度，灵敏性
58. dynamic range 动态范围
59. bistable [baiˈsteibl] adj. 双稳（态）的
60. aging processes 老化过程
61. photon-gated 光子选通

Notes

① 无论是磁技术还是一般的光学数据存储技术，都是在记录介质表面以不同磁或光学变化存储单个位，这样的存储技术正接近存储介质的物理极限，超过物理极限会导致单个位太小或难以存储。

② 全息技术是一种可以记录物体散射光并且可以重建的技术，重建过程中通过存储介质而显示的像和记录时原物体的位置一致。当观察系统改变方向和位置时，产生的像也会以同样方式改变，就好像物体依然存在，因而记录的像呈现出三维结构。

③ 因此，记录干涉条纹的实际层与感光乳剂表面平行，条纹间大约有半个波长的距离。

④ 当使用记录过程中两束光波中的任意一束照射存储的干涉光栅时，入射波被光栅所衍射进而再现了另一束波的信息。

⑤ 当衍射效率变得很高时，薄全息图并不适用于前面提到的理论——博恩近似。因为在高衍射效率情况下，照射光波通过光栅时会产生大量的损耗。

⑥ 参考光波通过存储的干涉光栅而产生对应的衍射波的强度与我们所要查询的图样和特定的数据页的内容之间的相似度成正比。

Optical Tweezers

第 10 章

PREVIEW

Traditionally the problem of how cells send and receive information has been *tackled*[1] in a number of different ways: The techniques of *biochemistry*[2], *genetics*[3], *cell biology*[4], *physiology*[5] and *electrophysiology*[6] have all to some extent been applied to the study of signaling. In recent years it has proved possible in many cases to synthesize the information from these seemingly *disparate*[7] areas of research to powerful effect. This has resulted in many significant advances and the field of *cell signaling*[8] is expanding throughout the world. Much of the success has been made possible by the development and application of new technologies. In many cases infusion of a technique from one research area to another has enabled rapid progress on a problem that had previously proved *intractable*[9]. One of the most exciting developments in the field of physics recently has been the realization of a technique for trapping and manipulating objects of widely different sizes with beams of light.

In 1970, it was discovered for the first time that the forces of radiation pressure from lasers can accelerate and trap neutral particles, since then, based on this effect, the technology of optical tweezers are being increasing developed in the world. In recent years, this technique, optical tweezers, has been applied to a number of biological systems with extremely encouraging results. It has been found that optical tweezers have the potential to allow non-destructive manipulation of objects within living *organisms*[10]. Optical tweezers is a technique that is built upon the principle that small particles can be trapped in the waist of a *strongly focused laser beam*[11], enabling its user to access tiny objects without any mechanical contact. The optical trap results from the fact that the objects that are trapped in the focus of the laser beam experience a *restoring force*[12] if they try to leave the high intensity.

In this paper, we first interpret the concept of optical tweezers and the brief history of this technology and then describe the basic theory of optical tweezers and its system, Finally the application of this technology are briefly characterized.

10.1 Concept of Optical Tweezers

In 1970, Ashkin showed that one could use the forces of radiation pressure from focused laser beams to significantly affect the *dynamics*[13] of small transparent neutral particles. Two basic light pressure forces were identified: a *scattering force*[14] in the direction of the incident light beam, and a *gradient force*[15] in the direction of the intensity gradient of the beam. It was shown experimentally that, using just these forces, one could accelerate, decelerate, and even stably trap small sized neutral particles using mildly focused laser beams. It was not known previously that one could use radiation pressure forces to make a stable 3-dimensional optical trap. Such a trap has an *equilibrium*[16] point in space, with the property that any displacement of a particle away from this point results in a restoring force.

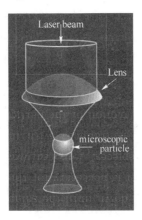

Fig. 10-1 Diagram of optical tweezers.

So what are optical tweezers? An optical tweezer is a scientific instrument that uses a focused laser beam to provide an attractive or repulsive force, depending on the index mismatch (typically on the order of piconewtons) to physically hold and move microscopic dielectric objects. As seen from Fig. 10-1, A low power, continuous wave laser that is focused through a high N.A. objective can trap particles and can move the trapped particle by moving the laser or stage, hence the laser acts as a "tweezer" by picking up and moving an individual particle. Optical tweezer is a three-dimensional trap that based on a strongly focused laser beam creates gradient optical force. Now this technology have been used as versatile tools for non-contact manipulation of micrometer-sized particles, such as grabbing living cells and organelles; measuring stretching of large molecules such as DNA, etc. It is also a useful tool for learning various optics procedures, and it is easy to build a simple setup.

10.2 History of Optical Tweezers

Now let us review the history of optical trapping and manipulation of small *neutral particles*[17], with particular emphasis on the origins of the field. This subject, which did not even exist before the advent of lasers, now plays a major role in single particle studies in physics, chemistry, and biology. It was known from physics and the early history of optics that light had linear and *angular momentum*[18], and, therefore, could exert radiation pressure and torques on physical objects. These effects were so small, however, that they were not easily detected. The study of radiation pressure was considered exciting physics, but not very practical at the turn of the previous century when Nichols and Hull and Lebedev first succeeded in experimentally detecting radiation pressure on macroscopic objects and absorbing gases. The subject essentially *dropped into obscurity*[19] until the invention of the laser in 1960. Laser physics range a large field of science. A subfield within laser physics is optical trapping and an optical tweezer is an example of an optical trap. A strongly focused laser beam has the ability to catch and hold particles (of dielectric material) in a size range from nm to um. This technique makes it possible to study and manipulate particles like atoms, molecules (even larger) and small dielectric spheres.

Most of the early work in this field was done by Arthur Ashkin of Bell Labs. He invented optical tweezers and did pioneering work in all the major areas of optical manipulation: in 1978: two opposing laser beams were used to trap and cool atoms; in 1986: a single laser focused through a microscope was used to trap *polystyrene balls*[20] with diameters of 10 um to 25 nm; in 1987: bacteria and *protozoa*[21] were trapped, first with a 514.5 nm Ar laser, followed by a 1064 nm Nd: YAG laser, in 2000: applications of tweezers to the study of single motor molecules, and DNA folding and sequencing.

Over the years, these newly found laser trapping and manipulation techniques were found to apply over a wide range of particle types, including particles as diverse as atoms, molecules, *submicron particles*[22] and macroscopic dielectric particles hundreds of micrometers in size. Even living biological cells and organelles within cells can be trapped and manipulated free of optical damage. The use of optical tweezer techniques has led to an explosion of new understanding of the mechanics, force generation, and *kinetics*[23] of a wide variety of motor molecules. With optics, we have fine control over forces from as low as hundredths of a piconewton up to several hundreds of piconewtons.

10.3 Basic Theory of Optical Tweezers

Light has the ability to produce radiation pressure. When light is absorbed, refracted by dielectric material, tiny forces on the order of piconewtons are generated. For reference, several milliwatts of power corresponding to a laser beam gives only a few piconewtons. However, a force of 10 pN is sufficient to pull a bacterium through water ten times faster than it can swim. The force is proportional to the power of the laser. These forces (radiation pressures) arise from the momentum change of the light itself. For every action force, there is a corresponding reaction force which is equal in magnitude and opposite in direction.

Arthur Ashkin tried a simple experiment to look for particle motion by laser radiation pressure. He used a sample of transparent *latex*[24] spheres of density 1, in water, to avoid any problems with heating or so called *radiometric effects*[25]. With just milliwatts of power, particle motion was observed in the direction of a mildly focused Gaussian beam. The particle velocity was in approximate agreement with their crude-force estimates, suggesting that this was indeed a radiation pressure effect. However, an additional unanticipated force component was soon discovered which strongly pulled particles located in the fringes of the beam into the high intensity region on the beam axis. Once on axis, particles stayed there and moved forward, even if the entire beam was slued back and forth within the chamber. Particles were being guided by the light! When the light was turned off, they wandered toward the fringes of the beam. When the light was turned on again, they were quickly pulled to the beam axis. Was this transverse force component light pressure, too?

Fig. 10-2 shows that both these force components do indeed originate from radiation pressure. Imagine a high index of refraction sphere, many wavelengths in diameter, placed off axis in a mildly focused Gaussian beam.

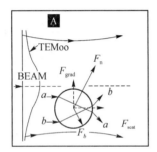

Fig. 10-2 Origin of and for high index sphere displaced from TEM beam axis.

Consider a typical pair of rays "a" and "b" striking the sphere symmetrically about its center. Neglecting relatively minor surface reflections, most of the rays refract through the particle, giving rise to forces F_a and F_b in the direction of the momentum change. Since the intensity of ray "a" is higher than ray "b", the force F_a is greater than F_b. Adding all such symmetrical pairs of rays striking the sphere, one sees that the net force can be resolved into two components F_{scat} called the scattering force component pointing in the direction of the incident light, and F_{grad}, a gradient component arising from the gradient in light intensity and pointing transversely toward the high intensity region of the beam. For a particle on axis or in a plane wave, $F_a = F_b$ and there is no net gradient force component. A more detailed calculation of the sum of the forces of all the rays striking the sphere gave a net force in excellent agreement with the observed velocity. For a low index particle placed off-axis, the refraction through the particle reverses, F_a is less than F_b and such a particle should be pushed out of the beam. One also observes by mixing large and small diameter spheres in the same sample that the large spheres move faster and pass right by the smaller spheres as they proceed along the beam. This is a form of particles separation and is expected from the simple ray-optic calculations. So basically optical trapping works because laser light refracts through transparent object in such a way that there is always more light pressure pushing the object towards the focal point than there is pushing it away from it.

Theoretical calculations of the force in optical tweezers acting on a particle are very time-consuming or even impossible. We are trying to give a qualitative explanation of the forces acting on a particle near the focus of the optical tweezers. If the object in question is sufficiently larger than the wavelength, one can take a *geometric optical approach*[26] (i.e. the *diffraction effects*[27] are negligible). Here is a ray optic representation of the gradient force valid for particles larger than the wavelength of laser light. Parallel rays enter a small, refractile sphere from above and are bent because the sphere acts like a lens. Before entering the rays travel vertically with zero horizontal momentum. After deflection however, they pick up horizontal momentum. Since momentum is conserved, an equal and opposite momentum change is conveyed to sphere. If the beam were uniform, the reaction forces would cancel and there would be no net sideways component. In a gradient status, however, the asymmetry in the light gives rise to an imbalance in the reaction forces and the object is pulled towards the brighter side. Near a diffraction-limited spot (i.e. for objects smaller than the wavelength of the laser light), Because the size of the focus is in the order of a wavelength the focus can be characterized as a dot which will simplify the calculations of the force acting on the object. If the object is placed below the center of the focus the resulting force of the trap will act in the upward direction, seen from Fig. 10-3 (a); If the object is placed above the center of the focus the resulting force of the trap will act in the downward direction, seen from Fig. 10-3 (b); If the object is placed to the right of the focus the resulting force of the trap force the object towards the center of the trap, seen from Fig. 10-3(c).

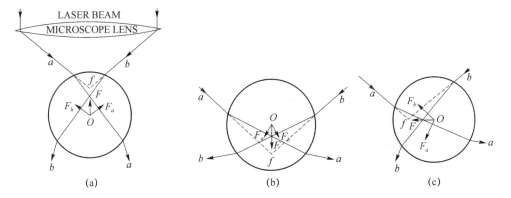

Fig. 10-3 Simple ray-optics picture of the stability of tweezer trap. Any displacement of a macroscopic sphere away from the focus, either axially as in (a) or (b), or transversely as in (c), results in a net restoring force.

Simply speaking, the magnitude of the optical trapping force is shown in the following formula: In which parameter Q is the trapping efficiency, for a spherical particle of radius equal to the light wavelength, $Q \sim 0.1$; c/n is the speed of light in medium; ν is the frequency of photon; h is *Planck constant*[28] and P_{power} is the laser power, the typical laser power used for optical trap are $1 \sim 100$ mW.

$$F=\frac{dP_{\text{momentum}}}{dt}=Q\times\frac{P_{\text{power}}}{h\nu}\times\frac{h}{\lambda}=Q\frac{nP_{\text{power}}}{c}$$

*In conclusion, in an optical trap, there is a scattering force which tends to push objects along the direction of light propagation and there is a gradient force which tends to push objects to the direction of the light gradient, so in order to make an optical trap, the steepest possible light gradients are needed to ensure that the gradient force overcomes the scattering force, which is not necessarily in the direction of the light gradient. A sufficiently steep three dimensional light gradient can be achieved by focusing laser light to a diameter on the order of the laser wavelength.*①

10.4 System of Optical Tweezers

An optical tweezers system is constructed by focusing light from a laser through a *microscope objective*[29] with a high numerical aperture (e.g. 100 * N.A. = 1.3) The objective serves two purposes, both imaging the object under investigation as well as focusing the laser beam to a small spot in the objective plan. Fig. 10-4 shows an typical optical tweezer system.

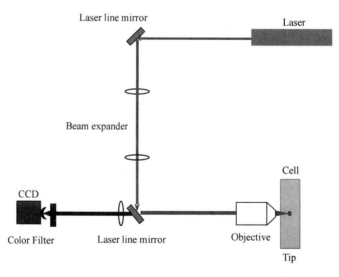

Fig. 10-4 Diagram of optical tweezers system.

Trapping can be done using lasers over a wide range of wavelengths. Visible lasers, such as the He-Ne laser used in the basic tweezer setup, have the advantage that they can be easily seen, and so are relatively easy to align. However, for *biological specimens*[30], the absorption of visible wavelength light can lead to the destruction of the specimen while being trapped. Therefore, for biological specimens, infrared lasers such as Nd:YAG or semiconductor lasers around 850 nm are commonly used. The infrared laser is chosen to avoid damage in the biological samples, and absorption of light in the water in the solution (shorter wavelengths is absorbed by biological samples, longer is absorbed by water). The optics between the laser and the microscope objective *expands and steers*[31] the laser beam. And the microscope objective is used both to focus the beam and to view the trapped object. A CCD camera is used to monitor the trapped object. Spectral analysis of fast movements in the trap, for example thermal motion, can be achieved by imaging the trapped object. It is important that the CCD camera's focus is the same as the trapping beam's focus, so that trapped particles are in focus when viewed on the monitor. This allows one to tell whether the specimen is properly trapped or not. To match these focuses properly, first get the camera at the proper distance above the trapping objective. One way is to just calculate the proper distance the video adapter must be from the back pupil of the objective, and fix the camera position according. A better way is to view a sample through the eyepieces of the microscope and move the camera up and down until the samples look the same on the monitor as they do in the eyepieces. No laser is necessary for this part of the alignment; be careful when looking into the mounted eyepieces. *Force calibration*[32] is performed by moving the microscope stage, while a bead is trapped, with increasing velocity until the bead escapes or by analyzing the Brownian motion of the particle in the trap.

Combining two beams of the same wavelength and opposite *polarization*[33] yields a dual-beam optical trap, as shown in Fig. 10-5. This makes possible a wide variety of experiments in which both the position and orientation of a particle can be controlled. Recently, the multiple optical tweezers and the dynamic optical tweezers can be seen in some references. Polystyrene balls make a good choice for initial trapping experiments. They are available in a variety of sizes,

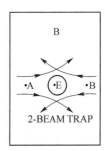

Fig. 10-5 Dual-beam optical trap.

have a long storage life, have an index of refraction of around 1.57, and can be trapped with a variety wavelengths without damage.

10.5 Application of Optical Tweezers

The laser tweezers can, in fact, not only move and sort individual bacteria or cells, it can also permit precise, non-destructive, repositioning of small structures inside a living cell, without recourse to *micromanipulators*[34] and without any damages to the cell surface. Moreover, since the power of the trap can be carefully and smoothly controlled, and since the trapping force acts on a large volume of the biological object, not only a specific part of its surface, no excessive force has to be applied to vulnerable biological systems.

Greulich and Berns were the first to use the tweezers technique in combination with the so called "*microbeam*" technique of pulsed laser cutting (sometimes called "*laser scissors*" or "*scalpel*") for cutting and moving cells and organelles. Laser Scalpel, on the other hand, is a technique for precise elimination or destruction of cells in various biological objects, penetration of cells in various biological objects, penetration of cell walls for artificial fertilization or for stimulated cell fusion, for DNA cutting etc. which is built upon the use of a well focused pulsed laser beam (whose intensity is carefully optimize).② Hence, it is expected that optical tweezers and laser scalpel very soon will become a most useful tool for manipulation of biological objects(e. g. , work with or in the interior of cells, with bacteria, *mitochondria*[35], DNA, for cell differentiation studies, etc.) that can replace and complement many presently existing micromechanical tools. Its extraordinary properties and potentialities also open up a number of new possibilities within the field of *biosciences*[36], even some yet unthought of.

Greulich's early work involved *ultraviolet cutting*[37] and tweezer manipulation of pieces of *chromosomes*[38] for gene isolation. Tweezers were also used to bring cells into contact with one another in order to effect cell fusion by cutting the common wall.

The early work of Ashkin et al. showed the ability of tweezers to distort the shape of red blood cells and confine many cells in a single trap. Svoboda and Block measured the *elastic properties*[39] of isolated red blood cell *membrane*[40]. Using three tweezer traps, Brakenhoff et al. developed a new *assay*[41] to sensitively measure the shape recovery time of single red blood cell, Significant differences in relaxation times were found for old and young cells. Measurements were made in *blood plasma*[42] and gave markedly different results from previous assays using pipettes in *buffer solution*[43], The three computer controlled tweezer traps used a multiple scanning trap system developed by Visscher et al.

Extensive use of optical trapping techniques has been made in the field of *microchemistry*[44], which studies the spectroscopy and chemistry of small um-sized domains. Experiments combining trapping with *fluorescence*[45] absorption spectroscopy, *photochemistry*[46], and *electrochemistry*[47] were performed. *Polymerization*[48], ablation and other micro fabrication techniques were demonstrated with micron samples. Beam scanning techniques were developed for trapping of um-sized metal particles, low index particles, and moving of particle arrays in complex patterns. These experiments are made by Masuhara et al.

10.6 Future of Optical Tweezers

It seems fair to predict that use of optical manipulation techniques will continue to grow at an increasingly rapid pace in the many subfields of physics, chemistry, and biology involving small particles. We are entering an era of increasing emphasis on the small for applications and for basic science. Microtechnology, small machines, small motors, motor molecules, gene sequencing, genetic engineering, and biological computers are already familiar terms. The role of laser tweezers and manipulation in basic sciences has been truly revolutionary. The impact of laser technology on the biological sciences may prove to be equally revolutionary.

References

1. A. Ashkin. acceleration and trapping of particles by Radiation Pressure. Phys. Rev. Lett., 1970, 24: 156.
2. A. Ashkin. Trapping of Atoms by Resonance Radiation Pressure. Phys. Rev. Lett., 1978, 40: 729-732.
3. A. Ashkin, J. M. Dziedzic. Observation of a single-beam Gradient Force Optical Trap for Dielectrical Particles. Optics Letters, 1986, 11: 288-290.
4. A. Ashkin, J. M. Dziedzic. Optical Trapping and Manipulation of Viruses and Bacteria. Science, 1987, 235(4795): 1517-1520.
5. R. W. Steubing, S. Cheng. Laser induced fusion in combination with optical tweezers: the laser cell fusion trap. Cytometry, 1991, 12: 505.
6. K. Svoboda, C. F. Schmidt, D. Branton, S. M. Block. Conformation and elasticity of the isolated red blood cell membrane skeleton. Biophys. J., 1992, 63: 784.
7. K. Visscher, G. J. Brakenhoff, J. J. Krol. Micromanipulation by 'multiple' optical traps created by a single fast scanning trap integrated with the bilateral confocal scanning microscope. Cytometry, 1993, 14: 105.
8. H. Masuhara, F. C. deSchryver, N. Kitamura, N. Tamai. Microchemistry Spectroscopy and Chemistry in Small Domains. North Holland, 1994.

New Words and Expressions

1. tackle: ['tækl] *vt.* 固定，应付（难事等），处理，解决，抓住
2. biochemistry ['baiəu'kemistri] *n.* 生物化学
3. genetics [dʒi'netiks] *n.* 遗传学
4. cell biology *n.* 细胞生物学
5. physiology [ˌfizi'ɔlədʒi] *n.* 生理学
6. electrophysiology [ɪ'lektrəuˌfɪzɪ'ɔlədʒɪ] *n.* [物]电生理学
7. disparate ['dispərit] *adj.* 全异的
8. cell signaling 细胞信号学
9. intractable [in'træktəkəbl] *adj.* 难处理的
10. organism ['ɔːgənizəm] *n.* 生物体，有机体
11. strongly focused laser beam 强聚焦激光束
12. restoring force 回复力
13. dynamics [dai'næmiks] *n.* 动力学

14. scattering force 散射力
15. gradient force 梯度力
16. equilibrium [ˌiːkwiˈlibriəm] n. 平衡，平静，均衡，保持平衡的能力，沉着，安静
17. neutral particles 中性粒子
18. angular momentum 角动量
19. dropped into obscurity 默默无闻，不受重视
20. polystyrene ball 聚苯乙烯小球
21. single motor molecules 单个分子运动
22. submicron particles 超微小粒子
23. kinetics：[kaiˈnetiks] n. 动力学
24. latex：[ˈleiteks] n. [植][化]乳汁，乳胶，橡胶
25. radiometric effects 辐射效应
26. geometric optical approach 几何光学方法
27. diffraction effects 衍射效应
28. Planck's constant 普朗克常数
29. microscope objective 显微镜物镜
30. biological specimens 生物样本
31. expands and steers 准直扩束
32. force calibration 力的标定
33. polarization [ˌpəʊlaraiˈzeiʃən] n. [物]偏振（现象），极化（作用），两极化，分化
34. micromanipulators [ˌmaikrəʊməˈnipjʊletə(r)] n [生]显微操纵器
35. mitochondria [ˌmaitəˈkɔndriə] [生]线粒体
36. bioscience [ˈbaiəʊˌsaiəns] n. 生物科学
37. ultraviolet cutting 紫外切割
38. chromosome [ˈkrəʊməsəum] n. [生物]染色体
39. elastic properties 弹性性质
40. membrane [ˈmembrein] n. 膜，隔膜
41. assay [əˈsei] n. 化验
42. blood plasma n. 血浆
43. buffer solution 缓冲液
44. microchemistry [ˌmaikrəʊˈkemistri] n. [化]微量化学
45. fluorescence [fluəˈresns] n. 荧光，荧光性
46. photochemistry [ˌfəutəʊˈkemistri] n 光化学
47. electrochemistry [ɪˌlektrəʊˈkemistri] n. [化]电化学
48. polymerization [ˌpɔliməraiˈzeiʃən] n. 聚合

Notes

① 总之，在一个光阱中，存在一个散射力，将物体推向光波的传播方向，还存在一个梯度力，将物体推向光强梯度变化的方向，因此，必须保证光强有足够陡的梯度以保证梯度力

能克服散射力的影响,从而形成光阱。一个足够陡的三维光强梯度可以通过将激光束直径聚焦到波长数量级大小来实现。

② Greulich 和 Berns 是最早将光镊技术和称为微光束的脉冲激光剪切技术(有时也称为"激光剪"或"激光刀")结合起来,用来剪切和移动细胞和细胞器官的。另外,激光微手术刀是一门基于准确聚焦的脉冲激光束(其强度最优化)的技术,用于在各种生物体中精确地消除或破坏细胞,或是穿透细胞壁实现显微授精,或是刺激细胞融合,或是用于 DNA 剪切。

Photonic Crystal Fiber

第11章

PREVIEW

Photonic crystal fibers (PCFs), also known as microstructured fibers or holey fibers, which are characterized by a periodic arrangement of air holes around the core along the entire length of the fiber have recently generated great interest in the scientific community in the recent decades thanks to the new ways provided to control and guide light, not obtainable with conventional optical fibers.[①] Proposed for the first time in 1996, PCFs have driven an exciting and irrepressible research activity all over the world, starting in the telecommunication field and then nonlinear optics, spectroscopy, touching metrology, microscopy, astronomy, micromachining, biomedicine, and sensing.

A variety of very interesting publications and high level books have been already presented, describing the different kinds of these new fibers, but do you know how did PCFs come into being? What's the difference between conventional optical fibers and PCFs and what do PCFs have predominance? Let's start with these questions.

11.1 The Origins of PCFs

Optical fibers are widely used in optical fiber telecommunications, which permits transmission over longer distances and at higher bandwidths (data rates) than other forms of communications. Fibers are used instead of metal wires because signals travel along them with less loss, and they are also immune to electromagnetic interference. Optical fibers are also used for sensors and other applications. Photonic crystals are periodic optical nanostructures that are designed to affect the motion of photons in a similar way that periodicity of a semiconductor crystal affects the motion of electrons. PCF is a new class of optical fiber based on the properties of photonic crystals.

11.1.1 Conventional Optical Fibers

Optical fibers, which rely on *total internal reflection*[1] (TIR) to guide light and transmit information in the form of short optical pulses over long distances at exceptionally high speeds, are one of the major technological successes of the 20th century. This technology has developed at an incredible rate, from the first low-loss single-mode waveguides in 1970 to being key components of the sophisticated global telecommunication network. *Charles K. Kao, widely regarded as the "father of fiber optics" or "father of fiber optic communications", was awarded half of the 2009 Nobel Prize in Physics for "groundbreaking achievements concerning the transmission of light in fibers for optical communication".* ② Optical fibers have also non-telecom applications, for example, in beam delivery for medicine, machining and diagnostics, sensing, and a lot of other fields. Modern optical fibers represent a careful trade-off between optical losses, optical nonlinearity, group velocity dispersion, and polarization effects. After 30 years of intensive research, incremental steps have refined the capabilities of the system and the fabrication technology nearly as far as they can go.

11.1.2 Photonic Crystal

Photonic crystals occur in nature and in various forms have been studied scientifically for the last 100 years. *The idea of photonic crystal originated in 1987 from work in the inhibition of spontaneous emission predicted by E. Yablonovitch and in the field of strong localization^2 of light predicted by S. John.* ③ It was subsequently shown that in periodic arrangements of ideally lossless dielectrics, the propagation of light can be totally suppressed at certain wavelengths regardless of propagation direction and polarization. The inhibition does not result from absorption but rather from the periodicity of the arrangement, and is possible (the so-called *photonic bandgap*[3], PBG), the density of possible states for the light vanishes, so that even spontaneous emission becomes impossible. Such periodic arrangements of dielectrics have been called photonic crystals, or photonic bandgap materials.

1. One-dimensional photonic crystals

The simplest device using the principles of photonic crystals is the one-dimensional photonic crystal, well known under the name of the Bragg mirror or the multilayer reflector. It consists of a periodic stack of two alternating dielectric layers. Light propagating in a direction normal to the layers undergoes successive reflection and transmission at each interface between adjacent layers. With an appropriate choice of layer thickness and refractive indices, waves reflected from each interface are in phase, whereas waves transmitted are out of phase. In that case, the transmitted wave components cancel each other out, and only the interference of the reflected components is constructive: the light is totally reflected. This works for a range of wavelengths. Bragg mirrors have been in use for decades, but it is only recently that they have come to be regarded as a special case of photonic crystals. The classical way of analyzing Bragg mirrors with a finite number of layers, uses reflection and transmission matrices for each layer, and it is then quite straightforward to prove through recurrence relationships that reflection call be perfect with an infinite number of layers. There is nevertheless another approach to deal with a stack having an infinite number of layers, originating from solid state physics. If the stack is infinite, it has a discrete translational symmetry. The Bloch Theorem then applies, and solutions to the propagation equation in the stack are Bloch waves. Hence two wave vectors differing by a vector of the reciprocal lattice associated with the periodic stacking are physically the same: the dispersion diagram "folds back" along the limits of the Brillouin zone. At the edge of the Brillouin zone, two solutions exist having the same wave vector but different frequencies, and in between those two frequencies no solutions exist at all. The gap of frequencies for which no solutions exist is called a photonic bandgap. Note that, reflection from Bragg mirrors was thought to be possible only within a relatively narrow range of angles of incidence.

2. Two and three-dimensional photonic crystals

Photonic crystals with two or three-dimensional periodicity can be seen as a generalization of Bragg mirrors. The simple approach with reflection and transmission matrices cannot be applied analytically here, and this is probably why their properties were discovered relatively recently, although, for example, important work on stacked grids for filtering in the far infrared was carried out by R. Ulrich in the 1960s. The Bloch approach can be used similarly, and shows that bandgaps can still open up. The point of using periodicities along two or three-dimensions is to open up an omnidirectional bandgap: for the Bragg mirror, bandgaps usually only exist for a narrow range of angles of incidence, and propagation parallel to the Bragg layers can never be inhibited. With photonic crystals having a two-dimensionally periodic arrangement of parallel rods, bandgaps can exist for all directions of propagation in the plane of periodicity, and for photonic crystals with three-dimensional periodicity propagation of light in all directions can be prohibited. When a bandgap exists regardless of direction of propagation and polarization, one speaks of a total photonic bandgap.

Photonic crystals with two-dimensional periodic arrangements are usually either made of parallel dielectric (or metallic) rods in air, or through drilling or etching holes in a dielectric material. In the field of integrated optics, holes of a fraction of a micrometer etched in slab waveguides are very promising for integrated photonic circuits, and have been successfully demonstrated experimentally. Photonic crystals with three-dimensional periodicity are a bit trickier to achieve. Yablonovitch suggested drilling an array of holes at three different angles into a dielectric material. The so-called wood-pile structure has attracted much attention and recent progress with artificial inverse opals is promising.

Note that the term photonic crystal was originally introduced to refer to photonic bandgap. It seems that it is now progressively more often used to any kind of periodic arrangement of dielectrics or materials, with or without photonic bandgaps. The latter generalization of the term makes sense considering that in solid state physics, a crystal is named so on account of the periodicity of its lattice, with bandgaps appearing in certain case. Usual practice is then to reserve the term photonic bandgap material for a photonic crystal having a photonic bandgap.

The interest of researchers and engineers in several laboratories, since the 1980s, has been attracted by the ability to structure materials on the scale of the optical wavelength, a fraction of micrometers or less, in order to develop new optical medium, known as photonic crystals. Photonic crystals rely on a regular morphological microstructure, incorporated into the material, which radically alters its optical properties. They represent the extension of the results obtained for semiconductors into optics. In fact, the band structure of semiconductors is the outcome of the interactions between electrons and the periodic variations in potential created by the crystal lattice. By solving the Schrödinger's wave equation for a periodic potential, electron energy states separated by forbidden bands are obtained. PBGs can be obtained in photonic crystals, where periodic variations in dielectric constant that is in refractive index substitute variations in electric potential, as well as the classical wave equation for the magnetic field replaces the Schrödinger's equation.

11.1.3 From Conventional Optical Fibers to PCFs

In 1991, Philip Russell, who was interested in Yablonovitch's research, got his big "crazy" idea for "something different", during CLEO/QELS conference. Russell's idea was that light could be trapped inside a fiber hollow core by creating a two-dimensional photonic crystal in the cladding that is a periodic wavelength-scale lattice of microscopic air-holes in the glass. The basic principle is the same which is the origin of the color in butterfly wings and peacock feathers, that is all wavelength-scale periodic structures exhibit ranges of angle and color, stop bands, where incident light is strongly reflected. When properly designed, the photonic crystal cladding running along the entire fiber length can prevent the escape of light from the hollow core. These new fibers are called PCFs, since they rely on the unusual properties of photonic crystals.

11.2 The History of PCFs

The first fiber with a photonic crystal structure was reported by Russell and his colleagues in 1996. Even if it was a very interesting research development, the first PCF did not have a hollow core, as shown in Fig. 11-1, and, consequently, it did not rely on a photonic bandgap for optical confinement. In fact, in 1996 Russell's group at University of Southampton could produce fiber with the necessary air-hole triangular lattice, but the air-holes were too small to achieve a large air-filling fraction, which is fundamental to realize a PBG. Measurements have shown that this solid core fiber formed a single-mode waveguide that is only the fundamental mode was transmitted, over a wide wavelength range. Moreover, the first PCF had very low intrinsic losses, due to the absence of doping elements in the core, and a silica core with an area about ten times larger than that of a conventional single-mode fiber (SMF), thus permitting a corresponding increase in optical power levels. In 1997 Birks reported an *endlessly single-mode*[4] (ESM) PCF, which is developed by embedding a central core in a two-dimensional photonic crystal with a micrometer-spaced hexagonal array of air holes. Such a fiber can be single mode for any wavelength. It is shown that its useful single-mode range is bounded by a bend-loss edge at short wavelength as well at long wavelengths. A high-speed optical-transmission experiment was successfully demonstrated in an ultra low-loss polarization maintaining PCF (shown in Fig. 11-2) by K. Suzuki in 2003. The fiber loss and modal birefringence at 1 550 nm were 1.3 dB/km and 1.4×10^{-3}, respectively. A 10 Gbit/s bi-directional optical signal was successfully transmitted through the 1.5 km fiber.

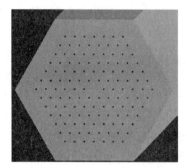
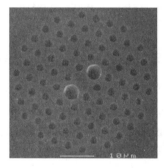

Fig. 11-1 Schematic of the cross-section of the first solid core PCF.

Fig. 11-2 Schematic of the cross-section of the ultra low-loss polarization maintaining PCF.

After moving his research group to the University of Bath in 1996, where PCF fabrication techniques were steadily refined, Russell and his co-workers were able to report, in 1999, the first single-mode hollow core fiber, in which confinement was due by a full two-dimensional PBG, as reported in Fig. 11-3. They realized that the photonic bandgap guiding mechanism is very robust, since light remains well confined in the hollow core, even if tight bends are formed in the fiber. However, it is highly sensitive to small fluctuations in the fiber geometry, for example, to variations in the air-hole size.

Fig. 11-3 Schematic of the cross-section of the first hollow core PCF.

Initial production techniques were directed simply at the task of making relatively short lengths of fiber in order to do the basic science, but many research teams are now working hard to optimize their PCF production techniques, in order to increase the lengths and to reduce the losses.

11.3 Guiding Light in PCFs

In order to form a guided mode in an optical fiber, it is necessary to introduce light into the core with a value of β that is the component of the propagation constant along the fiber axis, which cannot propagate in the cladding. The highest β value that can exist in an infinite homogeneous medium with refractive index n is $\beta = nk_0$, being k_0 the free-space propagation constant. All the smaller values of β are allowed. A two-dimensional photonic crystal, like any other material, is characterized by a maximum value of β which can propagate. At a particular wavelength, this corresponds to the fundamental mode of an infinite slab of the material, and this β value defines the elective refractive index of the material.

11.3.1 Modified Total Internal Reflection

It is possible to use a two-dimensional photonic crystal as a fiber cladding, by choosing a core material with a higher refractive index than the cladding effective index. An example of this kind of structures is the PCF with a silica solid core surrounded by a photonic crystal cladding with a triangular lattice of air-holes, shown in Fig. 11-4. These fibers, also known as index-guiding PCFs, guide light through a form of TIR, called modified TIR. However, they have many different properties with respect to conventional optical fibers.

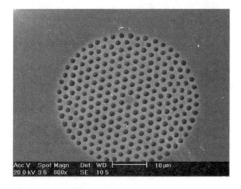

Fig. 11-4 Microscope picture of a fabricated solid core triangular PCF, which guides light for modified TIR.

11.3.2 Photonic Bandgap Guidance

Optical fiber designs completely different form the traditional ones result from the fact that the photonic crystal cladding have gaps in the ranges of the supported modal index β/k_0 where there are no propagating modes. These are the PBGs of the crystal, which are similar to the two-dimensional bandgaps which characterize planar light wave circuits, but in this case they have propagation with a non-zero value of β. It is important to underline that gaps can appear for values of modal index both greater and smaller than unity, enabling the formation of hollow core fibers with bandgap material as a cladding, as reported in Fig. 11-5. These fibers, which cannot be made using conventional optics, are related to Bragg fibers, since they do not rely on TIR to guide light. In fact, in order to guide light by TIR, it is necessary a lower-index cladding material surrounding the core, but there are no suitable low-loss materials with a refractive index lower than air at optical frequencies. The first PCF which exploited the PBG effect to guide light was reported in 1998, and it is shown in Fig. 11-6. Notice that its core is formed by an additional air-hole in a honeycomb lattice. This PCF could only guide light in silica that is in the higher-index material.

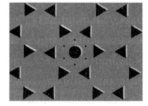

Fig. 11-5 Microscope picture of a fabricated hollow core triangular PCF, which guides light through the photonic bandgap effect.

Fig. 11-6 Schematic of the cross-section of the first photonic bandgap PCF with a honeycomb air-hole lattice.

Hollow core guidance had to wait until 1999, when the PCF fabrication technology had advanced to the point where larger air-filling fractions, required to achieve a PBG for air-guiding, became possible. Notice that an air guided mode must have $\beta/k_0 < 1$, since this condition guarantees that light is free to propagate and form a mode within the hollow core, while being unable to escape into the cladding. The first hollow core PCF had a simple triangular lattice of air-holes, and the core was formed by removing seven capillaries in the center of the fiber cross-section. By producing a relatively large core, the chances of finding a guided mode were improved. When white light is launched into the fiber core, colored modes are transmitted, thus indicating that light guiding exists only in restricted wavelength ranges, which coincide with the photonic bandgaps.

11.4 Properties of PCFs

Due to the huge variety of air-holes arrangements, PCFs offer a wide possibility to control the refractive index contrast between the core and the photonic crystal cladding and, as a consequence, novel and unique optical properties.

Since PCFs can be divided into two modes of operation, according to their mechanism for confinement. Those with a solid core, or a core with a higher average index than the photonic crystal cladding, can operate on the same index-guiding principle as conventional optical fiber, however, they can have a much higher effective-index contrast between core and cladding, and therefore can have much stronger confinement for applications in nonlinear optical devices, polarization-maintaining fibers. Alternatively, one can create a photonic bandgap fiber, in which the light is confined by a photonic bandgap created by the photonic crystal cladding, such a bandgap, properly designed, can confine light in a lower-index core and even a hollow (air) core. Bandgap fibers with hollow cores can potentially circumvent limits imposed by available materials, for example to create fibers that guide light in wavelengths for which transparent materials are not available (because the light is primarily in the air, not in the solid materials). Another potential advantage of a hollow core is that one can dynamically introduce materials into the core, such as a gas that is to be analyzed for the presence of some substance.

11.4.1 Solid Core PCFs

Index-guiding PCFs, with a solid glass region within a lattice of air-holes, offer a lot of new opportunities, not only for applications related to fundamental fiber optics. These opportunities are related to some special properties of the photonic crystal cladding, which are due to the large refractive index contrast and the two-dimensional nature of the microstructure, thus affecting the mode property, the birefringence, the dispersion, the smallest attainable core size, the number of guided modes and the numerical aperture and the birefringence.

1. Endlessly single-mode property

As already stated, the first solid core PCF, shown in Fig. 11-1, which consisted of a triangular lattice of air-holes with a diameter d of about 300 nm and a hole-to-hole spacing Λ of 2.3 μm, did not ever seem to become multi-mode in the experiments, even for short wavelengths. In fact, the guided mode always had a single strong central lobe filling the core.

Russell has explained that this particular ESM behavior can be understood by viewing the air-hole lattice as a modal filter or "sieve". Since light is evanescent in air, the air-holes act like strong barriers, so they are the "wire mesh" of the sieve. The field of the fundamental mode, which fits into the silica core with a single lobe of diameter between zeros slightly equal to 2Λ, is the "grain of rice" which cannot escape through the wire mesh, being the silica gaps between the air-holes belonging to the first ring around the core too narrow. On the contrary, the lobe dimensions for the higher-order modes are smaller, so they can slip between the gaps. When the ratio d/Λ, that is the air-filling fraction of the photonic crystal cladding, increases, successive higher-order modes become trapped. A proper geometry design of the fiber cross-section thus guarantees that only the fundamental mode is guided. More detailed studies of the properties of triangular PCFs have shown that this occurs for $d/\Lambda < 0.4$.

By exploiting this property, it is possible to design very large-mode area fibers, which can be successfully employed for high-power delivery, amplifiers, and lasers. Moreover, by doping the core in order to slightly reduce its refractive index, light guiding can be turned off completely at wavelengths shorter than a certain threshold value.

2. Dispersion tailoring

The tendency for different light wavelengths to travel at different speeds is a crucial factor in the telecommunication system design. A sequence of short light pulses carries the digitized information. Each of these is formed from a spread of wavelengths and, as a result of chromatic dispersion, it broadens as it travels, thus obscuring the signal. The magnitude of the dispersion changes with the wavelength, passing through zero at 1.3 μm in conventional optical fibers.

In PCFs, the dispersion can be controlled and tailored with unprecedented freedom. In fact, due to the high refractive index difference between silica and air, and to the flexibility of changing air-hole sizes and patterns, a much broader range of dispersion behaviors can be obtained with PCFs than with standard fibers.

For example, as the air-holes get larger, the PCF core becomes more and more isolated, until it resembles an isolated strand of silica glass suspended by six thin webs of glass, as it is shown in Fig. 11-7. If the whole structure is made very small, the zero-dispersion wavelength can be shifted to the visible, since the group velocity dispersion is radically affected by pure waveguide dispersion.

Fig. 11-7 Microscope picture of the cross-section of a highly nonlinear PCF, characterized by a small-silica core and large air-holes, with zero-dispersion wavelength shifted to the visible.

On the contrary, very flat dispersion curves can be obtained in certain wavelength ranges in PCFs with small air-holes, which is with low air-filling fraction.

3. High nonlinearity

An attractive property of solid core PCFs is that effective index contrasts much higher than in conventional optical fibers can be obtained by making large air-holes, or by reducing the core dimension, so that the light is forced into the silica core. The nonlinear coefficient γ (λ) of PCFs can be expressed as

$$\gamma(\lambda) = \frac{2\pi n_2}{\lambda A_{eff}} \tag{11-1}$$

where, A_{eff} is model effective area, and n_2 is the nonlinear index of silica. In this way a strong confinement of the guided-mode can be reached, thus leading to enhanced nonlinear effects, due to the high field intensity in the core. Moreover, a lot of nonlinear experiments require specific dispersion properties of the fibers. As a consequence, PCFs can be successfully exploited to realize nonlinear fiber devices, with a proper dispersion, and this is presently one of their most important applications.

4. Large-mode area

By changing the geometric characteristics of the fiber cross-section, it is possible to design PCFs with completely different a property, that is with large effective area. The typical cross-section of this kind of fibers, called *large mode area*[5] (LMA) PCFs, consists of a triangular lattice of air-holes where the core is defined by a missing air-hole. In this condition it is the core size or the pitch that determines the zero-dispersion wavelength λ_0, the *mode field diameter*[6] (MFD) and the *numerical aperture*[7] (NA) of the fiber. LMA PCFs are usually exploited for high-power applications, since fiber damage and nonlinear limitations are drastically reduced. In particular, LMA fibers are currently used for applications at short wavelengths, that is in ultraviolet (UV) and visible bands, like the generation and delivery of high-power optical beams for laser welding and machining, optical lasers, and amplifiers, providing significant advantages with respect to traditional optical fibers.

Conventional active fibers for lasers and amplifiers are basically standard transmission fibers whose core region has been doped with rare earth elements. These fibers, also known as "core-pumped", are usually pumped with single mode pump lasers. Due to its power limitations, this kind of fiber is unsuitable for high-power applications, on the order of 1 W, and upwards. High-power fibers are usually designed with a double-cladding structure, where a second low-index region acts as a cladding for a large pump core.

5. High birefringence

Birefringent fibers, where the two orthogonally polarized modes carried in a single-mode fiber propagate at different rates, are used to maintain polarization states in optical devices and subsystems. The guided modes become birefringent if the core microstructure is deliberately made twofold symmetric, for example, by introducing capillaries with different wall thicknesses above and below the core. By slightly changing the air-hole geometry, it is possible to produce levels of birefringence that exceed the performance of conventional birefringent fiber by an order of magnitude. It is important to underline that, unlike traditional polarization maintaining fibers, such as bow tie, elliptical-core or Panda, which contain at least two different glasses, each one with a different thermal expansion coefficient, the birefringence obtainable with PCFs is highly insensitive to temperature, which is an important feature in many applications. Some examples of the cross-section of highly birefringent PCFs are reported in Fig. 11-8.

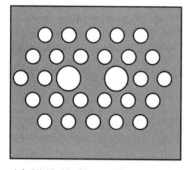

(a) Highly birefringent PCFs designed by NTT and Mitsubishi cable industry.

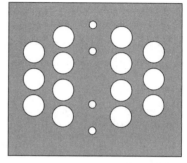

(b) Highly birefringent PCFs designed by University of Bath.

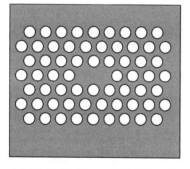

(c) Highly birefringent PCFs designed by Crystal Fiber A/S.

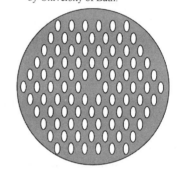

(d) Elliptical-hole highly birefringent PCFs designed by Columbia University.

Fig. 11-8 Several typical highly birefringent PCFs.

6. High numerical aperture

Highly numerical aperture (HNA) PCFs have a central part surrounded by a ring of relatively large air holes (Fig. 11-9). HNA-PCFs have the importance of minimizing the width of silica bridges in order to obtain a low cladding index. Several such fibers have been fabricated and the measured properties as a function of wavelength and web thickness follow the predictions well. These fibers show the highest NAs reported of 0.88 over a 41 m length at a wavelength of 1.1 μm, rising to NA at 1.54 μm, and decreasing to NA 0.65 at 450 nm. Such structures will lead to performance improvements for cladding-pumped lasers and increased sensitivity in collection of incoherent light.

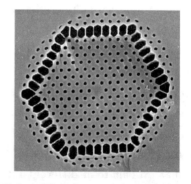

Fig. 11-9 Microscope picture of the cross-section of a HNA-PCF.

11.4.2 Hollow Core PCFs

Hollow core PCFs have great potential, since they exhibit low nonlinearity and high damage threshold, thanks to the air-guiding in the hollow core and the resulting small overlap between silica and the propagating mode. As a consequence, they are good candidates for future telecommunication transmission systems.

Another application, perhaps closer to fruition, which can successfully exploit these advantages, offered by air-guiding PCFs, is the delivery of high-power continuous wave (CW), nanosecond and sub-picosecond laser beams, which are useful for marking, machining and welding, laser-Doppler velocimetry, laser surgery, and THz generation. In fact, optical fibers would be the most suitable delivery means for many applications, but at present they are unusable, due to the fiber damage and the negative nonlinear effects caused by the high optical powers and energies, as well as to the fiber group-velocity dispersion, which disperses the short pulses. These limitations can be substantially relieved by considering hollow core fibers.

Moreover, air-guiding PCFs are suitable for nonlinear optical processes in gases, which require high intensities at low power, long interaction lengths and good-quality transverse beam profiles. For example, it has been demonstrated that the threshold for stimulated Raman scattering in hollow core fibers filled with hydrogen is orders of magnitude below that obtained in previous experiments. In a similar way, PCFs with a hollow core can be used for trace gas detection or monitoring, or as gain cells for gas lasers. Finally, the delivery of solid particles down a fiber by using optical radiation pressure has been demonstrated. In particular, only 80 mW of a 514 nm argon laser light was enough to levitate and guide 5 μm polystyrene spheres along a 15 cm length of PCF with a hollow core diameter of 20 μm.

11.5　Fabrication of PCFs

One of the most important aspects in designing and developing new fibers is their fabrication process. PCFs have been realized by "introducing" air-holes in a solid glass material. This has several advantages, since air is mechanically and thermally compatible with most materials, it is transparent over a broad spectral range, and it has a very low refractive index at optical frequencies. Fibers fabricated using silica and air have been accurately analyzed, partly because most conventional optical fibers are produced from fused silica. This is also an excellent material to work with, because viscosity does not change much with temperature and it is relatively cheap. Moreover, filling the holes of a silica-air structure opens up a wide range of interesting possibilities, such as the bandgap guidance in a low-index core made of silica when the holes are filled with a high-index liquid.

The traditional way of manufacturing optical fibers usually involves two main steps: fabrication a fiber *preform*[8] and drawing it with a high-temperature furnace in a tower setup. For conventional silica-based optical fibers, both techniques that are very mature. The different vapor deposition techniques, for example, the *modified chemical vapor deposition*[9] (MCVD), the *vapor axial deposition*[10] (VAD), and the *outside vapour deposition*[11] (OVD), are all tailored for the fabrication of circular symmetric fiber preforms. Thus, the deposition can be controlled in a very accurate way only in the radial direction without significant modifications of the methods. Moreover, producing conventional single-mode optical fibers requires core and cladding materials with similar refractive index values, which typically differ by around 1%, and are usually obtained by vapor deposition techniques. On the contrary, designing PCFs requires a far higher refractive index contrast, differing by perhaps 50%~100%. As a consequence, all the techniques previously described are not directly applicable to the fabrication of preforms for PCFs, whose structure is not characterized by a circular symmetry.

Differently from the drawing process of conventional optical fibers, where viscosity is the only really important material parameter, several forces are important in the case of PCFs, such as viscosity, gravity, and surface tension. This is due to the much larger surface area in a microstructured geometry, and to the fact that many of the surfaces are close to the fiber core, thus making surface tension relatively much more important. As a consequence, the choice of the base material strongly influences the technological issues and applications in the PCF fabrication process.

11.5.1 Stack-and-draw Technique

In order to fabricate a PCF, it is necessary, first, to create a preform, which contains the structure of interest, but on a macroscopic scale. One possibility to exploit for the PCF fabrication is the drilling of several tens to hundreds of holes in a periodic arrangement into one final preform. However, a different and relatively simple method, called *stack-and-draw*[12], introduced by Birks et al. in 1996, has become the preferred fabrication technique in the last years, since it allows relatively fast, clean, low-cost, and flexible preform manufacture.

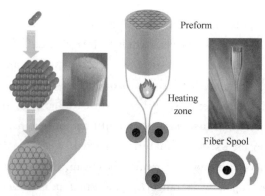

Fig. 11-10 Scheme of the PCF fabrication process.

The solid core PCF preform is realized by stacking by hand a number of capillary silica tubes and solid silica rods to form the desired air-silica structure, as reported in Fig. 11-10. This way of realizing the preform allows a high level of design flexibility, since the core size and shape, as well as the index profile throughout the cladding region can be controlled. After the stacking process, the capillaries and rods are held together by thin wires and fused together during an intermediate drawing process, where the preform is drawn into preform canes. This intermediate step is important in order to provide numerous preform canes for the development and optimization of the later drawing of the PCFs to their final dimensions. Then, the preform is drawn down on a conventional fiber drawing tower, greatly extending its length, while reducing its cross-section, from a diameter of 20 mm to an 80~200 μm one, as shown in Fig. 11-10. With respect to standard optical fibers, which are usually drawn at temperatures around 2 100 ℃, a lower temperature level, that is 1 900 ℃, is kept during the PCF drawing since the surface tension can otherwise lead to the air-hole collapse. In order to carefully control the air-hole size during the drawing process, it is useful to apply to the inside of the preform a slight overpressure relative to the surroundings, and to properly adjust the drawing speed. In summary, time dynamics, temperature, and pressure variations are all significant parameters which should be accurately controlled during the PCF fabrication. Finally, the PCFs are coated to provide a protective standard *jacket*[13], which allows the robust handling of the fibers. The final PCFs are comparable to standard fibers in both robustness and physical dimensions, and can be both striped and cleaved using standard tools.

The fabrication process of hollow core PCF preform is similar to the solid core PCF preform fabrication process. The different procedure is displacing rods and keeping air core, represented in Fig. 11-11. It is important to underline that the stack-and-draw procedure, represented in Fig. 11-12, proved highly versatile, allowing complex lattices to be assembled from individual stackable units of the correct size and shape. Solid, empty, or doped glass regions can be easily incorporated, as described in Fig. 11-10. A wide range of different structures have been made by exploiting this technique, each with different optical properties. Moreover, overall collapse ratios as large as about 50 000 times have been realized, and continuous holes as small as 25 nm in diameter have been demonstrated, earning an entry in the Guinness Book of Records in 1999 for the World's Longest Holes. A very important issue is the comparison of the PCF stack-and-draw procedure with the vapor deposition methods usually employed for standard optical fibers. Obviously, it is more difficult that the preforms for conventional optical fibers become contaminated, since their surface area is smaller. Moreover, the stacking method requires a very careful handling, and the control of air-hole dimensions, positions, and shapes in PCFs makes the drawing significantly more complex. Finally, it is important to underline that the fabrication process of PCFs with a hollow core, realized by removing some elements from the stack center, is much more difficult than that of standard optical fibers, even if at present fibers with low loss and practical lengths have been obtained.

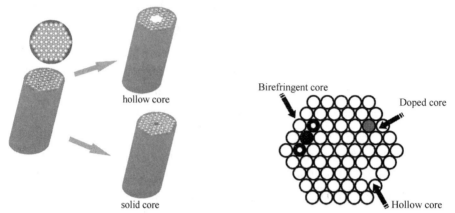

Fig. 11-11 Schematic diagram shown the fabrication of PCFs perform.

Fig. 11-12 PCF cross-section, showing the flexibility offered by the stack-and-draw fabrication process.

11.5.2 Extrusion Fabrication Process

Silica-air preforms have also been extruded, enabling the formation of structures not readily attainable by stacking capillaries. The extrusion process has been recently applied to other glasses, which are not as readily available in tube form as silica, like compound glasses. These materials, which provide a lot of interesting properties, like an extended wavelength range for transmission and higher values of the nonlinear coefficient, can be used to fabricate preforms through the extrusion process due to their lower softening temperatures, which make easier the fabrication procedure.

In this fabrication process a molten glass is forced through a die containing a suitably designed pattern of holes. Extrusion allows fiber to be drawn directly from bulk glass, using a fiber-drawing tower, and almost any structure, crystalline or amorphous, can be produced. It works for many materials, including *chalcogenides*[14], polymers, and compound glasses. However, selective doping of specified regions, in order to introduce rare earth ions or render the glass photosensitive, is much more difficult. Different PCFs produced by the extrusion process have been presented in literature. In particular, the fabrication of the first non-silica glass PCF by exploiting this technique has been reported in 2002 by Kiang *et al*. A commercial glass, called Schott SF57 glass, has been used, which has a softening temperature of only 519 ℃ and a high lead concentration, which causes a relatively high refractive index of 1.83 at a wavelength of 633 nm and of 1.80 at 1 530 nm. This material is interesting since its nonlinear refractive index that is 4.1×10^{-19} W^2/m at 1 060 nm, is more than one order of magnitude larger than that of pure silica. Another highly nonlinear PCF has been fabricated with the bismuth-oxide-based glass, which has proved to be an attractive novel material for nonlinear devices and compact

Er^{3+}-doped amplifiers. The fiber fabrication presented in consists of three steps. In the first step, the structured preform of 16 mm outer diameter and the jacket tube are extruded. In the second step, the preform is reduced in scale on a fiber-drawing tower to a cane of about 1.6 mm diameter. In the last step, the cane is inserted within the jacket tube, and this assembly is drawn down to the final fiber.

11.6 Application of PCFs

The diversity of new or improved features, beyond what conventional fiber offers, means that PCF is finding an increasing number of applications in ever-widening areas of science and technology. Let us sample a few of the more intriguing and important ones.

11.6.1 High Power and Energy Transmission

Larger mode areas allow higher power to be carried before the onset of intensity related nonlinearities or damage, with obvious benefits for delivery of high laser power, and for high-power fiber amplifiers and lasers. ESM-PCF's ability to remain single mode at all wavelengths where it guides, and for all scales of structure, means that the core area can be increased without the penalty of introducing higher order guided modes. This also suggests that it should have superior power-handling properties, with applications in, for example, the field of laser machining. A key issue is bend loss, and as we have seen, it turns out that PCF offers a wider bandwidth of useful single-mode guidance than high-delta SMF, because it can operate in the multimode regime of SMF while remaining single mode. This also shifts the long wavelength bend edge to longer wavelengths than is possible in standard fibers.

Hollow core PCF is also an excellent candidate for transmitting high continuous-wave power as well as ultra-short pulses with very high peak powers. Solitons have been reported at 800 nm using a Ti:sapphire laser and at 1 550 nm with durations of 100 fs and peak powers of 2 MW. The soliton energy is of course determined by the effective value of and the magnitude of the anomalous GVD. The GVD changes sign across the bandgap, permitting choice of normal or anomalous dispersion depending upon the application. Further studies have explored the ultimate power handling capacity of hollow core PCF.

11.6.2 Fiber Lasers and Amplifiers

PCF lasers can be straightforwardly produced by incorporating a rare-earth-doped cane in the preform stack. Many different designs can be realized, such as cores with ultra-large mode areas for high power, and structures with multiple lasing cores. Cladding-pumping geometries for ultrahigh power can be fashioned by incorporating a second core (much larger and multimode) around a large off-center ESM lasing core. Using microstructuring techniques, this "inner cladding waveguide" can be suspended by connecting it to an outer glass tube with very thin webs of glass. This results in a very large effective index step and thus a high-numerical aperture (>0.9), making it easy to launch and guide light from high-power diode-bar pump lasers. The multimode pump light is efficiently absorbed by the lasing core, and high-power single-mode operation can be achieved. Microchip-laser-seeded Yb^{3+}-doped PCF amplifiers, generating diffraction-limited 0.45 ns duration pulses with a peak power of 1.1 MW and a peak spectral brightness of greater than 10 kW/ (cm^2 · sr · Hz), have been reported.

Hollow core PCF with its superior power-handling and designable GVD is ideal as the last compression stage in chirped-pulse amplification schemes. This permits operation at power densities that would destroy conventional glass-core fibers.

11.6.3 Gas-based Nonlinear Optics

A longstanding challenge in photonics is how to maximize nonlinear interactions between laser light and low-density media such as gases. Efficient nonlinear processes require high intensities at low power, long interaction lengths, and good-quality transverse beam profiles. No existing solution comes close to the performance offered by hollow core PCF. At a bore diameter of 10 m, for example, a focused free-space laser beam is marginally preferable to a capillary, whereas a hollowcore PCF with 13 dB/km *attenuation*[15] is 105 times more effective. Such enhancements are rare in physics and point the way to improvements in all sorts of nonlinear laser-gas interactions. Discussed next are just two examples from a rich prospect of enhanced, and more practical, ultra-low-threshold gas-based nonlinear optical devices.

An example is ultra-low-threshold stimulated Raman scattering in molecular gases. Raman scattering is caused by molecular vibrations, typically in the multi-THz range, that interact spontaneously with the laser light, shifting its frequency both up (anti-Stokes) and down (Stokes) in two separate three-wave parametric interactions. At high intensities, the Stokes wave becomes strong and beats with the pump laser light, driving the molecular oscillations more strongly. This further enhances the Stokes signal, so that ultimately, above a certain threshold power, the major fraction of the pump power is converted to the Stokes frequency. The energy lost to molecular vibrations is dissipated as heat. A stimulated Raman threshold was recently observed in a hydrogen filled hollow core PCF at pulse energies 100 times lower than previously possible. Another field where hollowcore fiber is likely to have a major impact is that of high harmonic generation. When gases such as argon are subjected to ultra-short (few fs) high-energy (few mJ) pulses, usually from a Ti:sapphire laser system operating at 800 nm wavelength, the extremely high, short duration electric field momentarily ionizes the atoms, and very high harmonics of the laser frequency are generated during the recombination process. Ultraviolet and even x-ray radiation can be produced in this way. It is tantalizing to speculate that hollow core PCF could bring this process within the reach of compact diode-pumped laser systems, potentially leading to table-top x-ray sources for medicine, lithography, and x-ray diagnostics.

11.6.4 Supercontinuum Generation

PCFs with extremely small solid glass cores and very high air-filling fractions not only display unusual chromatic dispersion but also yield very high optical intensities per unit power. Thus one of the most successful applications of PCF is to nonlinear optics, where high effective nonlinearities, together with excellent control of chromatic dispersion, are essential for efficient devices.

A dramatic example is *supercontinuum*[16] generation. Supercontinuum generation is the formation of broad continuous spectra by propagation of high power pulses through nonlinear media. When ultra-short, high-energy pulses travel through a material, their frequency spectrum can experience giant broadening due to a range of interconnected nonlinear effects. Until recently this required a regeneratively amplified Ti-sapphire laser operating at 800 nm wavelength. Pulses from the master oscillator (100 MHz repetition rate, 100 fs duration, few nJ energy) are regeneratively amplified up to 1 mJ. Because the amplifier needs to be recharged between pulses, the repetition rate is only around 1 kHz. Thus, there was great excitement when it was discovered that highly nonlinear PCF, designed with zero chromatic dispersion close to 800 nm, displays giant spectral broadening when the 100 MHz pulse train from the master oscillator is launched into just a few cm of fiber. The pulses emerge from a tiny aperture and last only a few ps. They have the bandwidth of sunlight but are 10^4 times brighter. Not surprisingly, this source is finding many uses, e.g., in optical coherence tomography. The huge bandwidth and high spectral brightness of the supercontinuum source make it ideal for all sorts of spectroscopy. Measurements that used to take hours and involve counting individual photons can now be made in a fraction of a second. Furthermore, because the light emerges from a microscopic aperture it is uniquely easy to perform spectroscopy with very high spatial resolution.

11.6.5 Telecommunications

There are many potential applications of PCF or PCF-based structures in telecommunications, although whether these will be adopted remains an open question. One application that seems quite close to being implemented is the use of solid core PCF or "hole-assisted" SMF for fiber-to-the-home, where the lower bend-loss is the attractive additional advantage offered by the holey structure. Other possibilities include dispersion-compensating fiber and hollow core PCF for long-haul transmission. Additional opportunities exist in producing bright sources of correlated photon pairs for quantum cryptography, parametric amplifiers with improved characteristics, highly nonlinear fiber for all-optical switching and amplification, acetylene-filled hollow core PCF for frequency stabilization at 1 550 nm, and the use of sliced SC spectra as *wavelength division multiplexing*[17] (WDM) channels. There are also many possibilities for ultra-stable in-line devices based on permanent morphological changes in the local holey structure, induced by heating, collapse, stretching, or inflation. The best reported loss in solid core PCF, from a group in Japan, stands at 0.28 dB/km at 1 550 nm, with a Rayleigh scattering coefficient of 0.85 dB/(mm · km). A 100 km length of this fiber was used in the first PCF-based penalty-free dispersion-managed soliton transmission system at 10 Gbit/s. The slightly higher attenuation compared with that in SMF is due to roughness at the glass-air interfaces.

Hollow core PCF is radically different from solid core SMF in many ways. This makes it difficult to predict whether it could be successfully used in long-haul telecommunications as a realistic competitor for SMF-28. The much lower Kerr nonlinearities mean that WDM channels can be much more tightly packed without nonlinear crosstalk, and the higher power-handling characteristics mean that more overall power can be transmitted. The effective absence of bend losses is also a significant advantage, particularly for short-haul applications. On the other hand, work still needs to be done to reduce the losses to 0.2 dB/km or lower, and to understand and control effects such as polarization mode dispersion, differential group delay, and multipath interference. It is interesting that the low-loss window of a plausible hollow core PCF is centered at 1 900 nm, because light travels predominantly in the hollow regions, completely changing the balance between scattering and infrared absorption.

The large glass-air refractive index difference makes it possible to design and fabricate PCFs with high levels of group velocity dispersion. A PCF version of the classical W-profile dispersion-compensating fiber was reported in 2005, offering slope-matched dispersion compensation for SMF-28 fiber at least over the entire C-band (Fig. 11-13). The dispersion levels achieved (1 200 ps/(nm · km)) indicate that only 1 km of fiber is needed to compensate for 80 km of SMF-28. The PCF was made deliberately birefringent to allow control of polarization mode dispersion.

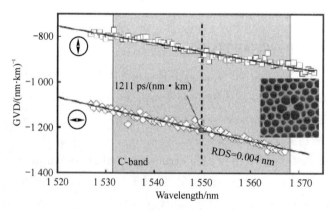

Fig. 11-13 Performance of a PCF designed to provide slope-matched dispersion compensation for

11.6.6 Optical Sensors

Sensing is so far a relatively unexplored area for PCFs, although the opportunities are myriad, spanning many fields including environmental monitoring, biomedical sensing, and structural monitoring. Solid core PCF has been used in hydrostatic pressure sensing. Multicore PCF has been used in bend and shape sensing and Doppler difference velocimetry. Fibers with a central single-mode core surrounded by a highly multimode cladding waveguide are useful in applications such as two-photon fluorescence sensing, where short pulses are delivered to the sample by the central single-mode core, and the resulting multiphoton *fluorescence*[18] efficiently collected by inner cladding waveguide, which has a large numerical aperture. Sensitivity enhancements of 20 times have been reported. Given the high level of interest, and large amount of effort internationally, it seems very likely that many more important sensing applications of PCF will emerge over the next few years.

11.6.7 Gratings in PCF

Bragg mirrors are normally written into the Ge-doped core of an SMF by UV light, using either two-beam interferometry or a zero-order nulled phase mask. The mechanism for refractive index change is related to the UV Corning SMF-28 over the C-band. Photosensitivity of the glass and is quite complex, with several different regimes of operation. In PCF, the presence of many holes in the cladding will inevitably scatter the UV light strongly and reduce (or enhance) the field amplitudes in the core. In addition, pure silica glass is only weakly photosensitive, requiring exposure to very intense light for formation of useful Bragg gratings. There have nevertheless been several reports of the inscription of Bragg gratings into pure-silica PCF, using 125 fs pulses at 800 nm wavelength and multiphoton processes. In the case of polymer PCF, low-power CW laser sources at 325 nm wavelength is sufficient to write Bragg gratings for 1 570 nm operation.

Although long-period fiber gratings (LPFGs) and PCFs have emerged at the same time and been around for almost ten years, the fabrications of fiber components in PCFs have attracted great attention in resent years. The potential applications of PCF-LPFG devices for gas sensing have been discussed. Unlike the PCF-based gas sensor that detects the analytes by the interaction of light with gases through the absorption of the evanescent wave in the holes of fiber cladding, the PCF-LPFG gas sensing works by the interrogating of the shifts of different resonance wavelength and strength of core-cladding mode coupling in the transmission spectrum. The advantages of the PCF-LPFG sensing devices are: high temperature insensitive and stability; compactness when packaged; practical use under hazardous conditions and in high temperature environment.

11.7 Future Perspectives

*PCFs have flexibility of design and can achieve many extraordinary characteristics, such as novel dispersion properties, high birefringence, single mode guidance over a wide spectral range, high nonlinearity, photonic bandgap guidance and others different from conventional fibers have.*① Although PCFs have only a near-20-year development history and the applications of PCFs are not diffuse, the developments of PCFs are rapid. As time progresses, there will doubtless be new scientists with new ideas and new experiments which will expand the role of PCFs in fiber optical research.

References

1. J. C. Knight, T. A. Birks, P. St. J. Russell, and et al. All-silica single-mode optical fiber with photonic crystal cladding. Optics Letters 1996, 21(19): 1547-1549.
2. A. Bjarklev, J. Broeng and A. S. Bjarklev. Photonic crystal fibres. Kluwer Academic Publishers Group, 2003, 19-42.
3. F. Poli, A. Cucinotta, and S. Selleri. Photonic crystal fibers: properties and applications. Springer Series in Materials Science, 2007, 7-42.
4. J. C. Knight, T. A. Birks, P. St. J. Russell, and et al. Two-dimensional photonic crystal material in fibre form. Proceedings of the 1996 Conference on Lasers and Electro-Optics Europe, CLEO/Europe, Hamburg, Germany, 1996, 75-79.
5. T. A. Birks, J. C. Knight, P. S. J. Russell. Endlessly single-mode photonic crystal fiber. Optics Letters, 1997, 22(13): 961-963.
6. K. Suzuki, H. Kubota, S. Kawanishi, et al. High-speed bi-directional polarisation division multiplexed optical transmission in ultra low-loss (1.3 dB/km) polarisation-maintaining photonic crystal fibre. Electronics Letters, 2001, 37(23): 1399-1401.
7. R. F. Cregan, B. J. Mangan, J. C. Knight, et al. Single-mode photonic band gap guidance of light in air. Science, 1999, 285: 1537-1539.
8. Ivan P. Kaminow, Tingye Li and Alan E. Willner. Optical fiber telecommunications V A (Fifth Edition), Academic Press is an imprint of Elsevier. 2008, 485-522.
9. P. Russell. Photonic Crystal Fibers. Science, 2003, 299: 358-362.
10. K. Suzjki, H. Kubota and S. Kawanishi. Optical properties of a low-Loss polarization-maintaining photonic crystal fiber. Optics Express, 2001, 9(13): 676-680.
11. A. O. Blanch, J. C. Knight, W. J. Wadsworth, et al. Highly birefringent photonic crystal Fibers. Optics Letters, 2000, 25(18): 1325-1327.
12. T. P. Hansen, J. Broeng, S. E. B. Libori, et al. Highly birefringent index-guiding photonic crystal fibers. IEEE Photonics Technology Letters, 2001, 13(6): 588-590.

13. M. J. Steel and R. M. Osgood. Elliptical-hole photonic crystal fibers. Optics Letters, 2001, 26(4): 229-231.

14. W. J. Wadsworth, R. M. Percival, J. C. Knight, and et al. Very High numerical aperture fibers. IEEE Photonics Technology Letters, 2004, 16(3): 843-845.

15. T. A. Birks, D. M. Atkin, P. St. J. Russell, and et al. Photonic band gap materials. Academic Publishers Group, 1996, 437-444.

16. K. M. Kiang, K. Frampton, T. M. Monro, and et al. Extruded single mode nonsilica glass holey optical fibres. Electronics Letters, 2002, 38(12):, 546-547.

17. D. Nodop, S. Linke, F. Jansen, and et al. Long period gratings written in large-mode area photonic crystal fiber. Applied Physics B, 2008 92: 509-512.

18. P. Russell. History and future of photonic crystal fibers. Optical Fiber Communication Conference, California, USA, 2009, 5-9.

19. http://www.nktphotonics.com/.

20. http://www.pcfiber.com/.

21. Zhaolun Liu. Simulation of optical properties and optimal designing of photonic crystal fibers. (Doctoral Thesis). Qinhuangdao: Yanshan University, 2008.

New Words and Expressions

1. total internal reflection 全内反射（当光线从具有较高折射系数的介质射入具有较低折射系数的介质时，如果入射角大于临界角，则光线不会发生折射，所有的光线都会被反射回原来的介质，这种现象称为全内反射现象）

2. localization [ˌləukəlaiˈzeiʃn] n. 局域化，局限，定位

3. photonic bandgap 光子带隙（不同介电常数的介质材料组成周期结构，比如在较高折射率材料中的某些位置周期性地引入低折射率材料，光波受到介质周期势场的影响而具有能带。这种能带结构叫做光子能带，而光子能带之间可能出现带隙，即为光子带隙）

4. endlessly single-mode 无截止波长单模（当光纤的归一化频率小于其归一化截止频率时，才能实现单模传输，即在光纤中仅有基模在传输，其余的高次模全部截止。也就是说，除了光纤的参量（如纤芯半径、数值孔径）必须满足一定条件外，要实现单模传输还必须使光波波长大于某个数值，这个数值就叫做单模光纤的截止波长。因此，无截止波长单模的含义是，能使光纤在整个运行波长范围内都支持单模传输）

5. large mode area 大模场面积

6. mode field diameter 模场直径

7. numerical aperture 数值孔径

8. preform [ˈpriːˈfɔːm] n. 预制棒

9. modified chemical vapor deposition 改进的化学汽相沉积（采用的 $SiCl_4$、$GeCl_4$ 等液态的原材料。原料在高温下发生氧化反应生成 SiO_2、B_2O_3、GeO_2、P_2O_5 微粉，沉积在石英反应管的内壁上。在沉积过程中需要精密地控制掺杂剂的流量，从而获得所设计的折射率分布）

10. vapor axial deposition 汽相轴向沉积（气化的原料进入火焰中水解形成的超细玻

璃粉堆积在作为靶子的种棒的端面上，形成轴向生长的光纤预制棒的方法）

11. outside vapour deposition 外汽相沉积（原料在氢氧焰中水解生成 SiO_2 微粉，然后经喷灯喷出，沉积在由石英、石墨或氧化铝材料制成的"母棒"外表面，经过多次沉积，去掉母棒，再将中空的预制棒在高温下脱水，烧结成透明的实心玻璃棒，即为光纤预制棒）

12. stack-and-draw 堆拉法

13. jacket ['dʒækit] n. 护套

14. chalcogenide ['kælkədʒə‚naid] n. 硫族(元素)化物，氧属(元素)化物

15. attenuation [ə‚tenju'eiʃen] n. 衰减

16. supercontinuum [‚sju:pkən'tinjuəm] n. 超连续谱（是指由频率在非常宽范围内是连续成分组成的谱）

17. wavelength division multiplexing 波分复用（指在同一根光纤中同时让两个或两个以上的光波长信号通过不同光信道各自传输信息）

18. fluorescence [fluə'resns] n. 荧光，荧光性

Notes

① 光子晶体光纤，也称为微结构光纤或者多孔光纤，它的纤芯周围有很多周期排列的贯穿整个光纤长度的空气孔，由于具有不同于常规光纤的新型导光机制，近十几年在科学界引起广泛关注。

② 高锟，被称为"光纤之父"或"光纤通信之父"，由于他在"有关光在纤维中的传输以用于光学通信方面"做出了突破性成就而获得一半的 2009 年诺贝尔物理学奖。

③ 光子晶体的概念最早出现在 1987 年，由 E. Yabnolovitch 和 S. John 分别在研究如何抑制自发辐射和光子的局域化特性时提出。

④ 光子晶体光纤具有灵活的设计，可以获得非凡的特性，比如新颖的色散特性、高双折射、宽带单模运行、高非线性、光子带隙及其他不同于常规光纤的特性。

第12章 科技文献检索

20世纪90年代以来,信息技术的高速发展和广泛应用引发了全球性的信息革命,信息被看成是一种战略资源,与物质、能源一起构成了现代社会的三大支柱。信息时代的到来和席卷全球的互联网的迅猛发展,给信息利用者带来了深远的影响,如何从浩瀚的信息海洋中获取所需的信息已成为科技人员科研工作中的首要问题。因此,熟悉和掌握科技文献的检索方法,对我们科研工作者的科研工作是非常必要的。

科技文献是用文字、图形、公式、代码、音频、视频等手段记录科技信息或知识的载体。科技文献包括科技图书、科技期刊、会议文献、专利文献、学位论文、科技报告、政府出版物、标准文献、报纸等。

科技文献检索是一门独特的科学知识。在知识爆炸、信息爆炸的今天,大学生不仅要掌握本专业所需的基础理论和专业知识,还要重视科技文献检索能力的培养与训练。在德国柏林图书馆的大门上刻有这样一段话:"这里是人类知识的宝库,如果你掌握它的钥匙的话,那么全部知识都是你的。图书馆目录是打开这大门的第一把钥匙。"这里明确指出了文献资料检索的重要性,掌握和运用检索文献资料的钥匙,及时有效地查到所需的学习和研究资料的方法,是我们必须具备的基本功。

怎样才能检索到我们在学习和研究中所需的文献资料?下面简单介绍一下文献资料的检索,然后谈谈在学习和研究中如何利用图书馆馆藏文献资料、数据库资源以及网络资源等检索文献资料。

12.1 信息检索的含义

信息检索(Information Retrieval),是指将信息按一定的方式组织和存储起来,并根据信息用户的需要找出有关的信息的过程和技术。信息检索有狭义和广义之分。

狭义的检索(Retrieval)是指依据一定的方法,从已经组织好的大量有关文献集合中,查找并获取特定的相关文献的过程。这里的文献集合,不是通常所指的文献本身,而是关于文献的信息或文献的线索。如果真正要获取文献中所记录的信息,那么还要依据检索所取得的文献线索索取原文。

广义的检索包括信息的存储(Storage)和检索两个过程。信息存储是指工作人员将大量无序的信息集中起来,根据信息源的外表特征和内容特征,经过整理、分类、浓缩、标引等处理,使其系统化、有序化,并按一定的技术要求建成一个具有检索功能的工具或检索系统,供人们检索和利用。而检索是指运用编制好的检索工具或检索系统,查找出满足用户要求的特定信息。

依据检索对象的不同,信息检索可分为3种类型:①以查找文献线索为对象的文献检索(Document Retrieval);②以查找数值与非数值混合情报为对象的事实检索(Fact Retrieval);③以查找数据、公式或图表为对象的数据检索(Data Retrieval)。

12.2 信息检索的基本原理

信息检索的基本原理是:通过对大量的、分散无序的文献信息进行搜集、加工、组织、存储,建立各种各样的检索系统,并通过一定的方法和手段使存储与检索这两个过程所采用的特征标识达到一致,以便有效地获得和利用信息源。其中存储是为了检索,而检索又必须先进行存储。

存储的过程,主要是对信息源进行标引,将其外表和内容的特征(如文献的标题、作者、来源和主题等)用特定的检索语言转化为一定的标识(如主题词、分类号和类目名称等),再将这些标识按一定的顺序编排后输入检索系统,从而为检索提供有规可循的途径。

为了保证文献信息能存得进、取得出,就必须使文献存储所依据的规则与文献信息检索所依据的规则尽量做到一致。也就是说,为了检索过程的顺利进行和达到较高的检索效率,除了在存储和检索过程的各个环节必须依据一定的方法和规则外,还必须有统一的检索语言和名称规范作为存储人员和检索人员的共同依据。

12.3 检索语言

检索语言是应文献信息的加工、存储和检索的共同需要而编制的专门语言,是表达一系列概括文献信息内容和检索课题内容的概念及其相互关系的一种概念标识系统。简言之,检索语言是用来描述信息源特征和进行检索的人工语言,可分为规范化语言和非规范化语言(自然语言)两类。

目前,世界上的信息检索语言有几千种,依其划分方法的不同,其类型也不一样。按照标识的性质与原理可分为分类语言、主题语言和代码语言三种;按照表达文献的特征可划分为表达文献外部特征的检索语言以及表达文献内容特征的检索语言。

检索语言在信息检索中起着极其重要的作用,它是沟通信息存储与信息检索两个过程的桥梁。在信息存储过程中,用它来描述信息的内容和外部特征,从而形成检索标识;在检索过程中,用它来描述检索提问,从而形成提问标识;当提问标识与检索标识完全匹配或部分匹配时,结果即为命中文献。

12.4 文献检索工具

文献检索工具是人们用来报道、存储和查找文献线索的工具。它是在对大量一次文献加工压缩的基础上形成有序的、体积较小的二次文献,并且成为有效的管理和利用文献信息的工具。一方面,它能将有关文献的特点著录下来,形成一条条的文献线索,并将它们按一定的方法排列起来,以供检索,这就是文献的存储过程;另一方面,它又能提供一定的检索途径,使人们按照一定的检索方法查出所需要的文献线索,这就是文献的检索过程。

12.4.1 检索工具应具备的条件

一般来说,检索工具应具备以下 5 个条件:
① 明确的收录范围;
② 完整明了的文献特征标识;
③ 每条文献条目中必须包含有多个有检索意义的文献特征标识,并标明供检索用的标识;
④ 全部条目科学地、按照一定规则组织成为一个有机整体;
⑤ 有索引部分,提供多种必要的检索途径。

目前可供人们使用的检索工具有很多,不同的检索工具各有特点,可以满足不同的信息检索的需求。

12.4.2 检索工具的类型

检索工具的种类繁多,按加工文献和处理信息的手段不同可分为手工和机械检索工具;按照出版形式不同可分为书本式、卡片式和计算机可读式检索工具;按照著录格式的不同可分为目录型、题录型、文摘型检索工具和索引。

12.5 检索文献资料的途径

查找文献资料,总是根据文献资料的不同特征来确定其查找的途径和选取引用的工具。文献的特征有两个方面:外表特征和内容特征。外表特征主要是指文献的篇名(题目)、作者姓名、出版者、报告号、专利号等。内容特征主要是指所论述的主题、观点、见解和结论等。一般来讲,检索途径可以分为以下 4 种:分类途径、主题途径、著者途径和其他途径。

(1) 分类途径

分类途径是指按照文献资料所属学科(专业)类别进行检索的途径,它所依据的是检索工具中的分类索引。

分类途径检索文献关键在于正确理解检索工具的分类表,将待查项目划分到相应的类目中去。一些检索工具如《中文科技资料目录》是按分类编排的,可以按照分类进行查找。

(2) 主题途径

主题途径是指通过文献资料的内容主题进行检索的途径,它依据的是各种主题索引或关键词索引,检索者只要根据项目确定检索词(主题词或关键词),便可以实施检索。

主题途径检索文献关键在于分析项目、提炼主题概念,运用词语来表达主题概念。主题途径是一种主要的检索途径。

(3) 著者途径

著者途径是指根据已知文献著者来查找文献的途径,它依据的是著者索引,包括个人著者索引和机关团体索引。

(4) 其他途径

其他途径包括利用检索工具的各种专用索引来检索的途径。专用索引的种类很多,常见的有各种号码索引(如专利号、入藏号、报告号等)、专用符号代码索引(如元素符号、分子式、结构式等)、专用名词术语索引(如地名、机构名、商品名、生物属名等)。

12.6 文献检索的基本方法

检索文献资料常用的方法有直接法、追溯法和综合法,现分别介绍如下。

1. 直接法

直接法是指直接利用检索工具(系统)检索文献信息的方法,这是文献检索中最常用的一种方法。它又分为顺查法、倒查法和抽查法。

(1) 顺查法

顺查法是指按照时间的顺序,由远及近地利用检索系统进行文献信息检索的方法。这种方法能收集到某一课题的系统文献,它适用于较大课题的文献检索。例如,已知某课题的起始年代,现在需要了解其发展的全过程,就可以用顺查法从最初的年代开始,逐渐向近期查找。

(2) 倒查法

倒查法是由近及远,从新到旧,逆着时间的顺序利用检索工具进行文献检索的方法。此法的重点是放在近期文献上。使用这种方法可以最快地获得最新资料。

(3) 抽查法

抽查法是指针对项目的特点,选择有关该项目的文献信息最可能出现或最多出现的时间段,利用检索工具进行重点检索的方法。

2. 追溯法

追溯法是指不利用一般的检索工具,而是利用已经掌握的文献末尾所列的参考文献,进行逐一地追溯查找"引文"的一种最简便的扩大情报来源的方法。它还可以从查到的"引文"中再追溯查找"引文",像滚雪球一样,依据文献间的引用关系,获得越来越多的与内容相关的文献。

3. 综合法

综合法又称为循环法,它是把上述两种方法加以综合运用的方法。综合法既要利用检索工具进行常规检索,又要利用文献后所附参考文献进行追溯检索,分期分段地交替使用这两种方法。即先利用检索工具(系统)检到一批文献,再以这些文献末尾的参考文献为线索进行查找，如此循环进行，直到满足要求时为止。

综合法兼有直接法和追溯法的优点，可以查得较为全面而准确的文献，是实际中采用较多的方法。

12.7 文献检索的一般步骤

文献检索工作是一项实践性和经验性很强的工作，对于不同的项目，可能采取不同的检索方法和步骤。检索程序与检索的具体要求有密切关系，大致可分为以下几个步骤。

1. 分析待查项目，明确主题概念

首先应分析待查项目的内容实质、所涉及的学科范围及其相互关系，明确要查证的文献内容、性质等，根据要查证的要点抽提出主题概念，明确哪些是主要概念，哪些是次要概念，并初步定出逻辑组配。

2. 选择检索工具，确定检索策略

选择恰当的检索工具，是成功实施检索的关键。选择检索工具一定要根据待查项目的内容、性质来确定，选择的检索工具要注意其所报道的学科专业范围、所包括的语种及其所收录的文献类型等，在选择中，要以专业性检索工具为主，再通过综合型检索工具相配合。如果一种检索工具同时具有机读数据库和刊物两种形式，应以检索数据库为主，这样不仅可以提高检索效率，而且还能提高查准率和查全率。为了避免检索工具在编辑出版过程中的滞后性，还应该在必要时补充查找若干主要相关期刊的现刊，以防止漏检。

3. 确定检索途径和检索标识

一般的检索工具都根据文献的内容特征和外部特征提供多种检索途径，除主要利用主题途径外，还应充分利用分类途径、著者途径等多方位进行补充检索，以避免一种途径不足所造成的漏检。

4. 查找文献线索，索取原文

应用检索工具实施检索后，获得的检索结果即为文献线索，对文献线索进行整理，分析其相关程度，根据需要，可利用文献线索中提供的文献出处，索取原文。

12.8 文献数据库检索

随着计算机信息技术的发展和文献资料的数字化，数据库成为主要的计算机检索信息资源，因此，学会一些基本的数据库检索技术有助于检索所需资料。

12.8.1 检索工具的类型

1. 布尔检索

利用布尔逻辑算符进行检索词或代码的逻辑组配，是现代信息检索系统中最常用的一种方法。常用的布尔逻辑算符有三种，分别是逻辑或"OR"、逻辑与"AND"、逻辑非"NOT"。用这些逻辑算符将检索词组配构成检索提问式，计算机将根据提问式与系统中的记录进行匹配,当两者相符时则命中,并自动输出该文献记录。

下面以"电子科学与技术"和"文献检索"两个词来解释三种逻辑算符的含义。

① "电子科学与技术"AND"文献检索",表示查找文献内容中既含有"电子科学与技术"又含有"文献检索"词的文献。

② "电子科学与技术"OR"文献检索",表示查找文献内容中含有"电子科学与技术"或含有"文献检索"以及两词都包含的文献。

③ "电子科学与技术"NOT"文献检索",表示查找文献内容中含有"电子科学与技术"而不含有"文献检索"的那部分文献。

检索中逻辑算符使用是最频繁的,对逻辑算符使用的技巧决定检索结果的满意程度。用布尔逻辑表达检索要求,除要掌握检索课题的相关因素外,还应在布尔算符对检索结果的影响方面引起注意。另外,对同一个布尔逻辑提问式来说,不同的运算次序会有不同的检索结果。布尔算符使用正确但不能达到应有检索效果的事情是很多的。

2. 截词检索

截词检索就是用截断的词的一个局部进行的检索,并认为凡满足这个词局部中的所有字符(串)的文献,都为命中的文献。按截断的位置来分,截词可有后截断、前截断、中截断三种类型。

不同的系统所用的截词符也不同,常用的有?、$、* 等。分为有限截词(即一个截词符只代表一个字符)和无限截词(一个截词符可代表多个字符)。下面以无限截词举例说明。

① 后截断,前方一致。如"comput?"表示 computer、computers、computing 等。

② 前截断,后方一致。如"?computer"表示 minicomputer、microcomputers 等。

③ 中截断,中间一致。如"?comput?"表示 minicomputer、microcomputers 等。

截词检索也是一种常用的检索技术,是防止漏检的有效工具,尤其在西文检索中,更是广泛应用。截断技术可以作为扩大检索范围的手段,具有方便用户、增强检索效果的特点,但一定要合理使用,否则会造成误检。

3. 原文检索

"原文"是指数据库中的原始记录,原文检索即以原始记录中的检索词与检索词间特定位置关系为对象的运算。原文检索可以说是一种不依赖叙词表而直接使用自由词的检索方法。

原文检索的运算方式,不同的检索系统有不同的规定,其差别是:规定的运算符不同;运算符的职能和使用范围不同。原文检索的运算符可以通称为位置运算符。从 RECON、ORBIT 和 STAIRS 三大软件对原文检索的规定,可以看出其运算符主要是以下 4 个级别。

① 记录级检索,要求检索词出现在同一记录中。

② 字段级检索,要求检索词出现在同一字段中。

③ 子字段或自然句级检索,要求检索词出现在同一子字段或同一自然句中。

④ 词位置检索,要求检索词之间的相互位置满足某些条件。

原文检索可以弥补布尔检索、截词检索的一些不足。运用原文检索方法,可以增强选词的灵活性,部分地解决布尔检索不能解决的问题,从而提高文献检索的水平和筛选能力。但是,原文检索的能力是有限的。从逻辑形式上看,它仅是更高级的布尔系统,因此存在着布尔逻辑本身的缺陷。

4. 扩检与缩检

扩检与缩检是网络搜索中为满足查全率和查准率要求而经常使用的两种检索策略与方法。

所谓扩检,即用较少的关键词和增加上位概念或同义词的方法扩大检索范围;所谓缩检,即用较多的关键词和增加专指性较强的概念或限制概念词来缩小检索范围。

在不同的搜索引擎中,可以用布尔符"OR(|)"、结果页面的相关关键词提示以及"link:"、"info:"等特殊检索语法进行扩检,用布尔符"and(+)"进行正向缩检,"not(-)"进行反向缩检,用"site:"和"filetype:"限定网页范围和文件类型范围进行缩检,以及用"Search within results(在结果中搜索)"缩检(注:在不同的搜索引擎中"或"、"与"、"非"可用不同的逻辑符表示)。

在制定检索策略时,对文献量较大或属于成熟学科的课题,应优先考虑查准率,从众多的相关文献中选取针对性较强的文献,对文献较少或新兴学科的课题,可适当放宽检索范围来保证查全率,以免遗漏重要的参考文献。

5. 模糊检索

模糊检索允许被检索信息和检索提问之间存在一定的差异,这种差异就是"模糊"在检索中的含义。比如,想查找"非挥发性存储"的信息,不知其在数据库中的标引词是什么,输入"非挥发存储"或"非挥发性的存储"都能得到想要的结果;模糊检索中所指的差异一方面来自用户在检索提问时输入错误;另一方面来自于某些词在不同国家的不同形式。

12.8.2 国内主要资源

(1) 维普

该数据库收录12 000余种社科类及自然科学类期刊的题录、文摘及全文。主题范畴为社科类、自然科学类、综合类,年代跨度为1989年至今。

(2) 万方

万方数据资源系统的数据库有百余个,应用最多的主要是包括了专业文献库、中国科技引文库、中国学位论文库、中国期刊会议论文库等。

(3) cnki

主要应用包括中国期刊全文数据库、中国优秀博士硕士论文全文数据库、中国重要报纸全文数据库、中国医院知识仓库、中国重要会议论文全文数据库。

(4) 超星图书馆、书生之家图书馆、中国数字图书馆

国内主要汇集各类图书资源的数据库。

12.8.3 国外主要资源

(1) SpringerLink

德国施普林格是世界著名的科技出版社,其检索系统名称为Link。出版物有期刊、丛书、图书、参考工具书等。目前共出版有2 100余种期刊。其电子期刊的学科覆盖有:化学和材料科学、计算机科学、商业和经济、工程学、建筑和设计、地球和环境科学、生物医学和生命科学、数学和统计学、医学、物理与天文学、计算机职业技术与专业计算机应用等学科,其中大部分期刊是被SCI和EI收录的核心期刊。

(2) IEEE/IEE

收录美国电气与电子工程师学会(IEEE)和英国电气工程师学会(IEE)自 1988 年以来出版的 12 000 多种 IEEE 和 IEE 的出版物，包括期刊、会议录和标准的全文信息。是电气电子和资讯科技最权威、先进的资讯来源。

(3) Scitation 平台

由 AIP(美国物理联合会)开发，为多个学会/协会的科技期刊、会议、标准等出版物提供电子访问服务。目前 Scitation 平台收录了 27 个出版社近 200 种科技期刊，是著名的物理学门户网站。

(4) ProQuest

收录了 1861 年以来全世界一千多所著名大学理工科 180 万份博士、硕士学位论文的摘要及索引，学科覆盖了数学、物理、化学、农业、生物、商业、经济、工程和计算机科学等，是学术研究中十分重要的参考信息源。

(5) Engineering Village

是由美国 Engineering Information Inc. 出版的工程类电子数据库，其中 Ei Compendex 数据库是工程人员与相关研究者最佳、最权威的信息来源。

(6) SCIENCE DIRECT 数据库

是荷兰 Elsevier Science 公司推出的在线全文数据库，该数据库将其出版的 2500 余种期刊全部数字化。该数据库涵盖了数学、物理、化学、天文学、医学、生命科学、商业及经济管理、计算机科学、工程技术、能源科学、环境科学、材料科学、社会科学等众多学科。

(7) OCLC(Online Computer Library Center)即联机计算机图书馆中心

是世界上最大的提供文献信息服务的机构之一，其数据库绝大多数由一些美国的国家机构、联合会、研究院、图书馆和大公司等单位提供。数据库的记录中有文献信息、馆藏信息、索引、名录、全文资料等内容。资料的类型有书籍、连续出版物、报纸、杂志、胶片、计算机软件、音频资料、视频资料、乐谱等。

12.8.4 进入数据库的方法和思路

(1) 购买权限，理论上这些资源都是收费的。查阅时，只能到购买权限的单位，才能进入数据库，一般高校或者科研院所都购买了许多数据库，在其设置的 IP 段可以免费下载，而在 IP 段外，可以通过购买阅读卡方式来获得权限。

(2) 采用公共的用户名和密码。这种方法用起来是最好最省事情的，但是搜索可就费时间了。密码来源多是试用形式的，一段时间会过期。取得这种密码，要看用户的搜索能力了。

(3) 使用高校或者科研单位代理。

12.9 其他检索文献途径

除了进入数据库检索外，因特网上有许多方法可以找到所需的文献，其中一种有效的方式就是使用搜索引擎。

搜索引擎其实是因特网上的一类网站，它事先将网上各网站的信息进行分类并且建立索引,然后将内容索引存放在一个地址数据库中,当人们向搜索引擎发出搜索请求时,搜索引擎便在其数据库中搜索,找到一系列相关信息后将结果以网页形式返回。目前比较有代表性的搜索引擎有 Google、AltaVista、Hotbot、Lycos、百度等。

如果通过以上方式还没有找到文献全文,那么还可以试一试以下几种方法。

(1) 根据作者 E-mail 地址,向作者索要,这是最有效的方法之一,一般作者都愿意提供,但信件一定要简洁! 为了更方便读者向作者索取原文,下面是信件模板:

Dear Professor ×××

I am a postgraduate student in College of ×××, ××× university. I am writing to request your assistance. I search one of your papers:"_____"(你想要的文献题目), but I can not read full-text content, would you mind sending your papers by E-mail? Thank you for your assistance.

Best wishes! (or best regards)

下面是网络上常见的一个模板,也可参考,信的内容如下:

Dear Mr./Mrs. _____(作者名):I am a graduate student of "_____"(你的单位)in China. I major in "_____"(您的专业). Recently, I found one of your articles, titled "_____"(文章名)in "_____"(杂志名). I found it may help me achieve my goals in this research field. This would make a really positive contribution to my work. I would like to be able to read the full text of this article. The abstract makes the article sound very interesting. I know there is usually a fee required to obtain the full article from "_____"(杂志名); however, as a student, my only income is a small scholarship which is about US $30.00 per month. I wonder if you would consider sending me the full text by Email. Perhaps you would consider this as an act of friendship between our two countries. Thank you for your kind consideration of this request. Sincerely: _____(您的名字)My Email address is:_____(你的 E-mail 地址)

出于礼貌,如果你要的文献作者发 E-mail 给你了,千万别忘记回信致谢。

(2) 让所在的研究所图书馆的管理员帮忙从外面的图书馆进行文献传递,不过有的文献可能是收费的。

(3) 到网络资源上求助,如果需要的文献目前还没有电子版,也可以通过馆藏求助获得全文。在找到中文文献之后,就可以通过其中的英文关键词来查找英文文献。

总的来说,现在获得文献的途径很多,越来越容易,但是对文献的消化吸收严重不够。我们不能变成文献的收集者,要做文献的利用者和使用者,研读关键文献,注重基础学习才是关键;要让信息成为财富,关键是消化吸收,而不能成为信息的奴隶,徒增信息的容量,而自己却无丝毫长进。

附:光电子领域常用科技文献网站推荐

http://www.sciencemag.org/ Science(科学网站)

http://www.nature.com/ Nature(自然网站)

http://www.osa.org/ the Optical Society of America(OSA,美国光学学会)

http://www.spie.org/ the International Society for Optical Engineering

http://www.nasa.gov/ National Aeronautics and Space administration (NASA)
http://www.aip.org/ American institute of physics
http://www.iop.org（英国物理学会）
http://wwwsoc.nii.ac.jp/jps/（日本物理学会）
http://www.ieee.org/portal/site Institute of Electrical and Electronics Engineers(IEEE)
http://www.sipo.gov.cn/sipo/（中华人民共和国国家知识产权局）
http://www.uspto.gov/ The United States Patent and Trademark Office
http://www.european-patent-office.org/European Patent Office
http://www.nist.gov/ National institute of standards and technology
http://opticsky.cn/（光行天下）
http://www.33tt.com/（飞达光学网）
http://www.cnopt.com/（中国光学在线）
http://www.opto-tech.com/index.php（光学设计论坛）
http://www.cscbbs.com/omp/index.php（光机人）
http://bbs.oecr.com/（光电论坛）
http://www.oeol.org/bbs/（光电在线）
http://coema.org.cn/（中国光学光电子论坛）
http://www.2ic.cn/（半导体技术天地）
http://www.smcrystal.net/（光学光电子元件网）
http://www.cndzz.com/（电子电路图站）
http://www.eeworld.com.cn/（电子工程世界）
http://www.cnele.com/（中国电子电器网）
http://www.chinacomponents.com.cn/（中国电子元器件网）
http://www.elec.cc/（国际电子网）
http://www.etuni.com/（电子爱好者网）
http://www.eetchina.com/（电子工程专辑）
http://www.cellphone.eetchina.com/（手机设计）
http://www.datasheet5.com/（集成电路速查网）
http://www.eefocus.com/（与非网）
http://www.ednchina.com/ EDN(电子设计技术)

本章参考文献

1. 谢小苑. 科技英语翻译技巧与实践. 北京：国防工业出版社，2008.
2. www.baidu.com.
3. www.google.com.
4. 小木虫网站（http://emuch.net/）.

第13章 英语科技论文写作

在世界科学技术飞速发展的今天,科技领域的交流日渐频繁,竞争也更加激烈,因此如何及时准确地将自己的科研成果公诸于众,是每一个科技工作者刻不容缓的工作。由于世界各国之间交流科技信息最通用的语种是英语,因此英语科技论文写作能力则是极为重要的环节。著名物理学家 M. Faraday 指出有价值的研究分成三步:"开拓、研究完成、发表"(There are three necessary steps in useful research: the first to begin it, the second to end it and the third to publish it.),可见发表论文或公开科研成果已经成为科学研究不可缺少的一部分。科技论文的发表不仅可以促进学术交流还有利于科学积累,同时又是发现人才的重要渠道,是考核科技工作者业务成绩的重要依据。因此如何进行英语科技论文写作将是每一个科研人员的必修课。

13.1 科技论文的概念和特点

科技论文(学术论文)是某一科学研究课题,在实验性、理论性或观测性(含调查研究性)上,具有新的科学研究成果或创新见解或创新知识的科学记录;或是已知原理被应用于实际中取得新的进展的科学总结;或是在某一学科领域对其某一方面研究进展与发展前景的综合论述。

从科技论文的定义上我们不难看出,一篇好的科技论文应该具备三个基本条件:①原创性成果;②采用一定的形式,使作者的同行能重复实验、审查作者的结论;③在杂志或其他能为科学界利用的原始文件上发表。

科技论文具有科学性、创新性(或独特性)、理论性(或学术性)、准确性以及规范性和可读性等突出特点。

13.2 如何撰写英语科技论文

从我们阅读的文章中可以总结出来,一篇好的科技论文应该在其内容原创性、成果的新颖性、可读性方面给人留下较深印象。要使论文给评审者或最终读者留下深刻的好印象,首先论文内容要是原创的,对前人工作的评价深入透彻、恰如其分。还必须有自己独特的研究方法,或用现有方法得到独特的发现,或有新的应用。

论文写作上，必须思路清晰、逻辑性强、语句通顺、表格信息丰富、图像图形能够达到弥补文字描述所不易达到的效果，有丰富的信息且可读性强。下面进一步介绍论文撰写时应注意的一些方面。

13.2.1 构建论文写作提纲

撰写提纲是作者动笔行文前的必要准备。从提纲本身来讲，它是一篇论文的写作计划，是作者构思谋篇的具体体现。

提纲撰写的常规方法是用一张空白纸写下能想到的关于论文主题的所有重要观点。然后问自己一些问题："Why did I do this work?"、"What does it mean?"、"What hypotheses did I mean to test?"、"What ones did I actually test?"、"What were the results?"、"Did this work yield a new method of compound? What?"、"What measurements did I make?"、"How were they characterized?"。列出所有可能的方程式、图和方案，得到主要的思想是非常重要的，当你开始实验来验证一个想法，但却发现数据会支持另外一种想法时，不要担心，把想法都写出来，并且从中找到猜想、目标和数据的最佳组合。论文的目标经常会随着论文的完成而发生变化，并且会产生出大量的优秀观点。

以上工作完成后，再拿出一张纸来开始组织论文的思路，将观点列为以下三条。
① 绪论：我为什么要做这项工作，中心目的和想法是什么？
② 结果与讨论：结果是什么？这些结果是怎么产生以及表征的？如何测量？
③ 结论：哪些想法被证明或者否定了？我学到什么了？为什么会不同？

接下来组织数据，将数据用图、表等形式表示出来。最后将提纲、示意图、表和方程式按顺序编排好。提纲确定后，就要进行论文的撰写。

13.2.2 撰写英语科技论文

典型的科学论文包括：题目（Title）、作者（Authors）、作者单位和联络方式（Affiliation and Communication Address）、论文摘要（Abstract）、关键词（Key words）、引言（Introduction）、研究目标（Research Objective）、实验设计（Experimental Design）、实验结果及其分析（Results and Analysis）、对方法和结果的讨论（Discussion）、结论（Conclusion）、致谢（Acknowledgement）、辅助材料（Appendix）、参考文献（References）以及表和图。从引言到结论为正文。有些论文由于推导繁琐，或需要附带程序等，为不影响阅读效果，需要把这类内容放在辅助材料里供有兴趣的读者进一步阅读。

这样的结构是用来帮助读者快速找到他们感兴趣的信息的，把信息放错地方会使读者糊涂。常犯的错误是混淆事实（结果）和解释（讨论）。讨论是对结果的解释及说明它的意义，而不是重复结果的描述。

一篇论文是从摘要、引言开始，本书建议从方法和结果部分开始写，因为作者对方法和结果最熟悉，此外只有更好地理解方法和结果，才能确定中心命题。而标题、引言和讨论的写作都需要中心命题。我们应该从最熟悉的事情开始，就像读者从他们最熟悉的地方开始理解一样。

1. 论文题目

读者阅读文献时，首先阅读标题，然后考虑是否阅读摘要和全文。某些文献往往只列出标题和出处,这就要求标题简单明了,既能概括全篇,又能引人注目。不恰当的标题往往会使真正需要它的读者错过阅读此篇论文的机会,从而使标题完全失去了它应起的作用。

一个令人满意的标题,既不要过于概括,以致流于空泛、一般化;也不宜过于烦琐,使人得不出鲜明印象,难以记忆和引证。论文题目一定要达意、简练、清楚。

写标题时应注意的问题如下。

(1) 标题是一种"标记",而不是句子(也有少数作者使用句子做标题)。一个句子一般要有主语、谓语、宾语,标题通常不采用句子形式,比句子简洁,但词的先后顺序很重要,词序错误是标题写作中常犯的错误。

(2) 下列词语会增加标题的长度,一般在标题中省略不用:"Some Thoughts on"、"A Few Observations on"、"Study of"、"Investigation of"、"A Final Report on"、"A Complete Investigation of"等。

(3) 标题中不要使用缩略语、化学分子式、专利商标名称、行话、罕见的或过时的术语,如果标题包含缩略语无法标明全称时,摘要中出现相同缩略语则必须标明全称,且尽量少用新的缩略语。

(4) 按惯例,英语标题第一个词和每个实词的第一个字母要大写。

2. 作者及作者单位

论文的署名作者应满足下列条件:①必须参与过本项研究的设计和开创工作,如在后期参加工作,必须赞同研究的设计;②必须参加过论文中的某项观察和获取数据工作;③必须参与过对所观察的现象和所取得的数据的解释,并从中得出论文的结论;④必须参加过论文的撰写。仅对这项科研工作给予过支持和帮助,但不符合上述条件者,不能列为作者。科技文章可以个人署名,也可以用集体名义署名,并写明工作单位和地址,便于联系。

如果作者不只一位,作者名单排列的顺序目前尚没有统一的规则。一般按对论文的贡献大小排列。英国有些杂志按作者姓名的字母顺序排列,这种方法未能得到普遍的承认。

作者单位应反映署名作者从事这项研究时所在的单位。如果作者的研究是在不同单位完成,应列出各个单位。如果作者在某单位做完研究后调往另一单位,在作者单位中不应列新调单位。但是可以在联络方式处注明:已换工作单位。论文发表时可以注明联系作者或者通讯作者(Corresponding Author)。通讯作者一般是研究工作开展单位有固定职位的研究人员。如果学生或访问学者与合作导师联合发表论文,一般通讯作者应是合作导师。其实,这与合作导师参与的程度并无直接关系,只是为了便于读者能向一个较长久有效的地址索要材料或提供批评意见。论文从开始投稿开始,联系方式便不可缺少。在论文投稿阶段可以使用负责投送的作者的联系地址、电话、电邮等,但是当论文发表时应该改成通讯作者的地址。

3. 摘要

摘要应能使读者迅速准确地判明该论文的主要内容,是否合乎自己所需,有无通读全文的必要。因此作者应从读者角度出发,在醒目的标题下,精心撰写摘要,让一次文献(原始文献)的读者便于浏览,并且稍加修改,甚至原封不动就能供二次文献(人工检索的文摘、索引、题录、文献卡,以及机读磁带)利用。

论文摘要应反映论文的主要信息,简明而不晦涩难懂。内容应包括如下五个方面:①研究的背景——研究的现状和尚存在的问题;②目的——研究的目的及重要性;③方法——研究的内容、方法和手段以及取得的进展,应该详而不繁;④成果——主要成果及贡献;⑤结论——评议论文的价值及建议。其中研究成果、结论为重点内容。

一般来说,一篇较短的论文,摘要不超过全文的3%可能是比较恰当的。写摘要的注意事项如下。

1) 规范

摘要虽然通常摆在正文前面,但往往是在最后写作。写摘要应使用正规英语、标准术语,避免使用缩写字。最好用第三人称,避免把各种时态混在一起使用,也避免把陈述式和命令式混合使用。

2) 精炼

文摘摘要要精练,不宜列举例证,不宜与其他研究工作对比。要取消背景性情况介绍,取消对既有研究情况的陈述,仅限于表达新的研究进展信息。

精简英语摘要,要注意以下几个方面。

(1) 不用开场白

早年常用的开场白为:

This is a report on...	这是关于……的一篇报道
In this paper the author presents...	在这篇论文中,作者介绍……
The purpose of this article is to...	本文的目的在于……

这类套话,应简写成:

The paper/author suggests/presents... 本文(作者)提出(介绍)……

(2) 不用标题语

摘要开头处,不可将标题中用过的词语再重复一遍。此外,摘要中也不要用图表、方程式、结构式等非文字性内容。

(3) 不用重复词

按修辞学要求,英语中最忌重复。省略是多方面的,这里只提一些在摘要中常见、不仅不增加内涵反而容易引起混乱的可删除词语作为示例。

① An hour in the morning is worth two(省 hours) in the evening.

一日之计在于晨。

省去后一个 hours 便觉行文洒脱而不唠叨。

② Potatoes are an important source of starchy food in temperate countries and bananas(省 are an important source of starchy food) in tropics.

淀粉食品的重要来源,在温带国家是土豆,在热带地区是香蕉。

英、汉语省略部分一致,句型结构不同。括号中的谓语部分 are 和表语 an important source of starchy food 同前面并列句中的重复,因此删除,节约篇幅;又用 tropics 代替 tropic countries。

(4) 少用形式主语

有些作者不主张多用形式主语,认为多用存在下列问题:①占去句首醒目的强调位置,平添一个 that 主语从句,使重要概念和事实不能及早入目,先睹为快;②主句用平淡无力的存在动词 be,而有表现力的行为动词反隐藏在后随从句中;③好像所提看法并非出自论文作者本人,使人怀疑作者有论据不足,因而不敢肯定之嫌。因此下列①②句不如分别简化为

③④句：

① It is concluded that a new method has to be devised.

② It will be seen that further research is needed.

③ （Conclusion：）A new method has to be devised.

（结论：）不得不想出一个新方法。

④ Further research is needed.

需要作进一步的研究。

3) 具体

摘要的每个论点都要具体鲜明。一般不笼统地讲论文"与什么有关"，而直接讲论文"说明什么"。

4) 完整

摘要本身要完整。有些读者是利用杂志摘要或索引卡片进行研究工作的，很可能得不到全篇论文，因此要注意不要引用论文某节或某张插图来代替说明。

5) 全面

不要过于简单地只把论文标题加以扩展，使读者无法得到全文梗概，了解论文的创新特点。这种写法在文献中是有的，要注意避免。

各国最有影响的电子科学、物理和材料等杂志对文摘写作有些共同要求。归纳起来有以下三条。

① 要说明实验或论证中新观察的事实、结论。如有可能，还要说明新的理论、处理、仪器、技术等的要点。

② 要说明新材料名称、新数据，包括物理常数等。如不能说明，也要提到这些。提到新的项目和新的观察是很重要的，哪怕它们对本论文的主旨来说仅仅是附带而已。

③ 在说明实验结果时，要说明采用的方法。如果是新方法，还得说明其基本原理、操作范围和准确度。

4. 关键词或者国际通用分类代码

按照惯例，摘要的末尾要加关键词，作为索引和检索系统的补充，表明文章的特性。关键词是英语科技论文的文献检索标识，用以表达文献主题概念的自然语言词汇。论文的关键词经由文题和层次标题选出。国际重要检索系统均用关键词来检索当前最新发表的论文。关键词一般为3～10个，根据"自由词汇表"或根据最新的权威性专业词汇从论文中选出。

人们在检索文献和投稿时，需要知道文献和稿件所属有关代码。并且国际期刊通常要求作者在文章中列出国际通用分类代码。学科不同，国别不同，分类代码也不相同。目前与光电类期刊有关的分类代码有 PACC 代码、PACS 代码、EEACC 等。

PACC (Physics Abstracts, Classification and Contents)是国际物理学分类表，是英国《科学文摘》分辑 A(Science Abstracts Series A)——《物理文摘》(Physical Abstracts)——的分类方法，PACC 被广泛应用在全球物理学期刊及有关数据库中，一些编辑部要求作者提供 PACC，详情可参见中文《物理学报》的网站：http://gjj.cc/Bao/ZaZhi/PeiXun/XiaoKan/wulixb.htm。

EEACC (Electrical and Electronics Abstracts Classification and Contents)是国际电气

电子学分类表,是英国《科学文摘》(Science Abstracts Series B)数据库分类体系的一个分辑(Electrical and Electronics Abstracts),详情可参照中文《半导体学报》的网站:http://www.cjs.ac.cn/new_cn/ch/common_item.aspx?parent_id=31&menu_id=66&flag=1&child=0&is_three_menu=0。

PACS (Physics and Astronomy Classification Scheme)是物理天文学分类表,由美国物理学会(American Institute of Physics,AIP)提供,从1975年开始应用于"Physical Review"系列期刊。详情可见网站:http://www.aip.org/pacs/index.html。

5. 引言

引言(Introduction),又称绪论或前言,是一篇论文的引导部分。一般简要地介绍论文的目的、宗旨,以及课题的价值和意义;综述有关学者在这个领域里已作过的工作、对目前成果产生过影响的重大发现和观点、研究进程以及遗留问题;限定本论文的论述范围;描述实验方法、研究手段和资料来源;介绍本论文的结构。一些首创性较强的论文则可能在绪论部分着重提供背景知识(概念、术语、定义、定理、历史沿革等)。

引言的主要目的是提出研究动机和目的。因此要指出目前所研究领域的知识缺陷,提出研究问题。这要求作者必须参考引证最新的相关研究文献。但是注意避免仅引用文章,不指出别人真正的贡献,特别是理论、方法、结果方面的贡献。当然,写作时不一定要用贡献之类的词来表述他人的工作。也可以将别人工作的不足作为自己研究的动机。在分析目前已知和不足之后,清晰地提出自己的研究目标或假设,着重指出自己研究的贡献。

因论文具有不同的类型和论题,绪论的内容也就不可避免地要有所侧重。但一般来说,在绪论中大多包括下述内容:①阐述本文的目的、宗旨和中心议题;②综述前人在本领域内做过的工作;③介绍背景知识;④探讨本课题的价值和意义;⑤介绍本课题的研究手段及数据和资料的来源等;⑥介绍正文的框架结构。

引言中一些常用的句型:

The experiments (research) on ... was carried by...

Recent experiments by... have suggested that...

The previous work on... has indicated that...

The paper is divided into five major sections as follows...

6. 实验设计、实验结果及其分析

实验设计主要应与研究目标呼应。内容包括完整提出理论、方法或模型,实验的内容和方法,如研制需要的某种仪器的原理,针对所提出的理论、方法和模型进行检验的方法,收集和观测数据的方法,对获取的数据进行处理和分析的方法等。应明确给出所使用的数据的来源、日期、比例尺等元数据内容。描述清楚处理数据的步骤,适当使用流程图。总之,提供的介绍应足以使读者可以重复同类实验。在结果部分,主要介绍按实验设计完成实验后所取得的结果,应该与处理方法相呼应。对结果的解释需要深入透彻,指出新的发现。适当使用图表,分析出现偏差的原因。

7. 讨论

讨论部分的内容包括整个研究与其他研究从理论、方法到结果的相同和不同点;理论与实验结果的一致性分析,方法和模型的灵敏性,出现误差的原因,指出本研究的局限;提出结论和概括性论点;对不确定或无法到达目标的结果进行更广泛的阐述。结构上,如果介绍结

果时必须对不确定的结果进行讨论,可以将讨论与结果部分合并。有时将讨论部分与结论合并。不管怎样,对于作者来说,这部分往往是写作的难点。也是反映作者对自己领域积累深浅的重要部分。做得好,对论文能起到画龙点睛的作用。一篇论文的贡献常常在讨论部分得到注释。

8. 结论

结论要与引言中的假设或研究目标相呼应,总结出实验结果能够支持的论点。有时为了使结论更易于理解,需要先对所用方法和实验设计进行归纳。

结论部分在写作手法上也有其特别的要求。它经常用到的语法时态是现在完成时和一般过去时,以表示上述所做的研究或实验客观的描述。也经常用到很多固定或常见的句型结构和表达方式,它们能开门见山地表明作者及实验、研究的目的、结果等。在结束语中还常用一些连接词,使段落与段落之间、结论与结论之间、句与句之间连接紧凑,从而起到突出主题、圆满结束全文的作用。

结论常用的句型:

On the basis of..., the following conclusion can be made...

From..., we now conclude (sum up) that...

We have demonstrated in this paper...

The results of experiment (simulation) indicate (show)...

Finally, a summary is given of...

9. 致谢

致谢部分不能流于形式,而应客观恰当地反映他人的帮助。要全面准确地列出资助论文研究的课题和编号。

This work is supported by Project supported by the National Natural Science Foundation of China (Grant No. _____) and Project supported by the National High Technology Research and Development Program of China (Grant No. _____). We are thankful to Prof. ... for use of their spectroscope and Dr. ... for his guidance while using the apparatus. We would like to thank ... for fruitful discussions. The excellent technical assistance of... is gratefully acknowledged.

10. 参考文献

撰写论文一般离不开参考资料。一旦引用了他人的任何材料,就必须向读者提供参考资料的来源(Documenting sources),说明作者是谁,书目或文章标题是什么,何年何月由谁在何处发表或出版,何处可以查得到,等等。这样做的目的,首先是为了向原作者表达引用者的谢意(Acknowledgement);其次是向读者表明论文作者的研究广度和深度,并以此来加强论文的可靠性和权威性;最后是为了能让那些对所引用的文献资料感兴趣的读者顺利地查找到引证之处。此外,恰当地引证参考资料还可以使论文作者避免"剽窃"之嫌,证明论文作者的学者风范。

一般来说,学术刊物在约稿时都会对论文作者提出比较详细的格式要求。论文作者在准备论文时要严格按照这些要求编排自己的论文,尤其是在引证注释方面,应该自始至终遵循刊物所规范的格式要求。参考文献不是多多宜善,而是能够充分反映目前在论文研究领域的知识面貌——所有结论和所用方法。不应漏掉关键的方法和结论,一般应引用概念、方法和发现的原创论文及对此做出贡献的相关发展。当然,如果对某一方面已有综述性论文和教材做出概括,应当引用。

11. 图、表

通常 SCI 收录的刊物,在投稿时,手稿正文不插入论文图表,而是置于文献之后,先表后图。图表分别编号要清楚,标题要清晰,表的标题放在表前。而图题置于图后。列图之前要加一个图的编号和图题清单。图例清楚,图题中的缩略语要给出解释。图表必须专业化地完成。考虑到发表时图形会缩小,因此要保证缩小一定倍数时也要清晰可读。

总之,在稿件投出之前,一定要注意以下几点。

① 认真对待写作,尽最大努力花时间写作。它是科学研究的重要一环。文章没写好,没人看,没人用,等于没发表。

② 除非这个研究是全面彻底的,而且你试了所有可以支持你结论的方法,否则不要去发表。

③ 重新思考,并合理解释为什么做这项工作,做了什么?什么是最重要的发现?为什么用这个方法?为什么用这些参数?什么是以前做过的(更新文献搜索)?不同在什么地方?

④ 要从批判的角度来看你的工作。只有这样,才能找到弱点,进一步发展。许多论文是在反复讨论中大幅度修改,许多计算经常要重做。只有理顺和理解结果,文章才会更有意义。

⑤ 要能回答所有合理的质疑。如果你自己有疑问,一定要搞清楚,否则别人又怎会相信。

⑥ 不要隐藏任何事实,不做假,不要低估其他科学家的智慧。让你的研究可重复,把所有的材料和数据上网。

⑦ 从头(标题)到尾(结论或讨论)要从旧信息过渡到新信息。永远不要在句子的开头引入新信息。切忌在术语被定义之前使用它们。

⑧ 在段首要有阐明整段主题的句子,在段尾要有连到下段的过渡句。从标题到结论都要连贯。研究什么问题、问题的位置,在引言中回答;怎样研究这个问题,在材料和方法章节中回答;新的发现,在结果一章中体现;新发现的意义在讨论中回答。这样句句相扣,段段相连,让一篇论文是一个整体而不是杂乱无章地把句子堆积在一起。才能使读者享受阅读你的文章。

⑨ 写,重写,再重写。没有人能第一次就写好。在修订阶段,应该仔细、彻底,并不断反复,如有可能,最好请母语是英语的编辑人员帮助编辑一遍。

13.3 英语科技论文的写作技巧

1. 如何指出当前研究的不足以及有目的地引导出自己的研究的重要性

通常在叙述了前人成果之后,用 however 来引导不足,比如:

However, little information (attention, work, data, or research)…

few studies (investigations, researchers, or attempts)…

none of these studies have been done on...
focused on...
attempted to...
conducted...
investigated...
studied...

Previous research (studies, or records) has (have)
failed to consider...
ignored...
misinterpreted...
neglected to...
overestimated,
underestimated
misleaded...

以上引导一般提出一种新方法，或者一种新方向。如果研究的方法以及方向和前人一样，可以通过下面的方式强调自己工作的作用：

However, data is still scarce (rare, less accurate)
there is still dearth of...

We need to
　aim to
　have to
　　provide more documents (data, records, or studies).
　　increase the dataset.

Further studies are still necessary...

一定要注意绝对不能全面否定前人的成果，即使在你看来前人的结论完全不对。这是对前人工作最起码的尊重，英文叫做给别人的工作 credits。

所以文章不要出现非常 negative 的评价，比如：

Their results are wrong, very questionable, have no commonsense, etc.

遇到这类情况，可以婉转地提出：

Their studies may be more reasonable if they had considered this situation.

Their results could be better convinced if they... Or Their conclusion may remain some uncertainties.

如果自己的研究完全是新的，没有前人的工作进行对比，在这种情况下，你可以自信地说，根据提出的过程，存在这种可能的结果，本文就是要证实这种结果。

We aim to test the feasibility (reliability) of the...

It is hoped that the question will be resolved (fall away) with our proposed method (approach).

2. 如何提出自己的观点

在提出自己的观点时，采取什么样的策略很重要。不合适的句子通常会遭到 reviewer

的置疑。常用的句型有：

We aim to
This paper reports on...
　　　　provides results
　　　　extends the method...
　　　　focus on...
The purpose of this paper is to...
Furthermore, Moreover, In addition, we will also discuss...

① 如果观点不是这篇文章最新提出的,通常要用：
We confirm that...

② 对于自己很自信的观点,可用：
We believe that...

③ 在更通常的情况下,由数据推断出一定的结论,可用：
Results indicate, infer, suggest, imply that...

④ 在极其特别的情况才可以用：We put forward (discover, observe) ..."for the first time"来强调自己的创新。

⑤ 如果自己对所提出的观点不完全肯定,可用：
It should be noted that this study has examined only...
We concentrate (focus) on only...
We have to point out that we do not...
Some limitations of this study are...
The results do not imply...
The results can not be used to determine...
　　　　be taken as evidence of...
Unfortunately, we can not determine this from this data...
Our results are lack of...

但是,在指出这些不足之后,随后一定要再一次强调本文的重要性以及可能采取的手段来解决这些不足,为别人或者自己的下一步研究打下伏笔。

Notwithstanding its limitation, this study does suggest...
However, these problems could be solved if we consider...
Despite its preliminary character, this study can clearly indicate...

3. 怎样圈定自己的研究范围

前言的另外一个作用就是告诉读者(包括 reviewer)文章的主要研究内容。如果处理不好,reviewer 会提出严厉的建议,比如没有考虑某种可能性、某种研究手段等。为了减少这种争论,在前言的结尾就要明确提出本文研究的范围。

(1) 时间尺度问题

如果问题涉及比较长的时序,可以明确地提出本文只关心这一时间范围的问题：
We preliminarily focus on the older (younger)...

如果有两种时间尺度的问题 (long-term and short-term),可以说两者都重要,但是本文只涉及其中一种。

（2）研究区域的问题

和时间问题一样,明确提出你只关心这一地区。

4. 最后的圆场

在前言的最后,还可以总结性地提出,这一研究对其他研究的帮助。或者说:further studies on ... will be summarized in our next study (or elsewhere).

总之,其目的就是让读者把思路集中到你要讨论的问题上来,减少争论(arguments)。

5. 用好连接词与逻辑

写英文论文最常见的一个毛病就是文章的逻辑不清楚。解决的方法如下。

（1）句子上下要有连贯,不能让句子之间独立

常见的连接词语有,However, also, in addition, consequently, afterwards, moreover, Furthermore, further, although, unlike, in contrast, Similarly, Unfortunately, alternatively, parallel results, In order to, despite, For example, Compared with other results, thus, therefore...

用好这些连接词,能够使观点表达得有层次,更加明确。

① 比如,如果叙述有时间顺序的事件或者文献,最早的文献可用"AA advocated it for the first time..."接下来,可用"Then BB further demonstrated that..."再接下来,可用"Afterwards, CC..."如果还有,可用"More recent studies by DD..."

② 如果叙述两种观点,要把它们截然分开:

AA put forward that... In contrast, BB believe...

Unlike AA, BB suggest...

On the contrary（表明前面的观点错误,如果只是表明两种对立的观点,用 in contrast）, BB...

③ 如果两种观点相近,可用:

AA suggest... Similarly (Alternatively), BB...

AA suggest..., BB also does...

④ 表示因果或者前后关系,可用 consequently, therefore, as a result。

⑤ 表明递进关系,可用 furthermore, further, moreover, in addition,当写完一段英文,最好首先检查一下是否较好地应用了这些连接词。

（2）段落的整体逻辑

我们经常要叙述一个问题的几个方面。这种情况下,一定要注意逻辑结构。

首先第一段要明确告诉读者你要讨论几个部分:

... Therefore, there are three aspects of this problem have to be addressed.

The first question involves...

The second problem relates to...

The third aspect deals with...

上面的例子可以清晰地把观点逐层叙述。或者可以直接用 First, Second, Third, Finally。当然,Furthermore, in addition 等可以用来补充说明。

总之,写文章的目的是要让读者读懂,读得清晰,并且采取各种措施方便于读者。

13.4 投稿过程

首先决定投哪份刊物。作者一般在撰写论文时就已经做出决定。主要决策依据应是主题内容合适,学术声誉好,读者多。当然也要看自己成果的大小,论文的质量而定。勿一稿两投。论文完成后,要按照每份刊物的投稿要求投稿。一般的投稿清单包括:投稿信(cover letter)、足够的稿件数、所有图表以及其他要求的材料。将上述内容打包邮寄,或通过电子网络按要求投递稿件。

投稿信中应该简述所投稿件的核心内容、主要发现和意义,拟投期刊时对稿件处理有无特殊要求等(如"not to review" list)。另外,请附上主要作者的姓名、通讯地址、电话传真和E-mail 地址。此外许多杂志要求推荐几位审稿人及其联系方式。投稿信范例如下。

例1:

Dear Prof. ...

We are submitting a manuscript named "AAA" by BBB et al. to "Journal name". This paper is new. Neither the entire paper nor any part of its content has been published or has been accepted elsewhere. It is not being submitted to any other Journal. We believe the paper may be of particular interest to the readers of your Journal as it... Correspondence should be addressed to * * at the following address, phone number, fax number and email address...

Thanks very much for your attention to our paper.

Sincerely yours

NAME,ADDRESS,E-mail,FAX.

例2:

Dear Editors,

On behalf of my co-authors, I am submitting the enclosed material "TITLE" for possible publication in JOURNAL "Journal name".

We certify that we have participated sufficiently in the work to take public responsibility for the appropriateness of the experimental design and method, and the collection, analysis, and interpretation of the data.

We have reviewed the final version of the manuscript and approve it for publication. To the best of our knowledge and belief, this manuscript has not been published in whole or in part nor is it being considered for publication elsewhere.

Best Regards.

Yours Sincerely,

NAME, ADDRESS, E-mail, FAX

论文投出后,一般刊物编辑部会给投稿作者发送收到稿件通知(Manuscript received by Editorial Office)。如果编辑觉得论文题材不适合所投刊物,会回信退稿。否则,作者就进入等待期(Under review)。收到稿件后，编辑挑选 2~3 名同行对论文进行评审。论文评审是对作者采用匿名形式。评审者不是专职，是自愿花时间评阅论文(并无评审费)。由于评阅人一般已经在本领域建立了地位，比较忙，因此往往需要花较长时间。投稿者应对此予以理解。

另外，由于评阅人较忙或其他原因，有的评审意见不一定贴切。是值得商榷的。编辑在审稿过程中是仲裁和最后决策者。审稿期间，作者一般应耐心等待。除按收稿通知建议时间与编辑联系外，一般应给评审 1~3 个月时间。若仍无消息，可以与编辑联系催促一下。

Dear Editor,

  I want to know the status about my manuscript (ID: JAP067942) titled "＊＊＊" to "＊＊＊" being reviewed on Aug. 28, 2006. And I wonder if it has been finished review and what is the result.

  I would be greatly appreciated if you could spend some of your time check the status for me.

Best regards!

Sincerely yours,

NAME, ADDRESS, E-mail, FAX

论文评审分一般内容和专业内容两部分。

一般评审内容包括：

① 稿件是否适合所投刊物；

② 若发表此文读者面会有多大；

③ 是否有现势性——即是否需要尽快发表；

④ 论文的理论、方法和数据等是否有创新性；

⑤ 论文有无重大缺陷(理论、方法、实验结果等)；

⑥ 论文结果是否重要；

⑦ 论文可读性如何；

⑧ 长短是否合适——与论文重要性是否平衡；

⑨ 图表是否必需，质量如何；

⑩ 有没有忽略重要前人工作。

专业内容是评审者对论文中不正确或存有疑问的内容、表述方法、写作缺陷等提出批评。没有具体形式。

审稿结束，作者迟早会收到稿件评审意见和编辑的仲裁结果。一般有四种情况：

① 接收(Accepted with or without minor revision)；

② 修改后可接收(conditional acceptance upon satisfactory revision)；

③ 可以修改后再投(Minor revision/Major revision)；

④ 拒绝(Rejected)。

对第一种情况，作者会收到投递最终稿的指南。一般需要提供数字文件，按要求提供图表。

对第二种情况，应按照评审意见修改论文，或者提出拒绝修改某些部分的理由。将修改部分单独写成报告提供给编辑。一般来说编辑比评审者更具同情心。因此，一般可以期望收到像第一种情况那样的论文接收信。

对第三种情况,看看评审意见,这种决定一般是由于论文需要补充材料,编辑希望继续修改提高。不要轻易放弃。修改后被接收的机会还是很大的。对于高质量的杂志,多数论文第一次投稿时都会被按这种情况退回来。作者应根据评审意见认真修改。当然也可以提出对某些部分不修改的理由。

若得到最后一种情况的答复,应根据评审意见修改文稿,然后投往其他刊物。国外刊物的拒稿率高低不等,一般专业刊物拒稿率在 30% 以上。不妨投到拒稿率低些或引用率低些的刊物上。

论文被接收后,按照提供印刷稿件要求重新投稿后,下一个回合就是收到印刷编辑寄回的校样。校样一般需要尽快寄还给印刷编辑。寄校样时,出版商会要求填写版权转让书(Transfer of copy Right),并告知支付版面费的办法和订购单行本的方法。许多刊物不收版面费,但对特殊印刷(如彩版印刷)收费。有的对超过定额免费页数的页面按页收费。不少收版面费的刊物费用都较高。如 Optical Express、IEEE Transactions 的系列刊物收费可以高达数千美元。必须有所准备。版面费一般可以用信用卡支付。对校样要认真细读,特别注意公式和图表。订购单行本的数量应够交流用即可。

Dear editor,

I have read carefully the Transfer of copyright agreement and signed it. Now I e-mailed it to you. Inaddition, we will not order the offprints at the present time. Please send me a back E-mail if you receive this messenge. Thank you very much.

Yours sincerely,

...

13.5 论文发表后的工作

论文发表后,一般不会有后续工作。除非论文观点引发争议,特别是遇到读者撰文批驳作者观点、方法或发现时。这时编辑一般会邀请作者对自己的论文进行辩护。当然也有可能论文印刷出错,这时应及时要求纠正,即在下期刊物上发表勘误——Erratum。最后就是满足读者获取单行本的请求。

本章参考文献

1. http://blog.csdn.net/ltbing/archive/2006/10/25/1350527.aspx.
2. G. M. Whitesides. Whitesides' Group: Writing a Paper. Advanced Materials,2004,16 (15):1375-1377.
3. 李美成,李洪涛. 信息功能材料专业英语. 哈尔滨:哈尔滨工业大学出版社,2003.
4. 小木虫网站(http://emuch.net/).

附录A 常用前缀、后缀和构词成分

1. 前缀

(1) 表示"否定"意思的

a-：apolar	非极性的
ab-：abnormal	反常的
an-：anaerobic	厌氧的
dis-：discharge	放电,放出
disjoin	分开
de-：deceleration	降速
degeneration	退化
in-：inflexible	不可弯曲的
ir-：irregular	不规则的
il-：illiterate	不识字的
im-：impossible	不可能的
non-：nondeformable	不变形的
un-：unsuitable	不适合的
unfit	不适宜的

(2) 表示"先"、"前"意思的

pre-：predetermine	预定
pre-set	预置
pro-：proceed	前进,进行
project	突出,投射
fore-：foresee	遇见
foreword	前言

(3) 表示"后"、"退"意思的

post-：post-position	后位
postdoctor	博士后
retro-：retrograde	后退的,逆转的
re-：retrace	回描,返回

(4) 表示"在上"、"超越"意思的

hyper-：hyperactive	活动过度的

hyperconcentration	超浓缩
over-：overburden	负担过重
overaccumulation	积累过多
sur-：surface	表面
surpass	超过
super-：superantiferromagnetism	超反铁磁性
supersonic	超音速的
ultra-：ultrasound	超声
ultra-short	超短波

（5）表示"在下"意思的

sub-：subway	地下铁道
subsonic	亚音速的
under-：underwater	水下的
underactor	次要演员
infra-：infrastructure	基础设施
infrasonic	次声的,亚声的

（6）表示"在内"意思的

in-：inside	内部的
include	包括
intro-：intronuclear	原子核内的
intra-：intracity	市内的
intradisciplinary	学科内的

（7）表示"在外"意思的

ex-：exclude	除去
extract	抽出
out-：outside	外部
outcurve	外曲

（8）表示"共同,一起"意思的

co-：co-operate	合作
cohesion	凝聚
col-：collect	收集
collision	碰撞
com-：compress	压缩
combine	结合
con-：concentrate	集中
cor-：correlative	相关的
correspond	符合,对应
syn-：synthesis	合成
synchrotron	同步加速器

(9) 表示"相互"、"在…之间"意思的
inter-：interaction 相互作用
　　　　intermolecular 分子间的
(10) 表示"太"、"过分"意思的
over-：overload 超载
　　　　overcharge 过量充电
(11) 表示数字的
bi-：bi-weekly 双周的
　　　biabsorption 双吸收
di-：diode 二极管
　　　dioxide 二氧化物
tri-：triangle 三角形
　　　tricycle 三轮车
quadr-：quadrangle 四角形
　　　　quadraline 四声道线路
penta-：pentagon 五角形
　　　　pentode 五极管
quinque-：quinquangular 五角形的
　　　　　quinquevalence 五价
hex(a)-：hexagon 六角形
　　　　hexangular 六角的
sept-：septangle 七角的
　　　　septavalence 七价
oct(a,o)-：octagon 八角形
　　　　　octocyclic 八环的
deca-：decagon 十角形
　　　　decade 十年
hecto-：hectogram 百克
　　　　hectometer 百米
centi-：centigrade 百分度的
　　　　centimetre 公分
kilo-：kilowatt 千瓦
　　　　kilometer 千米
milli-：millimeter 毫米
　　　　milliampere 毫安
semi-：semicircle 半圆
　　　　semiconductor 半导体
multi-：multitude 多数,大量
　　　　multimedia 多媒体

poly-:	polycentric	多元的
	polygon	多边形
macro-:	macromolecule	大分子的
	macroworld	宏观世界
micro-:	microworld	微观世界
	microelement	微量元素

（12）表示动词意思的

en-:	encircle	包围
	enlarge	扩大
im-:	imperil	危及
in-:	insure	保证

（13）表示"视线，光线"意思的

opt-:	optic	视力的，光学的
	optics	光学

2. 后缀

（1）表示形容词意思的

-able:	adjustable	可调的
	exchangeable	可互换的
-ant:	important	重要的
	resistant	抵抗的
-ent:	dependent	依赖的
	different	不同的
-ar:	angular	成角的
	linear	线的
-ary:	stationary	静止的
	secondary	次的
-ial:	special	特别的
	radial	半径的，辐射状的
-ful:	useful	有用的
	powerful	作用大的
-ic:	specific	特殊的
	metallic	金属的
-ical:	political	政治的
	metallurgical	冶金学的
-ible:	visible	能见的
	compressible	可压缩的
-ile:	tensile	张力的
	fragile	易碎的
-ious:	various	不同的

glorious	光荣的
-ish：reddish	微红的
childish	孩子气的
-less：useless	无用的
stainless	不锈的
-like：needle-like	针状的
glass-like	似玻璃的
-ous：precious	珍贵的
porous	多孔的

（2）表示名词意思的

-ability：acceptability	可接受性
permeability	渗透性
-acy：accuracy	精确性
fallacy	谬误，谬论
-age：usage	使用
storage	存储
-ance：importance	重要性
resistance	电阻
-ation：application	应用
installation	装置
-ence：independence	独立
difference	差异
-ency：tendency	倾向
efficiency	效率
-er：worker	工人
computer	计算机
-ion：union	联合
action	作用
-ist：chemist	化学家
metallurgist	冶金家
-ition：composition	组成
addition	附加
-ity：electricity	电
machinability	机械加工性
-(o)logy：biology	生物学
technology	技术,工艺学
-ment：development	发展
movement	运动
-ness：usefulness	有用

hardness	硬度
-or：operator	操作者
conductor	导体
-ory：factory	工厂
depository	储藏室
-ship：relationship	关系
leadership	领导
-sion：conversion	转换
precision	精密度
-ture：mixture	混合
creature	生物

（3）表示动词意思的

-ate：generate	产生
formulate	规划
-en：harden	使硬
strengthen	加强
-(i)fy：solidify	使坚固
electrify	电气化
-ish：accomplish	完成
establish	建立
-ize(-ise)：industrialize	工业比
oxidize	氧化

（4）表示副词意思的

-ly：completely	完全地
automatically	自动地
-ward(s)：upwards	向上
backward(s)	向后
-wish：clockwish	顺时针方向地
likewish	同样
-wise：likewise	同样地
batchwise	分批地

常用数学符号及数学式表达 附录B

符号	英文/中文
$+$	plus, positive 加号；正号
$-$	minus, negative 减号；负号
$\pm$	plus or minus 正负号
$\times$ ($*$)	multiplied by, times 乘号
$\div$	divided by 除号
$=$	is equal to, equals 等于号
$\neq$	is not equal to 不等于号
$\equiv$	is equivalent to, is identically equal to 全等于号
$\approx$	is approximately equal to, approximately equals 约等于号
$\simeq$	is equal to or approximately equal to 等于或约等于
( )	parentheses, round brackets 圆括号
[ ]	square brackets 方括号
{ }	braces 大括号
《 》	French quotes 法文引号；书名号
$\rightarrow$	maps into 建立映射；arrow 箭号
$<$	is less than 小于号
$>$	is more than 大于号
$\not<$	is not less than 不小于号
$\not>$	is not more than 不大于号
$\leqslant$	is less than or equal to 小于或等于号
$\geqslant$	is more than or equal to 大于或等于号
$\%$	percent 百分之
$‰$	permill 千分之
∞	infinity 无限大号
$\propto$	vary directly as
$\sqrt{\ }$	(square) root 平方根
$\because$	since; because 因为
$\therefore$	hence 所以
$\angle$	angle 角
$\frown$	semicircle 半圆

$\odot$	circle 圆
$\bigcirc$	circumference 圆周
π	pi 圆周率
$\triangle$	triangle 三角形
$\perp$	perpendicular to 垂直于
$\cup$	union of 并,合集
$\cap$	intersection of 交,通集
$\int$	the integral of ……的积分
$\sum$	(sigma) summation of 总和
$^\circ$	degree 度
$'$	minute 分
$''$	second 秒
$\&$	ampersand, and, reference 和,引用
$\log_n x$	log x to the base n
$\log_e x$ 或 $\ln x$	log$x$ to the base e, natural logarithm
x^n	the nth power of x, x to the nth power
$x^{\frac{1}{n}}$ 或 $\sqrt[n]{x}$	the nth root of x; x to the power one over n
$x \to a$	x approaches the limit a
$|x|$	the absolute value of x
$\bar{x}$	the mean value of x, x bar
b'	b prime
b''	b double prime, b second prime
b_m	b sub m
$f(x), F(x)$	function of x
$y = f(x)$	y is a function of x
$\dfrac{dy}{dx}$ 或 D_{xy}	the differential coefficient of y with respect to x, the first derivative of y with respect to x
$\dfrac{d^2 y}{dx^2}$	the second derivative of y with respect to x
$\int_a^b$	integral between limits a and b
$\vec{F}$	vector F
$(a + b)$	bracket a plus b bracket closed
$(a+b)(a-b)=a^2-b^2$	(The quantity) a plus b times a minus b equals a squared minus b squared
$a = b$	a equals b, a is equal to b
$a \neq b$	a is not equal to b, a is not b
$a \approx b$	a is approximately equal to b
$a > b$	a is greater than b

$a \gg b$	a is much (far) greater than b
$a \geqslant b$	a is greater than or equal to b
$a \ngtr b$	a is not great than b
$a < b$	a is less than b
$a \perp b$	a is perpendicular to b
$a // b$	a is parallel to b
$a \propto b$	a varies directly as b
$1:2$	the ratio of one to two
x^2	x squared, the square of x, the second power of x, x to the second power
y^3	y cubed, the cube of y, y to third power
y^{-10}	y to the minus tenth (power)
$\sqrt{x}$	the square root of x
$\sqrt[3]{a}$	the cubic root of a
$\sqrt[7]{a}$	the seventh root of a
$\dfrac{x^4}{y^2} = z^3$	x to the fourth power divided by y squared equals z cubed
8%	eight percent
6‰	six per mille
$3/4$ km	three quarters kilometer
$60°$	sixty degrees
$100℃$	one(a) hundred degrees Centigrade
$28°F$	Twenty-eight degrees of Fahrenheit

常用的符号和单位

附录C

C-1 SI Base Units

Physical Quantity	Unit	Abbreviation
length	meter	m
mass	kilogram	kg
time	second	s
electric current	ampere	A
temperature	kelvin	K
luminous intensity	candela	cd
amount of substance	mole	mol
plane angle	radian	rad
solid angle	steradian	sr

C-2 SI Prefixes

Multiply	Prefix	Abbreviation	Submultiple	Prefix	Abbreviation
10^{18}	exa	E	10^{-1}	deci	d
10^{15}	peta	P	10^{-2}	centi	c
10^{12}	tera	T	10^{-3}	milli	m
10^{9}	giga	G	10^{-6}	micro	μ
10^{6}	mega	M	10^{-9}	nano	n
10^{3}	kilo	k	10^{-12}	pico	p
10^{2}	hector	h	10^{-15}	femto	f
10^{1}	deka	da	10^{-18}	atto	a

C-3 Directly Derived Unit

Physical Quantity	Unit	Abbreviation
area	square meter	m^2
volumn	cubic meter	m^3
velocity	meter per second	$m \cdot s^{-1}$
acceleration	meter per second squared	$m \cdot s^{-2}$
density	kilogram per mole	$kg \cdot m^{-3}$
molar mass	kilogram meter per mole	$kg \cdot mol^{-1}$
molar volumn	cubic meter per mole	$m^3 \cdot mol^{-1}$
molar concentration	mole per cubic meter	$mol \cdot m^{-3}$

C-4 Special Names of Derived Unit

Physical Quantity	Unit	Abbreviation	In Terms of SI Units
frequency	hertz	Hz	s^{-1}
force	newton	N	$kg \cdot m \cdot s^{-2}$
pressure	pascal	Pa	$N \cdot m^{-2}$
energy	joule	J	$kg \cdot m^2 s^{-2}$
power	watt	W	$J \cdot s^{-1}$
electric charge	coulomb	C	$A \cdot s$
electric potential difference	volt	V	$J \cdot A^{-1} \cdot s^{-1}$
electric resistance	ohm	Ω	$V \cdot A^{-1}$

C-5 Units to be Discouraged or Abandoned

Physical Quantity	unit	Abbreviation	Definition in SI Units
length	angstrom	Å	1×10^{-10} m
force	dyne	dyn	1×10^{-5} N
energy	erg	erg	1×10^{-7} J
energy	calorie	cal	4.184 J
pressure	atmosphere	atm	101325 Pa
pressure	millimeter of mercury	mmHg	133.322 Pa
pressure	torr	torr	133.322 Pa

C-6 Some Physical Constants

Constant	Symbol	Value
Velocity of light in vacuum	c	2.988×10^8 m/s
Electronic charge (magnitude)	$\|e\|$	1.602×10^{-19} C
Electronic mass	m	9.107×10^{-31} kg
Electronic charge to mass ratio	$\|e\|/m$	1.759×10^{11} C/kg
Radius of electron	R	2.81×10^{-5} m
Permeability of free charge	μ_0	$4\pi \times 10^{-7}$ H/m
Permeability of free space	ε_0	8.854×10^{-12} F/m
Electron volt (energy)	$\|e\|V$	1.602×10^{-19} J
Boltzmann constant	k	1.381×10^{-23} J/K
Planck's constant	H	6.626×10^{-34} J·s

附录 D SCI收录的光电类期刊

D-1 530 物理学

(1) 530B0002-1A ISSN 1050-2947 IF：2.908

Physical Review A：Atomic，Molecular，and Optical Physics. 1970. 12/yr. American Physics Society.

http://pra.aps.org/

《物理评论 A 辑：原子、分子和光物理学》刊载原子、分子、光物理领域的最近进展及其相关基本概念。包括量子信息理论、原子和分子结构、物质波以及量子光学等内容。

(2) 530B002-2 ISSN：1098-0121 IF：3.322

Physical Review B：Condensed Matt and Materials Physics. 1978. 48/yr. American Physics Society.

http://prb.aps.org/

《物理评论 B 辑：凝聚态材料》刊载凝聚态材料和材料物理的最新进展。

(3) 530B0003 ISSN 0031-9007 IF：7.180

Physical Review Letters. 1958. 52/yr. American Physics Society.

http://prl.aps.org/

《物理评论快报》刊载物理学领域重要发现和当前热门论题的快报。期刊限定于短篇的文章。

(4) 530B0004 ISSN 0034-6861 IF：33.985

Reviews of Modern Physics. 1930. 4/yr. American Physics Society.

http://rmp.aps.org/

《现代物理学评论》刊载现代物理学当前研究进展和成就的评论。

(5) 530C0001 ISSN 1478-6435 IF：1.384

Philosophical Magazine. 1798. 36/yr. Taylor & Francis.

http://rmp.aps.org/

《哲学杂志》刊载凝聚态材料结构和性能的理论、概念、实验和应用方面的研究论文。

(6) 530C0002 ISSN 0950-0839 IF：1.548

Philosophical Magazine Letters. 1798. 12/yr. Taylor & Francis.

http://rmp.aps.org/

《哲学杂志》刊载凝聚态材料结构和性能等方面研究成果的短文。

(7) 530D0002 ISSN 0031-9015 IF：2.058
Journal of the Physical Society of Japan. 1946. 12/yr. Physical Society of Japan.
http://jpsj.ipap.jp/

《日本物理学会志》刊载物理学及其相关领域的理论和实验方面的研究论文和快报。

(8) 530E0005 ISSN 1434-6060 IF：1.397
European Physics Journal D：Atoms，Molecules and Cluster and Optical Physics. 1998. 12/yr. Springer Verlag.
http://www.springer.com/physics/atoms/journal/10053

《欧洲物理学杂志D辑：原子、分子、原子团和光学物理》刊载原子、分子和光学物理学等领域的研究论文。包括原子物理、分子物理和化学物理、原子和分子撞击、纳米结构、等离子体物理、非线性动态学、光学现象和光子学、量子光学、超强超短激光领域等内容。

D-2 537 光学

(1) 537B0001 ISSN 0003-7028 IF：2.062
Applied Spectroscopy. 1946. 6/yr. Society for Applied Spectroscopy.
http://www.s-a-s.org/

《应用光谱学》刊载光谱学，包括吸收光谱、发射、散射光谱、荧光、拉曼效应、X射线、质谱测定以及电与核磁共振光谱学等方面的理论和实践研究论文。

(2) 537B0002 ISSN 0022-2852 IF：1.636
Journal of Molecular Spectrometry. 1957. 12/yr. Elsevier.
http://ees.elsevier.com/jms/

《分子光谱学杂志》刊载分子光谱学的实验、理论和应用方面的研究论文。

(3) 537B0003-1 ISSN 1084-7529 IF：1.87
Journal of the Optical Society of America A：Optics，Imaging Science and Vision. 1917. 12/yr. Optical Society of America.
http://www.opticsinfobase.org/josaa/Issue.cfm

《美国光学会志A辑：光学、图像科学与显示》刊载光学现象原理与方法的理论和实验研究论文。

(4) 537B0003-2 ISSN 0740-3224 IF：2.181
Journal of the Optical Society of America B：Optical Physics. 1984. 12/yr. Optical Society of America.
http://www.opticsinfobase.org/josab/Issue.cfm

《美国光学会志B辑：光物理学》刊载量子光学、非线性光学、激光物理学等研究论文。

(5) 537B0004 ISSN 0003-6935 IF：1.763
Applied Optics. 1962. 36/yr. Optical Society of America.

http://www.opticsinfobase.org/ao/Issue.cfm

《应用光学》刊载应用光学的研究论文和报告,包括光学技术、信息处理、激光、光子学和环境光学等。

(6) 537B0006 ISSN 0570-4928 IF:4.144
Applied Spectroscopy Reviews. 1967. 6/yr. Taylor & Francis.
http://www.informaworld.com/0570-4928

《应用光谱评论》主要刊载与物理概念和化学应用有关的谱分析方法应用方面的研究成果。范围从 X 射线、红外、拉曼、原子能吸收、微波的 ESR、质谱、NQR、NMR 和 ICP。

(7) 537B0008 ISSN 0038-7010 IF:0.866
Spectroscopy Letters. 1968. 8/yr. Taylor & Francis.
http://www.informaworld.com/0038-7010

《光谱学快报》发表光谱学实验与理论研究进展简报。

(8) 537B0056 ISSN 1043-8092 IF:0.245
Laser Focus World. 1965. 12/yr. PennWell Publishing Co.
www.laserfocusworld.com/

《激光聚焦世界》介绍激光、光学和成像系统的新进展、分析和应用。

(9) 537B0057 ISSN 0195-5373 IF:1.076
Atomic Spectroscopy. 1962. 6/yr. Perkin-Elmer Corp.
http://atomicspectroscopyjournal.com/

《原子光谱学》刊载原子吸收光谱、原子荧光、原子发射和 ICP 质谱的分析数据及应用方面的研究论文。

(10) 537B0071 ISSN 0030-400X IF:0.584
Optics and Spectroscopy. 1956. 12/yr. Springer.
http://www.springer.com/physics/optics/journal/11449

《光学与光谱学》刊载从无线电波到 X 波长整个波段范围的光谱和现代光学各领域的原始文章。内容包括理论和实验的原子分子、凝聚态光谱、激光与物质相互作用的激光辐射,物理和几何光学,全息术和光学仪器制造的物理原理等。

(11) 537B0078 ISSN 0146-9592 IF:3.772
Optics Letters. 1977. 24/yr. Optical Society of American.
http://www.opticsinfobase.org/ol/

《光学快报》快速传播光学领域研究成果的学术简报。

(12) 537B0084 ISSN 1866-6892 IF:0.692
International Journal of Infrared, Millimeter and Terahertz Waves. 1987. 12/yr. Springer.
http://www.editorialmanager.com/ijim/

2009 年 1 月 1 日,由原 International Journal of Infrared and Millimeter Waves 更名。《国际红外、毫米以及太赫兹波杂志》刊载频率范围为 10 GHz 到 100 THz,主题包括波源、

探测器、其他仪器系统、光谱、传感以及电磁波与物质相互作用机理及应用等。

(13) 537B0108 ISSN 1053-0509 IF:1.88
Journal of Fluorescence. 1991. 4/yr. Springer.
http://www.editorialmanager.com/jofl/
《荧光杂志》刊载荧光光谱技术的理论和数据分析的新进展。

(14) 537B0116 ISSN 0887-6703 IF:0.597
Spectroscopy. 1985. 12/yr. Advanstar communications Inc.
https://advanstar.replycentral.com/? PID=581
《光谱学》刊载各种光谱仪器设备在应用研究、质量控制、环境测试以及生命科学等领域研究与应用方面的文章。

(15) 537C0002 ISSN 0022-4073 IF:1.635
Journal of Quantitative Spectroscopy&Radiative Transfer. 1988. 16/yr. Elsevier.
http://ees.elsevier.com/jqsrt/
《定量光谱与辐射传递杂志》刊载物质光学的特性、光谱分析、热辐射性质及辐射传递方面的论文。

(16) 537C0004 ISSN 0950-0340 IF:1.062
Journal of Modem Optics. 1954. 12/yr. Taylor & Francis.
http://mc.manuscriptcentral.com/tmop
《现代光学杂志》刊载基于经典光学与量子光学的现代光学方面的研究论文和评论,对重要问题出专刊。

(17) 537C0005 1SSN 0030-3992 IF:0.892
Optics and Laser Technology. 1968. 6/yr. Elsevier.
http://ees.elsevier.com/jolt/
《光学与激光技术》刊载各种光学和激光技术在实际应用方面的原始论文和评论文章。

(18) 537C0009 ISSN 0263-0346 IF:4.42
Laser and Particle Beams. 1983. 4/yr. Cambridge Univ Press.
http://journals.cambridge.org/
《激光与粒子束》刊载研究强激光产生、粒子束及其与其他物质相互作用和应用等问题的文章,涉及高能量密度物理学、热稠密物质和相应的原子、等离子体和流体动力物理学、束波相互作用微波、x射线等领域。

(19) 537C0057 ISSN 0306-8919 IF:0.761
Optical and Quantum Electronics. 1969. 12/yr. Springer.
http://www.editorialmanager.com/oqel/
《光电子学与量子电子学》刊载光物理学、光学工程及光电子学方面的研究论文、评论和通信,涉及半导体固态与气态激光、光通讯系统、纤维与平面波导、非线性光学、光电子装置、超速现象、光存储等。

(20) 537C0066 ISSN 0377-0486 IF:3.526
Journal of Raman Spectroscopy. 1973. 12/yr. John Wiley&Sons Ltd.
http://mc.manuscriptcentral.com/jrs
《拉曼光谱学杂志》报道拉曼光谱学领域研究成果,包括高阶过程以及布里渊与瑞利散射的研究。

(21) 537C0070 ISSN 0143-8166 IF:1.103
Optics and Lasers in Engineering. 1980. 12/yr. Elsevier.
http://ees.elsevier.com/olen/
《工程中的光学与激光》刊载应用于工程领域的光学与激光技术方面的研究论文,侧重实用器件与方法、效果评价以及理论研究与实验进展。

(22) 537C0091-A ISSN 1464-4258 IF:1.742
Journal of Optics A:Pure and Applied Optics. 1999. 6/yr. IOP Publishing Ltd.
http://www.iop.org/EJ/journal/2040-8986
从 2010 年起,"Journal of Optics A:Pure and Applied Optics"将改为"Journal of Optics"。刊载纳米光子学、非线性和超快光学、信息和通信光学集成光学系统和器件、基于光的材料加工以及传播、衍射和散射等方面的原始论文。

(23) 537E001 ISSN 0030-4026 IF:0.507
Optik. 1946. 12/yr. Urban&Fischer Verlag, Germany.
Authors can send their manuscript to the Editor either by post or by e-mail:Professor Theo Tschudi, Institute of Applied Physics, Darmstadt University of Technology, Hochschulstrasse 6, 64289 Darmstadt, Germany,
E-mail:theo.tschudi@physik.tu-darmstadt.de.
http://shop.elsevier.de/ijleo
《光学》刊载光学、光学设计、几何光学、波动光学、光学和微光学元件、衍射光学、光电子器件等领域的理论和应用方面的研究论文,用德文或英文发表。

(24) 537LB005 ISSN 1350-4495 IF:1.037
Infrared Physics&Technology. 1995. 6/yr. Elsevier.
http://ees.elsevier.com/infphy/
《红外线物理与技术》刊载红外线物理与技术的各个领域,包括原理、试验、设备与仪器等。其核心内容可以概括为红外射线的产生、传播和检测、相关光学、材料与装置。

(25) 537LB052 ISSN 0030-4018 IF:1.552
Optics Communications. 1969. 84/yr. Elsevier.
http://ees.elsevier.com/optics/default.asp
《光学通讯》刊载光学以及光与物质相互作用方面的研究成果简报。

(26) 537LB053 ISSN 0022-2313 IF:1.628
Journal of Luminescence. 1884, 12/yr. Elsevier.
http://ees.elsevier.com/lumin/

《发光杂志》刊载凝聚态物质中受激态过程基础与应用方面的原始研究论文。

D-3　539　应用物理学

(1) 539B0001 ISSN 0021-8979 IF：2.201

Journal of Applied Physics. 1937. 24/yr. American Institute of Physics.

http://ojps.aip.org/japo

《应用物理学杂志》本刊有美国物理学会研究论文及简报，包括普通物理及其他自然科学和工程技术领域的应用。

(2) 539B0052 ISSN 0003-6951 IF：3.726

Applied Physics Letters. 1962. 52/yr. American Institute of Physics.

http://ojps.aip.org/aplo

《应用物理学快报》刊载应用物理学，包括光、声、流体、等离子体及放电、力学与热性质、半导体、超导体等领域最新发展和研究成果的快报。

(3) 539C001 ISSN 0022-3727 IF：2.104

Journal Physics D：Applied Physics. 1968. 12/yr. IOP Publishing Ltd.

http://www.iop.org/journals/jd

《物理学杂志 D 辑：应用物理学》刊载研究物质性质的文章，主要涉及科学、工程和工业中物理学的新理论和实验，包括各种新材料的特性、电子现象、光学现象、辐射作用、气体转化、固体的结构与形成、凝聚物质的有关性质问题。

(4) 539D0003 ISSN 0021-4922 IF：1.309

Japanese journal of Applied Physics Part 2-Letters. 1962. 24/yr. Japanese Society of Applied Physics.

http://www.jjap.or.jp/index.shtml

《日本应用物理学杂志：第二分册》刊载应用物理学研究论文和研究札记，是《应用物理》(539D0002)的英文版。第二分册刊载超导体和半导体的研究快报。

(5) 539E0001-B ISSN 0946-2171 IF：2.167

Applied Physics B：Laser and Optics. 1994. 12/yr. German Physical Society. Springer-Verlag.

Email：svserv@vax.ntp.springer.de

http://link.springer.de/link/servece/journals/00340/edboard.htm

《应用物理学 B 辑：激光与光学》刊载光学物理学方面研究成果，侧重激光与光学方面的内容。由德国物理学会编辑，用英文出版。

D-4　730　电工与电子技术

(1) 7308000 1 TVLS ISSN 1063-8210 IF：1.373

IEEE Transactions on Very Large Scale Integration Systems，1993. 6/yr. IEEE-Inst Electrical Electronics Engineers Inc.

《IEEE 超大规模集成系统汇刊》刊载 VLSI/ULSI 及微电子系统的设计与实现，包括系统规范、设计与划分、高性能计算、通信系统、神经网络、多模块系统及应用等方面的原始论文。

(2) 730B0001 TCP2 ISSN 1521-3323 IF：1.253

IEEE Transactions on Advanced Packaging，1999. 4/yr. IEEE-Inst Electrical Electronics Engineers Inc.

http：//mc. manuscriptcentral. com/cpmt-trans-ieee

《IEEE 高级封装汇刊》刊载封装和制造技术方面的研究论文。主要涉及 IC 封装、激光束焊接、芯片与线路板、封装的计算机辅助设计、粘接及其材料、电路可靠性与模拟、涂层及其材料、接触阻抗研究。

(3) 730B0001 TCPl ISSN 1521-3331 IF：0.968

IEEE Transactions on Components and Packaging Technologies. 1999. 4/yr. IEEE-Inst Electrical Electronics Engineers Inc.

http：//mc. manuscriptcentral. com/tcpt-ieee

《IEEE 部件与封装技术汇刊》刊载电子、光子、MEMS、传感器封装和制造技术方面的原始性研究论文。主要涉及有源和无源元件、电子接点和连接、焊接、互联、器件的可靠性和失败模式、电子材料、热管理等领域的新进展。

(4) 730B0001EDL ISSN 0741-3106 IF：3.049

IEEE Electron Device Letters. 1980. 12/yr. IEEE-Inst Electrical Electronics Engineers Inc.

http：//mc. manuscriptcentral. com/edl

《IEEE 电子器件快报》刊载电子、光电子、纳米级器件、固态、集成电路、能源、显示、传感、机电设备、量子设备和电子管的技术理论、设计、性能、可靠性等方面的最新研究成果和简报。

(5) 730B0001JLT ISSN 0733-8724 IF：2.736

Journal of Lightwave Technology. 1983. 24/yr. IEEE-Inst Electrical Electronics Engineers Inc.

http：//mc. manuscriptcentral. com/jlt-ieee

《光波技术杂志》为 IEEE 与 OSA（美国物理联合会中的美国光学学会）联合编辑出版。刊载光学导波科学、技术与工程方面的研究论文。涉及光纤与光缆技术、有源与无源导波部件、集成光学与光电子学、系统与子系统、网络技术与转换系统、光传感器、光学导波技术的最新应用等。

(6) 730B0001JQE ISSN 0018-9197 IF：2.413

IEEE Journal of Quantum Electronics. 1965. 12/yr. IEEE Photonics Society.

http：//mc. manuscriptcentral. com/pho-ieee

《IEEE 量子电子学杂志》刊载量子电子学现象、新器件、系统及应用方面研究论文，论文侧重于器件的量子电子学原理，涉及 1 毫米以下波段相干电磁波的产生、传播、探测和应用等。

(7) 730B0001JSS ISSN 0018-9200 IF：3.466

IEEE Journal of Solid-State Circuits. 1966. 12/yr. IEEE Solid-State Circuits Society.

jssc-subm@ieee.org

《IEEE 固体电路杂志》刊载晶体管基集成电路设计的研究论文。涉及器件模拟、系统设计、布线和测试，侧重于集成电路和 VLSI 的原理，很少发表分立电路设计方面的论文。

(8) 730B0001JSTQ ISSN 1077-260X IF：2.518

IEEE Journal of Selected Topics in Quantum Electronics. 1995. 6/yr. IEEE Photonics Society.

http://mc.manuscriptcentral.com/jstqe-pho

《IEEE 量子电子学专题杂志》刊载量子电子学器件和技术最新理论和应用方面的研究论文。涉及通信、医疗、遥测术、传感、固态激光、消费电子、半导体激光、集成光路、光纤等领域。每期只刊载某个主题方面的论文。

(9) 730B0001PTL ISSN 1041-1135 IF：2.173

IEEE Photonics Technology Letters. 1989. 24/yr. IEEE Photonics Society.

http://mc.manuscriptcentral.com/pho-ieee

《IEEE 光子学技术快报》及时报道光子学技术研究成果和进展。侧重激光与光电子技术、激光物理学与系统、光纤和波导技术、光学滤波器、控制开关设备、光学传感器、自由空间光纤传输系统、太赫兹波等器件及其应用等。

(10) 730B0001TCA ISSN 0278-0070 IF：1.466

IEEE Transactions on Computer-Aided Design of Integrated Circuits & Systems. 1982. 12/yr. IEEE Circuits and Systems Society.

http://tcad.polito.it/

《IEEE 集成电路与系统的计算机辅助设计汇刊》刊载集成电路与系统结构设计和逻辑合成的方法、算法和人-机接口、过程控制与器件的建模、数值方法、计算机辅助设计理论，以及模拟、数字、光纤、微波、相关的规划、综合、划分、布局、验证、测试、文件编制等方面的理论研究和实际应用文章。

(11) 730B0001TED ISSN 0018-9383 IF：2.73

IEEE Transactions on Electron Devices. 1952. 12/yr. IEEE Electron Devices Society.

m.james@ieee.org

《IEEE 电子器件汇刊》刊载研究论文，兼载研究进展简讯，不定期出版专题特辑。涉及绝缘体、金属、有机材料、微等离子体、半导体、量子效应结构、真空设备、生物电子学应用、新材料、生物医学电子学、计算机、通信、显示器、微型电子电路、成像、微致动器、纳米技术、光电子、光电、功率集成电路和微型传感器等。

(12) 730B0001TMT ISSN 0018-9480 IF：2.711

IEEE Transactions on Microwave Theory and Techniques. 1953. 12/yr. IEEE

Microwave Theory and Techniques Society.

http://www.mtt.org/publications/index.htm

microwave.editor@ieee.org

《IEEE 微波理论与技术汇刊》刊载微波理论与技术方面的研究论文，涉及与微波的发生、传输和检测相关的元器件、有源与无源滤波器、组件与器件、电路和系统等。

(13) 730B0001TOS ISSN 0894-6507 IF：0.957

IEEE Transactions on Semiconductor Manufacturing. 1988. 4/yr. IEEE Solid-State Circuits Society, etal.

http://www.cpmt.org/trans/trans-sm.html

boning@mtl.mit.edu

《IEEE 半导体制造汇刊》刊载集成电路制造的新进展，包括过程和设备控制、工艺过程的模拟和建模、缺陷控制、产量分析、产品设计和规划以及专家系统应用等方面的研究论文。

(14) 730B0001TSP ISSN 1053-587X IF：2.335

IEEE Transactions on Signal Processing. 1974. 12/yr. IEEE-INST Electrical Electronics Engineers Inc.

E-mail：trans@ieee.org

http://ewh.ieee.org/soc/sps/tsp/

http://mc.manuscriptcentral.com/sps-ieee

《IEEE 信号处理汇刊》刊载语音声频波、数字、电子、声学、机械和光学信号等的传输、记录、再现和处理、测量技术和所需元器件与系统，以及相关的环境、心理学和生理学问题的研究论文。

(15) 730C0010 ISSN 0098-9886 IF：2.389

International Journal of Circuit Theory and Applications. 1973. 6/yr. John Wiley & Sons Inc.

http://www3.interscience.wiley.com/journal/1976/home/ProductInformation.html

http://mc.manuscriptcentral.com/ijcta

《国际电路理论及应用杂志》刊载有关基本电路理论、器件电路模型、滤波器和有源电路的设计、神经网络、非线性和混沌电路、信号处理和 VLSI、开关和模拟电路、功率电子学、固态设备以及 CAD 和模拟等方面的研究论文。

(16) 730C0093 ISSN 0894-3370 IF：0.509

International Journal of Numerical Modelling：Electronic Networks, Devices and Fields. 1988. 6/yr. John Wiley & Sons Inc.

http://www3.interscience.wiley.com/journal/4673/home

http://mc.manuscriptcentral.com/ijnm

《国际数字模拟杂志：电子网络、元件与电磁场》刊载研讨电气和电子电路以及电磁场的数字模拟技术及数据准备方法的文章，涉及电气与电子工程、输配电网络、集成电路、静电电磁场、模拟和数字电路、固态设备、电子管、电子元件、微波技术与光学设计等方面。

(17) 730E0002 ISSN 0948-7921 IF:0.378

Electrical Engineering. 1910. 6/yr. Springer.

http://www.springer.com/engineering/electronics/journal/202

https://www.editorialmanager.com/elen

《电气工程》刊载电气和电子工程领域的各类论文。除了报道理论和实验工作，期刊偏向对电子工程的发展和应用起到基础性作用的论文。

D-5　736 电子技术

(1) 736B0034 ISSN 0361-5235 IF：1.283

Journal of Electronic Materials. 1972. 12/yr. Springer.

http://www.tms.org/pubs/journals/JEM/jem.html

http://jems.edmgr.com/

《电子材料》本刊由 IEEE 电子器件学会和 AIME 矿物、金属、与材料学会合办。刊载电子材料的加工和应用方面的研究成果，设计用于存储、逻辑、显示、探测、互联元件、发射体封装、大量存储和硬拷贝等的电子材料。

(2) 736B0254 ISSN 0278-081X IF：0.396

Circuit, Systems and Signal Processing. 1891. 6/yr. Springer.

http://www.springer.com/birkhauser/engineering/journal/34

《电路、系统和信号处理》刊载从数学基础到工程设计方面的研究论文，设计线性与非线性网络、分布电路和系统、模拟滤波器和信号处理、多维信号与系统、数字滤波器和信号处理、统计信号处理、多媒体、计算机辅助设计、图论、神经网络、通讯电路与系统、大规模集成电路等。

(3) 736C0004 ISSN 0020-7217 IF：0.567

International Journal of Electronics. 1965. 12/yr. Taylor & Francis.

http://www.tandf.co.uk/journals/titles/00207217.asp

http://mc.manuscriptcentral.com/intjelectron

《国际电子学杂志》刊载电子学理论和实验方面的研究论文，题材广泛，包括模拟和数字电路设计、微波电路和系统、光电子电路、光生伏打、半导体器件、传感技术、电子材料中的传输、VLSI 技术和器件处理等。

(4) 736C005 ISSN 0038-1101 IF：1.422

Solid-State Electronics. 1960. 12/yr. Pengamon-Elesvier Science Ltd.

http://ees.elsevier.com/sse/

《固体电子学》刊载有关应用固体物理学研究论文，包括固态物理和技术在电子和光电子上的应用，包括理论和器件的设计；光学、电子及形貌表征技术和参数优化；半导体器件的制备及相关材料的生长、表征和评价；亚微米和纳米微电子和光电子器件的物理特性和模型等方面。

(5) 736C0006 ISSN 0026-2714 IF：1.290

Microelectronic Reliability. 1961. 12/yr. Pergamoon-Elservier Science Ltd.

http://ees.elsevier.com/mr/

《微电子学可靠性》刊载微电子器件、电路和系统可靠性分析的最新研究成果和相关信息。

(6) 736C0020 ISSN 0268-1242 IF：1.434

Semiconductor Science and Technology. 1986. 12/yr. IOP Publishing Ltd.

http://www.iop.org/EJ/sst

《半导体科学与技术》刊载关于半导体和界面性能的研究与应用的文章，内容包括：电气性能、光学特性、器件设计、器件制备、材料加工、材料和器件分析、过程监控和可靠性等方面。

(7) 736C0061 ISSN 0013-5194 IF：1.14

Electronics Letters. 1965. 25/yr. IET-The Institution of Engineering & Technology.

http://ieeexplore.ieee.org/xpl/RecentIssue.jsp?punumber=2220

《电子学快报》包含现代电子学的全部领域，刊载无线电与自动控制、电子产品研制与开发、电信、光电、光通信等电子科学与技术领域最新研究成果的快报。

(8) 73LB03 ISSN 0167-9317 IF：1.583

Microelectronic Engineering. 1983. 12/yr. Elsevier.

http://ees.elsevier.com/mee/

《微电子工程》刊载电子器件、电子电路和系统的微纳加工方面的论文，包括纳米光刻、图像转移、材料、纳米形态学、先进加工和纳米制作、先进器件等内容。

(9) 736LB005 ISSN 0925-1030 IF：0.591

Analog Integrated Circuits and Signal Processing. 1991. 12/yr. Springer.

E-mail：roderdept@wkap.nl

http://www.editorialmanager.com/alog/

《模拟集成电路和信号处理》刊载模拟、射频和混合信号集成电路以及信号处理电路及系统的设计和应用研究论文及评论，包括模拟和混合信号界面电路与系统、数据转换、有源-RC、开关电容、联系时间集成滤波器、混合模数 VLSI 系统、无线射频接收器、时钟和数据恢复电路以及高速光电子电路和系统等内容。

注：本书收录的期刊以 ISI 网站上下载到的 SCI 来源出版物为准，其中影响因子以 2008 年 JCR 数据为准。

正文中各来源期刊款目的的著录格式：

(10) 53780001① ISSN 0003.7028②IF：1.752③

---

① 中图公司报刊刊号。
② 国际标准刊号。
③ 影响因子。

Applied Spectroscopy. ①1994. 6/yr. ②Soc Applied Spectroscopy. ③ http://www.s-a-s.org/④

《应用光谱学》刊载光谱学,包括吸收光谱、发射、散射光谱、荧光、拉曼效应、X射线、质谱测定以及电与核磁共振光谱学等方面的理论和实践研究论文。⑤

---

① 刊名。
② 创刊年及出版周期(或全年刊数)。
③ 出版机构名称。
④ 网址。
⑤ 译名和内容简介。

附录 E

2009年EI收录的中国科技期刊（光电类可投期刊）

序号	期刊名	网址
01	Chinese Journal of Electronics	http://je.ie.ac.cn/
02	Chinese Optics Letters	http://www.opticsjournal.net/col.htm
03	High Technology Letters	http://www.hitech863.com/emain2.asp
04	Journal of Rare Earths	http://www.cre-ol.com/jrechina/
05	Journal of Semiconductors	http://www.iop.org/EJ/journal/jos
06	Journal of Systems Engineering and Electronics	http://xtgj.chinajournal.net.cn/
07	Science in China, Series B: Chemistry	http://219.238.6.200/journal?code=04
08	Science in China, Series G: Physics, Astronomy	http://219.238.6.200/journal?code=14
09	The Journal of China Universities of Posts and Telecommunications	http://www.buptjournal.cn/xben/en/qkjs.asp
10	Journal of Beijing Institute of Technology (English Edition)	http://www.ilib.cn/P-bjlgdxxb-e.html
11	Journal of Central South University of Technology	http://www.zndxzk.com.cn/
12	Journal of Donghua University (English Edition)	http://www.ilib.cn/P-dhdxxb-e.html
13	Journal of Harbin Institute of Technology (New Series)	http://journal.hit.edu.cn/jhit_cn/ch/index.aspx
14	Journal of Shanghai Jiaotong University (Science)	http://www.sjtu.edu.cn/research/journals/j3.htm
15	Journal of Southeast University (English Edition)	http://www.ilib.cn/P-dndxxb-e.html
16	Journal of Zhejiang University SCIENCE A	http://www.zju.edu.cn/jzus/
17	Transactions of Nanjing University of Aeronautics and Astronautics	http://www.ceps.com.tw/ec/ecJnlIntro.aspx?Jnliid=1294
18	Transactions of Tianjin University	http://admin.chinajournal.net.cn/model01/index.asp?rwbh='TJDY'
19	Tsinghua Science and Technology	http://qhxb.lib.tsinghua.edu.cn:8080/webpage/xuebao/eng/index.jsp
20	电波科学学报	http://dbkxxb.periodicals.net.cn/gyjs.asp?ID=4750649
21	电工技术学报	http://www.eage.com.cn/xb.asp
22	电机与控制学报	http://emc.hrbust.edu.cn/

23	电子学报	http://www.elecjournal.org/
24	电子与信息学报	http://jeit.ie.ac.cn/cn/dqml.asp
25	系统工程与电子技术	http://www.sys-ele.com/
26	高电压技术	http://gdyjs.periodicals.net.cn/gyjs.asp?ID=4751294
27	高技术通信	http://www.hitech863.com/
28	通信学报	http://www.periodicals.net.cn/counter.asp?ID=4747099
29	仪器仪表学报	http://www.asiatest.org/yqyb.asp
30	功能材料	http://www.gncl.cn/
31	硅酸盐学报	http://www.jccsoc.com/
32	人工晶体学报	http://www.jtxb.cn/
33	光电子・激光	http://202.113.64.2:8080/xuebao/ol/index.htm
34	光谱学与光谱分析	http://www.gpxygpfx.com/
35	光学精密工程	http://gxjmgc.periodicals.net.cn/gyjs.asp?ID=4752066
36	光学学报	http://www.opticsjournal.net/gxxb.htm
37	红外与激光工程	http://www.irla.cn/
38	强激光与粒子束	http://www.hplpb.com.cn/
39	中国激光	http://www.opticsjournal.net/zgjg.htm
40	太阳能学报	http://www.tynxb.org.cn/
41	红外与毫米波学报	http://www.opticsjournal.net/hwyhmb.htm
42	计算机集成制造系统	http://cims.diamt.net.cn/
43	控制理论与应用	http://www.jcta.ac.cn/cta_cn/ch/index.aspx
44	模式识别与人工智能	http://prai.hfcas.ac.cn/
45	纳米技术与精密工程	http://www2.tju.edu.cn/orgs/journal/nami/index.htm
46	北京工业大学学报	http://xb.bjgydxxb.com/
47	北京航空航天大学学报	http://bhxb.buaa.edu.cn/
48	北京科技大学学报	http://www.ustb.edu.cn/xuebaozr/index.htm
49	北京理工大学学报	http://xuebao.bit.edu.cn/
50	北京邮电大学学报	http://www.bupt.edu.cn/journal/
51	大连理工大学学报	http://press.dlut.edu.cn/
52	电子科技大学学报	http://www.xb.uestc.edu.cn/
53	东北大学学报（自然科学版）	http://xuebao.neu.edu.cn/
54	东南大学学报（自然科学版）	http://dndxxb.periodicals.net.cn/gyjs.asp?ID=4750924
55	国防科技大学学报	http://www.gfkdcbs.com/xuebao/tougao.asp
56	哈尔滨工程大学学报	http://www.heuxb.com/

序号	期刊名称	网址
57	哈尔滨工业大学学报	http://journal.hit.edu.cn/hitxb_cn/ch/index.aspx
58	湖南大学学报（自然科学版）	http://www.hdxbzkb.cn/ch/index.aspx
59	华南理工大学学报（自然科学版）	http://202.38.194.234/
60	华中科技大学学报（自然科学版）	http://hzlgdxxb.periodicals.net.cn/gyjs.asp?ID=4752911
61	吉林大学学报（工学版）	http://xuebao.jlu.edu.cn/index.html
62	江苏大学学报（自然科学版）	http://zzs.ujs.edu.cn/pub/zzs/chn/zrkxb/jbxx/
63	解放军理工大学学报（自然科学版）	http://jfjl.chinajournal.net.cn/
64	南京航空航天大学学报	http://nhxb.qikan.com/
65	南京理工大学学报（自然科学版）	http://kjc.njust.edu.cn/zyzd.asp
66	清华大学学报（自然科学版）	http://qhxb.lib.tsinghua.edu.cn/
67	上海交通大学学报	http://xuebao.sjtu.edu.cn/
68	深圳大学学报（理工版）	http://sdxb.paperopen.cn/
69	沈阳工业大学学报	http://xb.sut.edu.cn/
70	四川大学学报（工程科学版）	http://jsuese.scu.edu.cn/jsuese_cn/ch/index.aspx
71	天津大学学报	http://www2.tju.edu.cn/orgs/journal/default.htm
72	同济大学学报（自然科学版）	http://journal.tongji.edu.cn/journal/default.aspx
73	武汉大学学报(信息科学版)	http://www.wuj.whu.edu.cn/BJB-INFO/index.htm
74	西安电子科技大学学报	http://www.xdxb.net/CN/volumn/home.shtml
75	西安交通大学学报	http://unit.xjtu.edu.cn/xb/zrb/
76	西北工业大学学报	http://admin.chinajournal.net.cn/model01/index.asp?rwbh=%27XBGD%27
77	西南交通大学学报	http://journal.swjtu.edu.cn/
78	浙江大学学报（工学版）	http://www.journals.zju.edu.cn/
79	中国矿业大学学报	http://xb.cumt.edu.cn/
80	中国石油大学学报（自然科学版）	http://sydxxb.periodicals.net.cn/default.html
81	中南大学学报（自然科学版）	http://www.csu.edu.cn/zdxbzkb/xbjj.html
82	重庆大学学报	http://qks.cqu.edu.cn/cqdxzrcn/ch/index.aspx